Practical Strangers

New Perspectives on the Civil War

Practical Strangers

The Courtship Correspondence of
Nathaniel Dawson and Elodie Todd,
Sister of Mary Todd Lincoln

Edited by Stephen Berry and Angela Esco Elder

The University of Georgia Press
ATHENS

Publication of this book was made possible in part by a grant
from the Watson-Brown Foundation.

Set in 10/13 ITC New Baskerville by
Graphic Composition, Inc., Bogart, Georgia

Most University of Georgia Press titles are
available from popular e-book vendors.

Printed digitally

Library of Congress Cataloging-in-Publication Data

Names: Dawson, Nathaniel Henry Rhodes, 1829–1895,
author. | Dawson, Elodie Todd, 1840–1877, author. | Berry,
Stephen William, editor. | Elder, Angela Esco, editor.
Title: Practical strangers : the courtship correspondence
of Nathaniel Dawson and Elodie Todd, sister of Mary Todd
Lincoln / edited by Stephen Berry and Angela Esco Elder.
Description: Athens : The University of Georgia Press,
[2017] | Series: New perspectives on the Civil War |
Includes bibliographical references and index.
Identifiers: LCCN 2016055817 | ISBN 9780820351018
(hardback : alk. paper) | ISBN 9780820351025 (pbk.
: alk. paper) | ISBN 9780820351001 (ebook)
Subjects: ISBN: Dawson, Nathaniel Henry Rhodes, 1829–
1895—Correspondence. | Dawson, Elodie Todd, 1840–
1877—Correspondence. | Confederate States of America.
Army—Officers—Correspondence. | United States—History—
Civil War, 1861–1865—Personal narratives, Confederate. |
Confederate States of America. Army. Alabama Infantry
Regiment, 4th. | Confederate States of America. Army—
Military life. | Alabama—History—Civil War, 1861–1865—
Women—Sources. | Women—Alabama—Social conditions—
19th century—Sources. | Bull Run, 1st Battle of, Va., 1861.
Classification: LCC E551.5 4th .D39 2017 | DDC 973.7/82—
dc23 LC record available at https://lccn.loc.gov/2016055817

Contents

Introduction *1*

Editorial Method *17*

———————

PART 1. To War *19*

Illustrations, the Todd Family, and the Magnolia Cadets *121*

PART 2. To the Altar *135*

———————

Selected Bibliography *321*

Index *323*

Practical Strangers

Introduction

"SURELY THERE IS NO OTHER FAMILY in the land placed in the exact situation of ours," lamented Elodie Breck Todd in the fall of 1861, "and I hope will never be [another] so unfortunate as to be surrounded by trials so numerous." Elodie was one of fourteen children born to Robert Smith Todd of Lexington, Kentucky. Six of those children, including Mary Todd Lincoln, sided with the Union during the American Civil War; eight, including Elodie, sided with the Confederacy. The Todds were not uniquely miserable in their division, however. Many Kentucky families found themselves in a similar bind. "Kentucky has not seceded & I believe never will," Kentucky congressman John Jordan Crittenden wrote to his son, George. "She loves the Union & will cling to it as long as possible. And so, I hope, will you." George joined the Confederacy without a note of explanation and rose to the level of major general. So did his brother Thomas—in the Union army. Then too, in all their divisions, white families were getting the merest taste of what slave families had endured for centuries as mothers, fathers, and children were sold away from all they knew and loved. Even so, Elodie was partly right in claiming that no other family was placed in the exact situation as the Todds. No other family was stretched between Confederate trenches and the federal White House.[1]

Students of Abraham Lincoln have not come fully to grips with what it meant to his understanding and experience of the Civil War that he had family ties to the enemy. The Todds' saga undoubtedly buttressed his "charity for all, malice toward none" approach to the conflict and encouraged him to see the Civil War as a divine punishment for the *national* sin of slavery. Lincoln's ties to the Todds probably had other, less salutary impacts. Preoccupied by Kentucky, he pursued too long a "Border State strategy" and realized relatively late that keeping the re-

---

1. Elodie Todd (1840–1877) to Nathaniel Dawson (1829–1895), September 1, 1861, in Nathaniel Henry Rhodes Dawson Papers, Southern Historical Collection, University of North Carolina at Chapel Hill (hereafter Dawson Papers); John Crittenden to George Crittenden, April 30, 1861, John J. Crittenden Papers, Filson Historical Society, Louisville, Ky.

maining slave states in the Union was militarily less important than mobilizing the enslaved themselves. Similarly, Lincoln's family connections probably helped make his early Reconstruction policies more lenient than they could have or should have been. Mary's relationship with the Confederate half of her family was more purely disastrous. Her blood ties to traitors, as they were seen in the North, helped make her a suspected and ultimately unpopular First Lady, even as she had to quietly mourn the wreck her extended family became.[2]

Owing to their ages, Elodie and Mary did not know each other well. By the time Elodie was born in Lexington in 1840, Mary was twenty-two, living with an older sister in Springfield and already embroiled in an off-again on-again courtship of Abraham Lincoln. Mary had been the fourth child born to Robert Todd and his first wife, Eliza Parker. Elodie was the second to last child born to Robert and his second wife, Elizabeth "Betsey" Humphreys. The fact that most of the Parker-Todds (including Mary) sided with the Union and most of the Humphreys-Todds (including Elodie) sided with the Confederacy has created an unfortunate assumption that they were essentially two families. This is patently untrue. Large families were common in the period and, regardless of age difference, members were expected to uphold their bonds of alliance and affection. Death in childbirth was also common, and widowers with young children almost always remarried. The Todd family pattern was not unusual then; they did not describe themselves as half brothers and half sisters and were not described that way by others. Since they understood themselves as one family, we should do the same, especially because it is critical to understanding both Elodie's and Mary's state of mind during the war. When Mary did visit her younger siblings in Lexington, moreover, she took a particular shine to the youngest girls, including Dee Dee (as she called Elodie), probably because they were a welcome respite from the rambunctious, all-male ensemble she oversaw at home.

Like Mary, when Elodie came of age, she was often sent to visit recently married sisters in the not-so-subtle nineteenth-century tradition of throwing women into the path of eligible men. One of her destinations was Selma, Alabama, where her older sister Martha (nicknamed Matt) had moved in 1852 to marry merchant and warehouse owner Clement Billingslea White. Matt and Elodie were close, although not particularly

---

2. For more on Lincoln and the Todds, see Stephen Berry, *House of Abraham: Lincoln and the Todds, a Family Divided by War* (New York: Houghton Mifflin, 2007).

alike. Matt was confident and brash; she laughed easily, talked a lot, and was comfortable giving orders to anybody who would take them. Elodie was more retiring and thought herself a little old lady trapped inside a young woman's body. She also thought herself perfectly plain. "I am just as they say in K[entucky]," she noted, "the ugliest of my Mother's handsome daughters and simply plain Dee Todd. I am used to being called so and I do not feel it at all." Elodie was too modest, however. With large eyes, a winning smile, and a cascade of black tresses rolling down her back, she was actually quite attractive, though growing up with men gawking at her prettier and more stylish sisters, she had somewhat resigned herself to being an old maid. Matt thought this idea perfectly ridiculous; Elodie was pretty, men were plentiful, and everyone, deep down, was open to romance. "We are always together and more company for each other than for anyone else," Elodie said of her and Matt, even if "[we are as] totally unlike as any two sisters I ever saw."[3]

To hear Nathaniel Dawson tell it, he fell in love with Elodie at first sight. He told this story later, however, when the couple was well into their courtship and had begun to coedit their romantic backstory into the tales they would tell their children. In truth, Nathaniel had been an unlikely suitor when they first met. At thirty-two, he was twelve years older than Elodie and deep in mourning for his second wife, who, like his first, had died after giving birth to a daughter. This was not an age when a single man would have been expected to raise young children, but Nathaniel appears to have been a gentle and attentive father. "I frequently think that I was intended for a woman," he said flatly, meaning only that he sometimes worried that he was too tenderhearted for the times. To compensate, he cloaked himself in a reserve that made him seem cold. He had a plantation outside Selma, although he rarely went there and rarely talked about it; he seemed to prefer his town house and his law practice. Prematurely balding, twice widowed, matured in his profession, and cocooned in his outer reserve, Nathaniel seemed older than he was and not likely to be carried away by Cupid. But having twice married for love and twice tasted the bliss of early marriage, he was desperate to try again. Whatever he was outwardly, inwardly he was the sort of man who only feels complete if he believes he is completing somebody else.[4]

3. Elodie Todd to Nathaniel Dawson, October 13, 1861, Dawson Papers; Elodie Todd to Nathaniel Dawson, July 23, 1861, Dawson Papers.
4. Nathaniel Dawson had grown up first in Charleston, South Carolina, and then in Carlowville, Alabama. Shortly after his father's death in 1848, he moved to Selma to study

By March 1861 both Elodie and Nathaniel were living in Selma, but they did not meet there. Instead they met in neighboring Montgomery, where both traveled to attend Jefferson Davis's inauguration. As Confederate sisters of Mary Todd Lincoln, Elodie and Matt were the belles of the inaugural ball, and Nathaniel was probably not alone in finding himself utterly smitten. "I fell in love with you in Montgomery," he later confessed to Elodie, "and tried to restrain my feelings, but they were too powerful." At night's end, he said, "I made up my mind to endeavor to make the star mine in whose beams I had wandered."[5]

After returning to Selma, Nathaniel began to send Elodie little presents—sheet music, flowers, produce from his garden—the kinds of things that could be explained away as tokens of kindness to a new neighbor. Gradually he also included short notes and little snippets of poetry, although nothing hinted at the proposal to come. In the meantime, he drilled with his new company and readied them to offer their services to the Confederate government. A few days before he and his men were to depart for Dalton, Georgia, where they would be mustered in as Company C of the Fourth Alabama, Nathaniel marched over to Matt's house and asked Elodie for her hand in marriage.

Elodie was flabbergasted. She liked the man well enough, but as she put it, they were "almost strangers." And then there were the family considerations. Whatever Matt might hope, Elodie had never thought of her sojourn in Selma as permanent. As war loomed, she found herself particularly keen to get back to her mother and to Kentucky while roads and rail lines were still open and safe. Her mother, moreover, would be apoplectic. "Ever since I can remember," Elodie said, "I have been looked upon and called the 'old maid' of the family and Mother seemed to think I was to be depended on to take care of her when all the rest of her handsomer daughters had left her." And even if her mother could be brought around, what about her older sisters, what about Mary? Even with all this Elodie said yes; some combination of the man and the times made her willing to take a chance. Most of all she wanted to feel that she

---

law under George R. Evans. In 1852 he married Anne Eliza Mathews (1833–1855), the daughter of Joel Early Mathews, a rich planter and owner of the Mathews Cotton Mill in Selma. Anne gave birth to a daughter, Elizabeth, in 1852 but died shortly after. In June 1857 Nathaniel remarried, this time to Mary Elizabeth Tarver (1833–1860), daughter of Benjamin J. Tarver. She also gave birth to a daughter, also named Mary. Both daughters are listed as living with Nathaniel in Selma in the 1860 census, though during the war he sent them to stay with family friends.

5. Nathaniel Dawson to Elodie Todd, June 26, 1861, Dawson Papers.

was in charge of her own life. "My family may think I am committing a sin to give a thought to any other than the arrangements they have made for me," she said, but "as this is the age when Secession, Freedom, and Rights are asserted, I am claiming mine."[6]

Over the following year, Nathaniel and Elodie fell in love by mail. A letter represents absence, and someone's attempt to compensate for absence. All the encounters Nathaniel and Elodie might have had had they courted under usual circumstances—all of the dances and stolen glances, all the moonlit strolls and hushed conversations in parks and lanes—all of those romantic opportunities would have to be created through paper and pen. There are some benefits, though, to falling in love by mail. We are often less guarded, more open, when we write our feelings than when we have to act them or speak them out. Blunt and yearning, shrewd and funny by turns, Elodie and Nathaniel's letters also carry the emotional energy of wartime. Desperate to connect—Elodie because her family was shattering, Nathaniel because he might die—the two were driven to inhabit their words and not to hide behind them. In these letters, two people flirt, fight, make up, and fumble toward each other, always trying to guess what the other is thinking, and what the other needs. "What can I do to be more worthy of the love and kindness you bestow, and how can I express the happiness or gratitude I feel? Words are inadequate to the task," wrote Elodie soon after Nathaniel's departure. And yet, words were all they had.

This, then—what you have in your hands—is the Dawsons' courtship. For all practical purposes, they had no earlier history. This is their origin story, the story they told as they wrote themselves into love. As a reader, you have all that they had—letters from a correspondence that constituted their sole lifeline to each other and their sole means of conveying to each other their hopes and fears for a marriage (and a Confederacy) they had rashly embraced in secession's spring.

Having both halves of a correspondence is relatively rare in Civil War studies. Rarer still is for the two parties to know each other so little and yet be driven to write each other so much. In his letters, Nathaniel seems more addicted to the idea of Elodie. "How singular that I should be engaged to the sister of Mrs. Lincoln," he wrote, "I wish you would write her to that effect so that in case of being taken prisoner I will not be too severely dealt with." For Elodie, the Todd family's drama is not a singu-

6. Elodie Todd to Nathaniel Dawson, May 9, 1861, Dawson Papers.

lar oddity but a tragedy and a trial. Though clearly committed to the Confederacy, she refused to let anyone speak ill of the Lincolns in her presence, and she admitted that "melancholy reflection" on her family's situation sometimes left her bedridden.[7]

All of this raises the question as to why Elodie was a Confederate in the first place. Both she and Nathaniel grew up amid slaves and slavery, and both wrote regularly (and fondly) about individual slaves. But the institution of slavery itself—the aggrieved rightness (as they probably saw it) or grotesque wrongness (as we see it) of the institution that lay at the root of a war that decimated her family—this they barely discussed. How can that be? Was it their mere politeness not to "talk politics"? Perhaps. But the truth is, people are often strangely capable of abstracting their "noble way of life" from the brutalities that make that life possible. We think that Southerners should have been obsessed with slavery because it seems so impossible to justify, but throughout history the impossible to justify often becomes routine. Enormous evils hide in plain sight because they become systemic; the more entrenched the interest, the more apt it is to be taken for granted.

These letters then are an intriguing case study into how, exactly, Confederates justified themselves. When Nathaniel says, without any reference whatever to slavery, that he believes he is fighting for Elodie, he may mean that he is fighting to ensure that his slave wealth is safe so that he can be a good provider. Or he may mean that he is fighting to ensure that the slaves do not go free and avenge themselves on the white population, especially its women. Or he may mean that he is fighting to ensure that the invading Yankees do not despoil the country. Or he may mean all of these at once. Then again, Nathaniel and Elodie would not have been the first or the last soldier and soldier's sweetheart not to give such things sufficient thought. Whatever the realities, Nathaniel may genuinely have believed that he was fighting for Elodie and for his country and for freedom and independence and liberty and for all the ideals that have ever sent American men to the battlefield.

To be sure, at the scale of the individual the most enormous political issues often yield to personal ones. For better or worse, what we have in these letters is not two people debating the great issues of the war but struggling with some success to fall into love. Nathaniel fell hardest and fastest. For a variety of reasons, Elodie needed more convincing. She

---

7. Nathaniel Dawson to Elodie Todd, May 16, 1861, Dawson Papers.

needed to know that Nathaniel loved her and not love itself. She needed
to know that he wasn't just temporarily smitten and that he could love
the way she could—for life. This raises another value of the collection—
the insights it provides into gender dynamics and courtship practices.
If courtship is, to some degree, a sort of emotional negotiation, what
we have here is an amazingly complete laying out of terms. In most ro-
mances, many aspects of these negotiations would be hidden from view.
Here it all plays out on paper: What religion are you? What profession
should I go into? Where do you want to live? Are you romantic or irrever-
ent? Do you have a sense of humor? Do you hold a grudge after a fight?
Throughout this correspondence, and particularly on Elodie's side, one
has a sense that the two are probing for information and subtly settling
the terms of their marriage.

Obviously the most important context for these letters is the Civil War
itself. Historians have been debating for years the exact relationship
between the battlefield and the home front. Did soldiers retreat into
FUBAR-worlds with their buddies and come home alienated from society?
Or were they mere extensions of that home-front society? The letters of
Elodie and Nathaniel offer a fascinating study of the relationship between two cities—the mobile, makeshift one of Nathaniel's camp and
the town of Selma itself—both riven by petty social politics. The world
of Nathaniel's "Camp Law" is alive with masculine friction as the officers
jostle for place and the privates adjust to being told what to do. Who's
getting promoted; who's getting credit; who's jealous of whom takes up
a lot of Nathaniel's ink. These fissures, in turn, make their way back to
Selma, or perhaps they had come with the boys from Selma in the first
place. Nathaniel's company, the "Magnolia Cadets," was drawn from "the
first young men of the place," as one witness put it, meaning the most
affluent members of the community; the "Selma Blues" were made up
of "the more sober, settled men of the city," meaning the middle class;
and the "Phoenix Reds," whom Nathaniel barely mentions at all, were
composed "almost entirely of working men." Nathaniel's Cadets had left
Selma in such a rush that the women of the town had barely had enough
time to organize a proper send-off. The Blues, by contrast, hung around
for weeks after they were organized, parading in their uniforms and indulging in local hospitalities.[8]

---

8. Harvey H. Jackson, *Inside Alabama: A Personal History of My State* (Tuscaloosa: University
of Alabama Press, 2004), 89–90.

That at least was how it looked to Cadet partisans who chided the Blues for being too dainty to eat army rations and too comfortable ever to leave Selma. The Blues did depart eventually, but these divisions remained an essential part of the city's social calculus. "It seems strange to me that so few are together and all helping for one and the same cause," Elodie noted. "I do not know of anything that has been tried that has not been opposed by another party." The divisions played themselves out most viciously at the tableaux, the fund-raising soirees organized by the Selma ladies' circle. Every month or so, the women of the town put together a program of charades, skits, dancing, and musical entertainments designed to solicit donations from the remaining local gentlemen. These donations then had to be distributed between the Blues and the Cadets, a process that became so bitter that Dawson threatened to return the money. The social politicking became even more rancorous when it was decided to hold separate tableaux for the two regiments, and it was Elodie's touchiness on the Lincoln issue that cemented the antagonisms for the remainder of the war. Fond of singing, Elodie had participated in several of the earlier soirees and had been present when an organizing committee suggested a skit that ridiculed Abraham Lincoln. Incensed, Elodie made it clear that she took personal offense at the suggestion and threatened to remove herself from the program. The committee relented, and the Lincoln scene did not appear at the tableaux. A few months later, however, Elodie received the program for the first soiree organized for the exclusive benefit of the Blues: the skit was on the evening's agenda. Elodie was irate. "I must confess that I have never been more hurt or indignant in my life," she wrote Dawson. "What have we ever done to deserve this attempt to personally insult and wound our feelings in so public a manner?" With this incident, the loose division in the Selma social circle became a deep rift. "Society [here] has undergone a change," Elodie explained, "and is now divided into two distinct classes." The first class, calling itself the Anti-Whites, contained the Weavers, the Weedows, the Fourniers, the Morrises, Mrs. Steele, the Perkinsons, the Watts, Miss Echols, and the Misses Sikes and Carroley. The second class, calling itself the Whites, was composed of Elodie, her sister Martha, Mrs. Mabry, and the Misses Goodwin, Elsberry, Ferguson, and Bell. "The rest of the inhabitants," Elodie noted, "have been allowed the privilege of placing their own positions." With everyone clear on the sides, women who had insulted each other only obliquely came straight to the point. "There has been a *war here in words*," Elodie reported, "and the *Victory* is not yet awarded." Both Elodie and Nathaniel, then, were fighting wars within

wars. The community of Selma itself, in all its fractiousness, had gone
to war, and both Elodie and Nathaniel had parts to play in determining
whether it could keep itself together.[9]

This volume is divided into two parts. Part 1, "To War," takes Elodie and
Nathaniel from April 1861, and the eve of the conflict, to July 1861, and
the eve of the Battle of First Manassas. The letters in this period betray
a couple struggling to discover and understand one another. Nathaniel is almost ludicrously ardent, writing often and vaguely, carried into
raptures by the strength of his own affection. "My whole soul seems to
swell with love for you," he tells Elodie typically, "and if I could die at this
moment, all my thoughts would be of you." Nathaniel in this period was
inclined to see Elodie as a glorious abstraction, a vessel for all his hopes
and dreams of outliving the war. "Under all these privations, I am supported by the will of my own loved angel, Elodie, which whispers me to
bear all and hereafter to be rewarded with her love and her affections.
Oh God, how deeply I love you, nay worship you," he writes. Elodie's letters are far fewer but far longer and more substantive. She seems driven
to present to Nathaniel a whole person, mirthful and depressed by turns.
Often in his reverie Nathaniel is oblivious to these ups and downs, but occasionally he seems to know exactly what Elodie needs. In a fit of pique,
for instance, when Elodie tells him that they are practically strangers, Nathaniel handles it perfectly. "You say we hardly know each other," he replies, "but I think differently. I know you from your letters intimately. . . .
Had I not been a volunteer, I never would have known how rich were the
imaginings of your mind and how pure and beautiful were the flowers
that grow in the garden of your heart." Elodie tended to correct such rosy
excesses, poking holes in his ego and his lavish language, but she loved it
too. "I am a troublesome somebody at all times," she assured him; "I am
a Todd, and some of these days you may be unfortunate enough to find
out what they are." Nathaniel seemed gradually to understand that these
were not warnings but invitations—to know and love Elodie whole.[10]

Part 2 of the collection, "To the Altar," takes Elodie and Nathaniel
from the Battle of First Manassas in July 1861 to their marriage (and
the end of their correspondence) in April 1862. Manassas was a turning
point in the couple's correspondence. Nathaniel was almost killed when

9. Elodie Todd to Nathaniel Dawson, September 29, 1861, August 4, 1861, and January 5, 1862, Dawson Papers.
10. Nathaniel Dawson to Elodie Todd, August 21, 1861, Dawson Papers.

a cannonball struck the fence he was negotiating during a retreat. He died another kind of death when a member of his regiment accused him of cowardice. Suddenly Nathaniel's visions, for romance and the Confederacy, became far less grand; his first taste of war had soured in his mouth. Elodie, too, was sobered by the bloodshed. "As much as I thought I loved you," she wrote Nathaniel after the battle, "it was not until yesterday and today which has caused me to realize the devotedness and depth of the love that is in my heart for you and how crushed and torn it would have been had you been snatched from me by death's restless hand." For the rest of the year, the couple dealt with the fallout from Manassas and the charge of cowardice. Their correspondence continues until April 1862, when Nathaniel returned for their wedding. After this, their correspondence (and courtship) was effectively over. At the end of the volume, both remain ardent Confederates, but the war has already become an unromantic slog. The loss of two of Elodie's Confederate brothers, Sam and Aleck, at the Battles of Shiloh and Baton Rouge, respectively, was far more than she ever expected to pay in asserting her "Secession, Freedom, and Rights." Her birth family effectively destroyed, she turned with Nathaniel to building a family of their own.[11]

Between April 1861 and April 1862, Nathaniel Dawson and Elodie Todd wrote more than two hundred thousand words to each other, the equivalent of a novel each. Then they took their vows and laid those novels aside, turning to write out a common life by living it together. Letter collections often allow us to see enough of other people's lives that we become frustrated when we cannot see more. At the end of their correspondence, Nathaniel and Elodie are barreling toward marriage even as a new gulf opens between them. Nathaniel is angry because Elodie won't set a firm date for their wedding. His urgency is easy to understand: He loved marriage, and he loved Elodie. He may also have been driven by emotions he was less aware of. The charge of cowardice, however false, was an existential threat to his social status and sense of self. His reputation damaged, his appetite for military politics soured, he needed a good excuse to come home; he needed to distract himself and others from Manassas; and he needed someone to nurse his bruised ego. He may have been right when he told Elodie that his men would have elected

---

11. Nathaniel Dawson to Elodie Todd, July 25, 1861, Dawson Papers; Elodie Todd to Nathaniel Dawson, July 23, 1861, Dawson Papers.

him again as captain, but when the Confederate government agreed to honor the one-year commitments of the officers (and not the enlisted men), he abandoned the Magnolia Cadets and returned to Selma.

By the time he arrived, Elodie was deep in mourning for her brother Sam, even as she planned her wedding. No account of the ceremony survives, but we know that Elodie's favorite brother, Aleck—the one she had called her "pet"—managed to attend. By then he was serving as aide-de-camp to his brother-in-law Benjamin Hardin Helm. Earlier in the war, Elodie had dreamed that Aleck was "dreadfully wounded, and the whole scene was so vivid and life-like in all its minutiae, and I was so distressed that I awoke myself sobbing." Such dreams are not portents but clues as to what a person fears most. Three months after Elodie's wedding, Aleck was shot through the forehead in a friendly fire incident before the Battle of Baton Rouge. By then Elodie's pregnancy was beginning to show, and six months later she gave birth to a boy and named him after her brother. "Our joy was [short-lived]," Nathaniel wrote a week later. "The little cherub died yesterday morning. . . . The body was christened & named Alex Todd."[12]

Whatever Elodie and Nathaniel had hoped for from the Civil War, they probably never imagined so desolating a result. Nathaniel had fought one battle and been branded a coward; Elodie had lost two brothers in four months. None of these military disasters had been particularly glorious. The Fourth Alabama had been a key to rebel victory at Manassas, but Stonewall Jackson's men had gotten most of the credit, and Nathaniel's own experience had been one of watching people he liked get shot until the survivors "retired in confusion [and] ran for their lives." Sam Todd, too, had been fleeing a field when the bullet entered his back and blew out through his stomach. Aleck Todd had been shot in the head by one of his own pickets. Neither of these men had held a sword aloft and led some noble charge as he had probably hoped to do. For them War itself had been a casualty of the war, at least War as Victorian men had supposed it would be.[13]

Drawn by their letters into all this suffering, we can forget that Elodie and Nathaniel brought it all on themselves. No one forced them to fight

12. Elodie Todd to Nathaniel Dawson, December 1, 1861, Dawson Papers; Nathaniel Dawson to Hardin Helm, January 14, 1863, Emilie Todd Helm Papers, Kentucky Historical Society.

13. Nathaniel Dawson to Elodie Todd, August 29, 1861, Dawson Papers.

on the wrong side of a great moral question. The fact that they never explicitly said they were fighting for slavery doesn't particularly matter. Deep down, they knew they were; they just preferred to call it their "way of life." Ulysses S. Grant said it best when he noted that the Confederates fought valiantly and "suffered . . . much for a cause, though that cause was, I believe, one of the worst for which a people ever fought, and one for which there was the least excuse."[14]

Nathaniel never returned to the Fourth Alabama, but his reputation was not grievously harmed. Indeed, in 1863 he was elected to the state legislature. By then the sleepy town of Selma, which Elodie had found so dull by comparison to Lexington, had become one of the more important industrial and logistical hubs in the Confederacy. Employing ten thousand people in more than a hundred buildings along the river, the Selma Ordnance and Naval Foundry was second only to the Tredegar Iron Works in Richmond in its importance as a manufacturing center of Confederate war matériel. Union high command made capturing Selma a priority, but it was never feasible until the spring of 1865, by which time the Confederacy was in its death throes. On April 2, Union commander James H. Wilson scattered Selma's meager defending force under Nathan Bedford Forrest and seized the city. The gleeful destruction of the ordnance factories then devolved into a general looting of the town. We do not know whether this was the cause of Nathaniel's abandoning his old home, but late in the war he and Elodie moved into a house around the corner from Clement and Matt. In 1864 Elodie had given birth to a boy whom the couple named Henry Rhodes Dawson, after Nathaniel's father. The boy's laugh, a cousin said, helped to "drown the troubles of the times." Elodie bore another son in 1869, whom the couple named Lawrence Percy Dawson, after Nathaniel's brother. Unfortunately, like her closest sisters (and like Nathaniel's first two wives), Elodie had difficult pregnancies. Sister Matt died of undisclosed causes in 1868 at the age of thirty-five. Sister Kitty died in 1875, ten days after giving birth to her fifth child at the age of thirty-three. In 1877 Elodie became pregnant a fourth time, which she correctly predicted might kill her. "I try to console myself," she told her sister Emilie, "that my health can scarcely be worse than for the past year without [my] being a permanent invalid or dying." On the morning of November 14, 1877, Elodie slipped into a coma,

---

14. Ulysses S. Grant, *Personal Memoirs of General U. S. Grant* (New York: Charles L. Webster & Company, 1885), 473.

probably the result of an overprescription of laudanum. She gave "birth to a still-born male suddenly (*in a moment*) without evidences of pain or consciousness" and died that evening at 7:35 p.m. She was thirty-seven.[15]

At her death, Elodie had been the head of Selma's Ladies Memorial Association, working to erect a monument to the Confederate dead in a newly purchased section of the Selma cemetery. In her honor, Nathaniel set to work turning the entire grounds into a monument to Elodie. He first commissioned an Italian sculptor to carve a life-size marble model of Elodie and ship it in pieces back to the United States for reassembly. Feeling that the sculptor had not done justice to Elodie's hair, he shipped the head back to be recarved. He also purchased eighty live oaks and eighty magnolias from Mobile and planted them throughout the grounds to create the umbrageous aesthetic he loved. "You know I am fond of such places," he had written to Elodie from a graveyard in Virginia. "In all my travels, I have uniformly sought an acquaintance with the living through the silent instructions of the cemetery. Show me a beautiful monument, with a chaste inscription, and I will always know that a warm heart and a virtuous mind erected it."[16]

Clearly, given his ability to buy a new home and outfit a new cemetery, Nathaniel was not ruined by the war. Almost immediately he had rejuvenated his law practice with his senior partner, Edmund Winston Pettus, a vocal opponent of Reconstruction who rose to become grand dragon of the Alabama Klan and later a U.S. senator. Given the closeness of the two men—Nathaniel had entrusted Pettus with the care of his daughter during the war—it seems probable that Nathaniel was a member of the Klan too. In honoring his life, the Alabama State Bar Association noted that Nathaniel "took an active part in politics" in the period and that "his whole sympathy and heart went out to our people who were so grievously wronged by the Reconstruction Acts, and he did what he could to assist in restoring the government of Alabama to her rightful rules." This probably did not include night-riding, burning crosses, or lynching, but Nathaniel had always believed that the "natural" hierarchies in society needed to be preserved. Certainly he would not have appreciated the

---

15. Preston to Elodie Todd Dawson, December 12, 1864, Dawson Papers; Elodie Todd Dawson to Emilie Todd Helm, September 16, 1877, Townsend Collection, University of Kentucky. For more on Selma's significance as a manufacturing center during the war, see Megan Bever, "Summer 1862: Josiah Gorgas, Confederate Ordnance, and the Selma Arsenal," *Alabama Heritage* (Summer 2012): 39–40; and James Pickett Jones, *Yankee Blitzkrieg: Wilson's Raid through Alabama and Georgia* (Athens: University of Georgia Press, 1976).

16. Nathaniel Dawson to Elodie Todd, December 11, 1861, Dawson Papers.

ironies that a bridge named after his partner has become an icon of the
civil rights Movement (and is now to be renamed).[17]

In 1884 the Democrats captured the White House for the first time
since 1856. To thank the South for its support, President Grover Cleveland appointed several Southerners to his cabinet, including the man
who had drafted Mississippi's Ordnance of Secession, Lucius Quintus
Cincinnatus Lamar. As the new secretary of the interior, Lamar in turn
nominated Nathaniel Dawson to head the Bureau of Education even
though Nathaniel had no particular qualification for office outside his
service as a university trustee. Even so, he proved a capable bureau chief
and was instrumental in commissioning guides to the educational history
of each of the individual states. He also made an important trip to sur-
vey the state of Alaska and did much to plant the seeds of a functioning
public education system in the state. As might be guessed, however, he
was not the champion of African American education that the Radical
Republicans had been; indeed, he believed that public education should
be available to all but not necessarily the same for all. "Natural selection
and the survival of the fittest are great needs in American schools, col-
leges and universities," he said. "[This] will deliver us on the one hand
from the over education of the mediocrity, and on the other from the under education of genius." When Republicans regained the White House
in 1888, Nathaniel's tenure was not renewed. He died at his home on
February 1, 1895, and was buried beside the woman he had called his
country.[18]

Having sketched these two lives to their end, we need now to return
to the beginning, to the moment of origin when two strangers took a
plunge together into the vortex of life. Here is a story of the Civil War,
of Abraham Lincoln's shattered family, of two people falling in love, of
soldiers and brothers dying nobly on the wrong side of history.

Days after proposing, Nathaniel left for war. He did not know his betrothed; if he was honest, he didn't know a lot of things. He did not know
how battle would shake him. He did not know how rumors would haunt
him. He did not know that Elodie's family, already fractured, would break

---

17. *Memorial Record of Alabama: A Concise Account of the State's Political, Military, Professional and Industrial Progress, Together with the Personal Memoirs of Many of Its People*, vol. 1 (Madison, Wis.: Brant & Fuller, 1893), 858–865.

18. "Report of the Commissioner of Education" (Washington, D.C.: Government Print-ing Office, 1889), 36–37.

into smaller and sadder pieces. Neither of them knew, really, that two people could fall in love with only ink and paper. Nathaniel knew only that he wanted to stand on the deck of the paddleboat bearing him away to war and watch as Elodie grew smaller and smaller on the shore, until eventually, her physical presence was gone. And when his eyes could strain no more, he sat down on the boat, got out his paper and ink, and began to write.

Editorial Method

BETWEEN APRIL 1861 AND APRIL 1862, Nathaniel Dawson and Elodie Todd exchanged more than three hundred letters. Concerned about privacy, Elodie suggested the letters be burned. Nathaniel would not hear of it. Elodie's letters were *"sacred writing,"* he said, and while he kept the most recent missives on his person for romantic inspiration, he returned the others in ones and twos to Elodie for safekeeping. Befitting their personalities, Nathaniel's hand is loose, hurried, and (mostly) intelligible; Elodie's is more compact, flowing, and attractive.

In this print edition, the Dawson's voluminous correspondence has been edited to focus tightly on their courtship—the story, in their own words, of how they improbably fell in love by mail despite Elodie's divided family and Nathaniel's first (traumatic) taste of war. To accomplish this we have made extensive cuts, both of entire letters and (occasionally) of sections within letters. Certainly the "through line" is more visible this way—Nathaniel and Elodie's marital negotiations, her broken family, everyone's rapid disillusionment. Even so, we would never have made these cuts if the Press had not also agreed to allow us to present every word, line, and letter of the correspondence online. Available electronically at www.practicalstrangers.ehistory.org, the full collection encompasses not only every piece of paper Nathaniel and Elodie exchanged during the war but additional letters sent to them that take readers into the Dawsons' pre- and postwar lives. Editorial excisions (letters and passages) are not marked in this print edition with intrusive ellipses; instead we direct interested readers to the electronic version, which includes every aside and comment on the weather or the roads, every repetitive rapture and halfhearted opinion about local rumors, gossip, and drama.

The nuances of Nathaniel and Elodie's original language—eccentricities of grammar, syntax, and spelling—are here kept without any "sic" notations. We did, however, make more trivial intrusions and adjustments for ease of understanding. Underlining in the original letters has here been converted to italics. Dates have been put into a single format, and Elodie's liberal use of the comma has been disciplined so as not to create odd clauses and pauses in the flow of the text. Where words were forgotten but clearly intended or where additional words or letters were necessary for clarity, we have added them in square brackets. Where words could not be deciphered in the original, or where a letter was ripped, damaged, or smudged, we have inserted [illegible] in brackets to stand for the missing word(s). Where we were not quite certain of a transcribed name or term, it appears here with a [?] at its end.

In our annotations, we tracked down most but by no means all the people met, books referenced, and skirmishes recorded in the text. Some allusions, to a "Mr. Jones," for instance, or "our friend, the ex-Lieutenant," were simply too obscure to uncover. Individuals who were mentioned multiple times, however, are usually footnoted with enough detail to serve as a point of departure for those interested in further investigation.

PART I

To War

Alabama River, April 26, 1861

I do not know that I can better express my appreciation of the goodness of my gentle and dear Elodie, in being present, this morning, to bid me goodby and God speed, than by writing her a few hurried lines.[1] For I know that to hold communion with her is the sweetest of all pleasures.

We are speeding on our way over the water, and at each revolution of the wheels, the distance between us is lengthened, but the ties which bind us are only increased. I watched you until you passed from my sight in the distance, and saw with pleasure that tho smiles wreathed your face, it was done to cheer and to animate one whose heart was almost bursting with sadness. But I must not indulge these feelings, but must turn to the brighter visions that flit across the mind at the hope of future happiness and our union in those solemn bonds that will make us one in all things. Like Ruth[2] thy country shall be my country, my God shall be your God, and your people shall be my people, and we will have to appreciate in happiness the deferred visions of Hope. Am I not fighting for you, am I not your sworn knight and soldier? If so, you must bid me God speed.

I requested Mr. Dennis[3] to get some of my hardiest geranium plants

---

1. Elodie and Nathaniel walked to the dock on the Alabama River south of town, where Nathaniel got on a paddleboat. He watched the shore until he could not see Elodie anymore, and then he sat down and wrote this letter. The Magnolia Cadets, Nathaniel's militia group, had been ordered to Dalton, Georgia, where they would be mustered in as Company C of the Fourth Alabama Infantry Regiment. From there they would head to Lynchburg and then to an encampment across the Potomac from Washington, D.C. Two days before this letter, Elodie and her sister Martha sewed the Cadets a company flag, which was presented in a ceremony at Watt's Hall.

2. Nathaniel is referring to Ruth, of the Bible's Old Testament, who accepted the God of the Israelites as her God and the Israelite people as her people. In Ruth 1:16–17, Ruth tells Naomi, her mother-in-law, "Don't urge me to leave you or to turn back from you. Where you go I will go, and where you stay I will stay. Your people will be my people and your God my God. Where you die I will die, and there I will be buried. May the Lord deal with me, be it ever so severely, if even death separates you and me."

3. Probably John Dennis, a friend of Nathaniel's living in Selma. 1860 U.S. Federal Census, Selma, Dallas County, Ala. Hereafter, this census will be marked as 1860 Census: Selma.

to have them sent to you. Will you blame me again? I wish these fragrant flowers to be the silent, living witnesses of my love, and I know you will water and cultivate them as the living memorials of my constant fidelity to your heart.

I think our friend, the ex-Lieutenant, is now convinced that I am in love with you. He evidently was shocked at the tableau of last night and seems to have all of the feelings of a jealous nature aroused. But I do not blame him [n]or do I dislike him for loving the same dear and noble lady whom I worship. I will never feel pained at your receiving the attention of any gentleman but am rather pleased. For I am willing and anxious that the beams of the sun which reflect upon me should warm others into happiness. I have no hesitancy in saying that I have confidence that can never be shaken—the same in your love and truth that the follower of Mohammet has in his prophet.[4] We have a large and noisy crew aboard, and what with the noise, frequent interruptions, and the shaking of the boat, I can hardly write, but I know you will take the trouble to read what is written. We will reach Mongom'y tonight, and in a few days will leave for Lynchburg Va. I will write you very frequently, if only a hurried line. I fear you will object to my frequent letters. Your love will make me a stronger and better man, able to resist the vices of a campaign life. And now, good bye. Again, I commend you to God and subscribe myself your own attached,

N. H. R. D.

Atlanta, April 28, 1861

I wrote you a few hurried lines, my own dear Elodie, from Newnan this morning, but you will not blame me for turning twice in the same day to the Mecca of all my hopes, again to convene with the gentle being whose life is a part of my own.[5]

The excitement and enthusiasm of the people is very great. At every station we have been cheered and bouquets of flowers and the smiles

---

4. Mohammet is an alternate spelling of Muhammad, the Islamic prophet whose followers had a reputation for intense loyalty and trust.

5. Mecca, a city in Saudi Arabia, is regarded as the holiest city in Islamic religion. As the birthplace of Muhammad and revelation site of the Quran, all able-bodied Muslims are encouraged to complete a pilgrimage to this city in their lifetime.

of fair women, maids and matrons, have bid us God speed. Many of the flowers have mottoes attached. I enclose you a piece of rosemary & the motto that accompanied it.[6] Our flag met with a serious accident this morning as we entered the city. The staff was broken, but I am glad to say that the flag is uninjured.[7]

After writing you at Newnan, a large band of citizens came down to the station and as the [illegible] train came in, called vociferously for myself and others. I made a speech, which I am vain enough to tell you was loudly cheered. Col. Keitt of So. Ca., Mr Howe of Miss, Mr Stone of the Cadets also replied in eloquent remarks.[8] We leave at 6 o'clock on train for Dalton, where we organize a regiment and elect our regimental officers.

You must excuse me for writing you so often, but it is a great pleasure to speak with you, and unless you command me otherwise, I will continue to do so until my duties will prevent me.

Please present me very kindly to Mr. and Mrs. White[9] and to your brother.

---

6. Nathaniel routinely sent Elodie little tokens of his affection from camp and battle-field—pressed flowers, leaves, pebbles, scraps of material, a lock of hair, a bit of gold lace from his sword belt, and so on—most of which survive in the collection.

7. The flag Elodie and her sister sewed still survives and is held by the Alabama Department of Archives and History, Montgomery, Ala.

8. Laurence Massillon Keitt (1824–1864) was a former U.S. congressman from South Carolina perhaps most famous for his role in the caning of Charles Sumner. When Preston Brooks began the attack, Keitt jumped in the aisle, drew a pistol, and announced, "Let them be!" He served as a delegate from South Carolina during the creation of the Confederate Constitution and was mortally wounded at the Battle of Cold Harbor on June 1, 1864. For more, see Holt Merchant, South Carolina Fire-Eater: The Life of Laurence Massillion Keitt, 1824–1864 (Columbia: University of South Carolina), 2014.

Mr. Howe is probably Chiliab Smith Howe (1809–1875), of Marengo County, Alabama, who married the daughter of U.S. congressman and Alabama governor Israel Pickens. For more, see the Chiliab Smith Howe Papers, 1814–1899, #3092, Southern Historical Collection, Wilson Library, University of North Carolina at Chapel Hill.

Mr. Stone is possibly private John H. Stone, age thirty-four, though there are other Stones in the Magnolia Cadets (one of whom dies at Manassas). 1860 U.S. Federal Census, Marion, Perry, Ala.

9. Martha Todd White (1833–1868) was Elodie's older sister; she is often referred to simply as Matt. Seven years older than Elodie, Martha had married Clement Billingslea White and moved with him to Selma in 1852. The Whites owned two slaves in 1860. Clement Billingslea White (1829–1903) was born in Dallas County, Alabama. He attended Centre College in Kentucky, graduating in 1848. He probably met Martha as a student. He is buried in Live Oak Cemetery, along with Nathaniel and Elodie. For more, see Berry, House of Abraham, 58.

Have I sent you any flowers since my departure? Will you not write
me at Lynchburg? Tell me how much I am missed? And now goodbye.
God bless and protect you and give me a safe return to my own dear
Elodie
    Your attached,
    N. H. R. Dawson

Dalton, April 29, 1861

We reached this place, my dear Elodie, last night at two o'clock. Our
passage from west point, over the whole route, was a continuous ovation
to the troops. At Atlanta we were received very hospitably but by the
citizens, and in the evening one of the prominent citizens addressed
and welcomed our company. I replied, and in reply to an allusion made
to our beautiful flag, which was recovered without injury, stated that it
was the creation of two ladies nearly related to the hostess of the White
House and had been presented to us by the fair women of Selma.[10] The
announcement was hailed in long and loud cheering. You will excuse the
allusion, but my heart was full of you at the time, and I could not resist
it. We were placed in an open house last night, and I slept with my shawl
over me on a blanket with a billet of wood for a pillow, but with all this
rough accommodation, I slept soundly, dreaming of my own noble and
cherished "Ladye Love," who was then, I hoped, reposing peacefully at
home. No I will not tell you so, for I flattered myself, that she was even
then probably thinking of me.

We are now in our tents with our camp fire and will bivouac around
them tonight. The regiment will be organized tomorrow and then we will
proceed to Lynchburg Va. I do not know who will be Colonel as all of
the companies have not yet arrived. The Guards will be here tonight or
tomorrow morning. I know all of the officers here and, as many of them
are personal friends, I hope to pass my time agreeably. I have not yet
heard from you but hope to get a letter this evening or before I leave. I
cannot tell how long we will remain at Lynchburg but will expect to hear
from you there.

---

10. Nathaniel is referring to Elodie and her sister Martha, who made the flag. The "hostess of the White House" is Elodie's sister Mary Todd Lincoln.

I am quite well, never felt better in my life, and if you were mine and I was at home with you to enjoy your cheerful laugh and sunny conversations, I would be happy indeed. How I long to sit again in my library with you presiding genius, surrounded by books, and with my dear Elodie to sing and play on the Piano. I feel certain that this happiness is in store for me, and how happy will be its fruition. If I deserve any distinction or promotion, it is on your account that I may be all that you will deserve in a husband. Goodbye. May God protect and guard you, and may I be worthy of you, my dear Elodie.

Ever your attached friend,

N. H. R. Dawson

Dalton, April 30, 1861

Mr. Averitt[11] brought me last night, my own dear Elodie, your beautiful and acceptable present with your sweet note accompanying it. The merest trifle from you is valuable, but how much more is one which testifies how much you are interested in my welfare.

Is it painful for you to think of me? I so much regret that you should feel badly on my account, and yet it is flattering to know that there is one heart where I am enthroned, which responds to its pulsations and beats in unison with mine. You say that I am thoughtful of you to the last. How could I be less selfish in thinking of you? I was doing a kindness to myself. I have just left my encampment and had to turn away to suppress my feelings. A party in one of the tents were singing the Southern Cross to the air of the Star Spangle Banner, accompanied by the violins. The music reminded me of the last evening I saw you. I lingered at the gate and heard you play on the piano, and I was almost overpowered. The

---

11. James Battle Avirett (1835–1912) was the son of Serana Thomas and John Alfred Averitt. Avirett (who adopted a different spelling of his name, though Nathaniel always used the original) graduated from North Carolina University in 1852 and practiced law until 1858, when he began to study for the ministry. During the war, he became chaplain of the Seventh Virginia Cavalry. Afterward, he conducted an Episcopal seminary for young ladies, served as rector for multiple churches, and authored four published works. In 1862 he married Mary Louise Dunbar Williams, of Winchester, Virginia; they had two sons before his death on February 16, 1912. Tucker Reed Littleton, "James Battle Avirett," in Dictionary of North Carolina Biography, vol. 1, A–C, ed. William S. Powell (Chapel Hill: University of North Carolina Press, 1979).

world gives me credit for having no feelings but those of selfishness. I am so happy that you know better, that you have seen into the chambers of my heart and have recognized feelings there that have won your affections. I have been requested on all sides to run for colonel and lieutenant colonel of the regiment. The latter position I could easily get, but though the temptation has been strong, I have resisted it and, at the solicitation of my company, have declined either position. I was anxious to accept as I thought it would please my Elodie to see me and have me so highly honored, but a sense of duty to the young men who have been attracted to me has required me to make this sacrifice. What do you think of it?

I wish you could peep into my quarters, a room with trunks, boxes, and blankets all over, without a chair or convenience of any kind. I sleep on the floor with two blanks and a piece of wood as a pillow. Yet I am as well as I ever was and eat with great relish the rations of bread and bacon which comprise our food.

Mr. A.[12] will act as the correspondent of the cadets and will keep you advised thro' the pen of this camp life, which will save me the necessity of telling you subsequently, but I do not feel satisfied unless I write you as often as I can.

I hear that your brother[13] has an idea of coming on and joining the guards. If he does come on, will he not take a place in my company and in my mess, but I would advise him not to join the ranks as a private. The duties are very tedious, he would not like them. A gentleman must feel the position irksome. We will not leave here for several days yet as the companies are not prepared fully.

Write me at once to Lynchburg Va. Fear not to write me as you feel. It will be flattering to hear from your own lips the words and cares of your heart. I would give all the world to be safely returned and the husband of your affections. Do you know I see thro' the darkness of the present the bright star of future happiness. Good bye. God bless and protect you always is the constant prayer of you own

Affectionate,

N. H. R. Dawson

12. Mr. A. is James Averitt.

13. Most probably Nathaniel is referring to Elodie's brother David, who was the most anxious to get into the Confederate army.

Selma, May 2, 1861

Sister Matt and Miss M.[14] have gone this evening to witness the presentation of two flags to the five companies. I did not feel as tho' I could go thro' another such scene so soon, besides preferred staying at home to write to you, which will now be my greatest pleasure after receiving your own communications. My brother[15] returned from Montgomery yesterday morning, remained with us sufficient length of time to bid us goodbye. He succeeded in getting the appointment or commission (I don't know which I should say) of 1st lieutenant with promise of promotion to a captaincy before three months elapse. Parting with him, together with the information of the departure of my two other brothers[16] for the war and the deplorable state of affairs in Kentucky, has made me sad. Our dear old state is poorly provided with arms and ammunition, and all attempts to supply the deficiency thus far have proved a failure, for what they ordered has been seized by the state of Ohio. Another trouble is the division in political sentiment. What is to be the fate of home? I cannot divine and will not think Kentucky, whose name has been written with pride and honor on History's page, must now be dimmed and dishonored, untrue to herself and her noble sister states.[17]

The Blues are making more music and commotion about going to the

---

14. Miss Laura Mims of Oak Grove, Alabama, was about twenty years old in 1860. Her younger brother, George Mims, was a member of Nathaniel's company. 1860 U.S. Federal Census, Oak Grove, Perry, Ala.

15. Elodie's brother David Humphreys Todd (1832–1871) ran away from home at fourteen to fight in the Mexican American War. He participated to some degree in the California gold rush in 1850 and in a Chilean revolution in 1851. By July 1861, he would be a controversial commandant of the Richmond prison system and would be relieved of duty. He commanded an artillery company with distinction during the siege of Vicksburg and settled and married in Huntsville, Alabama, after the war. Berry, House of Abraham, 44–45.

16. It is not perfectly clear to which brothers Elodie is referring. Possibly they are George Rogers Clark Todd (1825–1902), who secured a commission as a surgeon about this time, and Samuel Brown Todd (see May 26, 1861, note 87), who had signed on as a private in New Orleans.

17. Southern in its social customs, Northern in its economic interests, Kentucky was a unique hybrid of the two regions. It remains one of the war's enduring ironies that the two men battling for Kentucky were Kentuckians themselves—Abraham Lincoln and Jefferson Davis were both born in the Bluegrass State. Ultimately, Lincoln would win this ground. "I hope to have God on my side," he supposedly said, "but I must have Kentucky." For more, see Anne E. Marshall, Creating a Confederate Kentucky: The Lost Cause and Civil War Memory in a Border State (Chapel Hill: University of North Carolina Press, 2010).

War than when you left.[18] The church bells ring two or three times a day to call the ladies together in order to form arrangements concerning the making up of 110 uniforms for the chivalrous corps, who are so determined to fight their country's battles that rather than remain at home they intend going on their own expenses and responsibility. I hope you and your company will soon do your fighting and make way for this noble band who I doubt not will return their brows crowned with laurels. Mr. Dennis leaves tomorrow for New Orleans. I dislike really to see him go as he positively declares Bro. Clem must accompany him, and I believe he has consented to do so. I would not give Mr. D. permission to carry out the order you gave him regarding the flowers. I think *your sending* Bouquets twice a week is sufficient to gratify my taste for flowers.

[illegible] Hagood[19] has made his appearance twice but takes especial delight in being agreeable and polite to all save myself to whom he is cold and haughty. I am only waiting for him to recover his usual good and amiable disposition before I retaliate with cool dignity. I am writing you a long, dull letter and am not conscious of what I have written, owing to the many interruptions which have occurred since I began . . . Laura says I have been writing long enough to have accomplished 13 letters and must stop as she and Matt have talked themselves completely out just beside me all the time, but it seems as tho' my pen is as eager to continue as myself. However, I must now finish. Hoping to hear from you very soon, believe me

Ever yours,
Elodie

Dalton, May 2, 1861

My Dear Elodie, I have been greatly disappointed every day at not receiving a letter from you. This evening I am again denied the pleasure; the deferred hope has made my heart sick. We leave for Lynchburg tomorrow, and I hope indeed that letters will be there awaiting me from

18. By the summer of 1861, the town of Selma had uneasily grouped itself into two camps, one associated with the men of the Selma Blues regiment, and the other associated with the men of the Magnolia Cadets.

19. Robert Hagood was in business with Clement White. These two, along with Edward T. Watts and John W. Lapsley, incorporated the "Central Warehouse Company" in Selma, in February 1860. It is not clear why Hagood is snubbing Elodie, though at other points in the correspondence she seems vaguely aware that he likes her.

one who is so essential to my happiness. No minute passes but that your image is not before me, recalling the beautiful charmer that has again awakened me to life.

We have at last organized our regiment. Col. Jones[20] of Huntsville, Colonel; E. M. Law,[21] Lieut. Col.; Charles L. Scott,[22] a private from my company, Major. My company would not allow me to be elected, and I now feel quiet and contented again, but I confess it was a trial to resist the temptation. I am almost unwilling to send you such a scrawl as this, but if you are like me, it will be a pleasure to read anything from you.

After a speech made yesterday at the May celebration, I received from a fair young maiden a beautiful wreath of mountain laurel and flowers. I wish I could send it to crown the tresses of my own dear Elodie, but Hope permits me to [dream of] a happy reunion with her, when she will be the genius of my home and the beautiful bride of my affections.

Farewell Love. May God preserve and protect you.

From your affectionate,

N. H. R. Dawson

Dalton, May 3, 1861

Even at the hazard of being thought [illegible] my dear Elodie, upon the eve of my departure this morning with the Regt. for Lynchburg, I steal a moment to tell you of my continuous devotion to you. My whole soul seems to swell with love for you, and if I could die at this moment, all my thoughts would be of you.

When will I be able to hear from you, my own dear girl? When shall I read your letters breathing your love and devotion? You must not fear to express your feelings freely. You must have confidence in that man who worships you as the only idol of his heart.

---

20. Egbert J. Jones (1818–1861) of Huntsville, Alabama, had helped raise the Fourth Alabama and was appointed its first colonel, though he did not have the full confidence of his men. 1860 U.S. Federal Census, Huntsville, Madison, Ala.

21. Evander M. Law (1836–1920) was born in South Carolina and moved to Alabama to run a military preparatory school. 1860 U.S. Federal Census, Darlington, S.C.

22. Major Charles Lewis Scott (1827–1899) was born in Richmond and served as a congressman from Virginia but met and married a young woman he met in Mobile, Alabama. He resigned his seat in Congress with the outbreak of war and joined the Fourth Alabama as a major. Charles L. Scott, Adventures of Charles L. Scott, Esq., ed. Kathy McCoy (Monroeville, Ala.: Monroe County Heritage Museums, 1997).

I sent you by [illegible] Lide[23] yesterday the wreath and some of the flowers that were presented to me on May Day. They were directed to Mrs. White and yourself, and he promised me to call and deliver the packet. How does my place *(yours)* look? Have you received any flowers? Let them remind you of me. And now good bye. Pray for me and may God in his mercy keep and preserve my dear Elodie.

Affectionately yours,

N. H. R. Dawson

Lynchburg, May 6, 1861

We reached this city last night after three days of most uncomfortable travel from Dalton. It was pouring down rain, and we were placed in a tobacco warehouse and slept upon the floors with our blankets without supper. I slept upon my shawl between two hogsheads of the Va. Weed. This morning it is raining again, and our men are very uncomfortable. We go to our quarters at the Fair Grounds as soon as the weather will permit. Under all these privations, I am supported by the will of my own loved angel, Elodie, which whispers me to bear all and hereafter to be rewarded with her love and her affections. Oh God, how deeply I love you, nay worship you. This is the anniversary of the death of one whose place in my heart you have supplied, and I am sad and dispirited.[24] Her image, clothed in the habiliments of immortality, is near to cheer and comfort me and beckon me on to a purer and better life. You must excuse me for alluding to this, but you are to comfort and soothe all my sorrows, and I know you will permit me to dwell sometimes upon the virtues of one who deserved all the devoted love I gave her while living and whose memory will ever be sacred in my heart.

---

23. Cornelius Mandeville Lide (1824–1908), a planter in Talladega County, Alabama, had married Nathaniel's sister, Mary Huger Dawson, in January 1850. He served as a private in Company D of the Third Alabama Cavalry.

24. Nathaniel's second wife, Mary E. Tarver, had died in early May 1860 following complications after the February birth of their daughter, Mary Tarver Dawson. Nathaniel's grief was especially fresh because it was the second time he had lost a young wife. In January 1853, his first wife, Elizabeth Mathews, had given birth to a daughter, Elizabeth Mathews Dawson, after which she gradually weakened and passed away in October 1854. Both of Nathaniel's daughters were living with him before the war but had to be parceled out to friends and relatives after he left. His first daughter, Elizabeth, was staying with her maternal grandparents, the Mathews. His second daughter, Mary, was apparently under the care of Nathaniel's senior legal partner, Edmund Winston Pettus.

I went to the Post Office, expecting to hear from you but was disappointed. Please write me and tell me all of your thoughts. You have no idea how much you are loved.

We will remain here in our quarters for several weeks to be drilled and equipped. And now Goodbye. God bless and preserve you, my own angel.

Affectionately yours,

N. H. R. Dawson

Camp near Lynchburg, May 8, 1861

I have read repeatedly your sweet letter of May 2d and hope my dear Elodie will indulge frequently in the pleasure of writing. It is to me a luxury to read anything from you here, and I do not flatter you when I tell you that your heart must be full of goodness to write as you do, so easily, sweetly, sensibly. I love you too well to flatter as our relations are now too close to permit us to indulge in it. You must express your own feelings freely because it is a happiness to know that you are willing to confide them to me. I would speak all my thoughts aloud to you, and, as I have told you, I have as much confidence in your fidelity as I have in the existence of the world. How so pure and gentle a being could be willing to confide the keeping of her affections and her happiness to me is frequently a subject of reflection, and I confess the enigma remains unsolved.

We began our duties today in earnest. I rose at daylight, attended officers drill from six to eight, breakfasted at eight, mounted guard at nine, acting as officer of the day, drilled from nine to twelve, and in the interval am writing you this letter using the pen you gave me. This morning I plucked from the side of the mountain the wild violets which are enclosed. They cover the ground, and there is a blue flower, which covers the ground in clusters like the oxalis. Does John[25] supply you with flowers? I intended him to do so.

I am very anxious to hear from your mother, and I hope she will interpose no objections. What would you do if she did? I would feel very badly and deeply chagrined.

---

25. One of Nathaniel's enslaved house servants, John, was frequently called upon to deliver flowers to Elodie and was described by Nathaniel as an "excellent servant" both "honest and trustworthy." In 1860 Nathaniel owned fifty-three slaves, most of them residing on his plantation. "N H R Dawson," 1860 U.S. Federal Census—Slave Schedules, Selma, Dallas County, Ala.

I hope to return safely to claim your hand, and if I do not you will always know that I have regarded you, in all things save the ceremonials of
the Law, as mine. At this point, I have just been handed your letter of 3d
May,[26] which I have read with renewed pleasure. You are a noble woman,
worthy of all my love, and I should bless Heaven you have promised to
be mine.

I do not know when we will be one, nor do I know our destination.
Can't you prevail upon your brother-in-law, A. L., to change his policy
& make peace? It would add greatly to our happiness. I have thought
that in case of the continuance of the war during the year that I might
with your consent, during the summer, obtain a furlough and return to
claim your hand, if you will consent to do so. To wait for a long, weary
year [for] the fulfillment of all our hopes is hard. Are you willing to
share my dangers and my privations? I dare to ask you, as I love you too
well to have you subjected to them. You could remain at home and get
some one to stay with you in *our home*. I wish to see you there as its mistress. It would be pleasant perhaps to spend the summer in Va. near our
camp in company with Mrs. Hardie.[27] What do you answer to this my dear
angel, Elodie?

Should you not agree to this cheerfully, don't hesitate to decline as I
know you will have good reasons for anything that you do. I love you so
truly and so well that if you were to decline to marry me at all, I would not
have the desire to *blame* you, though it would almost craze me.

I long to be in a condition to gratify all my wishes in respect to your
happiness without your having it in your power to decline allowing me
to do so. My heart is full when I think that fortune may still separate us.
But even in Heaven, I will be able to claim that you gave me your love
on earth.

Goodby dear girl, sweet Elodie. Write me frequently. God keep and
preserve you always is my prayer.

Affectionately your own,
N. H. R. Dawson

26. This letter does not survive.

27. Twenty-three-year-old Margaret Isbell married Joseph Hardie in 1856 and traveled
with him throughout the war. Joseph had been born in 1833, took his bachelor's degree
from Princeton in 1855, and owned a grocery store in Selma before the war. A lieutenant
colonel in the Fourth Alabama, he helped R. T. Coles write the unit's regimental history
after the war. Thomas McAdory Owen, History of Alabama and Dictionary of Alabama
Biography, vol. 3 (Chicago: S. J. Clarke Publishing Company, 1921), 774.

Selma, May 9, 1861

I commenced a letter to you yesterday morning, but being interrupted by company, was unwillingly compelled to put aside writing materials until this morning. Last Monday night my mother[28] and youngest sister Kittie[29] very unexpectedly made their appearance, and it is needless to tell how delighted I was or to attempt it, for after a separation of several months the reunion of course was pleasant. She declares you brought her, for until receiving your letter and my own, she had abandoned all thoughts of visiting the South before next winter. But two days after such startling intelligence reached her, she left Kentucky and was as much surprised to find herself in Selma as we were pleased to see her. I am sorry that you are not here for I am convinced could she but see you some of her opposition to my marrying would be more easily banished. Ever since I can remember, I have been looked upon and called the "old maid" of the family, and Mother seemed to think I was to be depended on to take care of her when all the rest of her *handsomer daughters* left her, and I really believe they all think I am committing a sin to give a thought to any other than the arrangements they have made for me. But as this is the age when Secession, Freedom, and Rights are asserted, I am claiming mine and do not doubt but I shall succeed in obtaining them as I have *some one* to help me in my efforts.[30] Mother brings us distressing news from Ky. She says the impression there is that dreadful fighting will soon begin, and there is so much excitement and indignation that once commenced there will be no end, altho' Gov. Magoffin[31] is trying to pre-

28. Elizabeth "Betsey" Humphreys Todd (1800–1874) was the second wife of Robert Smith Todd. Mary Lincoln famously complained that her stepmother hustled all of her husband's first children out of the room, but with eight of her own she may just have needed the room. See Berry, House of Abraham.

29. Catherine "Kittie" Bodley Todd (1841–1875) was the youngest sibling in the Todd family. After Lincoln's election, she visited the Lincolns in Springfield and became infatuated with their young friend Elmer Ellsworth, the dashing captain of a nationally famous military drill team. As the war progressed, however, she became more staunchly Confederate. See Berry, House of Abraham, 71–75.

30. Numerous Southern belles declared independence from their families and married without their father's consent during the Civil War. Another example is Georgia Page King, whose letters are available at the Georgia Historical Society, King and Wilder Family Papers, 1817–1946, Georgia Historical Society, Savannah, Ga.

31. Beriah Magoffin (1815–1885), twenty-first governor of Kentucky, sympathized with secession but nevertheless enforced the Kentucky General Assembly's neutrality proclamation. See Kentucky's Governors, ed. Lowell H. Harrison (Lexington: University Press of Kentucky, 2004), 78–81.

pare for it—defer battling until the last moment. Indeed, she says Ky. is utterly ruined; however, they of the old Union party have taken a view of the dark side of the picture. Let them but throw off Northern tyranny, and they will see the brighter and more beautiful view when summoned by the sisterhood of Southern Independence.

Matt has just interrupted me to say there is a room full of company, among them Dr. and Mrs. Mabry[32] and Miss Scott,[33] but I experience myself thinking three quite enough to entertain all visitors until this letter is finished, and being too selfish to deny myself the pleasure of talking to you on paper, altho' I doubt whether I would contribute any to their gratification or even be missed. Last night Kittie and myself went over to the encampment of the Blues and spent a very pleasant evening dancing until 11 o'clock. The wit and beauty of Selma were assembled, and it was quite an interesting scene to see the groups of young people scattered here and there, engaged in lively conversation, others dancing, while Mr. Woods[34] and some others drew an admiring crowd to be entertained by their music. Capt. Kent[35] has invited the ladies to come and dance every night and arrangements are to be made to make things more comfortable and pleasant. I hear they will certainly be moved off by the end of ten days. Mr. Pegues[36] and company left for Pensacola Tuesday, so Mr. Hagood told me and he knows everything. I made some pleasant acquaintances and enjoyed the fine hand of music they had with them. The Greensboro company is composed of the handsomest men I ever saw and all seem to be selected gentlemen and so happy and merry. But it made me feel unpleasant to think how few of the many there would perhaps

---

32. Albert Gallatin Mabry (1810–1874) was a prominent Selma physician who served often in the Alabama legislature from 1857 to 1867. He and his wife, Martha Mabry, had six children, including Gertrude, who appears later in this correspondence. Thomas McAdory Owen, History of Alabama and Dictionary of Alabama Biography, vol. 4 (Chicago: S. J. Clarke Publishing Company, 1921), 1142–1143.

33. Likely Susan V. Scott, age twenty-three, sister of Charles Lewis Scott (see Nathaniel to Elodie, May 2, 1861, note 22).

34. Probably Charles Woods, mentioned in several later letters by Elodie.

35. Dr. James Kent had been born in Virginia in 1830 and married Mary Grey Alston of Marengo County, Alabama, in 1855. A physician living in Selma before the war, he ultimately rose to become colonel of the Forty-Fourth Alabama. 1860 Census: Selma; marriage certificate, James Kent and Mary G. Alston, Marengo, Ala., Alabama, Select Marriages, 1816–1942.

36. Christopher Claudius Pegues (1823–1862) was a partner, with Nathaniel, in the law firm of Pettus, Pegues, and Dawson. Christopher began, like Nathaniel, as a captain, in the Fifth Alabama, but he rose to colonel before being fatally wounded at Gaines Mill. Owen, History of Alabama, 4:1336.

return and of course yourself and your noble little band came immediately before my eyes and first in my thoughts. By this time you must be in Lynchburg, and I am expecting a letter from you every day to inform me of your safe arrival there and all the news and prospects for peace or War. I will not often allow myself to think of the latter in connection with yourself for then I grow so miserable. I can picture to myself you wounded, killed, and everything that is horrible and am so restless that I do not know what to do to compose myself again to calmness. If there was anything known that could relieve this terrible suspense and let us be certain of the worst and have it over, I believe I could bear it better and bravely, but as it is I am afraid you would be ashamed of me, altho' none but yourself know or dream of the fears that are continually haunting my mind. You see I take you at your word and express freely enough my feelings, and this must convince you of the entire confidence I feel in you to do so, and for aught I know you may think I make myself ridiculous. Do I? If so, just give a gentle hint, and I'll take it.

You ask me how your place looks. Well, I have only seen it twice, and then it looked desolate and dreary enough, altho' the flowers are blooming beautifully and that relieves the deserted look the place wears a little and which are brought to me regularly Tuesday and Friday evenings. It is quite amusing to hear the gossip concerning myself in Selma. Some know so much. Matt was asked the other day if it was true that I was engaged to you, and another lady yesterday intimated that she knew I was to marry Mr. H.[37] on the 18th, and I suppose Mother's arrival will be confirmation strong.

Matt says tell Mr. Dawson that at first she was opposed herself, thinking no one was good enough for me, but that she is now your best friend since Mother is inclined to urge some opposition. I told Mother that I thought she had better give her consent and approval at once for my mind was made up, and I felt myself more of a Todd than ever, and they are noted for their determination or, as *malicious people* would say, *obstinacy*, and I believe she is becoming more reconciled as I discuss the subject with her. But you must make all due allowance, of a Mother's love naturally blinds her to her daughter's faults, and my family all love me more than I deserve and are not willing to see the faults that to others are so perceptible. I write this because I am not willing you should have a better opinion of me than I deserve and perhaps some day be awakened to

37. Robert Hagood (see Elodie to Nathaniel, May 2, 1861, note 19).

all my faults and feel disappointed. I was not all you were lead to believe from what my own family, blinded by affection, gave you reason to think.

I am as usual writing a long letter, and you only write me a few lines. After you reach Lynchburg and have more leisure (I don't think of fighting for a moment), I hope to receive long letters also, and you will try to write to me every day when you are not too much engaged, won't you? I am safe here with friends to protect from dangers, and there is no necessity for you to trouble yourself about me. But I *know you are surrounded* by danger and feel uneasy when I do not hear, and you have been kind in writing to me so often on your way that I must not say another word and will here end my scrawl, hoping to receive cheering news very soon of no battles but a safe and speedy return to your

Affectionate Elodie

P.S. I am so commented on and teased for writing to you so much and often that I expect the next thing to have to beg houseroom from some one long enough to write you letters, for when I begin to write they all congregate around me and commence to chatter like birds and want to know how I commence my letters and end them, what I call you and etc. and I *dread* Bro. Clem's return. You know of course Mobile is blockaded, and we think Bro. C. will have to go half around the world before he can return, which he will do I hope by railroad. I enclose a letter from mother. Don't believe quite all she says about me. Mother traveled out with Gen'l Beauregard[38] and staff, to whom she was introduced, and he presented her with a handsome bouquet and my sister a secession flag, the first she ever saw.

Camp near Lynchburg, May 9, 1861

I have just read over your notes of 21 and 24th April[39] with a chapter of the bible from the bible you gave me. The sweet words of love and confidence in your notes are a comfort and a solace. You promise me your love unalterably and under all circumstances and sign yourself "your own Elodie." These indeed are flattering expressions, and I long to receive an-

---

38. P. G. T. Beauregard (1818–1893) served as a general of the Confederate States Army.
39. These letters, written while Nathaniel was still in Alabama, do not survive in any known collection.

other letter in which you will sign yourself my own Elodie. Why is woman
so jealous of expressing her feelings, so guarded in telling the prompt-
ings of her heart? If it were treason to love you, I could be found guilty
from any one of my letters for I cannot conceal the fact. Probably you do
not like my style of writing, but I cannot help it & even as my wife I would
love & write to you as passionately. I adore and worship you above all
things and would willingly labor seven long, weary years to win your love.

   In you, I see all that I want in a wife—the winning modesty, the cultivated intellect, the witching simplicity and ingeniousness of truthfulness
and sincerity. How welcome will be the hour when I shall lead you from
the altar to my home to bless me with your love and affections. There you
will be the gentle Egeria[40] who will woo me from evil and from sin and
train me in the paths of goodness and Christianity. In my library, how
sweet in the long winter evenings to listen to your conversation or to hear
your voice upon the piano or the guitar. Gentle, dear Elodie, how happy
you have made me. How much I owe you for having consented to be
mine. What induced you to love so undeserving a man, one whose head
has been steeped in the waters of sorrow and misery, whom the world
only knows unfavorably as a cold, selfish man? Take the enigma and be
prepared to realize the rashness of the act.

   I have no news. Troops are pouring in by every train. 1000 Miss. arrived yesterday, and still they are coming. 5000 Va. troops are collecting
here. The rumors of war and our destination are very conflicting. I hope
these difficulties will be settled without war, but I am almost alone in the
opinion. It may be that my anxiety about you makes me think so.

   The ladies visit the camp in large numbers every evening. I am vain
enough for your sake to think that they look favorably at me, but I am
very careful to tell them that I have no heart to give away. Is this right? I
have met with much kindness from various persons, some of whom I have
known heretofore, having met them in my travels. I have just declined an
invitation to tea as I do not feel disposed to take the trouble to dress for
such an occasion; indeed, I have no desire to extend my acquaintance
beyond the circle of my own dear Elodie. I was up until three o'clock last
night visiting the sentinels [and] have drilled four hours today. At three
I turn out again and will be on the pace till 7 o'clock this evening.

---

   40. In Roman mythology, Egeria was the nymph and consort to the second Sabine king
of Rome, whom she advised on matters of law and religious ritual. Her name became syn-
onymous with that of a wise female advisor to a male leader.

The drums are just beating, and I am called away from the pleasure of conversing with you. I will try to write you frequently, and you must remember that it will be done even at the expense of duty.

We are all well except a few men with colds. My boys are greatly attached to their captain and point me out on all occasions as the handsomest officer to the ladies in the regiment. I bear the flattery for your sake.

And now goodbye. God bless and protect you always, my dear Elodie.

Ever and affectionately yours,

N. H. R. Dawson

P.S. Please remember me very kindly to Mrs. White. No one here suspects our engagement. Is it suspected in Selma?

Lynchburg, May 10, 1861

I have come on to the city this morning upon business connected to my company and am now waiting patiently at the office of the adjutant general for my time to come. Does my dear Elodie blame me for occupying the time in writing to her instead of reading a newspaper? Does she not tire of my long, foolish letters so frequently received that the P[ost] M[aster] will imagine the distance of our relations? But until you forbid it, I will continue to write you as frequently as possible, and I ask you to pay me in the same coin. I have no time for studied language, and you must excuse all deficiencies in style and rhetoric.

We are roused daily at 4 o'clock by the beating of reveille; officers drill from 4½ o'clock to 7. Breakfast at 7½. General inspection at 8. Drill for companies from 9 to 12. Recess from 12 to 2½. Drill from 2½ to 5½. Dress parade at 5½. Supper at 6½. Roll call at 9. Tattoo at 9½ when lights are extinguished, and we are all required to retire. I have so much to do and so many things to occupy my attention that I have little leisure, and you will be flattered when I tell you that most of it is directed to you.

As I was directing your letter yesterday, writing at my trunk upon your little desk, the top of the trunk fell, and the desk struck me upon the forehead, cutting it open to the bone. Your scissors were used for the first time to cut a piece of adhesive plaster to close up the incision, so you see how kind you have been. The wound is not at all painful, only on a bad place. It may leave a scar. I am quite well. I really have improved on the rough fare, and if I can get through as well as I have commenced, [I] will have reason to be grateful. I find that you have exercised a great

influence upon me and that you have given me strength and will to resist the temptations of the campaign life. You have blessed me with your
confidence and love, and I will try to be worthy of you in many respects.
I wish it were so that the war had been put off until after our union, but
we must hope for the best, and I at least will endeavor to be patient.
Do you approve of long engagements under ordinary circumstances? If
there had been no war or if I could have remained at home, I would have
requested my loved Elodie to give me her hand at an early day for I see
no reason why there should have been delay. The earlier hearts that love
become united the sooner they enter upon the realization of happiness.
"The briefer life the earlier immortality" expresses my meaning better.
The day that you become the chosen partner of my [illegible] and home
will be to me a day of infinite happiness, and I am anxious to have it
placed at as early a time as circumstance will allow.

I gathered some wild violets for you this morning. I know you will value
them. I send with them a piece of the gold lace from my sword belt which
was torn off yesterday, which you may value hereafter.[41]

How amply, how fondly, you are adored, my loved angel Elodie. Should
you never be mine from the [illegible] of fate, I hope you will find another to love you as well as I do for I am not so selfish as to wish you to
be miserable on my account, and all I will ask is that he may love you as
directly and truly as I do and that he may be worthy of your love. 'Tis a
wealth that is worth all the days of the earth, and, with you as the partner
of my life, I will seek no other happiness. I have tired you with this long
letter, and I must close it.

Will you think of me always at 9 o'clock at night when I will devote
my thoughts to you? It will be pleasant to know that tho' distant we are
united in our thoughts.

Remember me very kindly to your sister. I expect she thinks me des-
perately in love. If she could see how many flowers are sent me by the
ladies, how polite I am in accepting them and in [illegible] my thanks,
she might imagine that I was in some danger here, but I assure you I am
made proof against any attack from any quarter save the battery of your
own black eyes. Good bye, my own dear girl. May God protect and keep
and preserve you from all danger and troubles is the constant prayer of
your own devoted and affectionate friend,

N. H. R. Dawson

---

41. Dawson's bit of gold braiding is still a part of the collection.

Harpers Ferry, May 10, 1861

I wrote you a hurried note this morning, my own dear Elodie, but as I am sitting alone in my tent, suffering a little from the effects of quinine[42] and I have a private opportunity of writing, I avail myself of it to do myself the pleasure of writing you a longer letter. I know what a pleasure it is for me to hear from you and am confident that it is a great pleasure for you to hear from me.

We are not as comfortably fixed as we were in our Ala. encampment but comfort is one of the articles we left at home and is therefore not to be regarded.

I sent my trunk yesterday to Winchester by Mr. Averitt. He will leave it with a friend of his, and I do not know when I will again have the benefit of the few little luxuries and comforts it contained. I am now reduced to one suit of clothing and the few articles that a knap sack will contain. I am sorry to say that there are some men in the company too nice to do many of the duties required of them, and I have frequently to [lead by] an example. Some demur to carrying their knapsacks. Yesterday you should have seen their astonishment when I came out of my tent with a knapsack on with all of my accoutrements, rifle, sword and pistol, and large overcoat. I am obliged to do many of these things for the sake of example, and I am subjected to much inconvenience in consequence. But I desire to share all of the hardships and dangers of my men as they have manifested much feeling for me on several occasions.

We are encamped just in the rear of our line of battle[43] and will be very near the post of danger should the enemy show his face in front. I am really indifferent to the dangers of battle, and if it were not for the love I bear you, would have little apprehension. I have great confidence in the justice of our cause and have an abiding faith that fewer of our men will be killed than circumstances would indicate. You will notice that in all of our battles so far, we have escaped almost miraculously while the enemy have suffered greatly in comparison.

Even now, with their large armies in the field and all the appearance to the contrary, I do not think we will have a long war. The idea of subju-

42. Quinine, which occurs naturally in the bark of the cinchona tree, reduces fevers, kills pain, and has a bitter taste. For more, see Glenna R. Schroeder-Lein, The Encyclopedia of Civil War Medicine (New York: Routledge, 2015), 257–258.

43. On May 1, Confederate troops under Colonel Thomas J. Jackson were sent to occupy Harpers Ferry and keep it out of Union hands.

gating us must be preposterous, and I think, if I could be allowed to have the ear of my future *brother-in-law*, I could persuade him to abandon the idea if he ever entertained it. Can't you use your influence or get your sister Miss Kittie to use hers? I am anxious to know your sister and more anxious to become her *brother*. Does she look like you? I hope her influence with Mr. Lincoln will save me the trouble of being hanged, should I fall into his power. Is it not strange that I should be so anxious to see Mr. Lincoln defeated in his policy and at the same time be so devoted to his sister-in-law? I love you above all things and wish to live to prove to you, my dearest, that my protestations are not unreal. I could be steeped to the very lips in poverty if I were allowed to fall down and bow to your love in compensation. I reflect frequently upon the course of our acquaintance and really believe that Providence sent you as an angel of mercy to cross my path. How else could you have loved me in so short a time? Did you have any other than a feeling of respect and esteem for me previous to a declaration of my own feelings? Many ladies, you know, never love until they are married and are so coy as to express indifference in place of love. I do not admire the class, however, and am much more partial to those who deem it no sin to express themselves in language that is plain.

Remember that your letters will always be safe. If I have not sent them off in my trunk yesterday, I would send them to you by Mr. Ware[44] who goes off tomorrow. But when I send them, you must remember that they are still *mine* and merely placed with you for safekeeping, as the others were previous to my leaving home. You must keep them safely for me as I expect to derive many pleasant reminiscences from their perusal with you.[45] How pleasant will it be to sit with you and to hear you talk. When

---

44. H. H. Ware, age thirty-four, was married to Inda Ware, age twenty-nine. The couple owned six slaves, including Ned Admins, "a free man of color about sixty years old," who used the 1860 voluntary enslavement ruling in Alabama to become a "slave for life to Mistress Inda Ware of the city of Selma, in the county of Dallas, to her sole and separate use." In Emily West's Family or Freedom: People of Color in the Antebellum South (Lexington: University Press of Kentucky, 2012), West speculates that Ned was trying to be near his enslaved wife, perhaps Cealy Adkins, a forty-five-year-old enslaved woman belonging to H. H. Ware. This familial situation became even more fraught when a "favorite and indulged" enslaved woman poisoned both H. H. Ware and his daughter, an incident Elodie notes in her letter of October 13, 1861.

45. Elodie later requested that her letters be burned after he read them, but Nathaniel refused. Many wartime letter collections contain letters written only by men because their wives, sisters, and mothers could more easily save them. Soldiering males more often burned, lost, or discarded letters sent to them. Certainly if Nathaniel had not sent Elodie's letters back home to her for safekeeping, we would not now have her thoughts and perspectives on their courtship.

we meet I intend to be a patient listener as it is much pleasanter to listen than to talk, at least it is to me when I am with one whom I love and who talks as well as you do. . . .

Now dearest, I have spent an hour in writing you anything but an interesting letter. I have written to convince you that under all circumstances I intend to make an effort to please you. Goodbye, my loved and affectionate Elodie. May God keep and protect you, and may your dreams be guarded by angels while you sleep.

Ever affectionately and sincerely yours,

N. H. R. Dawson

Camp Davis, Lynchburg, May 11, 1861

We received marching order for Harpers Ferry last night at 12 o'clock to leave at 5 this morning. The camp was aroused and orders given to cook two days rations. You cannot imagine the bustle and noise of the night. At four o'clock our Col. who is slower than a Yankee clock arrived from town and countermanded the order and put the time at ten o'clock. We are all anxious to reach the scene of danger, and I apprehend that most of the regiment wish for a fight. I must confess, however, that I have no great anxiety for a battle as the idea of not seeing my own loved Elodie is not a pleasant reflection. I wrote you upon the eve of leaving to testify to you that even in such a moment of noise and bustle, I turn with feelings of devotion to that spot where my gentle and loved Elodie is, to tell her of my constancy and love and to convince her that under all changes and circumstances, she is the divinity of my life. How deeply I love you is known alone to you and to my creator. Tis sweet to know that I have your prayers and love for my safety, and I think I will bear a charmed life thro' the perils of war on your account. I met with a beautiful young lady yesterday evening at dress parade. A gentleman handed me a card with the compliments of Mr. Morly. After the parade was dismissed a servant came up and desired me to go to a carriage near by. I did so and was introduced to Mr. Morly and his daughter, a very pretty and sweet lady. She wore on one ungloved finger a rich diamond and if you had not already occupied my heart, I might have fallen in love at sight. Mr. M. was very polite and pressed me to take tea this evening, which I of course consented to do, but our departure today breaks up this very pleasant episode in camp life. Another lady presented me with a beautiful bouquet. Are you not jealous

and afraid that I will wander from the influence of your charms? Never, ·
never, my own loved girl. I would not quit you for all the women in the
world. You are the soul of my life, my very existence, and it is all because
you love me and have warmed it to life, the bruised and broken ruins of
my bosom. Why do you hesitate to tell me that you love me? Is it a sin?
Or do you fear that I may forsake you? Have no fears. I will be as true as
the dial to the sun. When will you be mine at the altar? How happy will I
be when you will lean upon my arm as my wife, the wife who is to guide
and direct me to better pursuits and to whose counsels and persuasions
I am to lend obedience. I wish I could feel as deeply of things in Heaven
as I do of my faith in you. My heart overflows with love, and you must not
think me foolish for giving expression to my feelings. I will never be fit
for anything again until you have become mine. I know you would like
me to write differently, to speak of scenery and such things, but my feelings are engrossed by you alone. I hear that much excitement prevails at
Selma. I hope my home will not be burnt, as I wish to introduce you to it
as soon as you will consent to be its mistress and circumstances will allow.

Write me to Harpers Ferry. It is a beautiful spot. Mr. Jefferson said it
was worth a voyage across the ocean to see it, and I will try to give you
my impressions of its scenery.[46] Goodbye my own, dear-loved Elodie. May
God bless and preserve you.

Affectionately yours,
N. H. R. Dawson

Harpers Ferry, May 14, 1861

Since writing you from Strasbourg—not Port Royal as the letter was
dated yesterday—I have passed quite an eventful time. We marched 18
miles to Winchester and arrived during a heavy storm of wind, rain, and
hail and were all wet. I walked the *whole way* tho' a horse and buggy were
provided for me thro' a friend, as I wished to share with my company
all of their hardships. My feet were so blistered and swollen, and I was
so much fatigued, that I got a room at a hotel and went to bed and was
unable to come on here until this morning. I am very lame, have taken

---

46. In his Notes on the State of Virginia, Thomas Jefferson described the view and then
famously noted, "This scene alone is worth a voyage across the Atlantic."

· violent cold, and have been in bed, or rather on a blanket, since reaching the place, until within the last 20 minutes when I got up to write my own dear Elodie, if it were but a short note.

On the cars this morning, Mr. Hardie, who remained at Lynchburg to join his wife, handed me your long and welcome letter of the 6th May. I was sick, sad, and low-spirited, but it acted like a panacea, and I read it over several times. How affectionate you are to think me so generous in sharing wreaths with you. Is not all that is mine yours? Are you not, dear angel, the loved and promised partner of all my joys? How then am I generous in bestowing what is yours! *I love you fondly* and *truly*, and every *hour* but adds to the *depth* of that *love*. I hope and pray that I may return to be *blessed* with the *wealth* of *your love*.

About your writing to Mr. A.,[47] you will use your own *discretion*. He is a friend of both of us but is indiscreet in his friendship, and it might be well for you to turn him over to Mr. White. I have no means of knowing what will be the result of our difficulties. Rumors of all kinds prevail. Last night the troops were kept under arms all night from apprehension of an attack. About seven thousand troops are now here engaged in fortifying the heights, and I do not think the Federal army will attack us. Among the troops is a regiment from Kentucky under Col. Duncan.[48] I will endeavor for your sake to make acquaintances among them. There is, I hope, a probability that peace will yet obtain. I pray so *for our happiness*. Is this not selfish in me? I have not been able to see anything owing to my indisposition. When I do, I will write you of the scenery.

I bear all of my privations without a murmur as my own brave Elodie would have her lover and future husband bear all things well and patiently. My dear Elodie must not fear that the fascinations of the Virginia ladies will steal my affections from her. I have had opportunities innumerable in Ala. and elsewhere to win the favor of the fair women of the South, but none have ever been able to do it but your peerless self. I could tell you some things that might surprise you at the attempts that have been made to win me to the smiles of some ladies by their friends, but these are not *my secrets*, and I cannot discuss them even to my own

---

47. James Battle Avirett.

48. A wealthy lawyer from Louisville, Kentucky, Blanton Duncan (1811–1902) was the son of Congressman Garret Duncan, who went to Europe in 1861 to avoid choosing sides. At thirty-five, Blanton had no such hesitation, and formed the First Confederate Kentucky Infantry regiment with no prior military experience. Pierre Fricke, Confederate Currency (London: Shire Publications, 2012), 21.

affianced Elodie. I hope you will never have reason to regret that you have confided to me your heart. You may not admire the style of my letters, but you must excuse the unstudied language of my heart. You love naturalness, and for that reason you tell me that you *admire* yourself. I did not know you had so much *egotism*, but as I agree with you in this case you are excused.

There is no truth in the report about Mr. Brown being a spy, and you will see a note of mine in the Reporter in regard to it.[49] I left word with Mr. Williams[50] to send me his paper and have received it occasionally. I see Dr. Mabry is of the opinion that he is one of the two gentlemen who alone can represent Dallas.[51] I wish I were at home to undeceive him. Tell me, do you wish me to be a politician or do you wish me to pursue my profession? I wish to pursue that path in life which will most contribute to your comfort and happiness. To live for you will be the sole object of life, and, to do this, I must consult your feelings and wishes. I do not think it would be right or just to resolve upon any step in life now without consulting you. I regard you now as almost wedded to me as far as affection and mutual promises can bind us, wanting only the ceremonials of the church. It is singular that you should have been five days without a letter from me as I have written you almost daily and will continue to do so whenever I am able. You cannot write too frequently. The only pleasure I have is to receive one of your letters and next is the pleasure of writing to you. Tell me of yourself, how you think of me. It is flattering to know that you are sad on my account. You never told me when you first thought of me in your heart. Tell me, how did you come to fancy such a [illegible] man? I have been made to think better of myself since you loved me. Mr. Simpson[52]—you remember him at Montgomery—he also came down the river with us, is a Lieutenant in a company here with Alabama. He has spoken to me of you in very flattering terms. You are known widely and favorably as the sister of Mr. Lincoln, and I am proud of such an angel. I used to comply with your request to write you only *two lines* but have been beguiled into a long, prosy letter, but it has run along so imperceptibly that it has in a measure relieved the soreness of my bosom, the aching

---

49. The Selma Reporter, a local newspaper.

50. Philip Williams, of Winchester, Virginia, an attorney and father of Mary Williams, whom Averitt married in 1862. 1860 U.S. Federal Census, Winchester, Frederick, Va.

51. Dallas County, Alabama, had its county seat in the city of Selma.

52. John Simpson Jr. was a lieutenant in Company H of the Fourth Alabama; he would be killed at the Battle of First Manassas. Joel Campbell DuBose, *Notable Men of Alabama*, vol. 2 (Atlanta: Southern Historical Association, 1904), 240.

of my heart. I am so hoarse that I can hardly speak. I hope by tomorrow to be well. Write me at Harper's Ferry. Your letters to Lynchburg will be forwarded. Mrs. Mason's daughter, wife of Senator Mason of Va., came to the hotel yesterday evening to take me to their home.[53] What think you of the captain? I know Mr. Mason.

And now goodbye dear girl. I will never cease to love you and to dream of you with my last sighs.

Ever your attached,
N. H. R. Dawson

P.S. Does John supply you regularly with flowers? He is *trustworthy*, and you may occasionally tell him that I am well. I told him he must make you his *friend*, and I hope he has not forgotten the injunction. I wish I could personate the flowers and be with my own dear angel.

Goodbye and God bless you.
H.

Selma, May 15, 1861

Yesterday I commenced to write you five times and each time was compelled to put aside my desk by the arrival of company, which came so fast and stayed so long that my patience was almost exhausted. Only the hope of being able to accomplish my desire after tea kept a remaining particle, but, after our tea was over, in came two beaux to take us to either camp or to hear Judge Campbell (of Mobile)[54] speak. I declined going to either at first but was finally persuaded to go over to the camp where we can all enjoy ourselves dancing, altho' I was only a looker and did not participate all evening having heard that fighting had commenced at Pensacola and Harper's Ferry. Tho' I did not place much confidence in the rumor, I

---

53. James Murray Mason (1798–1874) was a former U.S. senator; he was married to Eliza M. Chew (1798–1874), and together they had eight children: three daughters and five sons. For more, see Robert W. Young, Senator James Murray Mason: Defender of the Old South (Knoxville: University of Tennessee Press, 1998).

54. John Archibald Campbell (1811–1889) was an Alabama jurist appointed by Franklin Pierce to the U.S. Supreme Court, serving until the outbreak of the Civil War. He was one of the three Confederate peace commissioners sent to meet with Abraham Lincoln at Hampton Roads near the end of the war. After the war, Campbell resumed his law practice in New Orleans, where he became one of the chief legal architects of the South's successful gutting of Reconstruction. For more, see Robert Saunders, John Archibald Campbell, Southern Moderate, 1811–1889 (Tuscaloosa: University of Alabama Press, 1997).

could not think of enjoying myself in such a gay manner when those I was so interested in were in danger. I received three letters from you while at Lynchburg yesterday and heard of your departure for Harper's Ferry, Mr. McCraw[55] having telegraphed to Dr. Shortridge[56] the morning your company left Lynchburg for that place. I was completely at a loss where to write and at last concluded that your letters would be forwarded. Ere this you have received a letter from myself and mother written the 9th, which I hope will please you. She is still with us and will I trust remain until Kentucky is more decided in her movement.

My brother-in-law, Mr. Helm,[57] writes from Louisville that they are daily and hourly fearing an attack from Federal troops at Jeffersonville and New Albany and that there will be terrible bloodshed and soon in different parts of the state. My sister, Mrs. Kellogg,[58] for expressing sympathy for the South, has been compelled to leave Cincinnati. Is it any wonder that I am inclined to be sad, but I am wrong in writing to you in such a strain. If you did request me to write and freely tell all my thoughts and feelings, and I am conscious of being selfish, when you have nothing very bright to look forward to and not even a very cheerful letter, to burden

---

55. S. Newton McCraw, age twenty-two, was second lieutenant in Nathaniel's company and is described as Nathaniel's "most intimate friend" on August 3, 1861. His sister, Ella L. McCraw, nineteen years old, became a good friend of Elodie's and is mentioned often in the correspondence. 1860 Census: Selma.

56. Possibly George David Shortridge (1814–1870), father of George D. Shortridge Jr., a lieutenant in Nathaniel's company. George D. Shortridge Jr. (1837–1868) married Victoria English Echols on June 10, 1862, twenty days before his brother Eli died in the Battle of Seven Pines. Owen, History of Alabama, 4:1555; marriage certificate, George D. Shortridge and Victoria Echols, Dallas County, Ala., Alabama, Select Marriages, 1816–1942.

57. Benjamin Hardin Helm (1831–1862) married Elodie's older sister Emilie in 1856. A lawyer before the war, Helm had been educated at West Point and had done a short stint in the prewar army. Shortly after Sumter, Lincoln summoned Helm to the White House and offered to appoint him major in the paymaster corps and post him to the West, where he could remain a neutral. The post was the highest Lincoln could make without congressional approval. Helm turned the offer down and joined the Confederate army, though he admitted to a friend it was "the most painful moment of my life." He rose to the rank of brigadier general before being killed at Chickamauga. After her husband's death, Emilie stayed a week at the White House despite her status as a grieving Confederate widow. For more on Emilie, see Angela Esco Elder, "'We Weep over Our Dead Together': Emilie Todd Helm and Confederate Widowhood," in Kentucky Women: Their Lives and Times, ed. Tom Appleton and Melissa McEuen (Athens: University of Georgia Press, 2015).

58. Margaret Todd (1828–1904), the eldest of the Humphreys-Todd siblings, was married to Charles Henry Kellogg, a Cincinnati merchant. Despite attending Lincoln's inaugural, both had strong ties to the Confederacy. Charles even traveled with the Confederate army for a few weeks around the Battle of Shiloh in the spring of 1862 before returning to the North. See Berry, House of Abraham, 117–120.

you with my foolish apprehensions. I felt gratified that when you were sad and lonely you turned to me for sympathy, and you will never hesitate to write and to speak always of subjects near your heart. I hoped indeed I shall claim as my special right and privilege to divide with you all *your cares and sorrows,* and you must not deny me. Nor would I hesitate for a moment to share and brave your dangers were it necessary but think for your own sake it were better not, for I would only be a care and trouble to you all the time, and as I am situated now by friends who watch carefully over me and am out of danger, you would be saved much anxiety and trouble. I do not think my presence would compensate you for your care and annoyance for I am a *troublesome somebody at all* times and should be sure to improve with the times. I always want to act as you desire me even tho' I sacrifice my own selfish feelings, but *this time I really think of your comfort* by writing as I do, and you must believe it is so for I could not suf-fer more from anxiety myself anywhere than I do at present here where I am sometimes for days without receiving a line from you as it takes four or five days for a letter to arrive. I go daily to the post office, sometimes accompanied by Matt, and *know* I have received all your letters safely and am looking forward with impatience to the arrival of the mail. As your time is occupied with duties and you have so little leisure, I will not ask that you devote so much to me but will try and content myself with receiving an occasional account of yourself.

I heard from Mr. Averitt Monday and am glad that he has not forgotten me yet for I feel it a compliment to be regarded as the friend of so noble a man as I think him and he has proved himself to be. We are looking for Bro. Clem and Mr. Davis every day, but I do not know whether they will return by railroad or water but do not fear any danger [in] either route.

You are so complimentary as to my style of letter-writing that you [are] getting yourself into trouble for I am vain enough to think *it all so* and when I believe you are in earnest will write letters just twice as long as I do now and think upon the reception of another letter as full of compli-ments as the last I must punish you with a *very long* letter for attempting to spoil me, for if you begin in this way I shall expect you to keep it up and all else that is *pleasant.* I give you fair warning I have no objection in the world to your obtaining furlough to come and *see me* for I *believe* I would prefer seeing *you* to *any one* I know and hope you will before the year is out.

I am sorry to hear that you are *battling* already and would prefer your escaping as many scars as possible, but do not think of returning *without some* as you will never be accounted *brave* and *bold*. Kittie says she fears you will come home limping or without arms, Matt says without a head, so you can see what a subject of thoughts you are in the family, only don't realize Matt's fears and a body can stand the test that is nothing but an inconvenience. Kittie says if you take her beau Col. Ellsworth[59] prisoner just send him to her and she will see that he does not escape.

I am ashamed to send you this hurried scrawl, but we are to have company to spend the day, and I have only a few moments to write in and no doubt you are glad that such is the case. The Blues are still making a great noise about going away, have succeeded in obtaining from the citizens 8 or more nice tents and are enjoying pound cake and all delicacies from the ladies in such quantities that they have requested no more to be sent for several days. What a pity you did not encamp for a few days prior to your departure from Selma. Pray remember to do so next time. I am indignant when I think of you all as in danger without tents and a pitiful sum in hand from the generous hearts of this community and Blues at home enjoying everything and peacefully protected without any intention or thought of going, or if they do it will be after the fighting is over. I will think of [you] at 9 o'clock and assure you that my last and first thought is of you, and I could add *look* also for I keep your daguerreotype close at hand and spend more time gazing at it than the *Virginia ladies* do the *original* I know. I am proud that so much attention is lavished on you and think you deserve it all. It is nothing more than you are entitled to, but all are not so fortunate as to receive their dues, and I hope the same good fortune may attend you all the war through.

At last I must say goodbye for a few days when I shall write again. Let me hear from you again soon. Will you grant me the request to destroy all my letters? I would not have them seen for a great deal. Does Mr. A. know of our engagement? I know he suspects. So far from being suspected here, all think I am to be married the 18th to Mr. H. and I am inclined to think *he believes* so too from his attention, but strange to say

---

59. Elmer Ephraim Ellsworth was the twenty-three-year-old captain of the famous Zouaves, a military company that had recently concluded a national tour, performing their synchronized drills in their trademark baggy trousers, high gaiters, brocaded blue jackets, and red fezzes. The Lincolns brought Ellsworth into their family circle, and in the fall of 1860 at Lincoln's urging Ellsworth relocated to Springfield, where he met Mary's youngest sister Kitty. Although Ellsworth had a fiancée to whom he was devoted, he proved a gracious flirt, and he and Kitty got on famously. By the end of her stay in Springfield, nineteen-year-old Kitty was smitten. See Berry, House of Abraham, 72–75.

I am a greater belle than ever and have more beaux *now than I want.* I have filled very space and could add more but declared I would not so once more goodby. Dodge all bullets and come home as soon as possible to your affectionate,
    Elodie

Harper's Ferry, May 17, 1861

Your long and interesting letter of the 9th was received yesterday evening with your mother's note. I have written an answer which you must read and deliver if you like it. I have written it hurriedly under all the inconveniences of camp life with interruptions enough to vex a saint, and you must, as my fair and all-powerful advocate, make up for all deficiencies of style and matter in your speeches upon the subject. It is flattering to a sick and weary soldier to know that he has turned towards him the eyes of so gentle and witching a lady as those of my own dear Elodie, one who is calculated in all things to make him happy. You write just as I wish, naturally and freely, flattering to me and indicating how pure is the stream from whence refreshing cups of pearly dew are allowed to escape. The more I read your letters the more singular it seems to me that I have been so fortunate as to win your love. Had I not been a volunteer, I never would have known how rich were the imaginings of your mind and how pure and beautiful were the flowers that grow in the garden of your heart. Each letter discovers some new beauty and each hour spent with you will but add to the number of your charms and increase the boundless love now burning in my bosom. As your mother loves you very much, I have no fears upon the subject of her consent being eventually obtained. It must be a great pleasure to Mrs. White and yourself to have your sister and herself with you, and I regret that I am denied the pleasure of seeing them, but you know I am to take you to Kentucky when I will have that honor and pleasure. Tell your sister Kate[60] that I must employ her as an advocate and that if she succeeds well the fee will be a large one, but I had forgotten that, in you, I have an advocate *con amore* who will charge nothing for her services and whose success with her mother upon this

---

60. Nathaniel is referring to Catherine (Kitty) Todd (1841–1875), the youngest of the Todd sisters. Like Elodie, as the war progressed she became more staunchly Confederate and ultimately married William Wallace Herr, the man who would help carry Benjamin Hardin Helm's body from the field at Chickamauga. See Berry, House of Abraham, 184–185.

point cannot be doubted. I hope sincerely that we may have peace, but the [illegible] of preparation is going on very briskly. . . .

Mr. Averitt went to Winchester yesterday and told me he was to write to Mr. White. He is a very clever gentleman, closely attached to me, but I fear is too tender for a soldier's life. I never dreamed that I could accommodate myself to all of the privations so readily. If you were to see me now you would hardly recognize me. I am burnt black and have generally a savage appearance. At the first convenient place I will have a photograph taken and send you as a natural curiosity. You say my letters are short. When you receive the latest you will think otherwise. We left Dalton on the 3d May, reached Lynchburg on the 5th, and I wrote you daily I believe. It is a pleasure to chat with you, greater than it was, in the morning of my attachment, to send you flowers and write you pretty notes. Tell John to bring you flowers *three* times a week. In the stereoscope you had there are several views of Harper's Ferry. Could you venture to have them brought to you by John? Your slightest intimation would find a ready obedience and the views would be interesting at this time. I love you dearly, ardently, entirely, devotedly. Do you object? Do you call me lovesick? And I would throw millions in the scales if I could command them to feel that I deserved your love. Why do you not tell me that you love me? Are you afraid to flatter me so much, or afraid that your letters will be captured?

My house must indeed look desolate and dreary.[61] Some times will not my own loved Elodie go by it, merely to tell me that she has seen the flowers? One of these days, I hope her own hands will plant the beautiful garden flowers, made more beautiful because they have grown under her culture. And now sweet angel, goodbye. May God preserve us safely and may He guard and protect you at all times is the prayer of one who loves you *fondly* but not *too well*.

Ever and affty yours,
N. H. R. Dawson

I am much obliged to Mrs. White for her friendship but have flattered myself that she had given it to me some time ago. I know she will be all powerful, and I hope she will prevail for *your* sake as well as mine.

---

61. Elodie and Matt lived at what is now called White-Force Cottage at 811 Mabry Street, an Italianate-style home built in 1859. It is not clear where Nathaniel lived before the war, but it may be that his house did not survive the Battle of Selma and its aftermath. Regardless, after their marriage and before the end of the war, Nathaniel and Elodie bought a home around the corner at 704 Tremont Street, which they had substantially renovated. See Berry, House of Abraham.

Harper's Ferry, May 18, 1861

This morning for the first time I was able to pull on my boots, and, taking an escort of one corporal, I left my quarters intending to see some of beauties of this celebrated spot. The town is built on the narrow and low banks of the Shenandoah and Potomac Rivers which unite here, coming together almost at a right angle and from different quarters of the compass. The buildings are principally machine shops in this quarter and brick cottages for the employees of the government, presenting a beautiful and regular appearance. Rows of the black locust tree shade the single and narrow street and add to the picturesque groupings of houses. A long street on the Potomac leads to the upper town, the residence of the better classes, and, from the elevation of this street, the eye wanders over a beautiful landscape of water, forest, and mountain. Just opposite, across the Potomac to the left, are the battling heights of Maryland, now occupied by the Kentuckians, rising almost perpendicularly above the railway track. Across and immediately in front and to the right are the Virginia heights rising far above the upper town and commanding the approaches on all sides. They are now occupied by the Virginia troops. These mountains are almost impregnable and will be made so by the sharpshooters and riflemen who will man them.

In a handsome, stuccoed home at the top of this hill, upon which the upper town is built, Col. Jackson, the commandant, has his headquarters. A Confederate flag floats from the flag staff and indicates our nationality. From this point you have a lovely view of the surrounding country, fields and farms, while, just at your feet, the waters of the two noble streams, which break thro' the walls of the mountains, mingle together in friendly sympathy after their rapid journey from their western source. I have seen much beautiful and sublime scenery, but I think this is next to the falls of Niagara—not so sublime but uniting more of the beautiful and, for this reason, more lovely to me. In the distant fields one sees flocks of sheep and herds of cattle browsing upon the rich clover and luxuriant blue grass. In a lower place and overhanging the bank of the Shenandoah is the Jefferson Rock from which you can see for one or two miles the Shenandoah rumbling over its rapids and winding thro' the range of mountains. You look in another direction and you see, within a short distance, the two rivers running together, the waters of the Potomac distinctly marked from those of the Shenandoah by their yellow color. Standing here and looking around upon the [illegible] and boundless horizon, do you know my thoughts turned sadly to the distant spot where my gentle and loved Elodie was and a prayer for her safety and happiness trembled upon my lips, and then, recovering from the morning reverie, I sat down and cut her initials in the rock. If fortune favors our loves and we live, I will bring you here that you may see for yourself this beautiful and picturesque spot, and I hope this wish of my heart will be fulfilled at no distant day. I visited the engine house where John Brown and his men were taken.[62] The shot holes are still to be seen and at the corner of one house is shown the bullet hole made by the ball that killed Mr. Bukam.[63] He was shot by old Brown. Other places of interest connected with this raid are pointed out and seem from the number of persons examining them to possess much interest.

The town is crowded with soldiers clothed in all the colors of the rainbow from red to blue. Most of the respectable families, anticipating a fight, have left the town, and the figure of a lady is seldom seen in the streets. I got a distant view of Mr. Averitt and Mrs. Jos. Hardie this morning but had no opportunity of paying my respects. Her headquarters are at Winchester, and she came in on a visit this morning. I am almost ashamed to send you this letter, but as you have requested me to write daily and will make due allowances for all imperfections, I will risk the consequences.

I begin to hope that Mr. Lincoln will not invade Va. and that our difficulties will be adjusted without bloodshed, but you must not make up your mind to this desirable result my own loved angel for it may be otherwise, and you must bravely be prepared for the worst. If battle and its horrors come, I will have to bear my part, and if I fall it will be the fate of thousands, and thousands of hearts as loving as yours will be bowed with sorrow. In that event, I will only ask of you that you will let me testify for you what my affections and my heart indicate and that you interpose no objections to my last wishes. You will not unravel this enigma until fate has deprived me of life, and, I assure you, I will yet live to hold you to my bosom as the loved partner of my joys and sorrows. I do not anticipate evil, but I am prepared for it.

I have read over your letter of the 9th with unfeigned pleasure and

---

62. On October 16, 1859, abolitionist John Brown led eighteen men into the town of Harpers Ferry and seized the federal armory in a failed attempt to incite a slave rebellion. For more, see Jonathan Earle, John Brown's Raid on Harpers Ferry: A Brief History with Documents (New York: Bedford/St. Martin's Press, 2008).

63. Likely a misspelling of Fontaine Beckham, the Charles Town mayor and one of the civilians killed during the Brown raid.

will repeat it again today as I was disappointed in receiving a letter from you today. Your mother's only obstacle to consenting to your marriage is her unwillingness to give you up, but I have written her that I hoped, as do you, my pretty pet, that this will not be insuperable. Do you not agree with me? Her love for you convinces me that you are more beautiful than you were before, and I will rely upon her opinion rather than your disparaging remarks. I love you for your unselfishness. You know we like our opposites. You are a noble specimen of female character, and I am one of the most lucky of men in having won your love. I believe that you can do no wrong. You are as perfect as humanity can become, and I long to be under your control and influence. I only fear that you will be disappointed in your expectations of me for I know they are high and your young and unsuspicious nature does not allow you for a moment to think that I am not perfect in many things. If I know myself as you say you know yourself, I cannot say as you have ingenuously said that I admire myself for I see too many blemishes on the picture, but I will say that I expect you to improve many of the defects and to prepare me for that better life above where the soul will be without spot or blemish.

I must now end this prosy letter. Goodby, God bless and protect and keep you always, my love Elodie

Ever and affectionately yours,

N. H. R. Dawson

Selma, May 19, 1861

I have been sitting for some moments, your daguerreotype in hand, gazing upon the face which I would be so overjoyed to behold this very morning, thinking until I am so sad that I imagine that nothing can do me the same amount of good as writing to you and giving expression to some of the thoughts and dark forebodings which haunt so continually my mind in the three weeks past which have placed so many long and intervening miles between us, surrounding you with perhaps imminent danger. I feel that I have lived in thought and feeling a long and dreary year so slowly does the wheel of time turn, and those days calculated to impress one with gloom and dread and thereby biding the longer from our view the others which may be for us fraught with much happiness for the future. It is well occasionally to indulge in bright anticipations and rear beautiful air castles altho' we see them the next moment totter on their base and fall to the ground a ruin of hopes dashed for at the time

we are happy and sadness springing from the disappointment is pleasurable, but I hope mine may all yet be realized. Tho' the sky be hung with
lowering clouds, soon the silver lining may appear and the sun's bright
beams illumine them.

I am impatiently waiting for Bro. Clem each moment to bring me a
letter from you and will be sadly disappointed if he does not for I have
not heard for two days and wish to know of your safe arrival at Harper's
Ferry and what you are going to do next, whether there is any probability
of our engagement soon at that point or if you are safe a little longer and
not going to be sent to Washington. I have no idea of your being ordered
to that place and would be more opposed to your going there than I was
to Virginia, to which place I would have prevented your journeying if I
could and which shows how I may try to *guide* and *direct* you. It does well
enough for you to *write about such things*, but you must remember I have
brothers-in-law and possess a wee portion of knowledge about gentlemen.
They always take advice when it suits what their minds are bent on doing,
and no doubt if you had not intended going and I advised you not you
would have stayed at home.

We had a very unexpected visit yesterday from Capt. no Major Gee (for
that is now his title) who had been to Montgomery on business. He looks
very badly, has been quite sick he told me, expects he may be ordered to
Va. So you may meet with him. I have a fine photograph of his standing,
dressed in his regimentals, and you have no idea what a handsome picture he makes. [illegible] H.[64] informed me last night when I showed it
to him that he had one of himself for me rather in the same way. I shall
have quite a picture gallery soon. Don't you think you could add yours to
the number [even] if you are *not as handsome*? I will *prize it quite as much
as either of theirs.*

I have just rec'd your last letter dated the 17th from Port Royal which
gave me a great deal of pleasure to know you were well at the time of
writing, but I do not see how you can undergo so many privations and
hardships after the life you have been leading without being made sick
and hope you may continue to get along all the time as now. By this you
must be quite at home at Harper's Ferry. I wish you really were at home
in Selma, but if the War continues as long as some think it will, many
months will elapse before I can have the pleasure of seeing you back for
I hear it is thought if War begins it will in all probability last two years,

---

64. Robert Hagood.

and the horrible pictures sometimes drawn make me shudder. Have you gone in for the war or for a year? I am under the impression for the latter, am I not correct? I read the article you enclosed but do not agree with you in thinking it so beautiful. I think two or three paragraphs worthy of admiration but suppose I do not appreciate it. I don't want you to be filling up your letters with paper. I have no objection to reading any article which you are good enough to send me, but they must not curtail your letters which are so much shorter than mine that I shall soon follow your example thinking they are intended for that purpose.

Last night we had an alarm of fire between 12 and 1 o'clock which created quite an excitement. The steamboat Selma caught fire just as it landed, but owing to the promptness of the fire company was saved with little difficulty. It was quite a relief to know that it was the boat and nothing serious for other fears generally enter our minds at first owing to the plots discovered some months ago, tho' I apprehend no danger myself. We have another company, or two indeed, organized since you left—the "Selma Grays," Mr. Wetmore,[65] Capt., also the "Dallas Rangers." Mr. Wetmore has declined going with the Blues for the war but is perfectly willing to go for a year. The Blues really start Tuesday night on the Republic. Mrs. Kent[66] accompanies the Dr. It is well poor Mrs. Hardie is not here or else another of her ridiculous scenes would be gone over with to the amusement of some of those she considers her best friends.

In looking over this I find it looks miserable and were I to read it I suppose a few moments would suffice to destroy it. I do not intend to apologize for it because were I to copy or take pains I do not know that I would succeed better. The truth is I cannot write to you. All the time I feel as if I could talk tho' and expect when next we meet I will talk so much you will beg me to stop. What I have done will not even be a sample. Do you not dread it? But here I am again as usual filling up so many pages and think for your comfort I will stop. Do take good care of yourself and don't get any bullets or on the sick list unless you can come home to be nursed by your friends.

---

65. Possibly Thomas B. Wetmore, who mustered in as a provost marshal and eventually became an acting assistant quartermaster famous for composing a little ditty about collecting women's urine to produce ammonium nitrate for use in gunpowder: "We thought the girls had work enough making shirts and kissing / But you have put the pretty dears to patriotic pissing." See Cameron C. Nickels, *Civil War Humor* (Jackson: University Press of Mississippi, 2010), 70–71.

66. M. G. Kent was the twenty-three-year-old wife of Dr. James Kent. 1860 Census: Selma.

I feel so blue and disconsolate this evening I am going to try and shut my troubles up in my eyes just as tight as I can for two or three hours.

My Bro. Mr. Helm[67] from Louisville was in Montgomery a few days ago for the purpose of enlisting in the Confederate Army. He was educated at W[est] P[oint] and served for three or four years in the regular army. I hope he may succeed as it's a life he prefers to all others and would willingly give up law for it. Now goodbye. If my prayers ever ascend and will be answered, you will be spared from harm and return once more to your own affectionate,

Dee

Bolivar Heights, May 19, 1861

We removed to this encampment yesterday evening and are now comfortably quartered in our tents. The heights are on the Potomac and are at the opening of a beautiful amphitheatre formed by the mountains. Our tents, regularly laid off in streets upon two hills, ranging together but separated by a deep ravine, present a beautiful appearance. We overlook the river which is on the right of the camp. In the distance the blue mountains lift their heads and nature holds sweet communion with the harmonious landscape. All save the spirit of man is divine.

I went to bed last night feeling quite unwell and fearing from my headache that I might have to become an inmate of the hospital, but I am better this morning than since reaching Harper's Ferry. Last night was as cold as a December night, and the wind howled terrible. Old Eolus must have opened the doors of his cave.[68] I have an addition to my comforts in the shape of a mattress filled with straw and slept comfortably, more so than I have since leaving home. The whole camp, however, was roused about one o'clock by the alarm that the enemy were approaching and most of the troops were under arms all night. These false alarms are unpleasant as they try our nerves unnecessarily, but we are told, upon what authority I am ignorant, that we are to be attacked in a few days, but I think otherwise. I am well armed with a sword, Adams fire shooter,[69] and

---

67. Benjamin Hardin Helm (see May 15, 1861, note 57).

68. "Old Eolus" refers to the Greek god of winds.

69. A revolver made by Robert Adams, a British gunsmith who in 1851 patented the first successful double-action revolver, a gun that cocked itself after the trigger was pulled. For

a Sharps rifle,[70] slung over my shoulder. This last is one that was taken from John Brown.

We are just returned from the inspection of our regiment by Col. Deas of the Confederate army and have written two pages without telling my own loved and cherished Elodie how much she is the subject of my dreams and thoughts. Tis Sunday and in place of reading my bible I prefer to sit at my trunk and with the pen she gave me talk and chat with her on paper at the distance of one thousand miles from home. I wear your likeness with the lock of hair in a locket in my watch pocket and have several times been innocently asked by some of my men why I wore *two watches*. I could have replied to speak true—to keep near me the face and smile of that distant loved one who is now my guardian angel. I walked down the ravine this morning to see a file of men discharge their piece and gather for you the flowers enclosed, heartsease and strawberry. Did you get those from Lynchburg?[71]

I almost forgot to tell you that the Maryland heights have been fired, and last night the burning mountain presented a grand and beautiful appearance. The line of fire extends completely across the mountain and reminded me of Bulwer's description of the eruption of Vesuvius.[72] I looked upon the beautiful scene and wandered back to the parlor and home where you promised to be mine and tried to imagine myself at your side. Do you think you have safely conquered me and that there is no danger of losing the conquest? You must have no fears upon the subject tho' you have warned me of the danger of the beautiful women of Va. Many of them are indeed beautiful, but none are the peers of my affianced bride. Like Helen[73] she is the peer of all her sex, and the world in arms could not seduce me from her allegiance. I really think that you should be flattered at the depth of my love. I am flattered at yours and feel that none but a gentleman could win your love, and I know that no ordinary lady could have inspired me as you have. What answer do you

---

more, see Michael C. C. Adams, *Living Hell: The Dark Side of the Civil War* (Baltimore: Johns Hopkins University Press, 2014), 60–63.

70. A breech-loading rifle that was easier to load and more accurate, the Sharps rifle quickly became a favorite among soldiers, especially in cavalry units. Adams, *Living Hell*, 60–63.

71. The flowers that Nathaniel sent with this letter survive in the collection.

72. A novel written by Edward Bulwer-Lytton in 1834, *The Last Days of Pompeii* culminates in the eruption of Mount Vesuvius and the destruction of the city.

73. In Greek mythology, Helen of Troy was regarded as one of the most beautiful women in the world.

make to this reasoning? Do you not think that many in the city of Selma and elsewhere, did they know it, would be jealous of me? Will you return to Kentucky with you mother or do you remain in Alabama? If you keep your [illegible] you will hardly get back to Kentucky for several months, as she will not leave before the action of Congress in July. But I really hope that we will have peace in time to let me take you there. If I live to return home, the remainder of my life shall be devoted to rendering you comfortable and happy. I imagine no picture of the future that is not gilded by your presence and think of no joy that is not doubled by having you to share it, and no privation that is not lessened because you will divide it with me.

Do you not believe that love like ours is immortal and will only be fully realized in a more beautiful existence adapted to the fine development of what here is called affection? If the world were peopled with inhabitants as nearly perfect as you are, my dear Elodie, omnipotence would not have inflicted death upon man as a means of refining him for a better existence. I do not believe Satan could induce you to eat of the forbidden fruit like our mother Eve and persuade you to seduce me into the same fatal sin. You must not tell me that you are not perfect because I might believe it, as you have told me, that you know yourself. I shall never look for faults and if you have any, I will be greatly disappointed.

I have been sadly disappointed in not receiving a letter from you since that of the 9th. I have written you daily since reaching Lynchburg and fear you will hardly have room to preserve my letters. I have not received so many that I will be unable to put them in a very small pocket to my trunk. You must hide yourself and write me if you are interrupted. You can go over to my library and find yourself secluded there. I will give it to you for that purpose.

Mr. Averitt has now encamped with us and will preach this evening. He has too exalted an opinion of me, and I fear will be indiscreet in expressing it. You know it is much harder to preserve a reputation than to make one, and constant praises will create jealously in the minds of strangers. He is very sensitive and almost too effeminate in his mode of thought and action to go through the world with satisfaction to himself and friends.

The messenger has returned from the office without a letter from you, and I will have to be satisfied with reading your old letters. When I tell you this, will you not have pity and write frequently? I love you, my own dear girl, more than I can find language to express. I wish I could write you in beautiful language how deeply you are loved and how much I feel your absence from me, but you will be satisfied with the plainer language of truth and write me in return your beautiful and easy letters. I love you because *you love yourself.* I put faith in your taste and judgment. And goodbye dearest. I will think of you when all else has died from my mind and will pray for you with my last sigh. God bless and protect you.

Ever and affectionately yours,

N. H. R. Dawson

Selma, May 22, 1861

You can scarcely imagine how disappointed I was both yesterday and today when Brother Clem returned with the intelligence of no letters from you. I immediately began to wonder what had occasioned your silence, could arrive at no conclusion that seemed so probable as that sickness or an engagement with our enemies had prevented my hearing from you. This with the news of a fight in Norfolk[74] has made me almost dread to hear from Harper's Ferry, fearing that something has happened to you, and pass as unhappy a day as was possible.

This morning the Blues left for Richmond leaving Selma a sad and desolate home for many. Tears flowed abundantly from the eyes of men, women, and children, and I do not think there was an undimmed eye in the entire company. It was truly a sad and impressive scene. I was thinking of a similar scene which transpired almost a month ago, one that separated you and I, and how little those around me knew that my smiling face was deceiving them and hiding from their views an aching heart. I felt they were now undergoing what I had undergone, [and I was] passing thro' a second time. Indeed I could well sympathize withthem for had I not parted with you, a brother, and friends also? But I did not regard it as right to their emotion [and] therefore struggled hard and mastered mine that you might remember me as a woman ready and willing to sacrifice *her all* if necessary to the advancement of so glorious a cause, one to save our country from shame and dishonor, to arrest it from a tyrant's grasp and live as we have ever done a free and independent people. We could none of us ever be happy as subjects under King Lincoln or wish to live if such was the case.

You asked for my feelings and opinions on the subject of your being a

---

74. The Battle of Sewell's Point was a small skirmish that lasted from May 18 to 19, 1861, and ended with no fatalities.

politician or pursuing your profession after wishing yourself at home but a sentence before to show Dr. Mabry he was laboring under a mistake. Now if you will have the kindness to inform me of your preference for either life I will then tell you my choice for you. One might suppose to behold Mr. Lincoln's political career that my family would be content with politics. I am used to such a life, my father having followed such a one himself. I wish you to use your pleasure without consulting me. I think everyone should select the pursuit that they evince most taste and talent for and they think will be most conducive to their happiness. I shall endeavor to assimilate my tastes to yours in everything, besides I would not think of giving advice to you.

Mother and Matt have gone to Summerfield to make a visit of a few days to Mrs. White's aunt, leaving Kittie and I to keep house and entertain during their absence. We really feel ourselves to be of some importance and consequence, but I miss them so much that I would cheerfully resign my consequence and key basket to have them back again for I do not love to be alone. While nothing pleases Kittie more and altho' we are the only two in the house, she is off busy in one room and I am in another and no doubt will spend a very agreeable day if she persists in being alone. The ladies have sent on for goods to make clothes for the Cadets and Guards. I went down yesterday to the hall to get some work, but the material has not yet arrived. I was really indignant at the partiality shown to the Blues, and indeed it has been so spoken of that they have interested themselves since the *pets* left. I was very glad to hear that Major Hayden[75] had sent on six capes and one was intended for you, yet I think of the other poor soldiers who have no kind friends to provide for them, and I wish I could do something for them myself. I hope you will not find the Ky. Regiment all composed of such men as Col. Blanton Duncan for he left for his country's good I am sure but hope you will find some among them who will cause you to have the same admiration and love for them that I do. Let the world say what it will concerning Kentucky and Kentuckians and blame her now and not sympathize with her unfortunate situation. There is not on earth a nobler or braver class of people, and I would rather be a Kentuckian if my state hangs on to the old wreck than a native of any other state, tho' I must confess that I am mystified and distressed that they are so blinded and duped to their own interest

75. Probably the family member of James G. Hayden (sometimes spelled Haden), a private in Nathaniel's regiment (see June 26, 1861, note 110).

and happiness, and my pity has caused me to love them more than ever for I do feel most deeply for my own dear home and for those who are with us heart and soul and yet are forced by circumstances to be silent and suffer.

I regret I did not wait to hear from you before answering Mr. Averitt's letter and will take your advice for the future about them. I enclose you a piece written on the departure of the Blues and as it may entertain you a little while will give you a chance to read it by ending my letter. Hoping to hear often and soon from you, believe me as ever your affectionate,

Elodie

Harper's Ferry, May 22, 1861

It seems an age since one of your cheering letters has reached me, and I feel much anxiety to hear from your own pen, my own loved Elodie, that it has not been occasioned by indisposition. You last was forwarded from Lynchburg, and I fear from your long silence that something has occurred to interfere with your correspondence. I wrote you from Lynchburg directing you how to address me and as some letters have been received directed here, I am at a loss to know why I am so unfortunate especially as you promised to write me daily. . . .

It is touching to see the members of the Cadets singing at night. Last evening at roll call I went out. The moon was shining brightly, and the white tents of the [illegible] Miss. troops with their camp fires presented a picture that I had never seen. A dozen of the young men were grouped together singing "Home Again." The effect upon me was electrical. I realized the fact that I was a thousand miles from you, my own loved Elodie, and my heart felt sick. I have just here received your letter of the 15th inst. You cannot imagine how happy it has made me. I take back all of my querulousness for which I pray your forgiveness.

You must not insist upon your letters being destroyed. I much prefer that they should be returned to you to be kept safely for me, but I am not willing to have such evidences of your love and affection for me consigned to the flames. If anything occurs to me a *friend here* will see that your letters are returned to you in a packet, but I hope to keep them myself to hold them safely. Mr. Averitt does not know of our engagement, but he knows, from having seen some of your letters delivered, that we correspond, and I have told him that I have obtained your permission to correspond with you. I assure you if the mere compliment of telling you how much your letters are admired by me would induce you to write oftener, I would deal in much more of the article, but I tell you what I think when I say that you are dearer to me than life and that your letters are sweeter far than Madame Sevigne[76] or any other person. For your own sake I think it well for the present that you decline to be married now, but will you tell me that when it can be done with prudence on your part that you will grant my request? You are an angel of love to me, and I hope it will be my privilege to prove how grateful I am to you for having given me your love. There is nothing in my power that I would not do for you and to die for you would be a pleasure. I have pity and contempt both for *some* of the valiant Blues. Their captain[77] is a *double-dealing man* for whom I have had a friendship, but it is all forfeited by his recent conduct. *Beware* of his *smiles*; they *wreathe* a hidden poison.

Tomorrow Va. votes upon the ordinance of secession. The troops are waiting here today as many anticipate an attack tomorrow by the Federal troops, probably tonight. I do not fear it, however, as we are now too strong to be easily whipped. We have near 15,000 troops here now, and they come in daily. Col. Duncan and Col. Harmon of Va. had a difficulty today. Col. D. commands the Kentuckians. From what we hear, Ky. will certainly secede. If she does not, I will be very much surprised. Tell Miss Kittie you will claim her and that she must live in Ala. but that I will not promise to let her throw herself away on Col. Ellsworth as she must have a Confederate Col. for her beau. I am anxious for your sake and your family that you should have peace for it must be unpleasant to have them divided.

I am much gratified that your feelings did not let you dance when you heard the rumors of battle at this point. I was much gratified at your mother's letter but did not regard it as a consent and replied to it under that impression, but I do not think she will long hold out against your persuasions for who could resist them.

You must excuse the rambling letters I send you. I will one of these days when I can find a better desk than my trunk endeavor to prepare one at least that will draw from you a compliment. You are indeed chary of compliments. Several very pretty ladies visited us this morning and gave me

---

76. Marie de Rabutin-Chantal, the Marquise de Sévigné, was renowned throughout Western culture as a famed writer of letters.

77. T. C. Daniels had been a cashier of the Selma Commercial Bank before becoming captain of the "Selma Blues." He was killed at the Battle of Second Manassas. D. M. Scott, "Selma and Dallas County, Ala.," *Confederate Veteran* 24 (1916): 214–224.

a basket of cakes. God bless the ladies, they are so kind, but I always tell them that a fair young girl in Ala., far away but much loved, has stolen my heart and that I have nothing to lose here. But they will not believe my candor and call me a flirt. What say you to such an impeachment? The drums are now beating ½ for drill & I must obey. Goodbye sweet angel. May God bless you and soon restore me to my "own affectionate Elodie."

 Ever & affectionately yours,

 N. H. R. Dawson

Selma, May 23, 1861

You cannot imagine how happy I felt a few moments since when Bro. Clem handed me your two letters dated the 14th and 16th. I have not heard before for three days and feared you were indisposed. I hope now perfectly well. I know you must have been lonesome and missed the comfort of home and sympathizing friends. It is unnecessary for me to say how glad I would have been to have been near you and as much as possible administered to your comfort and happiness for you know well enough. You do not mention having received scarcely any letters from me. I have written regularly every other day until this week. My last letter was written the 19th and directed to Harper's Ferry and surely you should have received a letter from me enclosing one from Mother written quite two weeks since, which will give you I think satisfaction (I mean Mother's), altho' I could hardly prevail upon her to write you a line as she declared when Emma[78] married she would never consent to give up another and that when such an idea entered my own and Kittie's head we must *run off*. I think however in time she will get over all trivial objections, which she fancies, for in reality she has none. I will take the subject you propose into consideration and give it all due thought and will be ready with an answer whenever peace is declared should there be any war which I am beginning to doubt. Just see what a cheering effect your letters have had. I have been nearly all evening trying to cheer up Ella Watts[79] who is crying and grieving herself over the departure of the Blues. I imagine we are *similarly situated*, both with sweethearts gone to

---

78. Emilie Todd Helm had married in 1856.

79. Ella F. Watts was the seventeen-year-old daughter of Louisa M. and Edward T. Watts, a wealthy farmer in Selma. Ella and Elodie remained quite close throughout the correspondence. 1860 Census: Selma.

the War. She did not tell me, and I would prefer not knowing as keeping my own secret is enough. She remarked that were she engaged, she
would never stay behind but go too, and if she had foreseen all this perhaps she would have been married. Altho' this conversation happened
before two or three, I believe she spoke from the heart and is as deeply
interested as her neighbor but in whom puzzles me. I cannot find out.
Altho' report says Mr. Bruce Thomas,[80] I don't believe it. I had a letter
from my dear friend Dr. Rodman who is anxious to know if I am not
going to be married, from Mother and Kittie's coming down, and insists
on my telling him all about it. I will some of these days, but I am going to
be so silent that I will surprise everyone, and it would give me pleasure to
outwit Selma for once and show the kind, good people I will marry whom
I please and then without their aid and interference and that it is none
of their affair but entirely my own.

I am out of temper with the people here for showing the Blues so
much partiality and not noticing the Guards and Cadets, and Sallie Bell[81]
and I speak our minds freely when we meet. You have a sample of my
amiability. I am a *Todd*, and some of these days you may be unfortunate
enough to find out what they are. I will send your pieces on to the *Mercury*
and am sorry I get more credit than I am deserving of in regard to the
flag. I can scarcely realize it is but a month since you left for the time has
seemed so much longer and I *believe* I am getting anxious and impatient
to see you again. What will I do if the war continues ten years, do you
imagine? Pray do you think to inform Bro. Abe would do any good? He
would make you suffer for yourself and my being such a secessionist too,
and you must be too cute to get into their hands.

Well, it is growing late, and I must tell you goodnight hoping the mor-
row will bring me another letter. Are you in earnest about fearing a *rival*?
If so I am provoked with you for doubting for one moment my constancy.
I know there is more danger of your forsaking me, at least quite as much.
How is George Mims[82] or do you ever see him? I think he is a deserving

---

80. Possibly Bruce P. Thomas of the Selma Blues, part of the Eighth Alabama Infantry.
Regardless, Elodie was correct that the two did not marry. Alabama Civil War Muster Rolls,
1861–1865, Alabama Department of Archives and History.

81. Sallie Bell was a dear friend of Elodie's, living in Selma, whose brothers, Benjamin and Burke, were members of Nathaniel's company. National Park Service, *Civil War
Soldiers and Sailors System*, https://www.nps.gov/civilwar/soldiers-and-sailors-database.htm,
accessed October 20, 2016 (hereafter *CWSS*).

82. George Mims was a private serving in Nathaniel's company and was badly wounded
at the Battle of First Manassas. He survived to become a schoolmaster in Louisiana and

youth and think kindly of him for the sake of his family. My bro. David
has been ordered I hear to North Carolina. Now, once more, goodnight
and believe me yrs. Always.
    Elodie

Harper's Ferry, May 24, 1861

I have tried and so far been able by adding a postscript to my letters to
write you daily since you made the request, as I wish to prove to my much
loved Elodie that her slightest wish is all-powerful with me. I fear from
the offer you make in your last letter of the 15th that you are becoming
wearied with my epistles and that you have been paid in uncurrent coin
for your letters to me. But I assure you that it is the gratification for a
selfish feeling to write you as it is to love you, for in doing both I add to
my comfort and happiness. I can never love you more ardently than at
this time, but as the partner of all my fortunes I hope that we will climb
the hill of life and draw from many sources happiness and comfort. You
are the last and first object of thought, and your likeness is *stealthily* ex-
amined as I am all day in the presence of others. My duties commence
at five o'clock A.M. and continue until one when I have one and a half
hours to devote to you and my books, but really most of it is used in
writing to you.
    Mr. Averitt has just returned from Winchester and has called to tell
me that Mrs. Hardie had come and was at the Col's tent, but I put him
off on the plea of important business as I wish to write to you. I am
much gratified that your mother had but one objection to our marriage, the unwillingness to lose you. But you should tell her that she
is not losing you but only adding a *son* to her family for from all I have
heard of her and from what I know of you, it will be an honor and pleasure to be connected with her. You know I have great reverence for all
who deserve it. I love Mrs. Mathews[83] almost as fondly as a boy does his
mother for she has ever been a kind and affectionate friend, and she is
next to you and my children in my heart. She will love you so much and

---

Mississippi and eventually married a woman twenty years his junior in 1884. George's sister,
Laura Mims, was a friend of Elodie's. *CWSS*.
    83. Elizabeth Mathews was Nathaniel's first mother-in-law and grandmother of Nathan-
iel's first daughter, Elizabeth. The Mathews are keeping Elizabeth during the war.

so tenderly that I am anxious that she should know you as one that is dear to me.

I have just now received your letter of 17th, and if I have caused you pain even jestingly I crave your pardon and forgiveness. I have not really thought your letters were wanting in love, but I thought that you were careful in overstepping the limits of maidenly caution, but your last letter is so affectionate and kind that I can never even in jest complain again.

My reason for wishing you to marry me at an early day was to take you entirely under my charge and keeping. That you would be an anxiety to me, I admit, but all the trouble would be compensated in the deep love I bear you and in the great satisfaction it would give me to know that you were dependent upon me *alone* for protection, and that you would bear all of the trials bravely and well I have not a doubt. The only hesitation I feel upon the subject is on your account, and I have thought it would be asking too much of you to make the sacrifices that would be necessary. You must remember my dear Elodie that though you will be a trouble, as you term it and as I understand it an addition to my cares and responsibilities, yet that half the pleasures of life arise from the troubles caused us by those whom we love. The more sensitive the nervous system generally the more exquisite is the pleasure. I assure you that no trouble, no trial on your account, would be regarded as unpleasant. If I could convince myself that duty to you permitted me to do so, to ask you to increase the ties that now unite us, I would not hesitate to insist upon our marriage in the course of a few months. If we have no fighting soon, I do not think we will have much of a war, and in that event it will not be necessary to take the step as you will then be willing to marry me at once, and as soon as we are released from service. But I still ask you to leave your decision open for further reflection as I may tell you that *I am willing to be troubled with you.*

I have just had a long talk with Mrs. Hardie. She is comfortably provided at Winchester and is much better satisfied than she could possibly be at Selma. Are you willing to risk all the trials, all the sorrows, that my death would entail on you as my wife? I know I ask a grave question, but I know you will answer it with your characteristic candor, and I ask it of you in that spirit. The waters of the Potomac, rolling rapidly over its shoals and rocks, will turn in another direction before the place you have in my heart will be given to another, and I should do injustice to you did I entertain for a moment a feeling of apprehension that anything save my own misconduct could replace me in your heart.

I never dream of such a thing for I could not love more sincerely or more *wisely*, and when you are mine at the altar I shall feel that God has compensated and rewarded me for many of the sorrows and griefs of my life. I have from my earliest boyhood yearned for the comforting love of woman and the blessings of home. I yearn now more anxiously than ever before. And I see in you the impersonation of all those beautiful excellencies of character and mind that are so essential to brighten home.

I have written a long letter simply of love, and I know you are tired, but as I have told you it is out of my power to do otherwise. A large party of ladies are here with Mrs. Hardie from Winchester. They have come over on a special visit to us. I have put on my best regimentals and been to see them, but I have made no attempt to make an impression but been candid to tell them that I have no heart to lose. Was this not right? Mr. Averitt received your long letter today. He is much attached to me, and his attachment is proverbial with the officers. He is too loving. He puts his hands on me and is guilty of many such, to me unpleasant, ways, as I do not think they become the conduct of a gentleman. I might act toward little Willie[84] in this way, and *it might be excusable in a very affectionate wife* to her husband. But you will say, very properly, that I should not be so critical. He is very much in love with some young lady at every stopping place. But why should I trouble you with such trifles, my loved Elodie?

Gen. Johnston[85] of Kentucky, I think, who commanded the Utah expedition, has taken command here. He is reputed to be a great man, and I am better satisfied than I have been at the condition of affairs. Last night we slept upon our arms, expecting an attack, but there was no alarm, and I do not think we need have any fears upon the subject as we are now too strong for a very large army. Since reading your letter of the 17th, I have greater desire than ever to write you daily. I feel with you for your absent brothers and hope they will pass through the ordeal with safety. Make my kind regards to Mrs. White and your sister, Miss Kate, and tell her that I

---

84. William King White, age six, is the son of Elodie's sister Matt and husband Clement White. 1860 Census: Selma.

85. Nathaniel would not be the first or the last student of the Civil War to confuse or conflate his General Johnstons. In the biographical particulars, he is clearly referring Albert Sidney Johnston (1803–1862), who was born in Kentucky, lived most of his life in Texas, and in 1857–1858 led U.S. forces in the "Utah War" against the Mormons. But the Johnston in command of forces in Nathaniel's eastern theater was Joseph Eggleston Johnston, commissioned as brigadier general in the Confederate States Army on May 14, 1861, when he began organizing the short-lived Confederate Army of the Shenandoah.

have a special desire to kill Col. Ellsworth of the Zouaves for her sake as
I do not think he is good enough for any sister of yours.[86]

Write me frequently and freely, my dear Elodie. Goodbye and believe
me ever affectionately and sincerely yours,

N. H. R. Dawson

May I ask that you will burn up all of my letters as I would be ashamed of
such specimens of chirography?

Selma, May 26, 1861

. . . . Saturday we received a letter from my Bro. at Pensacola.[87] He writes
everything is very quiet there and that they know nothing of what is going on in their midst and are forbidden to give what information they
possess. Today a letter came from my Bro. David who is in Raleigh, N.C.
but gives us no intelligence more than we are apprized of by the papers.
Another from my sister Mary[88] to whom I had written informing her of
my engagement. She receives the news seriously and writes me a long
letter on the subject of matrimony and adjoins me that I am a great deal
better off as I am. She ought to know as she committed the fatal step years
ago, and I believe another such letter would almost make me abandon
the idea. Do you believe it? Mother says, "do tell your captain I have no
intention of writing to him again nor will I make any more objections
seeing you are determined and there is no chance of persuading you
from it as he has filled your head with ideas that I have been all my life
trying to keep you from possessing." *I am much obliged* to you capt. for
suggesting the thoughts.

This morning before going to church Miss Truitt sent me with her love

---

86. Bizarrely, Ellsworth died this very day. Leading the Eleventh New York across the
Potomac and into Alexandria, he noticed a Confederate flag waving above the Marshall
House (a second-class inn) and took a small detachment up to the roof to cut it down.
Returning downstairs with the flag, he was shot in the chest by the inn owner, James W.
Jackson, with a shotgun. As the first notable casualty of the war, his death shocked the na-
tion, and the Lincolns mourned him almost as a son.

87. Samuel Brown Todd (1830–1862) attended Centre College and then moved to
New Orleans after his father's death in 1849. There he married Clelie Cecile Royer and
clerked for her father, a French gardener. Sam joined the Confederate army as a private
and was sent to Pensacola. He was later killed at the Battle of Shiloh. See Berry, *House of
Abraham*, 115–117.

88. Neither letter to or from Mary Lincoln survives in any known collection.

a magnolia, the first I ever saw and I think it so beautiful that I have been in raptures over it. A day or two since Mrs. Mabry sent me a bouquet. I cannot account for their kindness but nevertheless am I grateful for it is pleasant to be thought of and remembered. I ought to recollect how little it takes to give pleasure and that often I have it in my power to do so but am too selfish to trouble myself but will try and profit by Miss T's example. I think she must be in every respect one of the most lovely and gentle of girls, and I regret I do not see more of her as her presence might influence me to do better. Indeed Capt. Dawson when you write to me expressing your belief that I am faultless, good, and etc. I really feel hurt because I cannot bring myself to believing you really think so yet am far from thinking you *untruthful*, only I am afraid that absent from me you think of me *as I should be rather than what I am*, and surely if you do entertain at all times the thoughts you express you will be sadly, sadly disappointed in very many respects. You need not think I am modest and do not appreciate myself because such is not the case, and I wish you knew something of me. I would not like all faults to be seen, only wish you to be aware that I am human but not on the lookout for what you will see. I am thinking of going to Summerfield[89] and vicinity for a visit of perhaps two weeks. I may go Saturday but will write again before I depart. Your letters will be sent to me, but I don't know that you will hear often from me as I imagine I will have a poor opportunity of writing while absent. I do not know why my letters did not reach you unless they went to Washington for I declare I *have written three times a week* ever since you left. I am much obliged for the flowers you send and will put them away, also for you description of Harper's Ferry which must satisfy me as I would neither venture to send for your views or take advantage of your kind invitation to possess myself of the quiet of your library to write you *nicer* and more entertaining letters. I am but a poor scribe at best, and you must content yourself with what I send, knowing I would be delighted to do better. I must now finish this letter for I am *obliged* to write another this evening but will promise you a long one again day after tomorrow and add all I have forgotten this time. Now goodbye. Write to me soon a long letter and believe me ever yrs affectionately,

Dee

89. Summerfield, Alabama, is a town eight miles due north of Selma, also in Dallas County. In the Civil War era, it was most noted for its Centenary Institute, a school operated by the Methodist Episcopal Church. Anson West, *A History of Methodism in Alabama* (Nashville: Publishing House Methodist Episcopal Church, South, 1893), 726.

Selma, May 27, 1861

Matt and Kittie have gone to ride, Mother to attend a Union Prayer Meeting,[90] so I am entirely alone and take advantage of being so and will acknowledge your letter of today but not attempt to express the pleasure it gave me to hear from you. Indeed, you have good cause to think strangely of my seeming negligence and silence, but I assure you it is owing altogether to the mail for I have written often and always long letters and many since the 9th, yet I am astonished to find that your confidence in my constancy could be shaken for a moment by anything, much less such an occurrence as not receiving your letters in good time, but I must confess I would think something was wrong if I was so long without hearing from you, but after all your protestations of love and faithfulness I would attribute your silence to anything else than inconstancy. As there is nobody here and besides I am not in demand, hereafter you need have no fear of losing me. You will find me here waiting for you when you return no matter when or how long that time is if I am living in this great world. I would like to know what you are doing just at this moment. I am sitting on the porch (but Mother has just joined me) writing to you and thinking how nice it would be to have you with us.

A few days ago I met several girls with their faces and eyes crimson with the tears they had been shedding, and they all acknowledge how many hours they indulge in tears for the departed Blues. I know I must be considered hardhearted, but I return the compliment thinking they are very silly to show their grief to public eyes and think those who say the least oftener feel the deepest. I regard my grief as too sacred to be seen by every eye and am selfish enough to *enjoy it entirely alone* when I have the inclination to indulge which I very seldom do as I think matters will not be improved, and I have a great dread of an unhappy person who is a tax on any one, and you know the habit might increase. I am afraid of being

90. As might be imagined, Elizabeth "Betsey" Todd was by 1861 consumed with worry by the drift of events. Kentucky seemed stuck in neutral, and if she didn't return soon she would be a sixty-year-old widow cut off from home and all its securities. If she did make it back, she would be cut off from her Confederate sons and daughters. Elodie, whom she always counted on as a companion in her old age, seemed firm in her decision to marry a man she didn't know. Mary had invited her to the White House, and there was no good way to say no, though she would obviously have to say no, because most of her sons were in the Confederate army. She probably hoped Kentucky would secede, but she attended Union prayer meetings because they were one of the few places where people were still praying for peace. Berry, *House of Abraham*, 71.

like Mrs. Hardie, not only miserable myself but causing those around me to be so too. But I do pity her, *poor creature.*

Kittie is writing to sister Mary (Mrs. Abe Lincoln), and I requested her to mention the fact of my being interested in you and should you fall into the hands of the blk. Rep., hope you will be kindly received with care, but I am fearful since Ellsworth's death that the Southerners will fare badly if they get within their clutches and hope you will keep as far as possible from them.

Selma is so quiet that one passing thro' would imagine it was ready to be inhabited, the town finished, the carpenters and builders departed. Kittie declares it to be the last place in the world, and I think is perfectly willing to leave now for some other place more congenial to her tastes. The gaiety of Springfield and the extreme dullness of this place must indeed be striking, but I imagine it is the same everywhere now. I could not mingle with gay society and feel grateful that all is so quiet around me, and I am not worried with company for the ladies are working or grieving I think as very few visits have been paid in the last week. Last night John brought me a bouquet of Cape Jasmines and a waiter of apples. They reminded me of Kentucky and are so nice that I do not know whether to keep them to look at or eat them. I did not know before apples grew anywhere in the neighborhood of Selma.

I went to see Mrs. Parnell a few evenings ago and a cousin, Miss Serena Parnell,[91] who is living with her. Mrs. P. told me she heard I was going to marry Col. D. and I would not tell you for any consideration the complimentary speeches she made about you, and I agreed with her in all, for fear of making you too vain and that ill-becomes a man, and besides would encroach upon our rights, for that one trait belongs to woman as her prerogative exclusively. I am writing a long letter and have been reminded by Mother that it is growing quite late, and I will take her hint and finish this [but] not before begging you always to overlook all deficiencies in composition and penmanship.

As I received no letter today I will look for one tomorrow and hope hereafter you will receive all I write you. Goodbye. May god in his mercy

91. The Parnell family is mentioned often in the correspondence, but they could not be identified definitively. Probably they are J. M. Parnell, identified as a farmer in the 1850 U.S. Federal Census, Lexington, Dallas County, Ala.; his wife Amanda; and their children, J. C. Parnell and S. G. Parnell, who is likely the Miss Serena Parnell, a friend of Elodie's, who would have been twenty-four at the outbreak of the war.

watch over and protect you from all harm, granting us a speedy reunion is the prayer of your ever affectionate,

Elodie

May 30, 1861

I was unwell, my dearest, last evening when my letter was written and was disposed to tear it up, but as it was impossible to do better, I concluded to send it as our nearness should not require so much particularity. I am better this morning, free from the headaches which disturbed me last night. I feel when writing you as if engaged in some sort of devotion, like the penitent *Christian when he kneels to commune with a superior being,* and, like him, when the pleasant task is over I am a *better* and *purer man.* You must not laugh and think this the effusion of a mind diseased with love. It is the normal feeling of every man who sincerely loves and true and gentle maiden. You complain of my short letters and compare them with your long ones. Remember that any hour spent in writing to you is snatched and stolen from some hour of *rest* or of *duty,* and I know you will then pardon me, but I hope that you will not carry your threat into execution. Your letters are like the visits of angels and are refreshing vessels in the dreary path of life. And I know, as you love me, you will continue to lighten my life with them. I will not ask you to write me daily but hope you will twice or three times a week while I will pay you *double* as long as I can get the materials.

The day is bright and pleasant. Last night was very cold, and I found *four blankets* and a large shawl comfortable.

I am much troubled about the condition of the Regiment and fear the want of confidence in the Col. will be very injurious to its history. I shall have nothing to do with him farther than duty compels. This is the case with six of the captains. How will such a family prosper? I think from present indications that we will have no fighting for the present. I hope by the time congress meets that better and wiser counsels will rule the cabinet of Mr. Lincoln. Do you write frequently to Mrs. L? If taken prisoner you must get me released on parole, and I will return to you.

Dearest how blissful will be the hour when we shall meet to part no more, when you will be mine and when your smile will always lighten at my coming. I look forward with hope and confidence to a safe return. You must cheer up and have confidence in our success and in the ultimate safety of your *friends*. I am very *prudent* and *careful* and *temperate*. On your account, I have given up *smoking*, of which I was very fond, and seldom touch anything stronger than coffee. This is done for your sake. Our engagement has made me a better man as it has given me something to live for that I have not had before. See what a mission you have to fulfill and how well you have begun? I wrote to Mr. Wetmore asking him to get you the photograph or rather to send it to Mrs. White. There are two specimens, one standing in full uniform, which is the best. Mr. Averitt has gone to Winchester and will be ordained on Sunday by Bishop Meade.[92] How would you like him to marry us? You will have the selection of the minister.

I saw Judge King cry over a letter from his wife yesterday. Parts of it were very touching, exhorting him to remember his duty to God and his country. She is a true wife and noble woman.

When will I cry over one from my own loved Elodie? Must I confess that your experiences of love and affection have already brought them into eyes unused to weep. Dearest, goodbye. God bless and keep and preserve you from all dangers.

Every affty yours,
N. H. R. Dawson

Harper's Ferry, June 1, 1861

I have just returned to my tent from duty since yesterday morning at 8 o'clock—28 hours, during which time I have been acting as officer of the day and have either been in the saddle or on foot. We are now threatened with the enemy who are in considerable force at Louisville, distant about thirteen miles. Orders have just been issues for all the ladies to leave, with those who are too sick to do duty. Ammunition is also distributed to the different commands. I cannot go to sleep under such circumstances but must write to my loved Elodie to convince her that she has no rival and to tell her, in reply to the question she asks in her letter

---

92. Bishop William Meade (1789–1862) was a U.S. Episcopal bishop and the third bishop of Virginia. He preached against secession even after Virginia seceded but ultimately acquiesced and became a convert to the Confederate cause. He died in March 1862 but not (supposedly) before giving his last blessing to Robert E. Lee. *Virginia's Civil War*, ed. Peter Wallenstein and Bertram Wyatt-Brown (Charlottesville: University of Virginia Press), 82.

of 23rd, that my heart is free from any apprehension that I have one. I have too much confidence, my dearest, to doubt for one moment the sincerity and devotion of your feelings for one so little worthy of them as my humble self. I will die, if die I must, thinking of you as one true in all your promises and willing to give my memory a small chamber in your heart. So much upon this subject, and if you are *provoked*, I hope you will be satisfied that I at least have no idea that I have a rival and further that I flatter myself that I can have no one so formidable as to make me apprehensive.

In my rambling yesterday, I came upon an itinerant ambrotype gallery, and, fancying that you would like to see me an officer of the day in my uniform, I had two likenesses taken. I will send them both to you by Mr. Fiquet,[93] a gentleman of Marion, who will leave the package at Selma with Mr. White. Select the one you like best and please have the other directed to Miss E. M. Dawson,[94] Cahaba, care of Judge Pettus[95] and sent to him by some safe hand. I wish Lizzie to have it as it may be valuable to her in case of any accident to me. You must excuse the common cases, but they were the best he had.

When this letter reaches you, my dearest, the writer, with all his faults, may have fallen. If so remember me as one who loved you more than all the world, who was willing to sacrifice all that *you* would have him sacrifice to *serve you*, and *who wished to live to make you happy*. You must not grieve too much in that event but look forward in time to the bright sun that will be unveiled by the clouds, to the time when you can find in another one worthy of your affections. But you must do what I wish you to do, which will be made known by Judge Pettus.

---

93. William Fiquet was born in New York but moved to Marion, Alabama, with his family before the war. Twenty-one years old when the war broke out, Fiquet joined Company G of the Fourth Alabama and died of wounds sustained at the Battle of First Manassas. Alabama Civil War Soldiers Database, Alabama Department of Archives and History.

94. His daughter, Elizabeth.

95. Edmund Winston Pettus (1821–1907) was the senior partner in the law firm of Pettus, Pegues, and Dawson. A Mexican-American War veteran, he helped organize the Twentieth Alabama Infantry and ultimately rose to the level of brigadier general, participating in most of the major action of the Western theater, including Stones River, Vicksburg, Chattanooga, and the Atlanta and Carolinas campaigns. After the war, Pettus resumed the practice of law in Selma and was named grand dragon of the Alabama Ku Klux Klan in 1877. Partly as a result of his success in organizing the Klan, he was elected U.S. senator in 1897 and 1903. The Edmund Pettus Bridge, the site of the 1965 "Bloody Sunday" civil rights engagement, was named for him. Robert W. Dubay, *John Jones Pettus, Mississippi Fire-Eater: His Life and Times, 1813–1867* (Jackson: University Press of Mississippi, 1975).

If no battle takes place, and I live to return to you, this letter will be regarded by you probably as foolish, but if I do not, you will then appreciate it. I write as I feel for you, my dear angel, and I cannot upon the eve of an attack suppress my feelings. They will convince you that I have no rival and that I am as true as a knight errant. The *Baltimore Sun* of yesterday is full of war news. After reading it, I think a battle will take place at Manassas Junction or at [illegible] before we have one. I think we will beat them in either event, and their defeat at one place will defeat their general plan of operations. But why trouble myself with these reflections. All is involved in uncertainty. I trust in the mercy and goodness of our all-wise God, and I will commend myself to His keeping. In your prayers, my dearest, I know that I am remembered, and it is a source of happiness.

I must not write you more in this strain as it will make you sad to read such a letter, but it is pleasant to breathe into your ear the soft feelings of melancholy which now prevail in my mind. I turn always to you for sympathy. You will always be an angel of hope and happiness.

Now, dearest, goodbye. May God bless and preserve you and make you happy. Believe that I love you so well that *none* can remove your image from my mind or your love from my heart. Adieu.

Sincerely and affty yours,

N. H. R. Dawson

Evening, June 1.

Our outposts have been driven in. We expect an attack tonight. I pray god to let me go through safely and return me to my own loved Elodie.

Goodbye. God preserve you,

N. H. R. Dawson

Selma, June 2, 1861

Saturday Bro. Clem handed me three letters from you dated 24th, 25th, 26th, which gratified me exceedingly as I was beginning to despair of ever hearing from you again, these being the first letters for a week. I suppose this delay and all coming together was owing to the new mail arrangements, yet newspapers came from everywhere it seems to me to confirm the news of the battle at Harper's Ferry and Hampton, and your silence or I should say the non arrival of your letters made me think perhaps there was some truth in the telegram, and there were many who felt as sad as I did until we found the news false. I really think that to publish such a dispatch without knowing that it is reliable should be punishable. I am glad you are at last receiving your letters and hope all I write will fall into your own hands as I do not write for any other eyes, and I know my letters would not be read as well to anyone else as they do to you. Besides if they give you pleasure I do not wish you to be without them, and I thought if you never received them you might doubt whether they were written as you seem to possess the idea that I may flirt [with] you and marry someone else during your absence. Well I suppose you had better be on your guard for you know what Mr. Dennis says of me, and perhaps it is true that I am very tricky, but this much I promise that when I marry you shall be present to know more about it than any other person. Will this do? But of course I know you are only jesting when you give expression to such fears for did I believe you thought otherwise after *what I have told you*, I would never write you another line, for there can never come a period when we should have more confidence in each other than at this time, nor could I be possessed of more than I have now in you, and I know you feel the same way with regard to myself. If you do not, you may place confidence in me with perfect safety, if you take my word for it, for I shall not love anybody else, and, if you are not permitted to return, I will live a cross, spiteful, old maid to the discomfort of all who know me and make it my chief aim in life to annoy and worry as much as I can all who come near me. I imagine that would be the only thing I would take any pleasure in.

You will see from this that I did not go as I anticipated to Summerfield, having heard there was an indisposition in the family I proposed visiting, and I may not go for a week yet. I would prefer staying in Selma as I do not feel as tho' I would enjoy the visit and only go to comply with a promise made some time ago, tho' were you to see me visiting here sometimes you would think I enjoyed it exceedingly but to tell the truth if I do not go out and have a very smiling face at home, I am teased and tormented most unmercifully by the household who threaten to write and tell you how *mean* you were to say anything to me before going to Va. I often tell them I think they are interfering and meddling, and I fear I am not grateful enough for the interest they manifest, and I want to be let alone. I think myself a martyr, but how foolishly I have rattled on. I feel ashamed of myself and since I have found it out, I am puzzled to know what else is left me to add for Selma is as Kittie says the dullest, most quiet, out of the way place in the world. I told [her] the attraction left before she came, but I do not blame her for thinking as she does for there is very little visiting done among the ladies and still less by the few young gentlemen left here, and there is nothing for her to do but read a little and dine in the evening. I take interest in going thro [illegible] to get work for the poor soldiers and am happy to say most of the ladies are aiding in sewing and a day or two since there was complete 183 oil cloth caps, more than a hundred of those caps and a box of goods being cut out, so you will soon receive some boxes, and from the lint and bandages I believe they intend all Guards and Cadets to be wounded twice over.

I omitted in my last to answer a request you made and repeat in your letter of yesterday which is my permission to allow you to tell Mrs. Mathews of our engagement. If I am not mistaken it was granted before you left, and I supposed she had been informed long since. Of course I have no objection and hope I will be as kindly thought of by her as you seem to think, and I will endeavor to make myself agreeable to her as she has been so kind to you. I think it but right that she should have your confidence and hope I have not prevented your communicating the intelligence to her if an opportunity has presented itself. Nor am I selfish enough to wish you to love and think of no one else but me for I know there are others who have claims to your love and thoughts, and I would not wish to prevent them from being loved as I know and enjoy so much the pleasure it gives me to have someone to be loving and kind that I think it would be a happiness to divide with them my own feeling and your love. I hope I will not be happy when I rob others of their rights. Do you know that you have asked me to answer truthfully and candidly some questions I had rather not and have quite an inclination not to do and if I enjoyed being unkind to you as much as to others I would not, but with a desperate effort I proceed. After expressing my objections to you to going with you to Virginia which you attach no importance to, altho' you acknowledge that I will add to your anxiety and care and perhaps give you more trouble, yet you are or *may be willing* to take yourself the trouble. I am willing to make some sacrifices when I know that to do so would contribute both to your and my own happiness. I certainly would be far happier with you than so far away, yet think, when you were absent I would be surrounded with strangers and would have to hear from you just as I do now and then be separated from my family beside, but I do not hesitate to say that if I could be with you always that I would be happier and would prefer it, and [I am] willing to endure hardships and make sacrifices to be with you. *I won't say near you.* You ask would I be willing to *risk* all the trials and sorrows that your death would entail on me as your wife. I say yes and assure you that as such I could not feel your death more than I would now. Do you suppose for one moment that I could? But now that I have answered all the questions you asked me and *candidly* too, I will quit the subject for it does not add to my comfort to look on any but the bright side, and I will not think of your dying for I declare I am growing nervous since I began on this subject which indeed you may well say is serious.

Col. Ellsworth was only an acquaintance of Kittie's, but one with whom she was thrown much last winter and being agreeable I think they were excellent friends, *nothing more*. But had she then seen him in his true light, she could not surely have entertained even that feeling. Nothing but contempt and scorn would have been the emotion of a woman for such a man. I have been expecting your photograph but as yet have heard nothing of it. Kittie says she must claim one also. I wish you could see this sister and mother of mine for I think you would like them both. My mother is the dearest, best woman on earth and is the loveliest and most amiable of persons and so agreeable and I think *pretty*. Kittie is fatter and larger than myself with black hair and eyes, rosy cheeks, and, altho' with strangers *too dignified*, is just as lively as can be at home but is rather spoilt being the youngest. Once or twice I have been asked if she was not the eldest and when I told her what her dignity did for her, she said if I would behave as well for my age as she does for hers we would be properly placed. I sigh for dignity.

Of course Mr. Averitt is very fond of you and all unpleasant acts that he is guilty of should be attributed to a want of judgment and discretion on his part springing from a very affectionate disposition, and I suppose he has always been accustomed to show it and never conceal his real feelings. You are one of the few persons I ever saw that did not like to be loved and have it shown. Yet you admire Mrs. Hardie's affection for her husband if it does make her in my eyes ridiculous—not the affection but her way of expressing it I mean, for I like to see persons who are fond of each other show it. I have two gentlemen friends who if they meet twice a day *will kiss*, no matter who is present, and I think their devotion to each other was admired by all who knew them. I liked it, thought it was beautiful because it was unusual. Suppose Mr. A. was to kiss you, what would you do? Did he let you read my letter *which was not long* and written on small note paper? Matt received a letter of 12 pages I think yesterday giving her a description of the scenery. I told her she ought to have it published the description was so good. Bro. Clem says if her letter is published, he is determined *all shall be* and will call on me for mine, but we will see whether he gets them or not.

Gen. Johnston of Ky. married first a favorite cousin of my mother, Henrietta Preston,[96] and is I think the same one you speak of, but really I am forgetting myself and you will think only to end this letter which I believe is the worst I have written, but I am not well today and have written hurriedly in order to lie down when it is finished. I hope to get a letter very soon and must ask you to write as often as possible to me, and I will continue to write as frequently as heretofore. But now goodbye.

Ever and affectionately,

Elodie

Harper's Ferry, June 2, 1861

We are relieved from drill this morning, being Sunday, and I prefer to commune with my loved Elodie to attending the service of our chaplain. Another day has passed since I wrote you, no attack has been made, and I now wish that my letter had been couched in different tones as it was written in a spirit to make you sad and gloomy. But you have taken me for *better* or for *worse*, and I wrote you simply as I felt, desiring always to be treated in the same way. This letter, with the likeness, will be borne by Mr. Fiquet and will reach you in advance of my letter of yesterday. I heard from a gentleman yesterday, who was direct from Montgomery, that the whole state was excited upon the subject of a battle at this place in which we have been victorious. I regret that there was no foundation for the rumor and do not see how such intelligence had its origin.

A friend told me yesterday that he received a letter from Selma in which, with other news, it was remarked that you had become quite a *recluse* since my absence, which was the cause of your sadness. While this is a flattering circumstance to me, I regret that others have noticed it as it proves how deeply you feel on my account. The cause of your seclusion of course was only surmised. How much I feel that you should have so much anxiety upon this subject. Indeed, it troubles me and at the same time is pleasant to know that a fair and gentle star watches and looks down upon the pathway of one who loves and worships her with an eastern idolatry. This love is *immortal*, will survive the wreck of time, and will be realized in another world if not attained here. I wish I could describe my love as

96. Henrietta Preston (1803–1835) was Albert Sidney Johnston's first wife. She died of tuberculosis at the age of thirty-two. For more, see Charles P. Roland, *Albert Sidney Johnston, Soldier of Three Republics* (Lexington: University Press of Kentucky, 2001).

eloquently as Bulwer has made Claude Melnotte declare his for Pauline. Get the play and read it, imagining yourself Pauline addressed by me.[97]

If we are ever married, my dearest, I will endeavor, with your permission, to travel over all of this state with you, to point out the places where we have passed, to enjoy with you the beautiful scenery. You are very unwilling to tell me which calling to pursue, Law or Politics. I will ask you to add the profession of Arms and select one for me. Do you think that you will always be *neutral* in such matters of opinion? You cannot be for you love me too well not to express an opinion when asked, and you will be unlike many of your sex if you do not, but I think you superior to your sex in many qualities and have made up my mind not to be disappointed. Who is Dr. Rodman? If he is a minister & a friend of yours, you must request him to marry us. I would prefer any *friend* of *yours* to perform so interesting a ceremony. I envy some of the beautiful places here and would have a home for you like one now occupied by Gen. Johnston. Have you any desire to live in Kentucky? If she secedes, I would like very much to have a farm there to spend our summers! Or somewhere in the mountains of Va. or Tennessee. When I dream of such things, it is always in connection with your dear image. But the humblest cottage in the confederate states would be a Paradise if you were the one to share it with me. Yesterday the ladies again visited us and brought niceties of all kinds—pickles, pies, cakes, and butter. One old gentleman brought the regiment forty bushels of meal and quite a number of hams. The ladies also have some smoking caps but did not give me one. I will be more provident the next time they come, but, as I have told them I was to be married as soon as the war is over, I am not so popular as I was. I was pleased with a young officer here. A lady at Winchester commenced a flirtation with him when he told her he was engaged. This was candid and well, and if one was begun with me, I would act like him. I am not over anxious to be taken prisoner and carried to Washington. I would prefer to go there after the war as a Confederate officer. We will have peace in *one year*, I think, and probably in three months, but I will return home at the end of my enlistment. I have written you a long letter literally with nothing, but you must be content. It is the best I can do. Please write me

97. *The Lady of Lyons; or, Love and Pride*, written by Edward Bulwer-Lytton in 1838, is five-act play recounting the story of Claude Melnotte, the son of Pauline's gardener, who disguises himself as a foreign prince so that Pauline will marry him. When she discovers the trick, she annuls the marriage. Melnotte then joins the army and becomes a war hero, and Pauline realizes she really does love him.

as *often* as you *desire* and as *long* as you *will.* Goodbye. May God guard and protect you from all danger and trouble.

Ever and sincerely yours, my own loved Elodie,
    N. H. R. Dawson

June 3.

No fight yet, but great preparations are making to meet the enemy. We expect an attack now in the course of a few days. I will telegraph the result so as to remove your suspense. I am quite well today. Goodbye my dearest Elodie.

Ever and affty yrs,
    N. H. R. Dawson

Selma, June 12, 1861

I received your letter and daguerreotype on Monday which were very welcome altho' not flattering. You are indeed changed if they are faithful resemblances of you now. I would not exchange the small and handsome one given me on your departure for a dozen taken as *Officer-of-the-Day.* It must be the *regimentals* that render them, may I say *unpleasant for me to look at.* I will send the best to Lizzie and think an opportunity will come next week, and now I will have the etiquette to thank you, not only for them but for thinking of me and the pleasure such a gift would afford. Nothing could have pleased me more *except receiving the original*, which would indeed be enjoyed, but I must content myself with anticipating that happiness no matter how far distant in the future it is to be and admire you the more because you have sacrificed so much in leaving home to go forth and battle for the rights and liberties of your country. It is a just and noble cause and now that you have gone, I am proud of you and would not have desired you to remain at home and idle in the hour of need when your country demanded your services for any consideration. Yet do not infer from this that I regard *this profession* as the *one* I would select for you, nor do I intend to be a *Kentuckian* and think for one moment of being neutral on that subject, else, after a while, when like that state I desire to act, it will then be too late, and, as you have asked me again to select a profession for you, *I will make a few remarks* but decline making the selection which I insist upon your doing yourself, even if we should disagree in our choice, for your happiness will be more immediately concerned than mine. So long as your country is really in need of your services to defend it from the invasion of an enemy then that profession will do, and I have no objection to it if there is no one to fill your place, tho' I sincerely hope there will never be another vacancy for you in the army. As to a political life, I think almost any choice preferable and more conducive to happiness. It is a life of trials, vexations, and cares, and in the end a grand disappointment to all the views of the politicians himself and those of his friends. What are a few empty honors, and do they compensate when gained for the trouble of a laborious life to please the world, which does, indeed, turn every day—your friends today, your foes tomorrow, ready to tarnish your fair name with any untruth that will serve to promote party purposes? I know my father's life was embittered after the selection of a political life was made by his friends for him and he accepted it, and after all the sacrifices he made for them and to acquire for himself fame and name which lived only a few years after he slumbered in his grave, and it was well he did not live longer to plunge deeper in, for every other life had lost its charm and there was but the one that added, he thought, to his happiness. Yet I am wrong, I expect, to judge all by the few I have known to be otherwise than happy in such a choice as much depends upon disposition, and any life may have proved to have had the same effect. It may be that you would be far happier engaged in this pursuit than any other. You know best. I do not know much on this subject and speak from a little amount of observation and the opinion of friends in whom I place confidence and will only ask you not to laugh and to tell you also that I can like you no matter what profession you follow—'tis not that I love. Why is it that you are always drawing me out, making me render myself ridiculous and exposing my ignorance on subjects fit for your mental faculties? If I were you I would laugh myself over this letter, but you asked me to *say*, and I did my best and I hope have convinced you of my anxiety to do as you wished for me, for I do not desire else than to be successful in this undertaking and feel myself quite out of my element in assisting you in the choice of a profession which I think is your exclusive right.

Thursday, June 13th.

I have risen an hour or two earlier this morning to finish my letter. Mother would not allow me to sit up last night as I am not well yet and for two or three nights have been compelled to be up until small hours, and you must look upon my early rising as the greatest compliment I could pay you. I was astonished at the information contained in your last letter about myself. Perhaps the writer of that letter to Harper's Ferry has not seen much of me, but circumstances have been such that, with the exception of a few days when indisposition kept me in the house, I have visited daily with my mother or sister and assure you that I am not a recluse, and you need not let this idle rumor trouble you longer, and I am not weak enough to give way to *grief* in *this public manner* and when I know it would *delight some* to be aware that I *suffered*. The writer must have been one of my good, kind, and *knowing* friends who always have more knowledge of my own actions than myself and are so interested in me, and I would really like to know who it was and is spying in our camp. Our concert I fear and hope will prove a failure as already there has been two or three difficulties among the troops. Ella Watts and I have concluded to have as little to do with it as possible and nothing if we can avoid it and to keep clear of trouble, do our practicing at home and not with the entire company which have not met but once when they did not quarrel or have some misunderstanding. On Sunday last a large box which contained capes and caps that had been sent on to the Guards and Cadets was returned with the word that it could not go, so all the sewing hurry and etc. was for naught. Mr. Woodson, Mrs. Henden, and Mrs. Woodson[98] left a few days since for Virginia after hearing of the death of their father. I hear it is Mr. W's intention to take the place of a brother in the army who has a large family and will return to them and take charge of his mother's affairs. Selma is constantly losing someone and when a few more families leave for their summer residences will be quite deserted. Mother is beginning to grow impatient and anxious to return to Ky., but we beg her to remain just a little longer as a very short time will decide for that state now, and from all accounts fighting will soon commence there. I tell her that I am not going until Kentucky secedes and am beginning to think now I will never return if I do indeed wait for that event to transpire. No, drooping flags for Ellsworth's death, inviting Major Anderson[99] on, and giving him a public reception in Linville are almost enough to

---

98. Mr. F. A. Woodson and Mrs. Maria T. Woodson were born in Virginia and were living in Selma according to the 1860 Census: Selma. They are listed as living with the Henden family, also from Virginia.

99. Union major Robert Anderson (1805–1871) was in command of Fort Sumter when it surrendered to Confederate forces.

convince one that their sympathy is with the North. I have no desire to have anything more to do with them, for I never can forgive that state for behaving in such a shameful manner. I am one of the most unforgiving creatures you ever knew in my disposition, and if a wrong is done me and I am angered, I can never again be reconciled to the offender, altho' that person may have been my dearest friend. My confidence could never be placed again there, and I could not be persuaded to do anything more than speak to them. Does this not astonish you or did you know me well enough to find it out? I tried to show only the good traits of my character and will only allow you to see by degrees the unpleasant ones if I can keep them sufficiently under my control.

You asked me who Dr. Rodman was: Why he is just one of the noblest and best of men and *my friend*. He has been for several years our physician and is partial to our family, especially your honorable writer whom I am proud to say is his favorite and values and appreciates his friendship. I have no relation interested in my future welfare and many not so much so.

I have just received your letter of June 4th in which you mention having received from me but nine letters. I know of *twelve* and think I have written more but will not positively assert the fact of having sent more than twelve. They have always been so long that you should count *each one as two*. I will make with pleasurable willingness a cap for you but cannot understand from the mention of [the] *hood* how I am to make it. If you will take a newspaper [and] your scissors and cut me a pattern and tell me what to make it of—silk, merino, or velvet—I will do so and think I can send it on without trouble. If you are unable to send me the pattern, a drawing will do with as good a description as you are capable of giving. What is your favorite color, or what color would you prefer for this cap?

You mention my reading you such a lecture in my letter of the 23rd. Please return the letter to me so that I may see what I did write. I have no copy and have a poor memory and have puzzled my brain trying in vain to recall any portion of that letter, which indicates the Todd. What will you think of this? I have been engaged for two or three hours practicing for the concert. My fingers and throat fairly ache. Mrs. Lumpte and I have a duet (instrumental) together and I have a vocal duet. I have refused to sing alone or do anything more than to take part in these two duets, and if I could well avoid doing so would take no part. I wish as it is for the benefit of the absent soldiers, you could be here to attend. I think I would take some interest then. Today was appointed by our president for fasting and prayer. My intention was to attend church, but as the morning was warm concluded to go this evening, and just as I was ready to start company came in and prevented me doing so. Mother promised to do my share tonight while I remained at home to write to you. Willie today heard me say I was going to church this evening to pray for the soldiers and came and put his arms around me and begged to go with me. I promised provided he would add his prayers and tell me what he intended to say. He replied immediately, Aunt Dee I'll pray to God to give Mr. Averitt *Bread* every day and Captain Dawson *Butter*. It was the best thing he knew of to pray for. He often speaks of you and Mr. A. also, whom he imagines is my sweetheart and tells persons so who ask him questions pertaining to that subject the same thing. I am much obliged to you for all your promises, but am terribly *afraid of promising people. Just do*, without the former, what you have already said, and I'll ask no more. I will make no promises myself but try to do what is right and my duty and hope I may add to your happiness. Mr. Wetmore has not sent your photograph yet. He told me a night or two since it was not completed. I told him to hurry it up for I was very anxious to have it in my possession, that I intended having it myself, not Mrs. White. He looked surprised and remarked, "Are you in earnest?," but did not seem to believe me. You see when I begin a letter to you I never know when to stop. All ask me what on earth I find to say, and they feel so sorry for you that it must be a task, between the writing and length, not very pleasant. I feel sorry for you too and will prove it by stopping my pen, and before doing so want to know what is the matter with my signature that you quote it on so many occasions. I am going to avoid putting any if your offence is again repeated, but indeed I must stop. Hoping soon to hear again from you and that God will spare you granting a safe and speedy return to your,

    Attached,
    Elodie

Harper's Ferry, June 12, 1861

With a heart full of gratitude and pleasure, I have to acknowledge the receipt, on yesterday, of your letter of 2d June, postmarked 4th June. I hardly know how, my dear Elodie, to thank you for this letter. Its candor, its affectionate tone, have soothed and comforted me under circumstances that have calculated to make me feel unpleasantly the uncertainty of our situation. Just at this juncture when our movements are extremely uncertain, it was indeed pleasant to receive so refreshing a draught from the fine fountain of your heart.

Your replies to my questions are certainly satisfactory and several occurrences have combined to vindicate their wisdom and your own good sense. I will not ask you to marry me until I can have you not *near* me alone *but with me always*, and I thank you for having been so candid. I know you would have to be separated from me nearly all the time and your location, with strangers, would be necessarily unpleasant. Mrs. Hardie is an illustration of what you would have to suffer. She is now very sick at Winchester, connected by rail with this place, and on yesterday was very *ill*, and Mr. H. was telegraphed to go to see her. He applied to Gen. Johnston for leave of absence, but he declined to give it but told Mr. H. if the exigency required it he could *resign*. This I think, tho' in accordance with military usage, was a terrible alternative to a husband who loves his wife. Mr. H. however did not resign and had to remain. I will not ask you, my dearest, for the happiness it would give me to have you near me, to subject yourself to such an unpleasant position. But I would unhesitatingly in such a case resign my commission and afterwards enter the ranks. When I marry you, I wish to be able to command my own movements.

And now, dearest, upon the subject of your flirtation, I will treat you as you treat me, give you permission to fall in love with any gentleman that offers as I flatter myself that you will find none good enough. I have no *ability* to doubt when I love immensely, and I love you so entirely, so wholly, that I can have no power to doubt you. I will be ready to make my exit from this world and "to shuffle off this mortal coil." If anything could increase my love for you, the candor, the good sense, and the *true* affection you have manifested in this letter will have done so. And my heart is overflowing with gratitude and affection. I will not trouble you again with these questions but have the time of our marriage to be fixed by circumstances, only insisting that you will marry me at the earliest time after I am released from my present bonds.

Again, my dearest, you tell me that under no circumstances could you love me more than you do at this time. This is indeed gratifying to a poor soldier, and as it expresses my own feeling for you, I thank you most heartily. Do you imagine how much I love you? I measure your love for me by the measure of my own.

I thank you for your rebuke about Mr. Averitt, as I feel that I was wrong in writing you as I did of him. He loves me, I know, and I must ever consent cheerfully to be kissed by him for your sake. He has placed my trunk with Mr. Williams of Winchester, who has promised to keep it until I can reclaim it. I have the pleasure of knowing his family and have been kindly invited to make his home my home when I go to Winchester. Is this not kind? Mr. A. showed me your letter and of course you must not object as I have answered it candidly. I think he would be much pleased to see his letter in print. He read it to me, at least the descriptive part of it, which was quite pretty, and I think would read well in the *Reporter*. Now I have pled guilty, and I hope you will say I have made amends. But, I assure you, I would not like to be kissed by any friend three times a day, but I would expect it and desire it in my wife for I am extremely affectionate and think its exhibition, except publicly, is a duty and a most pleasant custom. I hope you understand me on this question of ethics. Dearest, you must never hesitate to speak to me candidly. I think of you as my wife and look forward to my return home as if we were already married. I hope you will not blame for telling you this much. I should really like to know what you think of me from my letters.

I wrote you yesterday and the day before but could not resist the pleasure of having a talk with you as Mr. Ware, the gentleman who takes these letters, will not leave until this morning. I do not think it prudent now to send any articles to our companies as we may move from here, nearer to Richmond, in the vicinity of Manassas Junction. A large federal force is certainly coming down on us from Washington, and one from Western Va. and we may have to retreat before their large numbers. If we do, we will have to give up a part of our present luggage and even some of our tents. You should have seen me in my tent today with one of my lieutenants mending the only pair of pantaloons that your captain now has. Excuse me for mentioning this circumstance as it illustrates how little baggage we have. When one of our officers wishes to pay a visit of ceremony, he borrows a blue coat from some brother officer. The young man, Overton,[100] of whom I write you, is now convalescing rapidly and will soon be well. I am really grateful to God. How I wish I were a Christian. Dearest you know that a good wife will save a bad husband, and I rely upon your prayers and intercessions to sustain me thro' all of these trials. They are

---

100. John B. Overton, from Summerfield, Alabama, was a private in Nathaniel's company. In an earlier letter, Nathaniel had described him as "a boy who has made a fine impression by his behavior and bearing. . . . I hope he will get well but fear the chances are against him. I will feel his loss much more than if he had fallen in battle. Poor fellow." 1860 U.S. Federal Census, Summerfield, Dallas County, Ala.

made sweet when I think of you as one who approves of my conduct, and who will be ready to receive me warmly and affectionately.

I ordered a friend to have a photograph sent you, and I sent you one from this place, both of which I hope you have received. If I would have imagined that your sister Miss Kittie would have accepted one, it would have been forwarded.

I have written John a letter telling him to observe to the letter my instructions about the flowers and fruit. He will understand my meaning. He will probably carry you with my compliments Motley's *Dutch Republic*,[101] which I think has been sent to me from New York since I left home. I ordered it for you as I heard you once desired to read it. Ask him no questions how he got it. Please let me know if he delivers it. Continue to write me to Winchester as you have until further directions. Present my most respectful compliments to your mother and sisters and Mr. White and with the assurance of my entire devotion, I remain, my dear Elodie,

Affectionately and sincerely yours,

N. H. R. Dawson

Selma, June 16, 1861

Altho but a day or two has passed since I wrote you last, I have become so accustomed to employ a part of my Sabbath writing to you that almost unconsciously I begin to collect my writing materials preparatory to commencing this letter. I have felt no compunction of conscience for all my Sunday letters to you yet, for I cannot think I am committing a sin when I just take a little quiet chat with you on paper, yet Mother cannot reconcile herself to seeing me do so, and I never remember to have seen her do such a thing in my life, and I always go away from her when I wish to indulge myself. Yesterday I received two letters from you and I did not expect any was pleasantly surprised and found one more agreeable than the other for two reasons. I refer to one in which you *make choice of a profession*, and speak cheerfully of the future losing sight of the battlefield. I had just written you a lengthy article on the subject of professions which will no doubt prove amusing to you, but as we agree in the selection I am satisfied and think *you exhibit the fine intellect I have given you credit for.*

101. John Lothrop Motley (1814–1877) was an American diplomat and historian whose *Rise of the Dutch Republic* (1856) proved wildly popular.

You have indeed *proved yourself a wise, prudent, proper man* in some things, but I can tell you better after a while whether I consider myself *fortunate or not* in entrapping you and escaping Mr. J. whom I never stood in danger of. I do not believe it is *my Mr. J.* but an elder brother who is I know very wild and has caused the family much trouble and unhappiness, a namesake of his Father's. Did I ever tell you anything concerning the gentleman? Or how did you know he and I were acquaintances? I have a most unfortunate memory and have no recollection of ever having to you mentioned his name.

Last evening Kittie, Matt, and myself spent at Mrs. Mabry's, who had a little musical soiree—Dr. and Mrs. LeComte, Mr. and Mrs. Wetmore, Bro. Clem and T. J. Smith making the party. I have spent an evening or two there very pleasantly but thought last night was one of the dullest and stiffest I ever spent in Selma. The company did not appear congenial, certainly not Mr. L. and myself, who were thrown together. His feelings are all with the North I am positive and can read him altho he thinks himself no doubt very smart in hiding up his sentiments, and I cannot meet him unless he commences on the subject of politics, and I do not forget to mention Mr. J. C. Breckenridge and have him my model for politicians and choice and hope for President of the Confederate States. This hurts a leetle as he does so greatly enjoy hating Mr. B., and his face tells what his tongue does not. I am not more partial to him than most of the young ladies and fear [I] do not treat him with the same politeness. Mr. Shortridge keeps him informed of affairs at Harper's Ferry, and he is always asking me when I heard, but surely I can find a more agreeable subject of conversation than this gentle*man* and will not entertain you longer with him.

Yesterday morning two large boxes were packed and sent on by a gentleman named Davidson for the Cadets and Guards, and I trust they will go safely. I cannot understand how they will be intercepted and such seems to be the fear here. Bro. Clem received your letter and will do as you desire. I am so glad that he did not go to Virginia as he is so unwell, quite thin and feeble, and I think he would have been sent back. His only Brother is now on a visit to him and has with him his wife, and as they have not met for some time they really enjoy each other's society and act as I imagine they did as children, so affectionate and kind in their manner to each other. I think to see an affectionate family one of the most beautiful sights in the world and yet one that is rare, tho' it seems strange that anything else should be, and I think it is a characteristic of many families never to know what they feel. We have always been happy together and never knew what the feeling was that prompted others to always seek happiness from home and to feel miserable when compelled to remain there. I love to visit sociably and think it is right to do so but believe I can content myself at home as well as most persons and have now a good opportunity to learn as soon Selma will be almost deserted and there will be so few places to visit when one is seized with the inclination.

My mother speaks of returning to Kentucky in two or three weeks. I really do not feel as tho' it will be safe for her to return and dread the summer here for her. I do not intend returning with her as I feel safe and secure in this portion of the world and Ky. has not yet *seceded* nor have I now any hope that she will. Having heard some gentlemen conversing on the never-ending subject of war a short time since, I was surprised that they spoke so freely of Col. Jones as being totally unfitted for the position he occupies and what a terrible thing it would be if they should have a fight at Harper's Ferry as was now daily expected, for no other fate but being cut to pieces awaited the 4th Regiment if he commanded or else they would disgrace themselves by running. Just imagine how I feel when so often persons speak in this manner before me and are watching my face all the time thinking I'll betray myself perhaps, and now since this conversation I have felt worse than before and am dreading to hear from a battle in which you must take part as your chances are worse than those who are well commanded, and I am so far from being a Spartan[102] that if you were here and I could influence you to remain at home, I would not hesitate to do so. I am getting selfish and do not see why some should be called upon to make so many more sacrifices than others. There are even some here who have all left to them that they possessed before these troubles began and whose mind or happiness is not disturbed by the absence of a very dear friend, and they think every man should go. Alla Parkman[103] remarked the same thing to me. I told her I noticed those whose *relations remained behind* generally spoke in that way, but when the time came that would cause her to part with a *brother* and those she loved then she could not say the same. I have passed thro' the ordeal and knew and would be willing to *push* the *kin* of *others* off to *keep my own at home too*. I really felt angry at her for speaking in that way and knew she was not

102. Spartans choose their brides for their physical sturdiness and warlike character.
103. Alla Parkman, age nineteen, of Selma, was the daughter of M. R. Parkman, age fifty. Her twenty-three-year-old brother James M. Parkman is listed as head of the household. 1860 Census: Selma.

sincere in doing so for when Johnny[104] spoke of going, and you know he *was not in earnest,* Alla nearly wept herself away when war was mentioned in her presence. I miss you more now and feel worse than I did when you first left, and I am growing so impatient to have the question settled at once, one way or another, and if there must be fighting I want it over. Of course, if you had not mentioned the subject you did to me before leaving, I would have been spared all this anxiety, at least no other thoughts than those that I possess sometimes for acquaintances to whom I am not entirely indifferent would I ever have entertained for you, but I am willing & prefer to suffer suspense and anxiety as you tell me it adds to your happiness. Yet were you never permitted to return, I am afraid, indeed I know, I could not bear the trial as I should and bow my head to the decree of an all wise, just and merciful God without murmuring, and I hope no such trouble is in store for me, for if I find the thought unbearable, what would be the trial? I would be perfectly satisfied with life then, but I am writing to you this, altho you told me you liked sad letters and wished me to write as I felt, but were I to attempt to give expression to one half my thoughts, I would find it utterly impossible and give up the task in despair for I scarcely allow myself to think all I do feel.

I do not regret your having told Mr. Averitt all, for seldom have I ever met another for whom I formed a greater friendship, and there is no telling what the consequences might have been if I had not believed him *engaged* and you not made *your appearance* in the *right time,* as I liked him better every time I met him. He suspected so much that you could have had very little to have informed him of. He has never answered my letter, perhaps has never received it. I am spared some annoyance, as I would not like to have his letter remain unanswered, and yet would not answer them as you prefer my not doing so. I am glad that you find my letters pleasing and will be more anxious now than ever to write as you say you derive pleasure from them. You must indeed see thro' *kindly glasses* and make all due allowances for me, and I am so much obliged to you for I believe if I had plenty to relate I could do no better. I never liked to write and cannot take the trouble and pains to compose, and write just as I talk, running as rapidly from one subject to another as always. I have not made my trip to Summerfield yet but will do so after the concert which will take place Thursday or Friday night and will write you from there as

---

104. John M. Parkman was the older brother of Alla Parkman. 1860 Census: Selma.

here. I hope you have not taken any more *naps* over your *Bible*, but read it as I gave it to you for that purpose, thinking if you did your Company would imitate your example and that you would all be a pious, religious set and could offer up prayers for yourselves for I really believe they even *pray more* for the *Blues* than for the other companies. But I see my page is almost filled, and this will be a long enough letter this time, and I will stop, hoping to receive often long letters, that peace may be restored, and that you will return safely and speedily to your affectionate,

Elodie

Winchester, Virginia, June 18, 1861

I read last night, my dearest Elodie, your long and welcome letter of the 7th and thank you from the bottom of my heart for your expressions of love and affection. Have you received the ambrotype sent you from Harper's Ferry by Mr. Fiquet? The package was directed to *Mr. White.* Please get him to call on Mr. Fiquet at Marion for the package. Did you receive the letters by him?

Just here Mr. Averitt interrupted me. He comes to take leave and to eat breakfast with me. Dearest, I also tell you what he has told me as a *secret*— he is *engaged* to Miss *Williams.*[105] The event transpired last night. He is very happy. He has also accepted the chaplaincy of Col. McDonald's regiment of Dragoons.[106] Col. M. has given him a beautiful horse to outfit. I think he has done right to accept the place as he had no position in our regiment. We will still see much of him. I feel this morning, dearest, that we are to live to enjoy the love we bear for each other so strongly. There are moments of joy which succeed hours of depression. So it is with me this morning. I see your image in the beautiful morning and in the beautiful country around me. You *color* everything. I have written you almost

---

105. Mary Louise Dunbar Williams was the daughter of Philip Williams. She was twenty-seven years old when she and Averitt married on February 26, 1862. 1860 U.S. Federal Census, Winchester, Frederick, Va.; marriage certificate, James Battle Aiverett and Mary Louise Dunbar Williams, Winchester, Frederick, Va., *Virginia, Select Marriages, 1785–1940.*

106. Angus William McDonald (1799–1864) had been educated at West Point and became wealthy in the fur trapping trade, earning the sobriquet "Big Knife" from the Native Americans. In the spring of 1861 he agreed to serve as the first colonel of the Seventh Virginia Cavalry, to which Averitt would be assigned. For more, see Flora McDonald Williams, *The Glengarry McDonalds of Virginia* (Louisville: G. G. Fetter, 1911).

daily from H. Ferry [except] on the march, [and] in the wagon I had no opportunity of doing so but was there, sick and lying down, [though] I made out to write you once. I am glad that you speak so properly of bearing any *trials* you may have. I will always *share* and *divide* them with you, my own dearest, and I hope God will send none so heavy that you will not be able, by the exercise of Christian faith and grace, to submit with resignation. I have had my share of them, but God has enabled me to bear them. The will sun will come from under the clouds, and now I am again *blessed* with the *light* of *your love.*

What more can I say, my dear girl, to cheer you up under the painful suspense in which you are. I will take every care of myself that prudence and honor will dictate and will not needlessly risk my life as it belongs to others. I will try to be a better man, to be a *Christian,* and it is pleasant to know that you will join me in this effort. I have no time now to reply to your lecture upon *napping* over your bible. I can only say you have a happy *faculty of imagining.* And now, dearest, I must tell you goodbye and command you to the protection of an all-wise God who doeth all things well. I hope you will soon be well. I wish I could have been your *nurse* in your recent sickness. I will write frequently, but you must not think I have forgotten you if you do not hear regularly.

Ever affty & sincerely yours,

N. H. R. Dawson

Winchester, Virginia, June 26, 1861

This day two months ago I bid you goodbye, and as the boat proceeded upon her way your image, my dearest Elodie, was lost in the distance, but not one moment has passed since that sacred hour when your image has been absent from my mind. It is so intimately associated with my thoughts that is has become a part of my existence, and I must be very busily occupied not to be able to abstract myself to be with you. Indeed, it would require a greater effort than I am capable of making not to think of you always. Is such love as I give you worth anything? Or is it simply the homage that man pays to your sex? I am much deceived if many men love as ardently as I do. God grant that this love of mine will be gratified in a speedier reunion with you than the dark clouds of war, which overhang the political skies, would indicate. I console myself with the reflection that others are as hardly situated as myself and that their fate is as bad as mine, but still this is a very uncharitable consolation. One sixth of my time has passed, and I hope the term will find me as well as I am now. I would send you my likeness again, but as you seem to dislike my face in uniform, I deem it hardly proper to disturb your equanimity.

Our regiment has been transferred to the brigade of Gen. Bee.[107] He is a West Point officer and lately resigned from the U. States army. He is a So. Carolinian and the son of an intimate friend of my father. He is a very fine officer as you can judge from Mr. Davis having raised him from a captain to the command of a brigade. We will be associated with two regiments from Miss. and one from Tennessee. The transfer will be a pleasant one. I have not formed a favorable opinion of Col. Duncan. He says Mr. Breckinridge[108] is buttering his own bread. I am so great an admirer of Mr. B. that I have no respect for any one who detracts from him. I do hope he will be able to accomplish something for his state and that with her three loving sisters, she will yet join her destiny to the galaxy of her southern sisters and become one of the arches of the Confederate states.

I love you so much that I love any object that you love, my dearest, and this will explain the *control* you will exercise over me. Yours will be a *reign* of *love*, and if you have any dexterity at all, you will preserve this influence so essential the happiness of husband and wife. I can conceive of no happiness where a wife has no influence over her husband. I mean of course a control obtained by the exercise of those gentle and winning offices of love, entirely different from the reign of terror acquired by some female despots. To live with you in the bonds of wedlock would seem to be a foretaste of paradise, and I look forward to the time with the most sanguine hopes of happiness and comfort. The separation to which we have been subject and the circumstances under which we have loved will do much to call into being all the love of our hearts, and we will have felt in advance many of the pleasures of love and friendship.

I love you as the friend and intimate sharer of all my thoughts, in whose ear I can think *aloud* and upon whose bosom, in the day of trial and trouble, I will have a right to confide and to ask sympathy. To be a part of yourself, to share your troubles, and to mingle my tears with yours,

---

107. Barnard Elliott Bee Jr. (1824–1861) was born in South Carolina, moved to Texas as a child, attended West Point, and spent most of his army career in the West. In June 1861 he was appointed brigadier general in the Confederate army and would lead Nathaniel's brigade at Bull Run, where he was mortally wounded. For more, see John H. Eicher and David J. Eicher, *Civil War High Commands* (Stanford: Stanford University Press, 2001), 125.

108. John Cabell Breckinridge (1821–1875) was a Kentucky lawyer, politician, and vice president of the United States from 1857 to 1861. He would serve as the final Confederate secretary of war and would flee to Cuba to avoid capture.

will be a duty and pleasure, while to do all to make you a happy and contented wife will be the great, leading object of my life. . . .

I find that I have filled three pages with sentences that you will probably say are foolish contributions to the literature of love, less florid perhaps than the effusions of Eloise and Abelard.[109] But they are intended
to indicate my love for you [so] you must pardon them. We move this
evening to another camp, in a grove alongside of our new friends, the
Mississippians. From present appearance we are here for some time—
at least this will be the headquarters for Gen. Johnston's "Army of the
Shenandoah."

The weather is now very warm and pretty, and we will find our duties
very fatiguing if we are put on a march. I will be very fatigued to march
down on Washington. I think Gen. Beauregard evidently contemplates
an advance movement upon the capital and whenever he does make it
this division will cut in concert with his. We have about *fourteen* thousand
men in the district and county commanded by Gen. Johnston, besides
the militia of the country. We do not get as many little niceties as eggs,
butter, and chickens, as we did at Harper's Ferry. I presume the reason is
that the city takes all of them.

I have been endeavoring to get up a band of brass instruments for the
Reg. We have the performers but can get only one set of instruments,
which will cost $800. We will decide on tomorrow whether we can afford
to pay such a price. Music will add greatly to our pleasures. I never hear
music but that I think of you, my own dear Elodie.

I have just received from Selma an [illegible] cloth cape, sent by Maj.
Haden, with one each for Grey Haden, Rev. Tanner, Lewis Thomas, and
Turner Vaughan.[110] Dearest, you are no doubt tired and will be relieved
by the ending of this letter. Think of me always as your dearest friend
who would do all that man would dare to defend you from harm and who
loves you fondly and well. With my most respectful regards to Mr. and
Mrs. White and your mother and sister, I remain,

    Very affty and sincerely yours,
    N. H. R. Dawson

---

109. Alexander Pope's 1717 poem *Eloisa to Abelard* was inspired by the twelfth-century
tale of Heloise's illicit love for (and secret marriage to) philosopher and teacher Peter Abelard. See Peter Abelard, *The Letters of Abelard and Heloise* (New York: Penguin Books, 2003).

110. James Grey Haden, age twenty-two; Lewis Thomas, age twenty-one; and P. Turner
Vaughan, age twenty-one, were all privates in Nathaniel's company. He thought especially
highly of Vaughan, noting "he has no superior [and] hardly any equal in the company."
Vaughan would rise to the rank of second lieutenant. Alabama Civil War Soldiers Database,
Alabama Department of Archives and History.

Summerfield, June 27, 1861

I have a few moments to write you this morning before leaving this place for a visit of two days to Miss Laura Mims and must acknowledge the receipt of two letters last night from you and the pleasure they afforded me. I have been, I will not say, *positively* expecting a letter for almost a *week*, but none came and I realized for once in my life what to be miserable was and all the horrors of true unhappiness. Knowing you had left Harper's Ferry, I was well aware of the dangers to which you would be exposed and would attend you every step and felt all the more because I could not know where you were, for even this information affords some pleasure. I did not think for a moment of your being sick and am afraid from your being so that you do not take proper care of yourself and all the privations and hardships you are now undergoing will prove too much for you. The oftener I think of your willingness to go and the ready cheerfulness with which you made all sacrifices necessary to such an event, the more is my love and admiration for you increased, and feel so proud of my *soldier sweetheart*, but would be very happy to have him at home nevertheless. I have missed the pleasure of writing to you for so long, but as I had *received orders not to do so* until I heard again from my Captain, *I could not but be obedient*, altho' I commenced two letters and would not have been *afraid of disobeying orders* had I know where to have sent them to. What would have been my punishment for disobedience?

Last week the ladies gave their concert in Selma and everything save Dr. LeConte's lecture passed pleasantly. He was hissed and all manner of ridicule made of him which of course made us feel badly. *The cause* enabled us to go thro with our parts well, and the applause which greeted my singing the Marseillaise[111] more than repaid me for all the trouble I had in practicing, and I believe Mr. Harman, who selected me to sing it, was more pleased at my success than I. The amount made was $175, and all were so pleased that they speak of having another. Last Thursday we were all so delighted by the arrival of my Bro. Sam from Pensacola. His term of enlistment had expired, and he was on his way to New Orleans to visit his wife and children and would leave then for Virginia. My Bro. David wrote from Richmond that he expected to leave in a day or two for Staunton and has been appointed one of Gen'l Holme's[112] aides. I

111. Composed by Claude Joseph Rouget de Lisle in 1792, "La Marseillaise" was the national anthem of France and credited with rallying soldiers to the French Revolution.
112. Confederate lieutenant general Theophilus Hunter Holmes (1804–1880) graduated from West Point near the bottom of his class and is usually regarded as having a

hope you may meet with them for I feel assured you will like them both.
I have also two young cousins in the N.C. Cadets [letter torn] Clarke,
also a friend Theodore Bigot, a young Frenchman who was educated in
Kentucky and spent his vacations with us. I think they have a new Captain
whose name is Bond since leaving so if you are thrown in the same parts
of the country with them you can look them up. My Mother leaves for
Kentucky Tuesday or Wednesday but promises to return and spend the
winter South. I regret so much to part with her but Kentucky has not *seceded*, and I think myself safer and better off in many respects down here
and have declined accompanying her. I will miss her so much and feel as
tho I am *deserted*, but the truth is I am a *deserter* myself, and you are much
to blame for my becoming such.

I wrote to you acknowledging the safe arrival of your daguerreotypes
and letters and wrote indeed several letters which perhaps reached
Harper's Ferry after you left. Kittie, Mrs. Hagood, and self came out here
Tuesday evening to attend the concert and will remain until next Monday I suppose. This is one of the most quiet spots I ever visited and the
people seem quite fifty years behind the fashionable world, and it is such
a pleasure to be with them for a *little while*, and as I am a favorite with
Bro. Clem's relations I get a larger share of petting which will spoil me
for Selma, especially as Mother is going away. I thought of so much a day
or two since I would have to tell you of when next I wrote to you, but
since I have commenced the noise around me (for there are only 8 or
10 children) and the hurry I write in has caused every idea to fly. Just at
the last word I was again interrupted to go in the parlor to see company
which, when I was writing to you, I regard as quite disagreeable and annoying, and have yet to write you a letter without having met with such
an interruption, sometimes several.

I was much astonished when I read such intelligence of Mr. Averitt for
I heard and believed him to be engaged to Miss Washington of N.C. He
was more in haste than *you* and the young lady faster than I and I hope
may be as well satisfied and happy and have Mr. A. never so far off as you
are from me. Do tell me something more of her. Is she beautiful, intelligent, and all that *she should be* as a wife for Mr. A., and being interested
in him I want to know all about her. Did he ever meet with her before?
I think she will have a kind good husband, but I would not like to take

mediocre military record as commander of the Trans-Mississippi Department for the Confederacy.

upon myself *were I good enough* the troubles and trials of a minister's wife, for they are numerous enough to anger a saint, and none but a truly amiable and good woman ought to marry a minister. Such is my opinion. But my time is almost at an end for writing, and I must finish my letter, such as it is, for indeed as much mortified as I have been in sending you some others, I am more so at this, but it is only to show you that you are not forgotten and still loved for I believe the *farther you go from me the better I love you*, and I hope your next retreat will be a voluntary one to Alabama. When I think there are still left *two months* it seems impossible to be so long content without seeing you, and I imagine I could be satisfied with meeting you for half-an-hour and rejoice at the ending of each week and think well I am that much nearer seeing you again. When I read my own letters to you, it amuses me to think of your telling me to *write to you just as I feel* and with candor. Do you know I can write of nothing else and in no other style and if I did not feel and place sufficient confidence in you to do so, I would not write to you a line? I am very certain you do not love me for my *beauty* for let me assure you that all you see is imaginary, and if you say anything more about it I shall think you have seen some one's you *liked better* and thought *more beautiful* and desired I should resemble. But you *have no idea how I have improved since you left.* It was not necessary for you to ask me to pray for you as I have not allowed a day to pass without doing so, nor will not, altho' my prayers may not be heard, and I regret each day more and more that I am not a good Christian. As such my prayer might be of some avail, but I fear from the life I have lead does not entitle me to hope for much, and it is so hard to be good, and I pity all if it requires as difficult an effort and they meet with no better success than I do. But now goodbye. Write and soon and often to your ever and affectionate,

Elodie

Confederate States of America, Selma, July 3, 1861

I returned from Summerfield yesterday evening and found awaiting me your last two letters for which receive my thanks. They afforded me much pleasure and it was gratifying to know again where you were, and I hope your location will be for some time the same, as moving so continually forces you to suffer so many more privations and exposure, and I am beginning to fear as much from your continued indisposition as the battles and other weapons of your Yankee neighbors. I hope you will soon be

able to command in person your company and take such good care of
yourself in future that you will be a stranger to your physician. When I
thought of you as being sick, perhaps ill and suffering for proper attention, I was miserable and would have given anything to have been near to
have administered to your comfort and showed you by my unceasing attention my sympathy and love and willingness to add as much as possible
to your comfort and happiness. Altho you I know believe what I so often
have asserted and it will require nothing else to convince you of its truth,
but it would have been a pleasure at such a moment to have proved it to
you. Do practice some of the good advice you gave me and see if it will
not enable you to keep off the sick list and then I shall have more confidence in following it myself. I greatly prefer the example. Next time you
get sick succeed well enough to be *sent home*, and I will promise to nurse
you so well that you will think it *quite nice* to be an invalid.

My mother speaks of returning to Kentucky perhaps tomorrow. I wish
I was going with her as I am getting impatient to go back but think at this
time it is better to remain a little longer and see if Ky will not secede or
affairs become more quiet. I am beginning already to regret Mother's
departure (anticipated) and fear I shall behave foolishly and mourn her
leaving by shedding some tears, but it will not be the first time, nor will
I ever be ashamed to cry just as *much* as *I want* after such a *good Mother* as
I have, and who I fear I do not love and appreciate as much as I should.
You must know this good mother of mine, and I am so provoked to think
her visit here should be when you were absent, and that I cannot do
justice to her in trying to tell you of her goodness and loveliness nor
describe her in amiability and piety for she is so gentle and good. Mr.
Hobbs[113] called a few moments since to request me to assist in singing
tomorrow. Mr. Alex White is to make a speech and they wish some music,
the Exercise in commemoration of the 4th. I most respectfully declined
to assist. There is also to be a ball or rather hop tomorrow night, but I
have no idea of attending and think it decidedly out of taste and place at
such a time to be indulging in such amusement and cannot myself when
those so dear to me are far away and surrounded by danger. I will think of
them and pray that God may spare them in his mercy and grant a speedy
and safe return of them once again to us. How dreadfully I would feel to

---

113. Probably S. J. Hobbs, age thirty-five, who had been born in Maine but was living
in Selma before the war. Nathaniel does not think too highly of him. 1860 Census: Selma.

attend such a scene and afterwards learn that upon that night anything
had happened to you or my brothers. I believe I would never forgive
myself for it, and I think there are so many who feel as I do that the affair
will be a glorious failure.

I have just read a letter from my youngest brother (Ellick) who lives
in Ky. He is very anxious to have Ky. secede and writes me that he is perfectly assured if the state was well-armed and provided with ammunition,
it would at once go with the South and is lengthy in his endeavors to
reconcile me to Kentucky's neutrality and winds up hoping to see me and
says how much he misses me all the time. I intend writing to him that he
must make up his mind to give me up to you without a word, but I believe
he will take the idea of my marrying very much to heart and grieve that I
would prefer any one to him. . . .

I did not intend you to think I did not value the daguerreotypes. I only
meant the small one I had was superior and on that account I thought
more of it but have really very little need of one at all as I have your features daguerreotyped on my heart indelibly. The photograph at Wylde's
has not been finished yet, and I fear I won't receive it much before your
return. Bro. Clem is far from well—only weighs 107. But goodbye. Hasten back and believe me ever and affectionately,

Elodie

Thursday, 4th

I see from the morning paper that you have left Winchester for the purpose of meeting Genl. Cadwallender and for that reason have directed
my letter to the care of Mr. Williams. We have been disappointed in celebrating our 4th by a terrible rain and perhaps as I write you may be celebrating yours by a Battle with the Enemy. If so God grant the victory may
be *ours* and that you will escape death or harm, and that the 4th of July
may still be memorable as the day of Independence for the Confederate
States. I do not fear or think for a moment of anything for the South but
Victory but dread what *that Victory may cost* me, and I cannot reconcile
myself entirely to giving you up for even so glorious a cause & which after
my love for you is next [in] my heart and I would willingly sacrifice much
to gain it, for what would we be without our liberty? The few left of us,
a poor unhappy set who would prefer Death a thousand times to recog-
nizing once a Blk Republican ruler, I would [illegible] altho' he is my

brother-in-law, but as such there is not one of us that cherish an unkind thought or feeling toward him and for this reason we feel so acutely every remark derogatory to him, except as a President. I never go in Public that my feelings are not wounded [n]or are we exempt in Matt's own house for people constantly wish he may be hung and all such evils may attend his footsteps. We would be devoid of all feeling and sympathy did we not feel for them and, had we no love for *Mary*, would love and respect her as the daughter of a Father much loved and whose memory is fondly cherished by those who were little children when he died. I wish I were not so sensitive, but it is [a] *decided weakness* of the entire family and to struggle against it seems for naught.

My thoughts seem to be flowing much too fast for my pen and I omit so many words that it will be almost impossible to understand what I have written. You must try and remember too, I am not so composed as usual and will be so uneasy and anxious until I hear from you again either by letter or from newspaper accounts. If the latter contains anything unpleasant I will not credit it until I have proof in another way. *But you must not be killed.* Think of those who will be watching for your return and whose hearts will be so saddened. But I must not write to you in such a strain, and as I cannot refrain from giving expression to my feelings must stop. May God bless you and restore you again to your affectionate,

Elodie

Who is the flag bearer of your company?

Confederate States of America, Selma, July 7, 1861

I have just read your letter of the 30th, and it is needless to express or endeavor to do so the pleasure it gave me as you must well know that a letter to one who is anxious always—and such a kind, affectionate, and long one as yours—is quite a relief. Friday and Saturday telegrams were received giving us information of the battle at Martinsburg, but none of the particulars made known and consequently my anxiety has been and is still great, and for two days I have been unfitted for anything and cannot be the same until I am relieved either by a letter or telegram telling me of your safety, for we are all in Selma of the belief that the Cadets and Guards were in the affray, and well I know fought well and bravely. You, I know, did *your part*, as it should have been done by a *brave, Southern soldier* and will upon every occasion that presents itself. I have never doubted but earnestly hoped you would not have an opportunity to display your courage and have hoped against hope for peace.

I cannot tell you nor can you imagine what I have suffered since hearing the war has actually begun, and I feel now like giving up and away to my sorrow. I who up to this time have been *complimenting myself* upon *bearing up so bravely* and thought I realized all the uneasiness and unhappiness I possibly could, yet all past is not equal to my suffering now, and I have just discovered how deep my love for you is and how essential you have become to my happiness, and what a blank life will be without you. I did not dream I was so *much in love*, or that my feelings would so completely overpower me, but I believe every day and mile that has separated us has but increased and strengthened my love for you, and I can easily solve what you call the enigma of loving a *poor Captain like yourself* and can tell you furthermore that I would prefer being *loved* and *admired* by *that Captain* than by *all the men in the world* and am not extravagant in my expressing myself so, and you need not remind me of what I have been guilty of for I am well aware of having placed in your possession and entrusted to your keeping *my heart*, overflowing with the first warm and youthful emotions of love, awakened into life by yourself, and so far from regretting it or fearing the entire confidence I have given may have been misplaced would act again in the same manner without a moment's hesitation, nor will I believe that I shall ever come to regret such an act and hope that *neither of us* may repent the step. As I told you before, I would make no promises but would always endeavor to do what was *right* and all that was in my power to add to your comfort and happiness, and it makes me happy to think I can do so for you tell me I am capable of increasing your happiness and softening your cares and sorrows thro' life, and it will be always my pleasure to alleviate them.

One trouble causes me to think of another, and I turn from *you* to my Mother who leaves us tomorrow. For many reasons it is necessary for her to return to Kentucky, but at such a moment when all is excitement, tumult, and alarm will make us all anxious for her safety. My Bro.[114] wrote me, does not think it possible for Ky. to remain neutral much longer and that the fighting there will be terrible and soon. My troubles seem to be coming much heavier than I can bear, and I can see no bow spanning

---

114. Probably Alexander Humphreys Todd (1839–1862), Elodie's youngest brother, who had remained in Kentucky. A favorite of most of the Todd girls, including Elodie and Mary Lincoln, by 1862 Aleck (also referred to as "Ellick") had joined up to serve his brother-in-law, Benjamin Hardin Helm, as aide-de-camp. See Berry, *House of Abraham*, 96.

the dark clouds nor catch a faint glimpse of the sun hidden by them. All appears sadness and gloom, and I feel disposed to murmur and repine, altho' I know it is wrong and that all the troubles are sent by an all-wise hand and much too light for our numerous sins and transgressions. 'Tis human nature to err and sin, and it is right to be punished. Yet notwithstanding, we cannot bear it or will not as we should.

I have written you three pages *somewhat as I felt* and should be ashamed to give way to my feelings to you while others fill their letters with words of encouragement to those who are exposed to danger and called upon to suffer so many privations, but you are *one* of the *few* who does not need it as you bear all without a word and will never have to be encouraged to fight for a cause you have sacrificed so much to engage in. Now don't I excuse myself nicely? . . .

How I wish I could divide with you some of the nice fruit which is beginning to be plentiful in the shape of watermelons and peaches. I always think of and wish for you. Mr. Hagood sent me a splendid melon on the 4th and came up to help me eat it. That I could have accomplished without him, if he had thought so. I see from the date of your letter you employed a portion of your Sabbath writing to me. I scarcely ever omit writing to you Sunday evening. I generally go to church in the morning with Mother who has made me go to the *Presbyterian* with her, and I am now almost a stranger at the Episcopal but would not be surprised if I found my way back there after she leaves. Much to my surprise I heard her say she intended writing to you, that really she had become quite pleased with you, altho' *determined not to like you.* So you see you have *spoken for yourself,* thro' occasional portions of your letters to me and writing so often, and I expect playing the *devoted.* She ought to know it *won't last long.* Do you not think so? But what a long letter I am writing you. I do take into consideration that your time is limited and you cannot always devote so much to me. You see I direct my last two letters to Mr. Williams. I thought you might be absent from Winchester some time, and he would know what to do with them. Your letter giving a description of that place was very interesting, but I imagined after drinking from the same well that Gen'l Washington did you signed your name larger than usual. But I must sign my own now hoping I may soon receive a long letter from you giving me a description of the battle or battles you have taken part in and that God will watch over and protect you and soon restore you safely to your own ever,

Affectionate,

Elodie

In Camp, Winchester, Virginia, July 8, 1861

I avail myself of the earliest moment after my return to tell you of my safety. I wrote you last on 2d July and sent you by the same mail my likeness.

I had just mailed the letter when news came of the advance of a large army under Gen. Patterson[115] across the Potomac into Virginia, and of an engagement between it and about 4,000 of our men under Gen. Jackson.[116] An order was immediately issued to march and in an hour our brigade was on its way to the seat of conflict. We started at 4 o'clock and marched to Bunker's Hill by 8, a distance of 12 miles. We bivouacked in an open field, having our blankets and the *velvet earth* for our beds. At one o'clock we were roused by the bugle and were again put upon the march. How can I describe the beauty of the scene? On our right the moon shed its soft rays upon the column of armed men, while upon our left a magnificent comet, with its long nebulous trail, beckoned us onward and threw around us the mantle of superstition. The soldiers all saw in the unannounced phenomenon the "in signo vinces"[117] of the Southern cross and enlivened their march by singing Dixie. At sunrise, we halted for breakfast and, after a scant and hurried meal, marched on to the battlefield near Darksville and were drawn up in the line of battle, awaiting the approach of the enemy. This was repeated Wednesday, Thursday, Friday, and Saturday. And on yesterday, our army returned to their quarters here. During all of this time, we have been without tents and with very scant rations. At night I slept on one of the capes sent us by our good ladies with my shawl wrapped around me, with clothes and boots on. Indeed for one week, I did not pull off my clothes as we expected an attack at any time and had to sleep upon our arms. I laid my head upon a rock, and thinking of you, my dearest, I generally fell asleep and rested quietly.

We expected a fight, but Gen. Patterson, with twenty thousand men, for days declined to join battle with barely *ten* thousand. Gen. Johnston

---

115. Union major general Robert Patterson (1792–1881) would become somewhat infamous for failing to tie up Confederate forces in the Shenandoah Valley under Joseph E. Johnston, thus allowing them to reinforce General Beauregard and helping to deliver a Confederate victory at the Battle of First Manassas. Patterson would be mustered out of the Union army shortly after.

116. Thomas J. Jackson and his brigade of Virginians would be among the reinforcements that would help turn the tide of the Battle of First Manassas.

117. *In hoc signo vinces* is a Latin rendering of a Greek phrase meaning "in this sign you will conquer."

then properly, I think, returned here, where we will await his approach. The suspense of being in a fight is great, but I have learned to look upon it with indifference. We become accustomed to dangers. Yesterday I was very much fatigued by the march of sixteen miles thro' as hot a sun as ever shone upon us and am suffering this morning from a bruised heel, which is very painful. I am however going into town to see one of my sick men, who has sent for me. I rode a part of the way on a *mule*, and you should have seen what a figure I cut.

My dear Elodie, at every moment of danger and of trial your sweet face has beamed upon me, and I have been sustained by the knowledge that you approve of what I am doing and looking forward to the time when we shall be united never, I hope, to be separated from each other.

I love, nay, worship you and cannot express the sadness of my heart. I have not heard from you since your letter of the 17th June and cannot divine the reason of your long silence. But as you know I refer it to any other reason than one of indifference and hope soon to have the pleasure of receiving a letter.

I have only time to write you this short letter as many rumors have gone abroad of our having had a battle, and I wish to dissipate your anxiety for the present.

Dearest, I am yours under all circumstances, without change, unalterably yours.

May God in his mercy guard and keep you is my constant prayer.

Ever affty and sincerely yours,
    N. H. R. Dawson

Winchester, Virginia, July 11, 1861

Yesterday I was gratified by receiving your long letter of the 3d and 4th inst., and I can find no words to thank you for the consolatory love and tender affection which it breathes. It was handed to me at a moment of excitement as the order had just been given to strike tents and prepare for battle. Under these circumstances you can readily imagine how grateful I was to commune with you. We expected an attack yesterday but were disappointed. We expect it today, but I am skeptical upon the subject as we have so frequently been disappointed. Our tents are all struck, the knapsacks packed, and the men engaged in cooking rations for twenty-four hours. I have breakfasted and am writing you with a pencil as my trunk has again been sent to my kind friend Mr. Williams at Winchester. We will make a stand here, but I doubt very much if we have a battle for some time to come. Our flag has been placed with Mr. Williams for safe-keeping as we could not carry it and take proper care of it in our marches. I did not wish to see it ruined. A company is not allowed to take a flag into battle. Mr. Boykin Goldsby[118] is the bearer.

How grateful I am to know that you have such proper feelings in regard to amusements at times when your friends are in danger. On the day of the 4th we were all day in line of battle and on that night slept on our arms. It would mortify me to think that at such a time, you could enjoy the festivities of a ball room or even sing with a contemptible person as Mr. Hobbs. He has no standing with those who know him.

I thank you for your affectionate expressions. They were not necessary to remind me of your love, my dear Elodie, for that is as *true* in my belief and confidence as any fact registered by the recording angel in the book of Time. To doubt you would make me insane, as I regard you as my own betrothed, whom God has given me, the ceremonials of the law alone being wanting to make us in the eyes of the world what we are in our own opinion. I look upon you as my wife, bound to me by all the ties of love, and I wish the requisites of the law had been complied with. No human power, except your own statement, could convince me that you did not love me. Hence I regret the remarks of my friend Mr. Pegues, but I hope you will not permit them to trouble you. I have no desire to see you secluded or to deny you the attentions of any gentleman, as I know you will be the *last* to *encourage* any thing like *courtship*. Above all things in the word, I desire to live and to return to you safely and trust that a kind providence will vouchsafe it.

I am really glad that you have such feelings about Mr. Lincoln. I have never been able to entertain for him any unkindness, save as an enemy to my country. I have never believed the slanders upon him as a man and accord to him the respect that is due a gentleman. It would indeed be strange if you felt otherwise and did not love your sister.

You speak of my desire to *gratify* all of your wishes. It is the greatest pleasure I have to think that I can do so, but you must remember how little I have done, and how you almost denied me the pleasure of doing even that little, and how *chary* you have been in permitting it. When I am anxious to give you myself, you can imagine how small other things are in comparison.

I will send you letters by the first opportunity, as they may be lost. In-

118. Twenty-seven-year-old Boykin T. Goldsby, of Woodlawn, Alabama, was a sergeant in Nathaniel's regiment. Alabama Civil War Soldiers Database, Alabama Department of Archives and History.

deed, I will send them enclosed to Mr. White by mail as soon as I get my trunk, but *you are to keep them for me.* I merely make you their custodian.

I wrote you that I had written to Mrs. Mabry[119] thanking her for the papers sent me. I like Miss Gertrude[120] but agree with her mother that she is "now too much of a child" for the wife of a grave, dignified man like myself. I can love a noble-minded, heroic, intellectual lady like my dear Elodie, and upon such a one alone could I lavish my love. You are indeed my beau ideal of womanhood, one in whom I can trust with confidence, whose presence will be a guarantee of happiness. How proudly will I feel when you appear as my wife? And how happy will be the home where you preside? You have all that I wish in the wife who is to adorn and [illegible] my home.

I see no reason why you should not shed tears at the departure of your mother. It is natural and right, and I would love you more, it seems to me, to see you in tears when tears should be shed. I have wept at times myself and felt that it was *manly*. I rejoice, however, that you are to remain in Ala. as you will be nearer to me, and I think safer than in Kentucky. That deluded state, I fear, has been sowing dragon's teeth[121] and will soon be the seat of a ruthless war. How long the war is to last is doubtful. If Mr. Lincoln can raise the means, he will prosecute it vigorously. We will have much trouble, though I have never doubted our final success. If he is unable to get the means he has called for, the war must end shortly. I have been so frequently disappointed in my opinions that I am afraid to venture to express one about the probability of the U. States being able to raise the sum called for in his message. I will promise you one thing, however, that when I return home it will be to remain there with you, and that my energies will be devoted to my country in a different field of color than that of the camp. *I owe duties to you and to my little girls that are paramount to all others.* Gens. Johnston and Bee, with their staff, have just passed, reconnoitering the grounds. They are both striking officers in their appearance.

---

119. Martha Riggs married Thomas E. Tartt and, after his passing, Virginia-born Dr. Albert Gallatin Mabry (1810–1874), a prominent Selma physician and member of the Alabama legislature. Owen, *History of Alabama,* 4:1142–1143.

120. Gertrude Tartt was the daughter of Martha Riggs Tartt and Thomas E. Tartt. After her father's death, her mother remarried Albert Gallatin Mabry. In an earlier letter, Elodie teased Nathaniel about Gertrude: "I think for *your own sake* it was a pity you did not fall in love with her as she is one of the loveliest persons in every particular, but at the same time *I am delighted you did not* for then I would not have been so fortunate or happy in being your choice."

121. In Greek legend, Cadmus and Jason sowed dragons' teeth that grew into initially uncontrollable warriors. The phrase essentially means that one's actions can result in unintended consequences.

Continue to write me here until advised to the contrary. You must not complain of my short letters. Remember how they are written in the open air or in a crowd. I must now close. Remember me kindly to Mr. and Mrs. White and to your sister Miss Kate. And now my dearest Elodie goodbye. I commend you to the care and keeping of God and trust that He will spare us to meet again and to have all of our proper expectations gratified.

    Affectionately and sincerely yours,

    N. H. R. Dawson

Selma, July 14, 1861

I have just received and read with pleasure your letter from Winchester dated the 8th telling me of your return and safety. I have written to you as often as usual with the exception of once or twice when you requested me to wait until I heard again from you, and my two last were written while you were absent and directed to the care of Mr. Williams. Need I tell you that I have suffered the greatest anxiety for two days and nights concerning your safety which nothing could dispel? I dreaded to receive intelligence for fear the information would be the worst and cause me greater sadness and yet miserable that I did not hear from your own pen, knowing all the time too how utterly impossible it was for us to write and that as soon as it was in your power you would kindly relieve my anxiety. Mother's departure also added to my sorrow. On Wednesday last she started, having found agreeable company to Nashville, from which point she will write us. I did not write to you but once last week. Mr. Herman decided to give a concert last Friday night, and as my pieces were all new I did not have time to write any but a short letter, and I knew you would prefer waiting until the affair was over and I could write one of my usual, lengthy letters. I wish you could have been present as the selection of music was beautiful and there were no failures. Mrs. Leroy Weaver[122] took part in this, and she sings so beautifully that you would have taken pleasure in listening to her. I sang two pieces, and the Marseillaise, which was requested. Mrs. Weaver was to have sung it. The notes, however, could not be procured and she forced me to take her place after we were on the stage as she did not feel confident she knew the words and would not *fail*

---

122. Legrand Weaver was the twenty-five-year-old wife of Leroy Weaver, with whom she had four children (Mary, Natalie, Legrand, and Eugenie). Though they seem to be getting along here, the Weavers would eventually form part of the "Anti-White" faction that opposed Matt and Elodie in "a war of words." 1860 Census: Selma.

happily. I did and succeeded I hear as well as I did before and could not
have done better with the notes, and I am so gratified that I carried my
part thro' with credit, for I resolved I would never take *part again* as I was
not treated *well* by *one or two*, and I would never for *any cause* subject myself again to unkind treatment from those who *were my inferiors in position*,
and that one thing hurt them so that they acknowledged it by publicly
wounding my feelings and I have resented it by ceasing to recognize the
man—I won't say gentleman—who was guilty of the offence. But two or
three others had difficulties and have expressed the same determination
as myself. I received your letter and daguerreotype last Tuesday. I am
so much obliged to you for it and think it is quite a good one. You have
grown somewhat *brown*, have you not, and increased in weight it seems
to me, and were you to see how often I gaze on it and compare it with
the others you would be amused and at the same time I imagine complimented to know that I devote so much of my time to looking at and
thinking of you, and every day my desire increases to see the original.

And bye the by that reminds me of a piece of news I heard which if it *be
true* I will see you before I am aware of it. The friend who sometimes re-
members you remarked that a recent letter in the *Reporter* had been sent
to her to have published, as you had no one else to send it to, and that
"you were to return very soon, remain for two or three days, and we were
to be married," and she had called for the express purpose of knowing
the truth. Sister Matt told her she had never heard it before, and if it was
so I had not informed her of it. The last time I saw her she thought I was
going to marry Mr. H. at once. It is a matter of astonishment to me how
such reports get started, and I am inclined to think from the way it affects
some that *more than one have looked at your house* and are opposed to our ar-
ranging matters to suit ourselves. But no matter, it is an affair that will not
and have not need of the assistance of many of the inhabitants of Selma.

I received a letter from Mr. Averitt yesterday which surprised somewhat, and I will give you an extract or two from it and hope you will
enlighten me for I do not exactly comprehend his meaning. He says,
"You know the intimacy between Col. D. and myself is not what it once
was. I fear I have had and still have a *Rival*. There has been as between
us no diminution of either confidence or regard, but we are not as we
once were, a second Damon and Pythias.[123] Do you know why? I ask you

---

123. In Greek myth, Pythias was accused of plotting against the king and sentenced to
death. Pythias was allowed to return home one last time, but if he failed to return, the king
said he would execute his friend, Damon. Pythias did return, in the nick of time, and the
king was so impressed by their friendship that he pardoned them both.

the question in propria persona[124] and hope when the war is over, when peace shall not only scatter plenty but all its consistent blessings on our land, I hope to have from you, Miss Elodie, a full and fair answer as to the true cause, you understand me." I must confess to perfect ignorance. He certainly cannot and has no right to believe me anything but a friend and surely does not think I have done or said anything to influence you to give up the friendship. Will you assure him of my innocence and friendship for him or shall I do so in answer to his letter? Write me what to do. He says again, "I had hoped to have heard from you thro' Capt. D., but I think he had had no recent tidings from home. To you I need not hesitate to say that albeit not in any degree a party to the same, I am in full confidence of both parties. *You* understand me." Perhaps it is the way he has expressed himself. At any rate, I am satisfied I do not clearly understand him. Does he wish me to make a confidant of him and confess all that you have told him? If so, I imagine that desire will not be gratified as I can see no necessity for doing so and consequently will not *until the war is over* in truth. Will you tell him also that Sister Matt has answered all his letters, directed them to Winchester. Unless *you intend to let me* answer his letter—if not then please deliver my messages. He explains his motive for leaving the Cadets and hopes I will not blame him.

Bro. Clem has been quite sick for three or four days and is not able yet to leave his room. He has been suffering two or more weeks with chills. Dr. Caball[125] however thinks him better today and so far has nursed his chill. I hope he will soon be well enough to leave Selma for a short time. I am anticipating a visit to a cousin in Marengo, Mrs. Craighead,[126] and I hope I will return improved as I am getting a little pale and thin, tho' not so much so as I really was in summer, but the heat and dust is unpleasant and a change will be pleasant, tho' I dislike being away as I cannot receive the telegraphic intelligence as soon as I wish and do when in Selma. Today the news is that Gen. McClellan has surrounded some of the Confederate forces, but where, in Va. or under whose command, cannot be found out, and thus it is continually a disagreeable report to cause anxiety, and

---

124. *Propria persona* means "for oneself" in Latin. In this case, Nathaniel means "I ask you personally."

125. P. H. Caball, age thirty-four, a Virginia-born physician living in Selma with his wife, Patter, two daughters, Anna and Mary, and seven slaves. Nathaniel thought highly of him and relied on him to oversee the health of his own slaves. 1860 Census: Selma.

126. Jane P. Craighead, age forty, was a recently widowed mother of six children, spanning ages three to thirteen. She lived in Marengo County, Alabama, and the Todd sisters visited her frequently. 1860 U.S. Federal Census, Township 16 Range 5 East, Marengo County, Ala.

I believe they sometimes are worded up in the telegraph office. Mr. Sam Carter wrote to his wife on the 4th that on the 3rd an engagement had taken place in which the Guards and Cadets were engaged and only two deaths occurred, both Servants, and one Capt. Goldsby[127] and I doubted it, knowing I would have heard as soon as Mrs. Carter or Mrs. Anybody else. Am I not vain? No, not vanity but entire confidence and belief in the truthfulness of your protestations of love, and of course if you did you would write to me and relieve my anxiety about such an event. My love would cause me to write to you, but I don't believe you give me credit for loving you much, or at least that your own for me is so much greater, and I believe might be influenced to think I could forget you while absent and like somebody else better. But don't you do it, for you know *I don't, won't, or can't* like another so well, and with so much around me to remind me of you I could not if I wished obliterate you from my memory and believe I think of you and love you better and miss you more than when you first went away than when I could not realize all that I have since and wish I never had and altho I would not wish you at home when you are needed for such a cause, still it is a painful saddening thought that you may never return, but one that often forces itself upon me, and I am farther than ever from reconciling myself to such an occurrence and cannot think calmly of it. I do not know what will become of me if there is to be really war, and there seems to be no prospect for anything else. We are all anxiety to know what the Confederate congress will do more so than when the federal met. I hope it will be impossible for the North to raise the means to prosecute this unnatural war, or rather that God will in some yet unforeseen manner avert it. I cannot think it will be a general thing, yet it is predicted that battles be fought in Kentucky in another month. I am still hoping almost against hope for peace. I hear Mrs. Pegues[128] has lost her second daughter and left a few days ago to join Mr. Pegues somewhere in Virginia, and I suppose by this time Mrs. Boykin Goldsby has

127. Thomas Jefferson Goldsby (1825–1916), age thirty-six, was captain of Company A (known as the Governor's Guard) and would ultimately be elected colonel of the Fourth Alabama over Nathaniel. He was married to Mary A. Goldsby and had two young children. 1860 Census: Selma.

128. Caroline A. Coleman married Christopher Claudius Pegues (see Elodie to Nathaniel, May 9, 1861, note 36) on October 13, 1847, and lived with him in Cahaba, Alabama, before the war. She became a widow in 1862 when Pegues died of wounds sustained at Gaines's Mill. Marriage certificate, Christopher C. Pegues and Caroline A. Coleman, Dallas County, Ala., *Alabama, Select Marriages, 1816–1942*; 1860 U.S. Federal Census, Cahaba, Dallas County, Ala.

arrived. She left more than a week, indeed I believe two weeks, ago. Mr. Wetmore told me a few days ago he had received a letter from you and acknowledged he had been trying to find out if there was anything between us, that he had suspected a little attachment on the part of both, indeed, knew of yours, but made me promise I would not breathe to anyone as you had told him in secrecy, and I believe he thinks you have not told me yet. What did you tell him? I don't care to commit myself and would like to know in order to be able to stand the attack he always makes whenever we meet. The ladies made $152 at the concert, and some others had a set supper in Mr. Young's[129] store the same night which was freely partaken of after the concert was over, but I don't know how much they realized. The sum is to be expended in yarn, and they are to knit it up. Some of the girls have begun, but I have not commenced yet or do not know whether I will or not. If I do it will be for my favorites. Capt Montgomery's Flying Artillery is encamped about two miles out on Beech Creek. I expect to go out to see them tomorrow. They want money, men, and horses before they leave Selma, but I do not know what success they will meet with as the people in Selma do not give cheerfully yet. I cannot think of anything more to write you of. Mr. Harrell has not returned has he? You will doubtless be glad I have nothing else to say, and I will now stop. Do write soon and as often as you can, long letters to me. I cannot help being so selfish, altho I know you have so few leisure moments. But goodbye. I hope to see you soon and that tidings of peace will speed over our land sooner than we ever think for may God watch over and protect you always, restore you home again, is the prayer of your ever affectionate and sincere,

Elodie

Monday morning, July 15

I saw from the Montgomery mail last evening Capt. R. H. Dawson's[130] company from Wilcox Co. was there. Is it not your brother's? Also the

129. Probably William Young, age twenty-eight, who had been born in Germany and was a master shoemaker living in Selma. 1860 Census: Selma.

130. Reginald Huger Dawson was Nathaniel's younger brother. Also a lawyer by training, he acted as solicitor of Alabama's eleventh circuit from 1860 to 1864, though he also became lieutenant colonel of the Thirteenth Alabama Infantry and served with particular distinction at the Battle of Seven Pines. He later became president of the Board of Inspectors of Convicts after the war. See Douglas A. Blackmon, *Slavery by Another Name: The Re-Enslavement of Black Americans from the Civil War to World War II* (New York: Icon Books, 2012).

death of my cousin Col. B. Gratz Brown[131] of Mo., formerly of Frankfort
Ky., but as he was on the *other side* I cannot say I grieve but sympathize
with his wife and the rest of his friends, and as he is dead I am glad he
fell so early in the fight. His turning Republican caused his father great
distress. I am happy to say Bro. Clem is up today and bids fair to recover
from his late indisposition. Suppose I were to tell you I had rewarded *John*
with the daguerreotype you sent me from Harper's Ferry. What would
you think? *Don't be afraid to say just what you do,* but Bro. Clem is waiting
for me so again goodbye.

  Ever yours truly,
  Dee

Write me a soon a *long letter.*

Winchester, Virginia, July 14, 1861

I have spent a part of the morning, after performing the regular duties
of inspection and as *officer* of the day, in reading the morning service and
a portion of the scriptures from your bible, my dear Elodie. Your last
letter is also near me to be read again when this letter is concluded. All
of my devotional feelings are aroused, and in the general effusion I find
that my affection for you leads me to have higher and finer aspirations
for Heaven. I realize the fact that my love for you has made me a *better*
and *wiser* man.

  Yesterday Mr. Averitt, Mr. McCraw, and myself dined at Mr. Williams
and spent a pleasant day. Mr. A. is very happy and showed me a letter
from his intended. I *hesitated* whether to receive and read it, but he insisted upon my doing so. The letter was exceedingly well written and was
as affectionate as such letters usually are but would not compare with
your sweet epistles. I say that I hesitated for I have very singular feelings
upon the subject. Your letters are *sacred writing* in my opinion, intended
for no eye but mine, and I could not entrust them to my dearest friend.
I was, therefore, surprised that another would treat me in a particular in

131. Colonel Benjamin Gratz Brown (1826–1885) had been born in Frankfort, Kentucky, but moved to Missouri and became a founding member of Missouri's Republican
Party. An unconditional Unionist, he raised a Union army regiment and served as colonel
before becoming a U.S. senator. Obviously the report of his death in a Montgomery newspaper was an error. Norma L. Peterson, *Freedom and Franchise: The Political Career of B. Gratz
Brown* (Columbia: University of Missouri Press, 1968).

which he could not hope to have his kindness reciprocated. Don't you think my feelings are proper?

I feel at a loss how to write you. The rehearsal of my love must have become tiresome as it has been the burden of at least fifty letters, and I am afraid that you either think me terribly in love or else an uninteresting correspondent—unless you are as much in love as your humble writer.

The details of camp life are tiresome, and I am becoming exceedingly lazy. My spare time is spent in studying tactics, and in reading papers. I wish to qualify myself for the office I hold and to be a good soldier at the end of my term of service. Gen. Bee[132] was at our last dress parade and after it was over said to the officers that we had the best parade he had seen since he left the United States service. We are said to be the best-drilled regiment in this brigade and equal to any regiment in the army of the Shenandoah, and I am inclined to think we deserve the compliment. I am glad to say that the Cadets are doing well. Our new uniform was finished and distributed yesterday and improves the appearance of the company very much. Excuse the vanity, but I must tell you a remark which I overheard one of my privates make the other day. I was walking down the road, and he said to a comrade if our captain had a little more *hair* on his head he would be the handsomest man in the regiment. I believe that I am tolerably popular with the company, but I have had to be firm and sometimes severe with a few of the members.

How much this horrible war has broken in upon our happiness. I might by this time have ventured to ask you to marry me, and we would have been probably on a bridal trip over the union. I am anxious to travel in Europe. Would you like to spend the first year of our marriage traveling over England, France, Italy, and Greece? If all things go on well, I may be able to obtain a foreign appointment. Of one thing I am determined, not to trouble my brains and destroy my peace of mind by engaging in politics. I rejoice that you have no aspiration for Washington or Richmond society. Indeed, when I allow my mind to wander into the future, I find that all of my hopes will be satisfied when you become *Mrs. Dawson.* You say Mr. Hagood, in many respects, has been your *best friend?* In what category do you place me? Or do you place me on another list, among your beaux? The term friend, applied by me to you, hardly expresses enough. You are more than friend, dearest than myself. I am not afraid of making you jealous any more than you could make me so, and whenever I have

---

132. Barnard Elliott Bee Jr. (see June 26, 1861, note 107).

the pleasure of meeting a *nice pretty* lady from Washington or any other place will endeavor to make myself agreeable in order that I may not lose the knowledge how to please you. But really I take very little pleasure in seeing the ladies and never go near one unless absolutely required by politeness.

I sent you five packages of letters by mail yesterday and wrote you besides. They contain all of your letters to me, except that of the 4th, which have been received by me.

Please tell me whether it was the 19th of April when you engaged yourself to me? Or what day of the month? The day has passed very quietly, and the evening has turned quite cool and clear. I have been all round our encampment with Capt. King[133] and his father, looking at our fortifications and admiring the beautiful scenery of which I have already written you. I can see Harper's Ferry and Charlestown, near thirty miles distant. What a pleasure it will be hereafter to travel over this country with you and to point out localities that have become interesting to me and to see your face brighten under the influence of the beauties I have admired so often and wished that you could be present with me to share the pleasure. I never see anything to admire but I wish you present. At Mr. Williams yesterday I found in one of his parlors the duplicates of two painting which I have, English pieces, and you cannot imagine how many associations were recalled at the unexpected sight. It was like the meeting of two old friends.

I am frequently joked about Miss Gertrude and yourself, and it seems to be a matter of doubt where I am most interested. I have so far been able to foil any discovery. We have been engaged near three months. The time recently has passed rapidly and will continue to pass quickly as every week now counts. When six months of my term have expired the remainder will seem much shorter. I hear that the twelve months volunteers will probably be discharged as soon as the campaign closes about the first of November. If this is so, I will see you much earlier than you anticipate, but you must not be too sanguine. My organ of hope is large, and I am much supported by indulging it. Col. Forney's[134] regt. has just arrived.

You know that even now, I think the war will soon end. Providence will bring it to a close. This is my belief, contrary to all the indications.

---

133. Porter King (1824–1890) was captain of Company G of the Fourth Alabama. Alabama Civil War Muster Rolls, 1861–1865, Alabama Department of Archives and History.

134. John Horace Forney (1829–1902) was born in Lincolnton, North Carolina, but moved to Alabama in 1835. A graduate of West Point, he was commissioned as colonel of the Tenth Alabama Infantry. Eicher and Eicher, *Civil War High Commands*, 239.

I have now to go upon duty and will be just in time for dress parade.
Goodbye. May God guard and support you, my own dear Elodie, and
vouchsafe a happy and speedy meeting with you.

Ever and sincerely and affty yours,

N. H. R. Dawson

Winchester, Virginia, July 16, 1861

I have just read your letter of the 7th, covering one from your good kind
mother, my dear Elodie, and cannot express how much gratified I am
that my attentions to you have won her consent to our engagement. The
deep feeling she has manifested for you, a solicitude which a mother
wrapt up in her child only can feel, has won my heart, and I know that
when I know her I will share with you some of the love you have for her. I
can love a lady like Mrs. Mathews, and I have imagined that your mother
resembles her in character. I rejoice that my letter of the 30th gave you
so much pleasure. I assure you that the affection you speak of in that
letter is what I have tried to express in all of them, and if sometimes I fail
to be affectionate it is that I fear you may think me tiresome. It gives me
so much pleasure to read the affectionate expressions in your letters, to
know that I am loved by one whom I worship with a Eastern idolatry is
indeed flattering; and as I have often told you I am humiliated when I
think and know how little deserving I am of the deep ardent love of such
a girl as my dear Elodie, and knowing this I fear that when weighed in
the balances I will be found wanting. But dearest, I hope I will be equal
to the task of keeping pure and undimmed the pearl of your affections
which you have given to me. I cannot praise one like you *too delicate* for
praise. The *sensitive plant* is not touched without *wounding its sensibility*. I
love you with my whole heart. I have no dreams of the future that are not
gilded by your image.

Please when you write to your mother thank her for her note of the
7th and tell her that when she sees you in our home, I trust her matronly
heart will have no cause to fear that her cherished child has misplaced
her confidence "in a stranger."

Yesterday it was reported that Gen. Patterson was advancing, and a
fight took place between our cavalry and his advance, but today it turns
out that it was merely a foraging party. We will be ready to give him a
warm reception when he comes, and I hope that I will bear myself as
becomes a Southern soldier and as becomes a man who has won the
heart of so brave a heroine as Miss Elodie. The anxiety you feel is terrible

I know as I have on several occasion known how awful it is to have your hopes imperiled in uncertainty. If we ever have a battle I will telegraph the result to Selma if it can be done. I have become now quite used to alarms and can sleep without regarding them. I feel more anxiety for you than for myself as I think how much trouble you are caused by your engagement to me. I value and appreciate a love that was given under *such circumstances* to one who was about to jeopardize the life he had made so essential to your happiness. You are indeed to me another life, more valuable and cherished than my own.

How grateful and soothing your affectionate letter has been, coupled with the note of your mother. "Tis like the gentle rain from Heaven, twice blessed, blessing him (her) that gives and him that takes."[135] How poor is language, except in poetic numbers, to express my feelings for you my own sweet angel. You are more beautiful to me than the beautiful mountains that encircle the sky, more loved than all the possessions of the world. I am not *extravagant.*

See how your letter has affected me? If you wish to make me do just as you wish in all things you have only to be *affectionate.* I will be unable to resist your *love.* It is all powerful and overpowering, and I hope your "poor captain" will live to exhibit it in your cheerful happiness.

I must now close and sign my name. May God protect and reward you for your kindness and goodness. Adieu.

Ever and affectionately yours,

N. H. R. Dawson

In camp, Winchester, Virginia, July 19, 1861

I feel an irresistible impulse, my dear Elodie, to commune with one whom I love so fondly this calm, quiet evening and have stolen off from the groups of recumbent soldier who cover the velvet carpeting of our umbrageous encampment and am seated in my markee, fronting the long crescent line of mountains of which I wrote you in a former letter. My position commands a full view of the perfectly clear western sky, the sun just sinking behind the blue mountain tops, gilding with its rays the skies, the mountains, and the woods at their base. The meadows and hill

---

135. Nathaniel is quoting act 4, scene 1 of Shakespeare's *The Merchant of Venice:* "It droppeth as the gentle rain from heaven upon the place beneath. It is twice blessed: It blesseth him that gives and him that takes."

around are covered with their golden crops, while the green fields of clover, like oases in the desert, lighten the picture. It is a scene of perfect beauty, a landscape no human hand can sketch with justice. Now the golden rays are fading into crimson and purple; the twilight is deepening, the shadows are lengthening, and the chirp of the cricket reminds me that another day is rapidly closing on me, and the recording angel is registering his account of the thoughts, words, and actions for that great day for which we must all prepare. All proclaims God's love to man. Forgive, oh my Father, the sins of Thy Servant, and grant that a scene of such beauty may be reserved for him to enjoy and share with that loved one whom he has wooed and won, whose happiness is wrapt up in one fate and one destiny.

I would give so much, my dearest, if you were seated by my side, looking out upon the beautiful and gorgeous sunset I have attempted to describe, but my heart leaps with joy when I know that if we should live, we may have the happiness of admiring together, in the future, the handiwork of nature.

For the first time since the 17th of June, I have today received your letter of the 27th of the same month and assure you it was welcome. Think of one who loves so ardently, who is surrounded by trials and danger, who has, within that time, been *four* different times marched out to the field of battle to await the expected attack of an enemy with not even a word from you to console him, you have an idea of what I have suffered. No doubt your own feelings have been much disturbed by the knowledge that I have been exposed to these dangers without the means of knowing the result.

I am glad to hear that you have passed your time so pleasantly and hope your visit to Summerfield ended without anything to disturb its pleasure.

In answer to your inquiries about Mr. Averitt and Miss Williams. I have been treated very kindly by the family and have every reason to like them. Miss. W. is a quiet and intelligent, accomplished, and sweet-looking girl, with soft and easy manners. A person whom you would love for her gentleness and goodness, but I fear is too delicate to stand the trials of life. Mr. W. is a leading lawyer here, is wealthy and is exceedingly charitable and kind. Mrs. W. is a lady of great ease of manner, fine looking, as no doubt in her younger days handsome. They live in great comfort and entertain a great deal of company, apparently without an effort, which you know shows that it is an every day thing. Their home is large and airy, furnished with furniture of the olden times, massive and comfortable. I have seen few families apparently as happy as this of the Williams. Mr. W. has aided me very much in getting up the uniforms for the Cadets. Mr. Averitt was here yesterday and went on to Richmond to see Miss Mary, who is on a visit to her relations in that section of the state. Inter nos,[136] I think he is doing better than his intended for he is extremely fickle and impressible and lacks many of the elements to make a successful man, which in my humble opinion, is one of the essentials to comfort in this life. Mr. A. is unstable, was in love with Miss Washington, a young lady at Lynchburg, and with Miss Williams all at once. How different has been my conduct? With many bright eyes to tempt me, I have been as true as the dial to the sun. I institute the comparison merely for your own satisfaction. If I could fall in love with another as soon as you were out of sight I should never be willing to marry. I am always in earnest.

I must, however, protest against your forbidding me to love you for your *beauty*. I insist that it is one of the *elements* of your *character, intellectually and personally*, which I do love, and that with all your persistency you will be unable to lessen the charms of *Miss Elodie* in my estimation. Why do you make me wish to disbelieve what my own eyes have approved? But, my dearest, we will not quarrel upon this point. My happiness will be complete whenever we shall be united, and I am willing to put off the discovery of your want of beauty to a future day.

Our position is now being strengthened by breastworks and fortifications, and we are receiving reinforcements. The enemy is advancing slowly, and we will no doubt have some hard fighting to do. And from the character of Mr. Lincoln's message,[137] which I read yesterday, we are to have war in earnest. Should I meet with your brothers or kinsmen, I have no doubt that I will be pleased with them. . . .

And now goodbye my dear Elodie, and may God guard and protect you.
    Ever affectionately yours,
    N. H. R. Dawson

---

136. Latin phrase meaning "between ourselves."

137. Nathaniel is probably referring to Lincoln's July Fourth message to Congress, in which he said, "It is now recommended that you give the legal means for making this contest a short and decisive one" and requested more money and men.

Elodie's signature locks are on display in this photo
taken about the time she met Nathaniel Dawson. Courtesy of
the Lincoln Financial Foundation Collection (#3431).

Nathaniel Henry Rhodes Dawson in uniform at the outset
of the Civil War. Courtesy of the Alabama Department
of Archives and History, Montgomery, Ala.

The Flag of the "Magnolia Cadets," Company C, Fourth Alabama Infantry Regiment, was designed and completed by Elodie and her sister Matt. Courtesy of the Alabama Department of Archives and History, Montgomery, Ala.

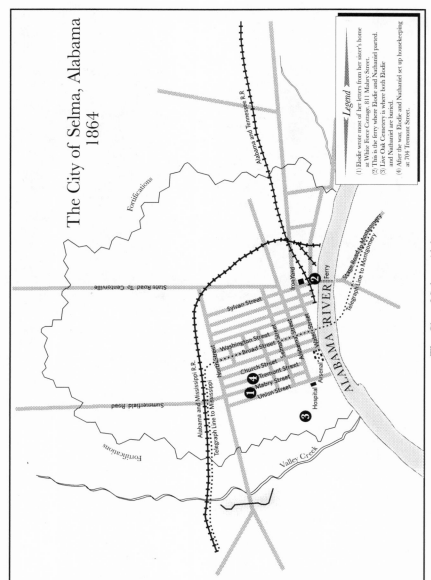

The City of Selma, Alabama
1864

Fortifications

Alabama and Tennessee R.R.

State Road To Centerville

Sylvan Street

Washington Street

Broad Street

Church Street

Tremont Street

Mabry Street

Union Street

North Street

Alabama and Mississippi R.R.

Telegraph Line to Mississippi

Summerfield Road

Fortifications

Valley Creek

Iron Yard

ALABAMA RIVER

Ferry

Stage Road to Montgomery

Telegraph Line to Montgomery

Hospital

Arsenal

Selma Street

Alabama Street

Water Street

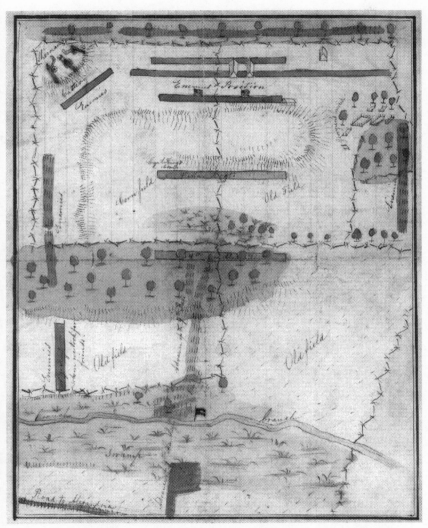

This depiction of the position of the Fourth Alabama early in the Battle of Bull Run conveys a sense of their encirclement. It also shows the fence where Nathaniel turned his ankle and was almost struck by a cannonball. The map was created by Nathaniel's fellow captain in the Fourth Alabama, Porter King. Courtesy of the Library of Congress.

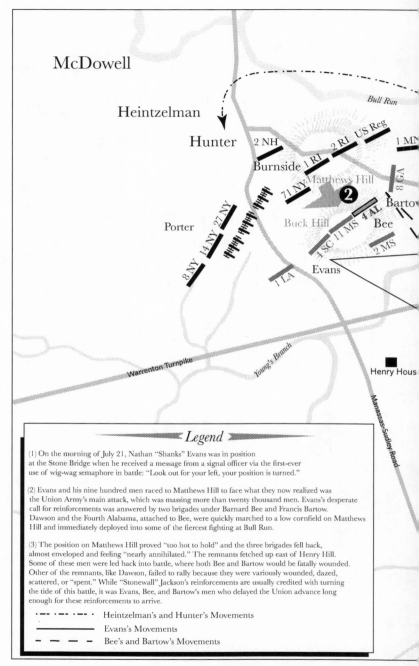

McDowell

Heintzelman

Hunter 2 NH 1 RI 2 RI US Reg 1 MN

Burnside 8 GA

Matthews Hill 71 NY

Buck Hill 4 AL Bartow

Porter 4 SC 11 MS Bee

2 MS

8 NY 14 NY 27 NY

1 LA Evans

Bull Run

Warrenton Turnpike Young's Branch Henry House

Manassas-Sudley Road

≡ *Legend* ≡

(1) On the morning of July 21, Nathan "Shanks" Evans was in position at the Stone Bridge when he received a message from a signal officer via the first-ever use of wig-wag semaphore in battle: "Look out for your left, your position is turned."

(2) Evans and his nine hundred men raced to Matthews Hill to face what they now realized was the Union Army's main attack, which was massing more than twenty thousand men. Evans's desperate call for reinforcements was answered by two brigades under Barnard Bee and Francis Bartow. Dawson and the Fourth Alabama, attached to Bee, were quickly marched to a low cornfield on Matthews Hill and immediately deployed into some of the fiercest fighting at Bull Run.

(3) The position on Matthews Hill proved "too hot to hold" and the three brigades fell back, almost enveloped and feeling "nearly annihilated." The remnants fetched up east of Henry Hill. Some of these men were led back into battle, where both Bee and Bartow would be fatally wounded. Other of the remnants, like Dawson, failed to rally because they were variously wounded, dazed, scattered, or "spent." While "Stonewall" Jackson's reinforcements are usually credited with turning the tide of this battle, it was Evans, Bee, and Bartow's men who delayed the Union advance long enough for these reinforcements to arrive.

∙—∙ ∙—∙∙ ∙—∙ ∙   Heintzelman's and Hunter's Movements

————————   Evans's Movements

— — — —   Bee's and Bartow's Movements

The Battle of Bull Run.

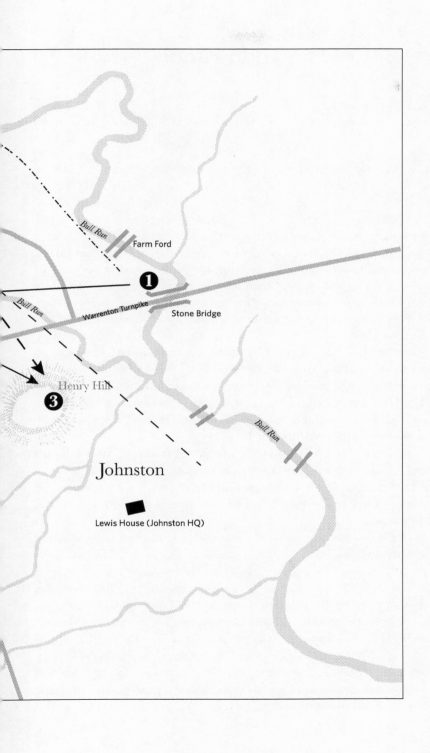

Farm Ford

1

Bull Run

Bull Run

Warrenton Turnpike

Stone Bridge

Henry Hill

3

Bull Run

Johnston

Lewis House (Johnston HQ)

The Todd Family

ROBERT SMITH TODD (1791–1849) married ELIZA PARKER in 1812. They had six children:

1. ELIZABETH PORTER TODD (1813–1888) married NINIAN WIRT EDWARDS in 1832 and moved with him to Springfield, Illinois. A "second mother" to her younger sisters, she invited Frances, Mary, and then Ann to stay with her—all of whom married Springfield men. Elizabeth attended Lincoln's inaugural, returned to Washington in 1862 to console Mary on the loss of her son, helped Mary during her confinement for insanity, and cared for her during her final days.

2. FRANCES JANE TODD (1815–1899) moved to Springfield shortly after the Edwards' arrival. She married WILLIAM SMITH WALLACE, a local doctor who owned the drug store beneath Lincoln's law office. The Lincolns' third son, Willie, was named for him, and Lincoln appointed him a paymaster in the Union army, saying, "He is needy . . . and I personally owe him much."

3. LEVI OWEN TODD (1817–1864) began in business with his father but floundered after the older man died. In 1859 his wife, LOUISA ANN SEARLES, divorced him for cruelty. Though a Union man, he did not serve in the Civil War and died in 1864 of "utter want and destitution."

4. MARY ANN TODD (1818–1882) moved permanently to Springfield shortly after the Wallaces were married. She and ABRAHAM LINCOLN met, became engaged, and became spectacularly disengaged in the winter of 1840–1841. A strange reconciliation followed, and they were hurriedly married in 1842. The Lincolns had four sons: Robert, Eddie, Willie, and Tad. Only Robert survived to adulthood.

5. ANN MARIE TODD (1824–1891) was the fourth Todd sister to make the move from Lexington to Springfield. She married CLARK MOULTON SMITH, a leading Springfield merchant, in 1846. She was a gifted seamstress but also "the most quick tempered and vituperative . . . of all the Todd sisters."

6. GEORGE ROGERS CLARK TODD (1825–1902?) was just a day old
   when his mother died of childbed fever. He graduated from Tran-
   sylvania's medical school in 1850 and became a gifted surgeon. Like
   his brother Levi, he had an irascible temper and a heavy thirst. And
   like his brother, his first wife (ANN CURRY) divorced him for cruelty.
   Serving as a surgeon in the Confederate army, he was, after the war,
   charged with the abuse of federal prisoners.

ROBERT SMITH TODD next married ELIZABETH "BETSEY" HUM-
PHREYS. They had eight children:

7. MARGARET TODD (1828–1904) married CHARLES HENRY KEL-
   LOGG, a Cincinnati merchant, in 1847. Both attended Lincoln's inaugural, but both had strong ties to the Confederacy, and Charles
   committed actual treason.
8. SAMUEL BROWN TODD (1830–1862) attended Centre College and
   then moved to New Orleans after his father's death. There he married CLELIE CECILE ROYER and clerked for her father, a French
   gardener. Sam served as a private in the Confederate army and was
   killed at the Battle of Shiloh in 1862.
9. DAVID HUMPHREYS TODD (1832–1871) ran away from home at
   fourteen to fight in the Mexican War. He participated in the California gold rush in 1850 and in a Chilean revolution in 1851. In July
   1861, he was in charge of the Richmond prisons but was relieved of
   duty amid allegations of prisoner abuse. He commanded an artillery
   company with distinction during the siege of Vicksburg.
10. MARTHA K. TODD (1833–1868) married CLEMENT WHITE in 1852
    and moved with him to Selma, Alabama. She attended Jefferson Da-
    vis's inauguration in 1861. In 1864 she was (erroneously) exposed
    as a smuggler and a spy, much to the embarrassment of the Lincoln
    administration.
11. EMILIE PARET TODD (1836–1930), called "Little Sister" by the Lin-
    colns, spent six months living with them and the Edwards in 1855.
    Ultimately, she married a Kentuckian, BENJAMIN HARDIN HELM,
    who rose to the level of brigadier general in the Confederate army
    before he was killed at Chickamauga. Despite being a Confederate
    widow, Emilie stayed at the White House for a week in December
    1863.
12. ALEXANDER HUMPHREYS TODD (1839–1862) was the youngest of
    the Todd boys and the one all the sisters united to coddle. Serving as
    Helm's aide-de-camp, he was killed in a friendly fire incident outside

Baton Rouge. While Mary Lincoln claimed not to care about her Confederate brothers, she admitted that Aleck's ghost occasionally comforted her at night.

13. ELODIE BRECK TODD (1840–1877) was on a visit from Kentucky when she met her future husband, NATHANIEL HENRY RHODES DAWSON, at Jefferson Davis's inauguration. Stranded in Selma, she was cut off from her home and her mother, and though she supported her husband and the Confederacy, she would not allow the Lincolns to be abused in her presence.

14. CATHERINE "KITTIE" BODLEY TODD (1841–1875) visited Springfield after Lincoln's election and became infatuated with his friend, ELMER ELLSWORTH, a dashing Union captain. As the war progressed, however, she became more staunchly Confederate and ultimately married WILLIAM WALLACE HERR, the man who had helped carry Hardin Helm's body from the field at Chickamauga.

The Magnolia Cadets

Company C of the Fourth Alabama Infantry

The Magnolia Cadets was enrolled for active service at Selma, Alabama, on April 26, 1861, and mustered into formal Confederate service on May 7, 1861, at Lynchburg, Virginia. The regimental commander was Colonel Ben Alston of the Fourth Alabama Regiment of Volunteers.

Dawson, N. H. R., Captain.
Shortbridge, Jr., George D., 1st Lieutenant.
McCraw, S. Newton, 2nd Lieutenant.
Wilson, John R. 3rd Lieutenant.
Waddell, Ed. R., 1st Sergeant.
Price, Alfred C., 2nd Sergeant.
Daniel, Lucian A., 3rd Sergeant.
Goldsby, Boykin, 4th Sergeant.
Bell, Bush W., 1st Corporal.
Garrett, Robert E., 2nd Corporal.
Brown, James G., 3rd Corporal.
Cohen, Lewis, 4th Corporal.
Melton, George F., Musician.
Marshall, Jacob, Musician.

PRIVATES.
1. Adkins, Agrippa
2. Adams, William S.
3. Avery, William C.
4. Byrd, William G.
5. Beattie, Thomas K.
6. Briggs, Charles H.
7. Bohannon, Robert B.
8. Baker, Eli W.
9. Bradley, Hugh C.
10. Cook, Thomas M.
11. Cook, James W.
12. Cook, Benson.
13. Caughtry, Joseph R.

14. Cole, George W.
15. Cleveland, George W.
16. Cleveland, Pulaski.
17. Cunningham, Frank M.
18. Coursey, William W.
19. Daniel, John R.
20. Densler, John E.
21. Donegay, James G.
22. Friday, Hilliard J.
23. Friday, James L.
24. Friday, John C.
25. Ford, Joseph H.
26. Grice, Henry F.
27. Haden, James G.
28. Harrill, Thornton R.
29. Hannon, Wm. H., Sr.
30. Hannon, Wm. H., Jr.
31. Hooks, William A.
32. Hodge, William L.
33. Jones, William.
34. Jordan, James M.
35. Jackson, Felix W.
36. King, William R.
37. Kennedy, Arch.
38. Kennedy, George D.
39. Lamson, Frank R.
40. Lane, William B.
41. Lowry, Uriah.
42. Lowry, William A.
43. Littleton, Thomas B.
44. Luske, John M.
45. Lamar, John H.
46. Mather, Thomas S.
47. Martin, James B.
48. May, Syd M.
49. May, William V.
50. Melton, Thomas J.
51. Miller, Stephen J.
52. Mimms, George A.
53. Moody, William R.

54. Mosely, Andrew B.
55. McNeal, George S.
56. McKerning, John W.
57. Overton, John B.
58. Overton, Thomas W.
59. O'Neal, William.
60. Paisley, Hugh S.
61. Pryor, John W.
62. Pryor, Robert O.
63. Peeples, Frank W.
64. Raiford, William C.
65. Reinhardt, George L.
66. Robbins, John L.
67. Rucker, Lindsay.
68. Rucker, Henry.
69. Shiner, David H.
70. Stokes, William C.
71. Stone, John W.
72. Stewett, Mayor D.
73. Turner, Daniel M.
74. Thomas, Lewis.
75. Tarver, Ben J.
76. Taylor, William E.
77. Terry, Thomas B.
78. Thompson, John S.
79. Thompson, William E.
80. Ursory, Edward G.
81. Vaughn, Turner P.
82. Wrenn, Theodore J.
83. Whallon, Daniel.

PART II
To the Altar

Manassas, July 21, 1861

We have had a terrible battle today, my dear Elodie, but have achieved a glorious victory. Our brigade was in the hottest of the engagement, and the 4th Ala. Reg. has been cut to pieces. I have had from twenty to thirty killed and wounded in the Cadets, but thanks to a merciful Creator and your prayers, I escaped unscathed. A cannon ball struck a fence which I was crossing and knocked me down, but the only harm done me was a dislocation of my ankle which I do not think will give me much pain. We have taken all the artillery of the enemy, their baggage and stores. Their loss is estimated at 4,000 to 5,000. But over this victory we have to mourn the loss of many of our best and bravest men. Mr. J. W. Stone, W. A. Lowry, E. G. Ursory, Bohannon, Taylor and several others are killed in the Cadets. W. H. Harrison, Jr. has lost his right arm. Rev. Turner is shot thro' one of his legs. Geo. Cleveland is slightly wounded in the heel and several others whom you do not know.[1]

---

1. John W. Stone, a private in Nathaniel's company. Alabama Civil War Muster Rolls, 1861–1865, Alabama Department of Archives and History, Montgomery, Ala.

William A. Lowry, a private in Nathaniel's company. Alabama Civil War Muster Rolls, 1861–1865, Alabama Department of Archives and History.

Edward G. Ursory, a private in Nathaniel's company. Alabama Civil War Muster Rolls, 1861–1865, Alabama Department of Archives and History.

Probably Robert B. Bohannon, a private in Nathaniel's company. Alabama Civil War Muster Rolls, 1861–1865, Alabama Department of Archives and History.

Probably William E. Taylor, a private in Nathaniel's company. Alabama Civil War Muster Rolls, 1861–1865, Alabama Department of Archives and History.

William H. Harrison Jr., age thirty-four, from Summerfield, whom Nathaniel especially liked. Nathaniel described his wounding in a later letter: "He is an excellent young man. He acted very bravely and was near me when he was shot. I had commanded the company to cease firing when he came to me and said, 'Captain, I am [illegible] and see a Yankee. Let me shoot him.' I answered and watched him as he fired and saw his hand fly up as if the gun had rebounded. He came to me and said, 'My arm is shattered.' I sent him from the field." 1860 U.S. Federal Census, Summerfield, Dallas County, Ala.

George W. Cleveland, a private in Nathaniel's company. Alabama Civil War Muster Rolls, 1861–1865, Alabama Department of Archives and History.

My dearest, I wrote you a few lines to inform you of our arrival this morning and wrote you at the earliest moment from Gen. Beauregard's headquarters of my safety and to thank God for it. My joy is great, and I attribute much to your prayers.

I have no time to write more fully. Dearest continue to pray for me. My escape is most miraculous. It is now near twelve o'clock at night.

Our Col. is killed, Lieut. Col. and major wounded.[2]

 Ever affty and sincerely,
  Your own devoted,
   N. H. R. Dawson

Selma, July 23, 1861

I wrote you a day or two since, but I cannot refrain from writing to tell, or try to do, my joy and happiness that you have escaped unhurt. Early this morning I sent to town a servant with orders not to return until he brought me news from the battle, which we received intelligence of late yesterday evening. He has just returned bringing me the telegram from yourself and Captain Goldsby relieving by it the anxiety of many hours. I was surprised and distressed when I heard of a battle being fought and you were engaged in it and could do nothing but grieve and anticipate the worst and trembled so violently that for several moments I was incapable of reading the dispatch until with a desperate effort I overcame it somewhat and opened it, my mind prepared to receive the worst. But imagine my joy if you can which possessed me when I read of your safety and the slight loss sustained by the Cadets and Guards. Would that you could now return and escape further exposure from such dangers, and this glorious victory, dearer to me because your noble heart and brave courageous arm helped to gain it, would satisfy our enemies and woo gentle peace to diffuse her gentle smiles again over our beloved country. Will they longer continue this terrible war, more so to them than us, even

---

2. Nathaniel was right that the wounds Egbert J. Jones received were mortal, but the colonel lingered for weeks before dying on September 1.

Evander M. Law suffered an arm wound at Bull Run that left the arm essentially immobilized and useless. He served with distinction throughout the war and was probably promoted to major general just before war's end. "The Sobriquet 'Stonewall,'" *Southern Historical Society Papers*, vol. 19 (Richmond, 1891), 165.

Charles L. Scott sustained a leg wound at Bull Run so severe he ultimately resigned his commission. "Sobriquet 'Stonewall,'" 165.

when they and we must believe god is one our side fighting for us against their wicked schemes and devices? Surely they have suffered enough and should be willing to cease hostilities.

As much as I thought I loved you, and you were dear to me yet, it was not until yesterday and today which has caused me to realize the devotedness and depth of the love that is in my heart for you and how crushed and torn it would have been had you been snatched from me by death's relentless hand or how darkened future anticipations which blessed by your love were adorned with the very tints of brightness and beauty, and it is with a thankful heart that I write and hear of your safety while too many others, more deserving of mercy than I, are sorrowing over their loved dead. Would I could see for a short time and hear from your lips all that has transpired I would indeed be happy. As it is, if the intelligence contained in your last letter be true, my face will brighten much sooner at your return than dared I hope for or thought of, and then you will never leave me again or go where I cannot with you. You ask me how I would like to travel in Europe. Why of course exceedingly, tho I could content myself with the idea very well that I would never see *any country* but *America*, which to enjoy all it affords is enough for anyone. Don't you think so?

I see from today's paper Mrs. Lincoln is indignant at my Bro. David's being in the Confederate service and declares "that by no word or act of hers should he escape punishment for his treason against her husband's government should he fall into their hands." I do not believe she ever said it and if she did and meant it she is no longer a sister of mine nor deserves to be called a woman of nobleness and truth and God grant my noble and brave-hearted brother will never fall into their hands and have to suffer *death twice over*, and he could do nothing which could make *me prouder of him* than he is doing now, *fighting for his country*. What would she do to me, do you suppose? I have as much to answer for.

Perhaps Mr. Averitt took my letter to him for a sample of the best I could do and wished you to see the contrast in letter writing and his lady love's superiority to your's, and you did not like to return the confidence or compliment, for I am ashamed of being so poor a scribe myself and certainly would not blame you for thinking so, but as you are satisfied I don't care what *Mr.* or Miss *Anybody thinks* of them or about them. No, I am not astonished that a gentleman of your delicacy and refinement would hesitate to read the letter of a lady, no matter if her lover had no hesitancy in urging you to do so and think the possession of such feeling should not only be appreciated but encouraged and admired as very proper. Speaking of lovers and etc. reminds me, Mr. T. Hall is to be married tomorrow night to Miss Coleman down on the river somewhere. Mr. Hagood and Hobbs, the attendants. Today I had sent me three baskets of fruit, two of which contained peaches and grapes, also two melons sent. Am I not in luck? But it has struck eleven, and I must say goodby and finish in the morning.

Wednesday morning, July 24, 1861

You ask among my list of friends your standing. Is it possible that I must tell that you are *my friend* and stand alone upon a list, receiving my love and admiration and esteem, while others I place together on another as *friends*, liking them with different degrees of affection and think of them in connection? Does my explanation of your position satisfy you?

Have you seen the speech of Vallandigham[3] of Ohio, and do you not like the courage, candor, and intellect of the man? I read some portions with interest and would have liked to have shaken him by the hand because he dared to speak his feelings openly and avowed his principles and even let them know that Mr. Lincoln had acted unconstitutionally. Many of the business houses were closed here yesterday. I understand after the news and deaths reached here also that Major Hayden and some other gentlemen had in their uneasiness gone on to Virginia. Mr. Hagood told me he came *very near going*, thinking his services would be acceptable as *nurse*, and I think perhaps if Bro. Clem had been at home he would have done so as Selma just at this time is misery to him. I wish he had and would have had to *fight* or *run* before he returned. Did I speak too hastily in regard to the flag? I was vexed at Mr. and not the young lady. I cannot govern my temper or tongue, and when I am angry say much that I am very sorry for afterwards and altho speak my feelings at the time, change them when I get a little cooler, but it is just the same next time. Mother has always predicted that my temper and tongue would get me into trouble, but I say no and if it does, I will stand up to what it utters. We heard from her yesterday. She was still in Nashville and must enjoy

---

3. Clement Laird Vallandigham (1820–1871) was a congressman from Ohio and leader of the antiwar wing of the Democratic Party. On July 10 he delivered a speech titled "Executive Usurpation" in which he lambasted Lincoln for "the wicked and hazardous experiment of calling thirty millions of people into arms . . . without the counsel and authority of Congress." For more, see Dan Monroe and Bruce Tap, *Shapers of the Great Debate on the Civil War: A Biographical Dictionary* (Westport, Conn.: Greenwood Press, 2005), 301–320.

her visit among persons she has known for so many years. I am expecting Matt back today and will be glad to see her. I miss her so much as we are always together and more company for each other than for anyone else, and she thinks so much alike in disposition, but I think us totally unlike as any two sisters I ever saw in disposition but resemble each other somewhat in appearance. You should see me sitting up knitting in the evening. It would amuse you. I only need glasses and a cap to make me an old lady, and I have [tried] on mother's and imagine I will be a very nice one but could never keep a straight enough countenance to judge well. Be sure and pick me out some *small somebody* that won't require much *work* as I am terribly opposed to doing anything I can help and am sure nothing but *great love of country* and *free speech* could have induced me to do so much. It will be three months on Friday next since you left, and on the 19th we were engaged the same number. Don't you feel ashamed to forget and don't I feel *bad* that you *did*. What a poor compliment for *a soldier*. I think you had better seek the acquaintance of some lady, else I think your conduct by end of *12 months*, if you continue to be *so ungallant*, will vex me considerably. But don't get too much interested, for I would not give you up to any one no matter how much later was their claim. You *belong to me*, and I mean to *keep you*. Please bear this in mind. But here I am without room for another word and think I had better try and finish. I shall expect a long letter soon giving me a glowing tho doubtless sad account of the battle at Manassas Junction. But goodbye. May God still bless and keep you is ever the prayer of your affectionate,

Elodie

Manassas, Virginia, July 24, 1861

We have in some measure recovered from the excitement following the battle, and I prepare to write you this morning, seated in a thicket, pencil in hand, some of the details of the late engagement—

We, the 4th Ala., with the 2d Miss. and 6th N.C. Rg., under Ben. Bee commenced the fight by attacking the advancing column of Yankees. Our reg. was supposed to attack 5,000 men and after keeping them in check for one hour, retreated, fell back upon the reserve. I was injured by a sprain in the ankle and missed the Reg. which was in advance and was not further engaged. About 200 of the reg. was collected but took no further active part in the battle. We have but about 200 killed and wounded. Among the former is Lieut. Simpson, whom you saw last win-

ter in Montgomery. He was to be married to Miss Collier. We lost about
1,000 killed and wounded. The loss of the Yankees is incalculable as they
were [illegible] for fifteen miles, all of their artillery—50 pieces—10,000
stand of arms, all of their hospital wagons, a large number of their baggage wagons, and a large number of prisoners have been taken. Their
dead line the road all the way.

I walked over the battlefield the next day after the fight. The scene
presented was horrible. I counted in one small spot—where Sherman's
battery was taken—thirty-seven horses that were dead and near one hundred dead yankees, besides the wounded who had been removed. Near
this place is a house, an old lady 90 years of age was killed by a cannon
ball. Her daughter told me this herself at the house.[4] The dead presented an awful appearance, and I thought perchance that the fortunes
of man might place me in a similar position. I have learned it seems,
however, to think philosophically of these things and am inclined to the
opinion that I am hard-hearted.

I have thought of you all the time, my own dear Elodie, have prayed
that I might be spared to see you again, and so far my prayer has been
granted, and I am deeply grateful to God. I am afraid you have been
troubled by rumors of my injury, as Mr. [illegible] and Mr. Smith, members of congress from Alabama who came up from Richmond yesterday
told me that I was reported killed. I telegraphed the *Selma Reporter* the
day after the battle and yesterday again and wrote you the night of the
battle of my safety and hope your apprehensions were not excited, but
I almost regret that I was not wounded that I might have had an excuse
for giving harm. But I am deeply thankful that so far I have escaped. Col.
Jones, Col. Law, and Major Scott are all wounded. Gen. Bee was killed. I
send you a flower plucked by me this morning from the spot. He was at
the head of our regiment at the time, or the remnant. We lost 185 killed
and wounded out of about 700 who went to battle.

You must write me at Manassas Junction, and I will get your letters. I
will write you as often as possible. I have sent to Winchester for my trunk
and will then have facilities. Excuse this miserable scrawl, but we are in
the woods without tents or baggage.

---

4. Born in 1776, the widow Judith Henry was bedridden and refused to leave the upstairs
bedroom of her home on what became the Bull Run battlefield. A Union shell, meant for
the Confederate snipers in her house, wounded her neck and side and blew off a portion
of her foot. She died later that afternoon. Her daughter was Ellen Henry. James Robertson,
The Untold Civil War: Exploring the Human Side of War, ed. Neil Kagan (Washington, D.C.:
National Geographic, 2011), 36–37.

Remember me to Mr. and Mrs. White. You are the idol of my heart, and I am so grateful for your love.

    Adieu, dearest Elodie,

        Ever and affectionately yours,

           N. H. R. Dawson

Near Manassas, July 25, 1861

I have written you three times since the late battle, my own dear Elodie, but it seems that for the first time today I am in a sufficiently quiet state of mind to commune with you. I feel like one who had accomplished a great work and was resting from his labors, and my first impulses after this are to lie down by your side and rest in the knowledge that your heart pulsates to every throb of mine. I come to pay tribute to you whom I love beyond all human beings and to whisper into your ear things that I dare not breathe to others, to tell you of the strength of that love which I bear you, and to seek comfort and peace in your sympathy. It is at such hours as this, when we rest from our labors, that man needs the comforting solace of woman, and I would give all that I have to be with you and to feel the influence of your kindness. How much I want you to be near me and to receive from your own lips the assurances of your love, I leave you to imagine.

During the night when the bullets fell like hail, I thought of you as far away, at church, on your knees, praying for my safety, and I was nerved and strengthened to do my duty. It seems a miracle that I was not killed as several of my men were shot down at my side. I attribute all to the providence of God, and I trust that I will endeavor to appreciate his mercy.

I went over the field yesterday. The scene was awful. The dead Yankees were still lying unburied in many places. I saw as many as one hundred in the space of an acre. They belong to Ellsworth's Zouaves who were reduced from 1,100 to 200 men. God seems specially to have marked them for vengeance. They wore blue pants and red shirts and are fierce looking fellows. They fought well.

To give you an idea of the extent of the forces, I will merely mention that our line of battle extended ten miles, but we were only attacked on a line of about three miles. The roar of artillery was incessant from 8 o'clock until 3 in the evening. The air resounded with the whistling balls and hissing shells. Trees as large as my body were cut down in the forests by the rifle cannon balls. I have gathered up some of the bullets on the field and will keep them for you.

Our regiment is in a state of disorganization. Capt. Goldsby being the senior captain is acting as Col. He has been absent since the battle, and I now have the command. I do not desire to retain it however as I am anxious that a competent U. States officer should be placed in charge. We have suffered greatly for want of competent field officers, and I will not permit any selfishness to interfere with the welfare of the regiment.

We are encamped on the battlefield, surrounded by all the evidences of the sanguinary contest—broken gun carriages, dead men, dead horses, and the graves of the dead. Every house in the neighborhood is a hospital for the wounded of the army. Our own have been sent to Culpepper and Charlottesville. The dead Yankees will all be buried today. Judge Walker arrived this morning to take the remains of Lieut. Simpson, his brother-in-law, home.[5] He will mail this letter in Richmond as there is some difficulty about sending letters off here. I telegraphed the *Reporter* to let you know that I was safe as I knew you would be very uneasy until you heard.

We have now been sleeping in the open air without tents since we left Winchester, and it seems we are to do without them for the balance of the season. We are indeed fast becoming used to all sorts of hardships. I am bearing them well and hope to pass thro them safely. It is now three months since I bid you goodbye, but it seems a long year. I cannot tell you how anxious I am to see you again. It will be one of the happiest days of my life when I meet you again safely. You are indeed, my dear Elodie, the star that I worship, and all the breadth of my love seems insufficient to repay you for yours. When I think how much this has cost me in the sacrifice of being absent from you, I almost wish it had not been commenced, but we are battling for our rights, and the feelings of an individual should not be allowed to interfere with our duties. But still I hope, and hope most earnestly, that I will be allowed to be reunited again to you. Our movements are uncertain. We will remain now on this line of operations and may go on to Alexandria, but we will hardly attempt to take the place by storm. The campaign will end in November on this line of operations, when the war may be transferred to the south.

You will write to me at Manassas Junction and your letters will be forwarded in case of our removal. I have not heard from you since the 11th of July. I hope to receive letters forwarded from Winchester today or to-

5. Probably John Simpson, a lieutenant in Company H of the Fourth Alabama. Alabama Civil War Muster Rolls, 1861–1865, Alabama Department of Archives and History.

morrow as I have sent a gentleman over there to see about our baggage. You can't imagine how much pleasure a letter from you will give me now. It will be so soothing to read your affectionate letters. I will continue to write you as often as I have an opportunity, but you must not expect to hear as regularly as you have heretofore done. I will always embrace any opportunity of advising you of my movements.

I have now to attend a meeting of our officers and must bid you adieu. Farewell, my dear Elodie. Pray for me and may God bless and preserve you always.

Ever and affectionately yours,
N. H. R. Dawson

I have attempted no rhetorical account of the battle and its incidents. You will see this from better hands. Besides I have no time and no power to do so. You will see in the *Charleston Mercury* a full account from Mr. Sprate, who is a friend of mine. Our regiment did great credit to itself.

Selma, July 28, 1861

I received quite unexpectedly two letters from you on Friday last, dated the 17th and 19th. I say unexpectedly because I did not think you would have time to write me before going to Manassas Junction. Nevertheless they were, as your letters always are, very welcome. I had hoped to have one today but upon reflection knew I was hoping against an impossibility and must content myself yet for a day or two before I can be gratified. I have no idea where you are at this time or where you went after the battle but am writing because it affords me pleasure and I take for granted Mr. Williams to whom I will enclose it will know where to forward it or what to do with it for me. Now that war has actually begun I am dreading every day to hear of another battle, fearing that you may not escape as well as before or your life be spared at all. We had a great many false rumors afloat here which caused much pain, among them the death of Boykin Goldsby which nearly distressed his mother to death and many others too numerous to mention. Mr. Robbins was expected on this morning's boat and from him we may get a true statement of affairs. Do you believe it that I would have given almost anything to have witnessed it, tho I do not think I would have been able to have looked long at such an awful sight, but when the victory was gained, then I would have forgotten all save the glory and exaltation of the moment? Oh how can *man* stay at home at such a time? I could never travel fast enough to get to the scene of battle, and yet there are plenty among us who call themselves so and stir not tho in *words such patriots*. I am so proud of you and think you are such a *great man* that I fear I shall never be able to realize the fact that *anybody else fought* for their country. Mother writes me that she never witnessed such excitement and joy in her life as at Nashville when the news was received. Cannons were fired, companies paraded and indeed every sign of joy that could be manifested. Here there was no rejoicing exhibited for sadness for the young and gallant dead filled our hearts, and we could not forget them to exalt in a victory that closed their lives in nobleness and honor and before they could see their loved country freed from Northern tyranny. God bless and be merciful to them and all who fall in our glorious cause of liberty and rest their souls in peace. You write me to be more cheerful and look on the brighter side. I look straight forward as far as I can and all around and above and yet all looks gloomy and dark. I have never for a moment doubted that anything but success would attend us, but I have thought of the many who would and must die to purchase it. Tis true there is not a man among you would not willingly prefer death to slavery, and you would yourself sacrifice your life gladly to gain it. Yet we who are left will find in freedom *poor* and *sad enjoyment* when those that are dear to us must die for it, and no matter how hard we try cannot reconcile ourselves to giving you up cheerfully for the cause. I do not now think of peace for a moment; fighting alone can accomplish our end and that hard and bloody. We are prepared for reverses, for we yet remember some lost battles in a similar struggle and notwithstanding them, success crowned our efforts. And when we lose now we will push forward again with redoubled courage and determination and must and will conquer. Everybody wanted to go on immediately to nurse and do what they could. Others (a few) were anxious to fill the places in the ranks of those who had fallen and for aught I know have gone.

We have no good news from Kentucky, yet my faith is not shaken. I still hope and am proud to say that many are leaving the state to join companies of others and endeavoring to do what they can. Perhaps those remaining will surprise us by doing the same. I know you will smile and *say yes it will surprise us,* but I don't care what Ky. does, I will acknowledge to the last I am a *good, old fashioned Kentuckian,* and be proud to say it.

I am thinking of paying a visit to my cousin Mrs. Craighead near Woodville this week, provided I hear from you—if not will wait until I do before I go. I have been trying to make up my mind to go for two weeks and am afraid some news will arrive that I cannot hear, therefore will not be gone long. We all laughed at me because I said I was going to see Mr. Robbins. Mr. Hagood wanted to know for what. I replied to hear from my sweetheart, but I would be ashamed to ask myself after I got there and would to send her (Matt) to see Mrs. Robbins. We are reading the life of Gen'l Quitman[6] which seems to be prophetic of the present times, especially some portions which are very striking. I cannot write you a *very long* letter this evening as I am anxious to write to my two brothers and an old schoolmate living in Louisiana and whom I have neglected for three months. I wrote you on Tuesday immediately upon the reception of your telegram and was so happy that you were safe that I do not remember what I wrote you or how I expressed myself, if I said I was glad, that was my object. Bro. Clem is still absent nor do we know when he will return. . . .

This morning I spent a part of in reading over some of your letters and tying them into bundles to empty the box they *filled*, to put more in. I find the last one written in just the same strain and believe you *like me yet*. But I have forgotten that my two brothers are doubtless anxious to receive letters and words of encouragement, and I must try and write more cheerfully to them. Goodbye. Write soon and believe me with a constant prayer for your safety.

    Yours affectionately,
    Elodie

Manassas, July 28, 1861

I have written you several times during the past week but cannot permit an opportunity presented by the departure of D. Jones to pass unused. I feel much depressed since our battle last Sunday and would give anything for peace and home. The cessation of hostilities unites me to you, and this may be the reason why I am so strong in favor of the measure. I have never before been placed in a situation where I had no volition. I am a soldier until next May and till then am the servant of the state. I must endeavor to do as you have enjoined me to behave, like a true Southern soldier. I was yesterday engaged in writing to the friends of our killed and wounded and found it a sad task. The absence of over twenty from our

---

6. Likely J. F. H. Claiborne's *Life and Correspondence of John A. Quitman* (New York: Harper & Brothers, 1860), which was released in two volumes in 1860.

ranks has made quite a gap in the company and cast a deep gloom over us all. I long to be yours, entirely yours. I will feel as if my labors were ended and that I had a right to enjoy the comforts of home under the soothing care and affection of my noble ladylove, one whom I adore and worship more than my country. When I think over the occurrences of the last week, the great dangers I have escaped, I feel how thankful we should be, and I hope I duly appreciate the mercy of God in having protected me. Oh dearest, we should place our trust on High, and I hope, one of these days, that we may be found kneeling at the same altar in public confession of the faith that we profess. I am anxious to know that you are prepared to take this step. The white robes of Christianity become and beautify the angel virtues of woman, and I long to see them encircling the fair form of my dear Elodie. I know that you have all the purity, all the essential qualifications, that would authorize you to take this step, that you are in all things, save the public confession, a Christian.

We are now about four miles from Manassas and I think will remain in this vicinity for some time, but you know enough of army life to be aware of the fact that the General alone knows when we are to move. The policy of Mr. Davis seems to be entirely defensive. The opinion prevails that the defeat of Mr. Lincoln's army will have no effect in making peace but will only stimulate renewed exertions. I hope it will at least have the effect of disheartening the Yankees and of opening their eyes to the utter impossibility of subjugating us. It will certainly strengthen the Peace party, and we may pass the remainder of the season without another great battle. I sincerely hope so.

I am glad to hear that Missouri and Kentucky will rise in the majesty of their people and now vindicate their rights. For your sake, my dearest, I hope that this may be true. Major Pope tells me he has hopes for the best from Kentucky. I saw a few days ago from the papers that your brother David had reached Raleigh, N.C. with forty prisoners in charge. I also see that a Dr. Todd[7] of Lexington, a brother of yours, had been arrested for incendiary language but was discharged. I know this is not true as you have no such brother. Our regiment is much disorganized, owing to the loss of our field officers. I have been acting as Col. Capt. Goldsby having been quite unwell. I was in command yesterday at dress parade. We have asked Gen. Johnston to detail a regular officer to command the regiment ad interim. Our wounded are all doing well. I receive

---

7. George Rogers Clark Todd.

intelligence from them daily, tho I am unable to go to see them as Gen. Johnston will not allow an officer to leave camp. The regiment lost 190 killed and wounded in battle. The full details of the loss on both sides are not yet made up, but enough is known to show that the Yankees have lost in killed, wounded, prisoners, and missing about 10,000 men. We took 70 pieces of artillery, beautiful guns, most of them brass pieces. Two of them are large rifle guns and must have cost from $5000 to $7000 each. The value of the property, munitions of war, taken is put at $2,000,000.

It is now ten days since we have had our tents or baggage and as you may imagine have been put to much trouble and inconvenience. We have had rain but once however, and this has made it more comfortable. We have sent to Winchester for them.

My dear Elodie, in all these trials, I have turned to you and imagined how deeply your sympathy was enlisted in my behalf. You have been the bright angel that has always whispered courage and strength in the hour of danger, and I always look with hope to the time when I shall find in your love all the rewards for these trials. It is pleasant to know that you like me to treat you affectionately. I love you so well that it delights me to do anything that pleases you. You must not object, when I shall have the right to do so, if I pet you like a little girl. You are as dear to me as the morning is to the early spring flowers, sweeter than the dews of the beautiful roses with which I was accustomed to tell you of my love and thro which I dared to win you. These were happy hours when I paid homage to you and happier when I was told by your own lips that you could return and reciprocate my love. I frequently lie on my blanket at night, looking up to the blue canopy of heaven studded with stars, and dream of those days as among the halcyon hours of my life. Do you often think of them? Why need I ask the question as I know you do and as I know your heart is as full of such thoughts as mine? As I write in a crowd, under a tree, with a book to hold the paper, you must excuse all deficiencies of chirography and of style. I make no attempt to observe the rules of either, as I am only anxious to write to you.

I have seen many of the prisoners and wounded of the Yankees. They all say they were deluded into the war that they never expected to come to invade the south, and that they never will return to attack us. I place little reliance upon such statements, but they indicated on their part some reluctance in the future to volunteering. Mr. Lincoln should now rise above party and give peace to the country, but I fear he will not be equal to the position. He is too much of a party man. I say this, my own dear girl, knowing how you feel and with no idea that I will give you pain.

For you know that for your sake I would refrain from doing or saying ought that could wound as sensitive a nature as yours. I love you too well and might add that I love myself too much to offend you.

Please write me regularly to Manassas Junction and your letters will be forwarded if our location is changed. I hope to hear from you tomorrow as I sent a man to Winchester to get our baggage. Mr. Averitt's command is here, but I have seen nothing of him. Remember me to Mr. and Mrs. White and, dear Elodie, now commending you to the care and providence of our merciful God, I remain,

Ever affectionately and sincerely yours,

N. H. R. Dawson

Selma, July 31, 1861

Your welcome letter of the 24th has just been read with pleasure, acquainting me with your own hand of your safety for altho I received one from you written the 21st at Manassas, as you did not even mention a battle nor was there any signs told of a fight, I concluded it was written before the battle began. I had not heard any rumor to the effect that you were wounded or killed but am not astonished at the latter getting out as you *said so yourself* when the *cannon ball knocked you and the fence* into the air and then *onto the earth* and as you are a *truthful man*, I would have been inclined to have placed confidence in the assertion myself had I heard you utter the exclamation. It must have been a funny sight and doubtless you felt so, never having had a cannon ball so near you before, and I am truly thankful you escaped so well while others were falling around you and your own company suffered so much, and I hope you may go safely thro the war if it is your destiny to fight it out. I shall not say or do anything I hope to influence you the one way or the other and will try to be content with [your] own decision at the end of year of your enlistment. *We must conquer,* no matter what it costs, and we must have brave men in the field to do it, and one does not suffer much more than another for we all have to make sacrifice, tho I am selfish and candid enough to say I would much prefer others to do it than myself and hope Mr. Wetmore or Dedman's[8] company will be ready to take your place as the idea of being separated from you perhaps for years is not agreeable. But one must do

---

8. James M. Dedman was a member of the Twentieth Alabama Infantry, Company B. Alabama Civil War Muster Rolls, 1861–1865, Alabama Department of Archives and History.

the best they can, and I am trying to bear up cheerfully, but sometimes I make a great failure, especially when I do not receive a letter, tho your kindness keeps me well posted, and that is quite a consolation I assure you. I have suffered much anxiety, but since hearing there is no possibility of a fight for three months—so completely has Gen'l Scott's[9] army been routed—that I think when you write me the same I can take the world a little more quietly.

I must tell of an honor I received. A day or two ago a large letter from Head Quarters, Fort Morgan,[10] from Col. Harry Maury commanding was handed me which notified me that I was a member of the "Magnolia Regiment" and a handsome silver badge (so he calls it), a Magnolia bed and two leaves, was enclosed with the request that I would assume and wear it. I was astonished! The honor was unexpected, and I wondered if the regiment was like the blockade, on *paper*, however the ornament is pretty and I will say I *belong* to the "Magnolia Cadets" with your permission, should I learn it is not in existence. I am glad to see Mr. Breckenridge has at last said something[11] but so sorry he was so long making up his mind that a Free State man, Vallandigham, expressed his sentiments freely and in a more noble, manly way before him. Alas, tis too true that Kentucky is no more Kentucky, and it is with sorrow and pain I must say and see it. My hope is getting fainter and fainter and were I *J. C. B.* I would have made my speech before and bowed myself out and taken the field a common soldier, seeing nothing was to be gained by longer subjecting myself to *insult*. I have written to you frequently lately and hope you did not have to go battle in reality without a letter. I directed them all to Winchester. How am I to keep up with you travelling all over the State? If I wait for you to write me word you always complain of my silence and then that makes me feel bad to think you would suppose I did not wish to write to you, so you must stay in one place if you want to hear from me.

Bro. Clem returned today from Livingston having gained 8 pounds,

---

9. Although Winfield Scott (1786–1866) was general-in-chief of all Union forces, he had not been in favor of the "On to Richmond!" strategy that ended in defeat at Bull Run, preferring what was derided as the Anaconda Plan. Nevertheless, he accepted responsibility for the rout and by the end of the year had been edged out in favor of George B. McClellan.

10. Fort Morgan was located at the mouth of Mobile Bay, Alabama.

11. Kentucky's John Cabell Breckinridge was increasingly isolated as one of the few U.S. senators supporting secession and slavery. In the July special session, he claimed that Lincoln was operating outside the Constitution, noting, "I infinitely prefer to see a peaceful separation of these States than to see endless, aimless, devastating war, at the end of which I see the grave of public liberty and of personal freedom." By the end of the year he was in Confederate uniform. For more, see William C. Davis, *Breckinridge: Statesman, Soldier, Symbol* (Lexington: University Press of Kentucky, 2010).

but I cannot see any change whatever as he still looks thin. Selma is quiet now that the excitement of the first battle has worn off, and we are all eager for some other news. If I had not received some from you this evening, I think I would have gone to bed sick as I had almost given up, thought I could stand it no longer. I have nothing to write you of and fear my letters are as similar to each other as you think yours are. I am hoping you may be able to return soon if but for a short visit and think what a nice time we could have together and as we are almost strangers am afraid if you do not that we will have to begin our acquaintance anew when you do return. How little we have seen of each other, but we made the *most* of it when we did meet and in few meetings, did we not? Well it is after ten o'clock. I have been busily engaged all day and feeling somewhat fatigued will finish this scrawl, which is written simply to let you know I still think of you often, all the time, indeed there is not a moment when you are absent from my memory and a constant wish to see you is also felt. Matt has been tiring herself tonight in the way of laughing and talking, and it is more than probably I have introduced some of her conversation. Write me when you can. Goodbye and believe that I am with much love and a prayer ever for your safe return,

    Yours affectionately,
    Elodie

Manassas Junction, August 1, 1861

I received yesterday your welcome letter of the 14th of July which was forwarded from Winchester. You have no idea how welcome it was. It was like balm to the wounded, like the soft gleam of the moon after the dust and glare of a summer day, and I thank you, my dearest, for its affectionate and interesting details. I can well imagine your anxiety and rejoice that your confidence in my promise to relieve it was not misplaced as I wrote to you on the night of the battle and telegraphed the *Reporter* to assure you of my safety.

I am glad you acquitted yourself so well at the concert, especially as it *gratified* some parties whom you do not mention. I am glad that you have punished the *man* as you have, and I will take pleasure when I know him to see that you are protected from his rudeness. Please tell me who he is. I am indeed complimented to think that my likeness is so often gazed upon by your beautiful eyes, that your love for me places value upon it. I am not as stout as when I left Selma but am much darker, having been bronzed by the exposure and sun. I cannot imagine how the lady friend who received my letter from the Soldier's Aid Society could have manufactured such a report, that I was soon to return home to be married, as you well know my good sense would avoid making her or anyone beside yourself the depository of such an intention. I told you that I had received and answered a letter from her.

Mr. Wetmore does know of my attachment and engagement to you, which was imparted to him for special reasons which I will explain at the right time. It was necessary that it should be entrusted to some one in view of a purpose, and I selected him as a friend of both of us.

Mr. Averitt's letter is mysterious, and I am out of temper that he should have written you as he has, and I hope you will not deign to reply. He evidently hints at my attachment to you which *good taste* and *propriety*, in which he is sadly deficient, should have prevented. I am no rival of his, and I presume his allusion to our diminished friendship has arisen from my not allowing him to read your letters, tho he has shown me those of his intended. He evidently thinks you are the *rival* that has supplanted him in my confidence, and it may be that he merely meant a little pleasantry, but I still think he should not tread upon the sacred ground of your affections. I would never dream of taking such a liberty with Miss Williams. I impute no bad motive to him but attribute it all to the want of proper *culture*. He has been educated well, but I am not confident that his early education was very gentle. He has been all his life depending upon others and lacks independence. But enough, I hope you will excuse me from delivering your message to him, but if you deem it right you have my permission as you ask it to write him. My dearest, I am very sensitive to anything that touches you, and I may take a wrong view of the matter, but you will attribute it to my love for one dearer to me than life itself. Let the conclusion of the war solve the mystery for him. I am outraged that he should hope even to be made your confidante. Just such things as these have changed my estimate of his character very much.

If John has been faithful in his duty to you, and he deserves in your opinion so valuable a reward as my likeness then dearest you can bestow it, and I will approve whatever you do. Tell John to get you melons. I expect they are plentiful at the plantation. Is it not a pity that you are deprived by this war of so many things that are yours? I do not permit myself to doubt that I will return to you in safety after the expiration of my term of service. I enclose you for your perusal and then for *safe-keeping* a letter received from Mr. Mathews to see his feeling and his great kindness. He will love you as his own child, and I am exceedingly anxious to introduce you to him as *my wife*. His love is worth millions, and I am proud of his friendship. I have some balls and mementoes of the battlefield which I will endeavor to have sent to you in some way by one of the gentlemen here from Selma. I will send them to Mr. Wetmore and ask him to *give* them to you. Have you any objections? I will send a hollow spherical cannon ball with some bullets in it which you can take out. I picked them up on the field after the battle. I also send you a *Harper's Weekly* containing some interesting views of the war, and one of Gen. Rees, our brigade, on review at Winchester. Mr. Woodson came to see me last night on his way from New York. He gives a very interesting account of the feelings there about the battle on the 21st and brought me a pile of newspapers. I do not think we are to have a speedy peace, tho I hope, even against hope, that in some unforeseen way God will vouchsafe it to our country. How pleasant it would be to have our expectations of a long war disappointed and soon return to those we love. Among the letters sent you is your mother's. I wish it preserved carefully that it may always remind me of a mother's love for a cherished daughter and of my duty to guard and protect her with my love. The two brief notes of your mother's have greatly impressed me in her favor as a lady of great *character* and *good sense*. How could such a *daughter* have a *different mother*? You wrong me in saying that I do not give you credit for loving me as much as I love you, my dear Elodie. My love for you is great, and that love teaches me to have in you the most perfect confidence, that does not permit a doubt to enter my mind upon the subject of your truthfulness and affection. To doubt you would make me mad, and I would roam the world a desolate and broken-hearted man. I am glad you are going to leave Selma on a visit to Marengo. I knew Col. Craighead[12] very well. I will feel uneasy should you remain in Selma in August and September, which are usually our sickliest months. Will you not tell me your birthday? I will tell you mine that you may not hesitate to grant me the favor, February 14, 1829. You see I am getting too old faster than you imagined when you told Mrs. Mabry you were not too young to marry me. You really have a happy faculty of foiling the assaults of your friends. Please tell her not to be uneasy, that I will make no claims to the hands of her fair daughter. Nine months wear away before we meet, unless peace throws its white mantle over the country. The time will pass more rapidly now, as events of an active character will take

---

12. James B. Craighead (1795–1859) was the late husband of Elodie's cousin Jane Preston Craighead of Marengo County, Alabama.

place. Our trials, however, are intended for a wise purpose, and we will love each other more warmly and know each other better than if we had been married earlier. Don't you think so, my dearest? I think of you as my wife, dear to me as you ever will be, and happy will be the home when you are given to my care and love. I am always at your side, when the moon beams brightly, and at the soft hour of nine, I turn to worship with you in the stars the God who made and protects us. I have written you a long letter and no doubt you already tire in deciphering its characters. Good-bye. May God guard and protect you ever shall be my constant prayer.

With my kind regards to Mr. and Mrs. White, I remain, dear Elodie,

Ever affectionately and sincerely your own devoted,

N. H. R. Dawson

Manassas Junction, Virginia, August 3, 1861

I have the pleasure of acknowledging the receipt of your two letters of the 22d and 24th ulto. written immediately after the late battle and the tidings of my safety had reached you.

How flattering to a wearied soldier to know from the lips of one dearer to him than life that his dangers have caused her so much anxiety and that her love is so deep and strong. You speak of those who doubt your attachment to me. I am angered and grieved that anyone could have expressed such an opinion. You truly say, my dear Elodie, that such un-kind expressions pass by you as the idle wind and make no impression upon you. You will never be doubted by *him* whose love is pledged to you. Indeed, *you belong to me and I belong to you and we intend to keep each other.* You were thus employed, while I was engaged in the battle, in writing to me your usual Sunday letter. Do you know that I thought of this on the battlefield and was consoled by the reflection that your spirit was there hovering around me? I have written you several times since the battle and sent you yesterday by Dr. Prestridge a package of letters with a number of *Harper's Weekly,* and also sent to Mr. Wetmore for you several mementoes from the battlefield. I hope you will receive the little articles safely as I know you will value them.

Mr. Daniels is now here and will bear this letter unless I mail it.

We have no news here. Our wounded are still doing well and will re-cover. I am so glad of this as I am warmly attached to all of my men. When I return safely and we are married I will want you to give the company an oyster supper, and I will be so proud to introduce them to such a bride.

My dearest, when I allow myself to look into the future and see you at my side, loved and cherished as you deserve to be, I feel that I will be far happier than I deserve. I do not think the world could have given me one more calculated to give me happiness and to shed its rays upon my home. You have all that I have learned to admire in woman. Intellect, intelligence, beauty of person in character, affection, and gentleness. But you will tell me that I am too complimentary. I answer that the *truth* will not offend you or make you vain. I am certainly very much in love with Miss Elodie, and she is well aware of it. I admire the speeches of Mr. Vallandigham and Mr. Breckenridge very much. I expected it of them both and hope their influence will gradually reverse public sentiment at the north.

We have Captain Davis of the Confederate service assigned to us as commander until the field officers resume their duties. Capt. Goldsby and myself are acting as Lieut. Col. and Major. I will now be allowed to keep a horse, which will be a great convenience.

We have been informed that our regiment will be ordered to western Virginia in all probability. The officers have all joined in remonstrance against the move. I am rather partial to it myself as we would be in a healthier and better country. My only objection would be the difficulty of communicating with you. It is still my opinion that the regiments from the south for twelve months will be sent southward in the fall. If so, I will hope to see you my dearest before the expiration of a year. What a happiness it will be to *kiss your hand*, my own, much loved Elodie. My heart leaps for joy at the hope of seeing you. But time is passing quickly. It is now going on *four* months since we left Selma, twice that period will compass the year & I hope restore us to those whom we love so dearly. I though the 19th of April was the day upon which we were engaged, but my mind was so much confused about dates at the time of our departure that I wished to know from you whether I was correct.

You ask me to find out some poor fellow in my company who has neither mother nor sister to care *especially* for him, and you will attend to his wants in knitting and sewing. I will do so most cheerfully and hope you will proceed at once with your knitting. I will even name myself as the man and hope you will be so good as to keep your promise. I will be very happy to receive a specimen of your needles and will agree with you that you will make a *nice looking old lady*, provided you do as I desire. I have neither mother nor sister who care specially for me.

If you will place the ambrotype in Mr. Wetmore's hands he will have it sent to Cahaba to Lizzie. I send you a letter received from her today.

I am gratified that you class me as your *friend* in our category above all others, "primer inter pares."[13]

I do not believe that Mrs. Lincoln ever expressed herself as you state about your brother David. If she did, it is in very bad taste and in worse temper and unlike all the representations I have seen of her character. But, you will learn my dearest, that a wife soon becomes wrapped up in the fortunes of her husband and will tolerate in her relatives no opposition to his wishes. I agree with you about the conduct of your brother and admire him for his patriotism and know that he will meet with his reward. How deplorable is this fratricidal war. Two brothers met in the battle of Manassas on opposite sides and are now here in the hospital, both wounded.

I am glad you like Miss McCraw. Her brother is a very fine young man and is my most intimate friend.[14] We mess together and occupy the same tent. We have had no meat for breakfast or dinner today. Provisions are very scarce, and we are unable to purchase them, though I am *now very* rich having been paid off for two months yesterday. I receive $130.00 per month, which is a large sum in a country where you cannot spend money. If the war continues, and I save thro it, I will be well off, will I not? It has cut me pecuniarily thousands and, in being separated from you, millions in happiness. Mrs. Hardie is in camp today and rode over the battlefield with Mr. Thos. Daniels. Should you visit Mr. Daniels he will be able to give you an idea of the danger of our position in the battle and may also give you some interesting details of your friends of the 4th Ala. Rgt.

I think Mr. Hagood would do well to go to the war. He may transfer his affection to Miss Kittie, but I should not like a sister of mine to wed such a man. Do you know that he is near fifty years old? He acknowledges that he is forty-five.

I was under the impression that your sister had returned to Ky and am glad that she remains in Ala. She will be a pleasant companion for you, and I hope will remain in Ala. long enough for me to know her. I am anxious to know and to love her. Present me to her kindly, if she will permit a stranger such a liberty.

Dearest it is a great happiness to love you and to know that one eye will grow bright with anticipation when I return, that one heart will be

13. Latin phrase meaning "first among equals."
14. Miss Ella McCraw and her brother S. Newton McCraw (see May 15, 1861, note 55).

opened to welcome me. I hope and pray that God will vouchsafe this happiness to us.

Should we leave Manassas Junction, I will inform you speedily.

Present me kindly to Mr. and Mrs. White. With a great deal of love and my earnest prayers that the blessings of God will be showered upon you my dear Elodie, I remain ever

Yours affectionately and sincerely,

N. H. R. Dawson

I do really admire your bravery in learning to shoot a pistol. I have a beautiful pair at home which I would be delighted to place in your hands, but they are locked up in a bureau. I have one here that will kill at 200 yards. I wore it in battle but did not use it. An officer has really no opportunity to use arms as the Yankees never will allow us too close with them. They are afraid of the cold steel and can't stand the bayonet. They ran whenever they were charged.

I met an old friend, Col. Burt[15] of So. Ca. by accident this morning. He is on Gen. Smith's[16] staff. I have met gentlemen in this way that I never expected to see again.

My brother R. H. Dawson is now in Richmond, and I hope will soon be near me. I love him very much but not half as much as a certain black-eyed, witching young lady of *seventeen summers.* You will never tell on your birthday that I might celebrate it?

Confederate States of America, Selma, August 4, 1861

I was considerably brightened up yesterday evening after reading your letter sent by Dr. Jones. I did not really expect to hear, was only indulging in the hope I would be so favored, for I had been thinking of you for an hour or two, wondering where you were, what doing, where going next,

15. Possibly Erasmus R. Burt (1820–1861), born in Edgefield County, South Carolina. Burt studied medicine in Alabama before moving to Mississippi, where he helped raise Company K, nicknamed "Burt Rifles," of the Eighteenth Mississippi Infantry. He received a mortal wound at the Battle of Balls Bluff in October 1861 and became the first Mississippi officer to be killed in battle. He left a widow and eight children. Jeff T. Giambrone, *Images of America: Remembering Mississippi's Confederates* (Charleston, S.C.: Arcadia Publishing, 2012), 34.

16. Possibly Edmund Kirby Smith (1824–1893).

when I would see you again, and a thousand other things but one of which was satisfied by your letter, as you expressed ignorance of your own movements and etc. and of course not enlightening me, and I could not arrive at any satisfactory conclusions myself but one which was the best thing I could do was to try and be patient and wait for time to reveal all that now seems hidden so completely from us. Tis no easy task, but I am endeavoring to bear everything as well and cheerfully as possible. Sometimes I fail entirely, but in a short time find myself persevering again in the struggle and may yet come out victorious. I do not think of peace and know well Mr. Lincoln is not *man enough* to dare to make it. He is but a tool in the hands of his party and would not brave their wrath by such a proposition. How nobly he could redeem himself if he had the courage. He is no more fitted for the office than many others who have recently occupied it, and we may date our trouble from the time when we allowed *party* to place in the chair a President entirely disregarding his *worth*, ability, or capacity for it, and I hope our Confederacy may guard against it. I would not be more for him than his party or than for any other Blk. *Rep. President*, and you do not say as much as I do, tho that is a privilege I allow myself exclusively, to abuse my relations as much as I desire, but no one else can do the same before me or even say a word against Kentucky. I told two gentlemen the other night that as they knew I was a Kentuckian and acknowledged myself as such, that I considered anything they said against my birthplace and home personal, and there were many subjects more entertaining to me than abuse of Kentucky. I thought if they desired to discuss her movements, they could take themselves off to do it, but as long as a drop of Ky. blood courses in my veins I see myself listening to people who just by a small majority threw off Northern tyranny themselves and before Ky. for I still have faith in her and will ever take her part knowing better than some all the disadvantages she is laboring under. But enough of that state and on to something that will interest you more, and it requires some thought to know what the subject shall be as I write so many long letters and discuss all the commonplace subjects of the day that it will be the same thing over.

I have here read a letter from my dear friend Dr. Rodman in which after hoping that my brother and yourself may be safe he says he cannot advise me about my sweetheart and knows if I love him he is *all right*, and he knows one so guileless, good, and honest as myself cannot unworthily bestow my affections, advises me not to marry until after the war is over, and extends an invitation for you to visit him as he is a good kind friend of mine, and we love each other so much. I am a particular pet of the

whole Rodman family, and I am very partial to them. Mr. Hagood came
up to dine with us today. I have been polite enough to excuse myself,
leaving the rest to the enjoyment of newspapers. Mr. H. comes up regularly every evening until I am so tired of his *sighs* and *eye rollings* that I am
almost outdone and amuse myself by talking to him of the sweetheart I
have fighting in Virginia, how bravely and nobly he has acted in sacrificing so much to go, and how proud I am of him. I believe he thinks there's
a chance for that sweetheart never to come back from the way he hangs
on. He says he will be so lonely when we go to Mrs. Craighead's. "Miss
Kittie how long will you be gone?" Kittie replied with a very mischievous
look, "a month, perhaps longer." He will derive a great deal of satisfaction from the answer. I am encouraging him to go to the war on every
occasion and really think he ought. Will you give him your captaincy if I
succeed in getting him off? You must not get discouraged. Next May will
roll around and then you will return so much better pleased that for a
year you have been doing your duty, fighting like a brave soldier for his
country, and I will be better pleased too. I could not love you if you had
staid at home content to remain inactive at such a moment. The separation with all the suspense is trying and painful to me, and sometimes I
almost feel disposed to give way to my feelings and never make another
effort to keep up, but I know it is but right that you should be where you
are and all I ask is that you continue to bear your hardships and trials as
bravely and cheerfully as you have done so far. It is needless to mention
a word as to fighting, for I know you are a brave, noble man and I would
willingly choose you as my knight. Indeed you are and I am confident
before the year is out you will distinguish yourself by your bravery. I am
counting time and find almost four months have passed, and I think if
you can contrive to come and *see a body* before a great while I can stand
it better. Please, if you can, come back for a little while. Can't you come
before December? I think as I have spared you so long, Gen'l Johnston
might spare you a little while for me. I shall not object to your petting me
when you have the *right* as I like it, and when one is as affectionate in their
disposition as myself they must have affection in return. To be loved is as
essential to my life and happiness as the air I breathe, and until I knew
you imagined you were so cold, not unfeeling, but reserved, undemon-
strative, and did not care for friendship or love either, but I don't think
so now. You must know that before our acquaintance began, and I never
saw you to know you until our meeting in Montgomery, I used to hear
very much of you and fancied I knew you, but I never was so mistaken
before in my life. I have been listening to Bro. Clem relating the proceed-

ings of the 21st at Manassas which he gleaned from Mr. Davidson. How I wish I could hear someone who was there relate the incidents of the day. I believe I have read every account given since in the Montgomery, Richmond, Mobile, Charleston, Louisville, and a New York paper, and am not satisfied yet, so you can prepare yourself to answer innumerable questions when we meet.

I wrote to my Bro. David to Richmond, where I hear he was, [and] have not had time to hear from him yet and hope I will as soon as possible for I have been quite uneasy about his long silence. Dr. George Todd is my father's youngest son by his first marriage but an almost total stranger to me for in my whole life I have never seen him but twice. The first time he was a practising physician, the next, after my father's death, and owing then to some unpleasant family disturbances there has never since existed between the older members of my family and himself and his older brother the same feeling as before or that is felt for our sisters.[17] I was too young at the time to even understand why the feeling was. When he called on David in Richmond, David would not see him or recognize him. This I feel sorry for and hope they will yet make friends. He should remember he is our father's son and for his sake endeavor to forget and forgive the past. Unforgiving as I am, I would do so.

I wish I were prepared to take the step you are so anxious that I should. For two years, I have wished to but dared not, never until there is a decided change in my heart will I dare to do so, and to speak candidly I am afraid you would be surprised did you know how far from being ready for such a step I am. You give me credit for more goodness and amiability than I am entitled to and so far from being able to assist you in your duty will require assistance from you. And you know I told you my choice of church did not agree with yours. I have been raised a Presbyterian, and I love them. For generations back my father's and mother's family have been such. Now what will you do with me? You will have a stubborn, hardheaded Presbyterian to convert and an ignorant one on religious matters too, altho in my young days so much attention was bestowed upon me. You see I am candid to you on all occasions and subjects and expect the

---

17. George Rogers Clark Todd is seen by most Todd biographers as the "black sheep" of the family. Notoriously irascible, in 1849 he contested his father's will on a technicality, eating into his widowed stepmother's financial support and forcing her to buy back some of her liquidated estate, including family furniture and mementos. The lawsuit also necessitated the sale of Todd family slaves. See Stephen Berry, *House of Abraham: Lincoln and the Todds, a Family Divided by War* (New York: Houghton Mifflin, 2007), 41–42.

same from you always. I should be much hurt did I think you would keep from me or hesitate to say anything you desired, as you know I would very soon inform you if anything was said I did not fancy.

By this time you have received all the letters written to Winchester but one which did not arrive before the second or third day of this month, and this time I have written the greatest number of letters. I have not received but two since the battle, one the 24th and 28th. I shall think you have forgotten me to fall in love with any of the beautiful and accomplished Va. ladies you see, and who must be so happy, having it in their power to do so much for our soldiers. I love all the soldiers, and if they were wounded and sick near me I would think I could not do enough for them. Speaking of soldiers reminds me of Jimmie Barker. You remember him—a young man from Summerfield who could not go with you on account of his deafness. Well, he and Miss Nannie Heard found out about the time he thought of going they were interested in each other and have concluded to be married on the 7th.[18] I think the war has performed many wonderful things. I feel the effects of it myself. I have not seen Mr. Wetmore for a week. He then told me he expected to receive from you soon a long and interesting letter, and I asked if he would read it to me, which caused him to look at me and finally to say yes, if there were no secrets. I told him I only wanted the war news. He says he suspected something, but he cannot find out, but he has *his heart set on one thing* and from the good words he spoke for it did not take me long to surmise what it was, and I could have told him *mine was set on the same thing too.* He begged me to tell him if I was engaged to Mr. H., said I must not consider him impertinent but for a particular reason he asked. I like to be with him sometimes. He has so much curiosity, and I tease him well. He is a good friend of yours and never omits an opportunity of saying something kind in your favor, and you have a rival in Bobby who comes to see me and declares he would not have anyone but Miss Todd, which he always called me, for his sweetheart. I'll try and prove true to you and not reciprocate his love.

I am annoyed to see how I have rattled on, and Bro. Clem will go down town and leave my letter which I am finishing before breakfast, which would disappoint me as I always send you a letter Monday morning and you know what day to expect it as certain.

18. James Barker, age twenty, and Nannie Heard, age eighteen, did indeed marry on August 7, 1861. Marriage certificate, James N. Barker and Nannie C. Heard, Dallas County, Ala., *Alabama, Select Marriages, 1816–1942.*

I wish I could talk to you in place of writing. I would have so much more to say and enjoy it more, for I always was averse to letter writing, tho from the length of mine you would not judge so, yet it is true and when you return I expect to be able to count all the letters I will write. But really I must cease. I hope to hear from you today. What has become of Mr. and Mrs. Hardie? Remember me kindly to Mr. Averitt when next you see him and assure him as I am *his friend.* Goodbye. May heaven bless you and your cause, watch over and protect you from danger and harm, is the ever constant prayer of your devoted,

Elodie

Manassas Junction, August 4, 1861

Since writing you last, my loved Elodie, we have changed our encampment to a much more pleasant location nearer the railroad and convenient to springs of fine water.

Capt. Davis of the Confederate army has been assigned to the command of the regiment until one of our field officers can resume his duties. I now rank as Major and am acting as second in command and as our Col. and Lieut. Col. are frequently absent have to act as commander. We are now halted at the idea of being sent to northwestern Va. and have petitioned for a transfer to another brigade, but I do not myself anticipate a move from this line for some time.

Speculations as to peace and war are frequent and make up the staple of camp conversation. If the North is as willing to have peace as we are, there would be little protestation of hostilities, but the leaders at the north are not yet satisfied and will no doubt make another effort to [illegible] their defeated arms.

It is Sunday evening, and I am seated at my trunk under the shadow of a pine tree writing to my dearest, knowing and believing that she is occupied in the same way in composing one of those beautiful letters which bring me so much love and so much pleasure. Next to seeing you in person, I would receive one of your letters. You have improved in one respect, my dearest, you no longer fear to express the deep feelings that live in your bosom for one so unworthy, in his own opinion, of the love and esteem of one so much purer and so much superior to the majority of her sex. I love and worship you and confess that you have me completely secured in the golden meshes of your heart. I could not, if I would, be released. Does it not argue great power to have affected such a conquest?

When I first felt the power of your love, I strove against it because I apprehended then that this war in which I am pledged to participate would interfere with my marriage, and I was unwilling to interest you at such a time, but your beauty of *mind* and *character* quite vanquished me, and I fell a victim at your feet. You have raised me up and bid me hope and love. I am deeply thankful and will ever try, my dearest, to love and guard you as you would wish me to love and guard your affections. I hope to be able to prove to your mother that her fear of your happiness will prove groundless and that she will never regret the consent she has given. Do you know I feel as if I were writing to one who was already mine, before God and in our hearts? I have for you at home a beautiful present, more substantial than flowers, which I will present when you take possession of the white house. I could give you the world and still think I had not done enough. Such are my feelings, and I should like to hear whether you object to my loving you in this way. I fancy that you will *pet me*. I yearn for the love of woman, to be loved by you will be a paradise of happiness. But I fear you will tire of this and think me a love sick swain.

I went to hear a sermon in camp this evening from Mr. Henderson of Tuskegee Ala. He preached an eloquent sermon upon the war and our trials and exhorted us to be Christian soldiers. Our chaplain, Mr. Chadwick,[19] who was in the late battle and had his clothes cut by several balls, delivered a most touching and feeling prayer, and when he alluded to our dead and wounded comrades, he was choked to suffocation, hardly able to express himself, and in the large assembly of bronzed and bearded soldiers, you could see almost every eye and cheek furrowed with big tears. It is singular how much attached we become when thrown together as we are in military life without knowing it. When I stood *alone* at the grave of our four killed men, I cannot express the feeling of my heart. It was akin to the feelings when I have stood at night and knelt at the tomb of one in whose existence my life has been wrapped. I prayed for the presence of the dead and desired to sink into the same grave.

But hope will beckon onwards and will induce us to find happiness where we had expected sorrow and gloom. I have been miserable. I am now happy, miserable only in being separated from you. But the time flies rapidly and our meeting, I hope, will be much earlier than we expect. I hope the regiment will be ordered south in the winter to garrison one of our forts, and if so, I will have the opportunity of seeing you. I cer-

19. Possibly S. W. Chadwick, transferred to the Fifth Alabama Infantry in August 1861. Alabama Civil War Muster Rolls, 1861–1865, Alabama Department of Archives and History.

tainly hope to be able to visit Selma in January even if we remain in this state. How joyful will be our meeting, but how much more joyful if it be a meeting when I marry you. As you ask me the question, I will never leave you or go where you cannot accompany me, unless for a short time. You will find me as unwilling to a separation as you will ever be, and I expect more fond of remaining at home, as I will never want other companionship than that of my beautiful wife. Her smile will make happiness and will bring peace and comfort. You ask why it is that you receive so many presents in the *eating line*. I suppose because you *appreciate them*. Do you remember the *oysters* I sent Mr. Hagood? I ordered the *very best* because I knew you liked them and would get some from him. Now are you any wiser after having your question answered? Do you know when I am in earnest? Have you yet learned my character? Your mother pays me a compliment in saying that I understand your disposition. Our tents have just arrived. Last night I slept under an open tree and the dews were very heavy. I got up Sunday morning, as it was, and gave the quartermaster a good abusing because he did not bring my tent yesterday, and as I am now an important personage it produced a fine effect.

Dearest, I have passed the evening in writing, knowing that you are employed in a similar manner. Most of our Sabbaths have been our busy days. I think our authorities should regard the Sabbath with more consideration.

I must now take up the bible you gave me and read a chapter for your sake. I will hope one of these days to read it to you in the soft light of our home, with your bright eye beaming its rays upon one who will always love you and who will endeavor with you to follow its sacred precepts.

I will keep you advised of all our movements and will write as often as circumstances will permit, Remember me to Mrs. White and your sister Miss Kate. Tell Mr. White that I am reading "The Woman in White."[20] With many prayers for your welfare and continued happiness, I remain, my dearest Elodie,

> Affectionately and sincerely yours,
> N. H. R. Dawson

After writing the preceding letter and reading over again your affectionate letter, I could not refrain from taking up my materials to add to its length, trusting that this long letter would be repaid by you with a long and affectionate one. Ours is not the first love affair in which the parties

---

20. Wilkie Collins's *The Woman in White* appeared in serial form from 1859 to 1860 in *Harper's Weekly* and was then published in book form.

were separated by time and distance, but it has produced its natural results. I think, tho I may be wrong, that if we had not been separated as we
have been, we would not have loved each other so much, but I am now
willing to compromise the discovery of any new beauties in your character by a speedy return home and peace.

Cols. Moore and Forney arrived on Sunday evening with their regiments. I went over to see them and found many friends—among the
officers, Dr. Talbid of Marion, who is one of the captains, is a cousin of
mine. Reuben Chapman, Mrs. Pettus's brother, commands a company.
It was really a pleasure to meet so many acquaintances, and I felt almost
at home again as many of them have been at my home and are intimate
associates.

Mr. Averitt was here this morning. He is awfully in love and thinks he
will never live to marry Miss W. as he expects to be killed. My word for it
the enemy will never catch him asleep. He talks of his intended familiarly
as Mary. I do not like such familiarity. Your name is *sacred*, and I would
never dream of speaking of you to any one except as Miss Elodie or Miss
Todd as I think it would be an unwarrantable liberty. My love, like your
sorrow, is too sacred to be paraded before the public, and I hope never
to lose my sense of propriety by profaning your name.

Let me cheer you up. You must take a brighter view of our affairs.
When victory has crowned our arms and our independence shall have
been vindicated, you will feel proud that I have acted my part in the
drama. Indeed, I do not see how I could have done otherwise than I
have. I am in the performance of a duty to my country, which, when
performed, will greatly add to my own satisfaction. The chances of my
safe return are greatly in my favor—one fourth of the term has passed
without a battle and in a battle, or in several, a very large majority escape
uninjured. To have one tenth of an army killed and wounded would be a
very large loss. More men usually die from sickness than from battle, and
I will always endeavor to take care of myself for your sake.

For your own private information, I can tell you that the enemy will
attack us here to great disadvantage as we have a strong natural position,
which has been strengthened by fortifications and cannon. We have also
received since our return from Martinsburg five or six large regiments.
This force will enable us to face the Lincolnites.

The enemy are said to be advancing, and we have been in line of battle.
I have returned merely to enclose this letter in an envelope [illegible].

Ever sincerely and affty, my dearest Elodie, your own faithful,

N. H. R. Dawson

Charlottesville, Virginia, August 15, 1861

I have not written to you since the middle of last week, my dear Elodie, on account of sickness, having been confined to my bed by fever for several days.

Yesterday I came down to this place, having been advised to leave by our physician for a few days in order to recoup my strength. I was also anxious to see Maj. Haden and our wounded soldiers. I am glad to say I found them all improving.

I am much better this morning and hope to return at the end of this week entirely well. I received on Monday your welcome letter of the 4th and 5th and am greatly obliged for the confidence you express in me. I hope that I have done my duty so far as a soldier and a brave man and, with God's help and your own encouragement, will do so to the end. It is a most gratifying truth that the love of a true woman never faileth, but like a spring is always gushing forth to refresh the weary and the unfortunate. I find the change from camp to the comforts of a hotel very grateful just at this time and almost wish I had never seen a camp. It is very certain that I will never remain in one longer than my duty requires, and at the end of my enlistment I mean to keep my promise to you and become your good and faithful soldier.

I am afraid you find my letters uninteresting since the late battle. It has had a most demoralizing effect upon the soldiers and seems to have made them careless and negligent. This is said always to be one of the effects of a victory. It has certainly made me feel indolent and lazy. But we have had so much to render us uncomfortable that this latter cause may have produced the effect. We have a great deal of sickness. In our brigade, numbering about 4,000 men, on Sunday we had 1,750 sick men. Gen. Whiting[21] stated this to my informant. You speak of receiving only two letters from me on the 24th and 28th ulto. I wrote you on the night of the 21st at 12 o'clock at night. You speak rather lightly of being knocked down by a cannon ball. I assure you if you had been as badly lamed and had been as much exhausted as I was on that day you would think it a serious matter. I was so tired that I was in the rear of our men and walked away in company with Col. Jones and two others, one of

---

21. William Henry Chase Whiting (1824–1865) had taken over brigade command after the death of Barnard Bee. Nathaniel repeatedly approached Whiting about a furlough, but was consistently denied. John H. Eicher and David J. Eicher, *Civil War High Commands* (Stanford: Stanford University Press, 2001), 566–567.

whom was shot near me and has since died. Co. Jones was shot in advance of me and was taken prisoner very shortly afterwards. The regiment was completely scattered and not more than 150 of them were ever collected again in one day, and they never got into a second fight. I myself became separated and never could hear of the regiment until late in the evening after the battle was over, and if I had known where it was, was in such a condition that I would not have rejoined it. No doubt the same was the condition of the whole regiment, who were worn down and exhausted by the march from Winchester and the fatiguing march at double quick of six miles that morning, previous to the fight. Our regiment did its duty gallantly while it was in the fight, as well as men could do, but after their retreat, owing to the want of a leader, were scattered everywhere.

I hope we will have a place in the next battle that we may redeem whatever of blame may attach to us for the scattering, but our regiment was guilty of a fault common to many other divisions of the army on that day and cannot alone be blamed.

There is hardly anything to write you of here. The war news you have from the papers. We never have any other. I hear a fight going on, under my window, between the servant girls but am not sufficiently interested to go and see the result. One seems to have come off the victor.

Prince Napoleon[22] was at Manassas on last Friday and rode over the battleground with Gen's Beauregard and Johnston. I did not see him, but Lieut. McCraw did. He was with our generals two days. It is thought that his visit is a political one, and I am inclined to believe so.

When I read your affectionate letters, they fill me with gratitude that I have won the love of one who has so warm and affectionate a nature. I too require love as much as the air to enable me to live, and I am so happy to find that your nature and mine correspond in this respect. With two hearts so warm, and one so pure and guileless as my Elodie's, we will hope for a great deal of happiness.

I noted what you say about your religious feelings. I give you credit for speaking as you do and am glad you are so candid. You tell me I will find you *"hard to consent"* and *"an obstinate Presbyterian."* Well, my dear Elodie, you know that it would give me greater pleasure to see you a member of my own church than of any other, but at the same time I would never

---

22. Prince Napoleon of France, a cousin of Emperor Napoleon III, arrived in the United States in July 1861. For his aide-de-camp's thoughts on the war, see Bayrd Still, *Mirror for Gotham: New York as Seen by Contemporaries from Dutch Days to the Present* (New York: Fordham University Press, 1994), 181–183.

object to see you a good Presbyterian, and I hope that even if one faith and one communion did not unite us that our hearts would be united in love and in one desire to discharge all of our duties. I will never undertake the office of converting you but will hope that time, as it mellows the light of your life, will bring about that change so essential to our eternal happiness. I trust to see you a *professing Christian*, even tho' of a *church different from mine.* Now I hope you will think me candid.

Four months, one third of the year, have almost passed, and I will endeavor for your sake to bear our trials and privations as patiently as those of the past have been borne. I will also endeavor to fight well and to bear myself as becomes your betrothed. I am so far conscious of having tried to do so and will to the end. If I live it will be to be worthy of you. If I die it will be that you may never be ashamed of my memory. But I pray God this war may end speedily and save the innocent loss of life that is now foreshadowed.

Mr. John Rollins left here a few days ago for home. It is said his friend acted impudently in removing him and fears are entertained that he will die. I do not know where he is. I found Billy Harrison sitting up in the parlor yesterday evening entertaining a lady. I regret the loss of his arm exceedingly. George Mims is at Warrenton and is improving. I am surprised that none of his friends have been in to see him. He was severely wounded in the shoulder.

The people here are a noble set. They have made hospitals of their homes, and the most refined ladies are the nurses. Our men have been shown every attention. Their own mothers and sisters could not have been more attentive and kind.

I have now written you a long letter, dear Elodie, too long I fear, and must come to a close. Write me to Manassas. With much love and a prayer that God will guide, guard, and protect you always, I remain,

Sincerely and affectionately yours,
N. H. R. Dawson

Charlottesville, Virginia, August 18, 1861

This is Sunday, the fourth since the battle of Manassas, and I have been spending the morning in my room, reading the bible you gave me upon the eve of my departure and also in reading over your last three letters of July 24, 30, and Aug. 5. This is frequently a consoling occupation with me, and when I feel the want of friend or of sympathy, I invariably turn

to you, my own loved and cherished Elodie. I sometimes reproach myself
that I have not as much love of sacred things as I have for you, but I hope
you will pardon me for loving you as I do for I can love Him through you.
I place all my hopes of earthly happiness in you, and were I to lose your
love I would become a wanderer and a fugitive from society. I would then
be willing to remain in the army and would on all occasions seek death
in the battles that we are to fight.

I hope I will yet be able to be more worthy of you than I am and that
the future will bring with it for you and for me many hours of happiness.
I live in your love and look to the departure of each day as bringing me
so much nearer to you. I have been repacking my trunk this morning and
putting out a number of superfluous articles, preparatory to an entire
campaign, which I think we will have. *Inter nos*, I think we will advance
before Washington, and you must not be surprised to hear that Washington has fallen by this time next month. If so, I hope to have a pleasanter
time for spending the winter than we now anticipate if we remained so,
but I still hope that we will be sent South. I spent an hour very pleasantly
yesterday at Mr. Cochran's, a relative of Mr. Mathews. I have known the
family for a long time. I found Miss Mary Preston[23] grown up to womanhood, a beautiful and interesting girl, resembling you in her cordial,
unaffected manners. I was really pleased and gratified at her cordial reception. I have promised Mrs. Cochran that I would come to her house
if I am sick or wounded, and you will certainly be in danger of losing a
part of my heart should I be so unfortunate for Miss Mary Preston is a
charming girl. She *lisps* a little which adds to her interesting appearance
and manners. I like her better than any lady I have seen in Va. Mr. Averitt's intended is near this place. I intend to get our flag and send it home
to you. Maj. Haden has seen her and is very much pleased.

The day is bad and rain still comes pouring down. I think of going
to camp tomorrow as I am now much better, only wanting my strength,
which will come back as soon as I take to exercise and drill once more.

Have you seen the official report of the 4th Ala. Rgt? It is published
in the dispatch of yesterday, also an account from the diary of G. T. Anderson of our regiment, a young man from Huntsville, who was killed
near me in the battle. I saw the poor fellow when he fell. He was a pious
lad, devoted to his sister Pauline. Six or eight men were killed near me.

---

23. Mary Preston Cochran, age nineteen, was the daughter of John Cochran and Margaret Lynn Lewis. She married John Montgomery Preston; 1860 U.S. Federal Census, Fred-
ericksville Parish, Albermarle, Va.

I almost wish I had been wounded. I must now bid you goodbye, dearest Elodie. I wrote you yesterday and hope you are writing me now.

Adieu. May God protect and spare you always.

Ever sincerely and affty yours,

N. H. R. Dawson

Marengo County, August 19, 1861

Last night I received your letters of the dates of Aug. 3rd and 4th—the first news I have had since my arrival here. I thought it was dreadful but owing to the incessant rain and terrible roads it was impossible to send to the office for the mail. I am delighted at the idea of your being sent South this winter and hope you are correct in your surmise of army engagements for then we may see something of each other and be allowed to spend some of these pleasant, quiet evenings, which we were so suddenly deprived of by this dreadful war. I am thinking of this night four months ago—do you remember it? You were then with me, and I so happy, little dreaming of what a short duration it was to be and that two weeks from that time would place so many long and weary miles between us and surround you with danger and many trying privations and trials and leaving me feeling sad, lonely, and anxious for your safety and fate. But I am getting accustomed to your absence and more reconciled, tho' occasionally the old feeling of rebellion against my fate comes over me, and I think myself the most *unfortunate creature* on Earth. Really you seem to anticipate my feeling and state of mind, for I generally receive a letter from you which dispels all my gloom and raises my spirits and cheers me almost to great bravery and my old patriotism. I wrote you a long letter yesterday as usual, but it was so full of complaints and its tenor so sad I concluded to destroy it and write another. I am determined to correct this bad habit of mine always writing you such complaining letters, and I hope you may soon be able to say I have *improved in two aspects*. I do not forget when I am *enduring all my great trials* that you have so much to discourage and try you and expend a great deal of sympathy on you that you are not aware of, and think of you very often, and wish I had wings that I might visit you sometimes when you write me that you would be *glad to see me*. But I have then to revert to sending you a winged messenger in the shape of a letter, one of those you consider so *beautiful*.

You ask me if I have learned your character. I can tell you I have learned you are a *great flatterer*, and you do not seem to know that I do not value

and appreciate flattery as much as some of my sex. Did Mr. Dennis give
you lessons in trying to make "people feel good?" It is a mania with him.
We have not heard from our old friend for several weeks and his silence
causes us to think he has departed for Europe. I would enjoy seeing
him so much. Indeed I do not intend sewing or knitting for you who
have Mrs. M. to keep you supplied with such beautiful specimens of her
needles. I will knit you a pair to prove to you that I can knit, but all the
rest must go to the young soldier I am so anxious to befriend and who
is really in need. I have almost completed two pair and think myself exceedingly smart and industrious and suppose I will return to Selma just in
time for my share of Fall sewing for the companies. I expect to make my
appearance there the last of this week. Altho the sun has only made itself
visible twice in thirteen days, I have had a pleasant visit and believe I will
be better for it. I find it a relief to be away from Selma. I am getting tired
of the place and long to return to Ky, and if I did not expect to see you
before next May believe I would go back and be content to witness the
fighting there, provided the secessionists came off victorious—otherwise
with my free speech I would fear for my neck. But you know I feel a
confidence in the success of all engaged on that side. My mother has
not written since her arrival there. I am anxious to receive a letter from
her giving me all the news. Kittie thanks you for your kind message and
reciprocates the desire to meet with and know you but fears she cannot
tolerate Selma long enough to see you. She is perfectly outdone with all
Alabama, but I beg her not to judge all by that one spot. The citizens have
not treated her with the same attention they did me or that a stranger
is entitled to, but I attribute all to the war, which has made a change in
every one and every place. She says she pities any one who lives in Selma
who has never been elsewhere—so with such feelings I do not think we
can retain her much longer in the South. I have not heard from my *Jailor*
brother in Richmond yet but hope I may have a letter awaiting me in
Selma. They only send me yours, thinking I suppose no others will prove
interesting or worthy of my notice. I am vexed that he has such employ-
ment. I was anxious that he might have an opportunity of displaying his
courage like the rest, and I would just as soon have had him remain at
home as to be so engaged.[24]

I believe I wrote you I had sent the daguerreotype some time ago to
Lizzie. She will soon write you very interesting letters and for her age

---

24. David Todd became infamous during the war and after for his stint as commandant
at what became Libby Prison in Richmond. See Berry, *House of Abraham*, 83–91.

writes very well. She is quite young yet I think. You know I have seen her. You seem to believe I am not like my sex as regards curiosity when you mention having such a beautiful present for me. I think as you have *never given me anything* I must claim it before the time you name as proper for its presentation, for should that time never come then I cannot be satisfied and think *how terrible* it is to have *ungratified curiosity*. I know you possess plenty of the article yourself and sometime I will retaliate in the same manner.

I hear Mr. B. Goldsby has returned. I hope it will be possible for me to see him before he returns as I am all curiosity to see some one who can answer some of the thousand queries I have to be propounded, and I think I will call on Mr. Daniels. I see from the papers that Mrs. Hardie is making herself a second Nightengale,[25] but I must see all that I have read to realize the transformation. Do not find out I am *envious of her place.* I wish to keep it a profound secret. I hope as you are opposed to going to Western Virginia that you will not be forced to go, but as you are away I do not know that the place you are sent to makes much difference. But David is ready to go to Dayton, and I must hasten and finish my letter— and excuse me for saying it will be a *relief* for I mean my pen gives me almost a bad temper. It is so indifferent and I can procure no other. I will write you from Selma a long letter and hope to be able to accumulate some interesting details by that time. You will have your patience tried in endeavoring to decipher this letter. All those little details of camp life are very interesting and with a wish to see you soon and that you will pass thro the anticipated battle about the first unharmed, I am ever yours affectionately and truly,

Elodie

Charlottesville, August 22, 1861

I enclose your three last letters, my dear Elodie, desiring that they should be in safe hands and out of reach of our enemy—not because I do not value them. You will keep them for me.

It seems that my whole object now in living is to love you and to be

25. Florence Nightingale (1820–1910), already famous for her *Notes on Nursing*, was consulted early in the war by the Union government. Though they did not take all of her advice, she helped inspire the U.S. Sanitary Commission. For more, see *Collected Works of Florence Nightingale*, ed. Lynn McDonald, vols. 1–16 (Waterloo, Ontario: Wilfrid Laurier University Press, 2001–2012).

loved in return. You are dearer than ever before, and I will willingly bear all the trials of the next eight months if I am to be rewarded by your love. I am in bed endeavoring to write you, tho I sent you a long letter yesterday—but it seems right that I should attempt what you have told me pleases you so much.

I have this morning written brief letters to my sister and our aunt in Charleston merely to gratify them and to let them know where I am.

We have no papers from Richmond this morning, and it has created quite a blank. I had a long conversation today with Col. Randolph,[26] the grandson of Mr. Jefferson. He is a very sensible man, and I like his views on the war. He thinks it will not last more than a year and that Mr. Lincoln will be impeached by the North and removed from office. The difficulty of raising men and money seems great, and unless we make a false move I think the war will be brought to an early and successful close. We have an enemy of at least 60,000 men at Manassas. We are now blocking up the navigation of the Potomac, and before Lincoln is aware of it we will have him besieged in his capital. I prophesy what may take place, but you must not hold me responsible for its failure. How much I have wished in my little sickness that you could have been near me to cool my feverish temples and to have breathed those soft words of comfort that fall as softly upon the ear as the sounds of music. Do I love you dearest? Ask the opening rose if it loves the dew drop. Yes, I love with all the ardor of youth and with the strength of maturer manhood. God has given you to me, and I only hope to be worthy of the trust, to be equal to the duty of protecting my Elodie as she deserves to be guarded and I rewarded in being loved. I must end. I merely intended to write you a note to say that I was better and will return to camp about Saturday. Goodbye dearest. May God keep you safely always.

Ever affectionately yours,
N. H. R. Dawson

Marengo County, August 24, 1861

I have just received and read your letter from Charlottesville dated August 15th, and hasten to reply to it for several reasons: first to express

26. A Confederate colonel, Thomas Jefferson Randolph was the oldest grandson of Thomas Jefferson, notable for the false information he gave a historian, claiming that his uncle, not Thomas Jefferson, was the father of Sally Hemings's children. See Annette Gordon-Reed, *The Hemingses of Monticello: An American Family* (New York: W. W. Norton, 2008).

(or rather try) my sympathy and sorrow that you are again indisposed and hope, ere this, you have recovered your usual health. I wish I felt in a quarrelsome mood that I might scold you for not taking better care of yourself. Your duties, service, the battle, have been too severe, and I am decidedly opposed to your being called upon again to do double duty, thereby fatiguing and exposing yourself unnecessarily or at least to a greater extent than is your share, and in the second place to tell you I am sorry to think I have written in a manner to *hurt you*. Upon so serious a subject, indeed, you must forgive me for writing in the light way I did in regard to so serious an accident. At the time I wrote you, you had not written me of it, and I had just heard it told in an amusing manner and that you were unhurt and really in no danger at the time, and I thought you would wonder and be surprised at my hearing of it and so soon. I only mentioned it to tease, the thought of offending or hurting you being the most distant in my brain. Could you see my long face, you would know how sorry I am and how determined to be more particular as to the subjects I select to indulge my teasing propensity in hereafter and would forgive me at once and dismiss the thought from your mind.

I have received now I think all your letters but the one written on the night of the twenty-first only, last Thursday. I have not written you as often or regularly as usual because the rain and roads prevented my cousin sending to Dayton for letters. I was surprised (pleasantly of course) on Tuesday at receiving a letter from your brother, who was in Richmond at the time of writing, tho' expecting to join you immediately at Manassas. It was so kind and affectionate in its tone that with it and what I have heard of him, I have a great desire to see and know him for myself.

You write as tho' you had been blamed for your, or rather I should say, the conduct of the regiment had been blamed on the day of battle. In all the accounts I have seen, the 4th Ala. has appeared conspicuous, and as far as you are concerned *no one could make me believe you had not acted noble and bravely* on that occasion and *will on any others of a similar nature*. I have *no fear of ever being ashamed of you living or dead* and know you will conduct yourself in a manner calculated to win from me more admiration than I now have for you, *if that is possible*. Tis you are candid, and I hope you will always be so with me and allow me to be so with you. Believe me, we will never have any unkind discussions upon religious subjects. We know each other's feelings and opinions and will respect them, and I do sincerely hope that I may act in this matter, and all others, in a manner to please you and will endeavor to get the *heart right*, which is the most important thing. You are more liberal in your feelings than many of those of other denominations.

The 26th will be four months since you left, but the time seems much longer, and I hope the remaining eight months may pass more quickly than those have done, and if you are only correct in your surmise of part of the army being sent south this winter and you are in that division, I will be so glad for I dread your spending a winter in the cold climate of Virginia, which you would feel very [illegible] after the pleasant winters of your sunny south. You will be surprised that I am still in Marengo, but my cousin was so urgent that I concluded to stay until Monday. Kittie declares she has enjoyed herself more up here than at any time or place since coming to Alabama but is not well enough pleased to remain in Ala. a day longer than she can help but will return at the first good opportunity to Kentucky.

Indeed, you are mistaken, we find no news in the papers. I see no change since the battle and feel as tho' I would be much better satisfied if I only knew what the programme was. I am prepared to hear any day of another engagement, but the feeling produces any other than one of happiness, and I will be happy when your term expires and hope you will keep to your promise unless it is necessary to break it in which case I will excuse you, but I hope never again to go thro' what I have endured so far. I would not write you in this way did I think it would make any difference with you or discourage you in the least, but I am obliged sometimes to give expression to my thoughts and feelings and to you alone. But really you will think me a very *love sick girl*, and I am not ashamed to acknowledge to being in love and never intend to get out. You did not act with judgment when you desired me to write you long letters and freely express my feelings. You will next have to write and desire the contrary. Upon my word you are *cool* giving the length of your foot when you do not even know whether I am going to knit for you or not, but I am engaged at present in knitting you a beautiful pair of socks of the finest yarn that can be spun. Now, do not *dare* to tell me you do not wear yarn for you are obliged after all my labour and patience to reward me by accepting and wearing them. I hope Mrs. M's box may yet reach you, and Mrs. Craighead invited I should knit for my *particular fancy* and furnished the material. I have just finished writing for her a business letter—my first attempt. I know you will think it was a terribly long one and not well-written as their chief beauty is brevity, but you are mistaken—it was actually, truthfully *short*. I will enclose in this a letter to your brother in answer to his which you will please send or give to him as I do not know where to send it. I am afraid if he judges me from my letter he will form a poor opinion as I am a poor scribe and the circumstances attending the answering of such a letter *new* and *trying*. You may read it if you will and send it if you think it will do. I am writing you after night, having been employed some time. My little cousins are impatient for me to walk on the porch with them. They seem very fond of us and are very interesting. I wish you to know them and their mother. At last, but reluctantly, I must stop writing and no doubt *you are satisfied*. Why do you always say that your letters are dull and tiresome and that I must weary of them? Do you judge the feeling produced by mine is felt by me when yours are received? No, indeed, they are *always welcome* and would be were they twice as long and often. And now with a wish that we may meet soon and a constant prayer for your safety and speedy return and a proclaimer of peace, I am every your,

    Affectionate,
    Elodie

Charlottesville, August 25, 1861

Not feeling strong enough to attend church this morning, I have read services with a portion of scripture from your bible, in the leaves of which are carefully preserved your two notes of 21 and 24th April last. In the note of 24, accompanying the gift, you use these consoling words: "I send you a bible and when you see it and read it, think of me as bending over mine and praying for your safety." The bible is never used without the remembrance of these words being in my mind, and I feel satisfied that your prayers have had an influence in my favor. May they always ascend on my behalf. In the note of the 21, the first in which you write to me as your accepted suitor, after speaking of the unsolved enigma of my love for you, you tell me, "I have nothing to give you save a heart overflowing with love, happiness undeserved, entirely your own, under any and all circumstances, unalterable by time or change."

Could I have asked for more, my dear Elodie, or could you have given more than you have promised? My heart felt sad then that you so con-fidingly loved one who might not prove equal to your high opinion, for the discovery would cause you more pain than it could give to anyone else except it were him who had forfeited your love. When I do so, I will have no desire to live but will wish to be quickly sent to that place where the "weary are at rest" and the "wicked cease from their troubles." I will not, however, anticipate such an evil but will tarry for its coming with the hope that it will never come. It is four months today since I bid you

adieu, but it seems to have been an age, and I hope that the next eight
months will pass more rapidly. I hope, at any rate, to be able to obtain
a furlough in December, when I will be able to make amends for all of
my failures to do my duty towards you. I love you with that adoration
which a man gives to a lady whom he feels to be greater and better than
himself, and my love, as I have frequently told you, is hardly distinguish-
able from religious feeling. I know that it is worthily bestowed and the
indulgence of the feeling, like the cultivation of any virtue, makes me
wiser and *better*. "But enough of this," I almost hear you say, "If thou lovest
me Hal . . ."[27]

There are rumors here this morning of the advance of Gen. McClellan
across the Potomac with a large force in the vicinity of Fairfax. If so, I
must rejoin my regiment tomorrow. I place no credit in the rumor, however, as I do not believe that the Federal army is in condition to resume
the offensive at this time. Our regiment is suffering greatly from sickness. Four captains are absent and several other officers. Lieut. McCraw
is among them and has gone to Richmond to Mrs. Hopkins'[28] hospital.
I hope he will soon be well. Alabama has done little for her soldiers
while other states are erecting hospitals and dispensing cordials, med-
icines, and clothing to their soldiers. So. Ca. has a hospital and a large
store here. Some of the first ladies and gentlemen in the state are the
superintendents.

A surgeon told me of a most remarkable case last night, and I will
venture to tell it to you. Among the wounded was a man who had been
shot in the head, at the junction of the occipital and parietal bones.
The wound was thought to be a mere superficial one as for two weeks
he walked about the town complaining of no pain. About that time he
complained of violent headaches and was thrown into convulsions. Upon
examining his head, it was found that the ball had entered and it was removed but at the end of a week the man died. His head was then opened,
and it was found that the ball had entered the brain and had penetrated

---

27. A reference to Shakespeare's *King Henry IV*, act 2, scene 4: "No more of that, Hal,
an thou lovest me!"

28. Juliet Hopkins (1818–1890) converted tobacco factories into hospitals when her
husband, Alabama businessman Arthur Hopkins, moved to Richmond to establish a hospi-
tal for Alabamians. She was widely known during and after the war for her devotion to the
Confederate cause and soldiers. See Bertram Wyatt-Brown, "Juliet Ann Opie Hopkins," in
Women in the American Civil War, ed. Lisa Tendrich Frank, vol. 1 (Santa Barbara, Calif.: ABC
Clio, 2008), 335–336.

it for near two inches, and two large pieces of the skull were also found driven into the brain. And yet this man had lived in this condition two weeks without inconvenience. Truth is frequently stranger than fiction.

Yesterday was a beautiful day, and in the evening I went out to see some of my wounded. It was a real October evening, and the soft atmosphere and the undulating scenery of mountain and meadow carried me back to "days of auld lang syne"[29] when as a boy I used to run over the hills of upper So. Ca. some twenty years ago. On that score, what changes have come and how little of life I have lived.

Evening.

I have just received your long letter from the Cane Brake and am delighted to know that you are well and have had a pleasant visit. I hope you have received some of the letters you were expecting from me before this time, but I fear they will not prove interesting as I begin to think I am a very uninteresting fellow and fear you will find me so before the end of ten years.

The rumors about a fight at Fairfax prove to be untrue. We must have other battles, and you must be prepared for the worst my dear Elodie. My escape in the last was almost a miracle as I was in the thickest of the fight and was alongside of many who were killed and wounded. In the next, I cannot hope to be so fortunate.

I will go to Manassas on Tuesday as my boy Andrew[30] is quite sick and will not be well enough before then to go up with me. The sun is now going down, and as I wish to write a letter to Mr. McCraw at Richmond, I must close.

I will hope now to receive a long, interesting letter from my dear Elodie. I assure her that her letters are more pleasant to me than the sounds of falling water. With much love and a *kiss for the ring* on your finger, I remain yours,

Very affectionately,

N. H. R. Dawson

---

29. A Scottish poem written by Robert Burns and set to music, the phrase means "days gone by."

30. Andrew is probably one of the twenty-four slaves owned by Nathaniel. "N H R Dawson," 1860 U.S. Federal Census—Slave Schedules, Selma, Dallas County, Ala.

Manassas Junction, August 29, 1861

I reached the camp yesterday safely and am once more in the midst of camp luxuries and comforts. I am glad to say, however, that I am very well. The love I bear you, my dear Elodie, and the intimate future and present relation that exists between us and my desire to let you know all that concerns me makes it proper, on account of rumors that I have heard have reached Selma, to make to you, if to no others, a personal explanation of my conduct at the battle of Manassas, for I have no concealment as I am conscious of having done my duty.

I was with my company and the regiment during the battle and fought as well as others did. When we retreated, I was among the last to retire for I was in the rear of Col. Jones, owing to an accident, when he was shot. I was near him with the chaplain and in crossing a fence in our way, a ball knocked it down, and those who saw have told me I was knocked ten feet on the ground. When I recovered I found my ankle badly sprained. I followed on and overtook the regiment almost a quarter of a mile ahead, when an attempt was made to rally it. Everything was in great confusion as the Yankees were following us and were then flanking us on both wings. I went up to the colors and called on the Cadets to rally. The disorder is indescribable. Col. Law was now wounded, Col. Jones reported dead, and either with or without an order, for I heard none, the regiment, or that part of it that was there, again retired in my confusion, and brave men had to run for their lives as the enemy now poured upon us a murderous fire of musketry and artillery. In passing thro this many were killed and wounded. Here I saw Major Scott fall to my right and in front of me. I was about to go to his assistance when others took him up, and I went on, as I assure you I was then anxious to get out of range of the enemy's fire. This I know was a common feeling. In a few moments, I came across Geo. Mims, who told me he was mortally wounded and asked me to help him along. I told him I was unable to do so from fatigue and lameness, but that I would not leave him and would get him assistance. This took place in a piece of woods in which we were. In a few moments a soldier came along who, at my request, took charge of George. We then separated. I met many members of the regiment, all of whom told me that the regiment was cut to pieces and two companies taken prisoner. I was fully of this impression. I met no troops coming to our aid but seeing a battery of artillery went toward it. Before I reached it, the battery hitched up and retreated. The shot from the enemy's artillery here was terrible and several balls fell very near, and the bombs burst on all sides. The next object I saw was a body of men around a house. I made for them, and before reaching the place they all ran off. I found some wounded men here, and among them Geo. Mims who was under a tree suffering terribly. He called to me and asked me to take him to a place where a surgeon could see him. I asked where the surgeons were, and he pointed to a piece of woods. I had George taken up by four men, and we went to the place where I found a number of wounded Alabamians had their wounds dressed and sent them on to Manassas. Before reaching this place, I met Lieut. Wilson[31] of my company who had just arrived from Piedmont, too late to be with us in the battle, much to his chagrin, as I have never known a man more anxious than he was to get into a battle, nor one who would bear himself more gallantly. This was between one and two o'clock. I was busily engaged until three o'clock about the wounded. After this time, I was so fatigued and lame that we got into the shade and remained there until the firing ceased and the prisoners were coming in and the battle over. We were then told that the regiment had gone to Manassas and, for the first time since my separation from the regiment, I was told by one of Gen. Bee's aids, who was carrying him off the field, that the remnant of the regiment was about a half mile behind and near Lein's house. It was then late, the battle was over, and at about *five* o'clock Lieut. Wilson and myself started for Manassas and reached there *after dark*. I found a number of the regiment there with their arms stacked and had got supper from the quartermaster.

This is a plain statement of the whole matter, and I make it for your satisfaction. Over three hundred of our regiment became separated and never fell into it after the retreat. As brave and gallant men as breathe. Why I have been made a victim I cannot understand. If I could find out the author of the reports, I will hold him to a strict account. No officer in the regiment, I am glad to say, attaches any importance to this slander, except that it is calculated to injure me. If it were only on my own account I would care little, but as all connected with me are liable to injury, I am much annoyed. I will take steps here to correct the reports. I was not aware of their existence until the day I went to Charlottesville, when Mr. Pegues wrote me of them, and I was not aware of their circulation at Selma until a few days ago.

I trust my dear Elodie has not believed them. I retract the expression,

---

31. John R. Wilson, age thirty, of Selma, was a lieutenant in Nathaniel's company. Alabama Civil War Muster Rolls, 1861–1865, Alabama Department of Archives and History.

for I know that she could not have done so. I fear many opportunities will be afforded me of vindicating my courage on the battlefield, and I am brave enough to admit that I am not over anxious to get into battles, for I know and appreciate their dangers.

I would do nothing to forfeit your love, but I am not willing that your name should be associated with one that was disgraced. I love you too well and too purely for that sacrifice. I will prefer to die on the battlefield than to live with a tarnished name.

I was with the regiment during the whole time it was engaged, had twenty-three men, out of fifty, killed and wounded, and exposed myself to all the perils of the fight. After I was separated about 150 of the regiment was rallied but never again taken into battle. If I staid out, I am like them, for they staid out also, but was separated by an accident and did not run off intentionally. A coward prefers to be with a crowd rather than to be alone and will generally shelter himself with his comrades. I would have much preferred to have been with the regiment than to have been separated from it.

I must now close this letter and will beg you to consider its contents.

Goodby dearest. Write me soon. May God preserve you always.

Ever affectionately yours,
N. H. R. Dawson

Selma, September 1, 1861

As usual I am writing you my Sunday letter and as I sit by my window looking at the bright sunshine I indulge in the wish that some of its beams could enter my heart and cause them to take the place of so much darkness and obscure some of the unhappy forebodings in possession there. Your long silence has made me anxious and uneasy and I cannot imagine what has become of you, whether you are ill or have gone from Manassas to some other portion of Virginia devoid of Post Offices, your last letters having been written the 22nd of August, and I have received none since. See how completely you have spoiled me by writing so often and how ungrateful I am, growling when you are silent a little while. But from the fact of your writing me you were sick have my fears that you may be ill arisen, and were I to know such were the case I would be so miserable I would not know what to do with myself.

I have spent a bad week. Your silence, my brother's indisposition, the unfortunate situation of Kentucky, and my Mother, brother and sister, besides other relatives and dear friends in the midst of her troubles, have given me food for melancholy reflection, and from the latter there is no hope of receiving any information, the mail arrangements having been again broken up. I wish I were with them or they with me so that our fate might be one or at least known to each other. Surely there is no other family in the land placed in the exact situation of ours, and I hope will never be so unfortunate as to be so surrounded by trials so numerous.

There is much conjecture in town as to the next movement of Gen'ls Beauregard and Johnston. Some contend that they will enter Maryland and help her to throw off her chains,[32] while others assert their belief in the immediate movement on the City of Washington. I know nothing, say nothing, however [I] wish that if another battle is in contemplation it will soon be fought and the victory ours and so great that the Federals will be willing to try peace and we willing and kind enough to give it to them. The ladies of the military aid society are anxious to raise funds for the winter clothing of the companies and expect to give tableaux and a concert combined next week for the accomplishment of their design. Matt, Mrs. Cabell[33] and Miss Donnell are the managers of the affair and all the young ladies in town, excepting your honorable writer, participants, and I think from the programme they will be beautiful.

Just here I have been handed your two last letters of the 23rd and 26th and as you write me your health is restored all my fears have flown to the wind, and I feel much relieved. You do not know how happy I am when I am the recipient of a letter from you. My face is all smiles, my thoughts all pleasant, and it is such a gratification to know that you have *remembered me four months*. How my letters must amuse you. I am such a rattle-tongue and write you doubtless many details uninteresting, but you must know by this time, mine is an original style of letter writing.

We have received a letter from my brother David this evening. He is better and says those terrible bleedings of his lungs were produced by the excitement of his arrest. I feel so sorry for him. He is so mortified and hurt at the manner in which he has been treated, declares he will play janitor no longer but go into active service.[34] I hope he will. It makes me angry to have anyone offend my brothers or sisters. I would prefer their harming me, and he says he has been unjustly wronged.

---

32. Elodie was not alone in supposing that Maryland was held in the Union only by force of arms. Robert E. Lee made much the same mistake in his Maryland campaign of 1862.

33. Patter Caball, age twenty-three, married to Dr. P. H. Caball (see July 14, 1861, note 125).

34. On August 9, David Todd was arrested for "having acted contrary to the orders . . . of the military department of Richmond" for his mismanagement of the Richmond prisons. Berry, *House of Abraham*, 88.

I was so sorry to hear F. Hatteras[35] had been retaken and so many prisoners. What a pity. I suppose now they think it will be nothing to reoccupy all the Southern forts and that will be the winter programme. If so I hope you will be sent South, or if not hope you may be able to make a visit in December. I shall be so disappointed if you do not and my admiration for Johnston all gone if he refuses you permission, but *twenty days is too short*. You say you are astonished at none of George Mim's family going on to see him. Mr. Mims received a letter from some gentleman who is or was nursing him and which assured him he should have every attention, and as they were poor, I suppose they did not wish to incur the expense. I had the pleasure of meeting Mr. Davidson in the Canebrake and amused him very much with my many questions and my great interest in the whole proceedings. Does Mr. McCraw know of our engagement? From a little circumstance I think he knows or suspects and has communicated it to Miss Ella, and the truth to tell a great many do know it, but I am so independent now that I do not care or would not deny it. Sometimes it seems hard to realize all that has transpired in the last five months. It appears more like a painful dream until something reminds me of the stern reality of the past and present condition of affairs. But I must finish off. I enclose a letter to your brother which you can read if you desire, but you will be as much ashamed of it as I am.

Manassas Junction, September 2, 1861

Your letter of the 24 and 26 ulto., my dear Elodie, was received this morning, and I assure you the expressions of sympathy and love running through its pages but add to the deep love I bear you. Woman, when she truly loves, loves more ardently when its object is in danger, and I have the great satisfaction of knowing that thro' evil and good report your love remains unchanged. You are indeed a ministering angel, and the devotion of a whole life to your happiness will be but a poor reward for your love.

I wrote you on my return to camp of the existence of certain rumors at Selma in regard to my conduct. The officers of the regiment and of my

35. The Battle of Forts Hatteras and Clark on August 28, 1861, marked an important transition in Union strategy from the "On to Richmond!" impulse that ended in debacle at Bull Run to the implementation of Scott's Anaconda Plan. With the fall of Hatteras, the Union blockade began its steady but relentless constriction of the Confederate coast.

own company, I hear, are very indignant and will take steps to vindicate me. Several officers like myself were separated, in the general *rout* of the regiment, from their commands and left the field early in the day. I was in such condition that I could not do so, even if I had desired, but if I had been well, I should not have attempted to rejoin the regiment when there was no probability of finding it. I do not know whether I shall notice these slanders thro' the papers, but I have written fully to my friends and asked them to do as they deemed best. I am no candidate for a pistol reputation, but any man who doubts my courage or who will impugn it can have the pleasure of testing it. But why should I trouble you, my dearest, with such an unpleasant topic.

I will wear the socks with a great deal of pleasure and will ever value them in after years as a mark of your love. I can never dare to leave you, even if you were to require it. I was sick all yesterday in my tent and spent a part of it in reading your bible and your letters. I am up again today, but am excused from brigade drill this afternoon as I was unwilling to undergo the fatigue. I have received Mrs. Mathews's box and luxuriated over the cordials and am now wearing a pair of boots sent by Mr. Mathews. Lizzie contributed a cake of nice soap. By the way, I am now using a cake sent me by you in the little writing case at Dalton. How greatly blessed in having such friends and sweetheart!

I beg your pardon for impressing the idea that I was hurt at any remark of yours. You must excuse me for having been so unfortunate. You have never irritated me, and I never expect you to do anything that will, as I know how sweet your temper is and how much you love me. I wrote to Mr. Averitt recently and sent him your message. He has been so kind that I felt it my duty to do so, and I am glad I did and know you will be pleased to hear it. I do not think he will be married shortly, tho it is merely an opinion. I wish my dearest I were married to you now, but it may be that it is put off to a time you have indicated. I hope to get a furlough in December for thirty days which will give me an opportunity of seeing you, and we will certainly be able to enjoy the evenings together. I hope God will permit us to be married as my whole desire to live is to be your husband and to discharge my duties to God and man. We know nothing of our movements, but I still think at the right time that we will be advanced toward Washington and perhaps into Maryland. We are now ordered to keep on hand three days' cooked rations in order to be ready for a march at any moment. Our troops are suffering very much from sickness. In several regiments near us about three deaths take place daily. We hear the volleys of musketry over the poor fellows very frequently.

I met with such kindness at Charlottesville and spent my last evening at
Mr. Cochran's. Miss Mary Preston Cochran is his daughter, and as I wrote
to you a cousin of yours and Mrs. Craighead. Miss Mary is like you in her
manners, and you would like her. I am to stay there if I am wounded.

I very much regret to hear of your brother David's sickness and truly
hope you will soon have better tidings from him.

I am so glad Reginald[36] wrote you. He is a noble fellow, and I hope
he will live to return home to reap all that he deserves. His regiment is
still at Richmond but will be ordered up to this point I presume. He will
be much gratified to hear from you I know. I have had him under my
charge since he was nine years old and of course feel a great interest in
his welfare. He will love you very much.

I have just heard that Col. Jones was dying this morning. Poor man. I
spoke to him last on the battlefield as we were coming off together. We
were separated in crossing the fence where I was knocked down, and he
was shot about forty steps in front of me. The evening before the battle
he told me he expected to be killed.

Mrs. Hardie left for home on Saturday. I have seen but little of her
since the battle. Mr. Hardie has been made quartermaster. He is a gallant gentleman and will make us an efficient officer. Our present commander, Col. Ben Allston of So. Ca., is a perfect martinet but exceedingly
courteous and pleasant. He is a young man of about thirty, small and
handsome. He is the son of Gov Allston[37] and is a graduate of West Point.
I am glad to hear such good accounts of John. Tell him that Andrew was
improving when I heard from him.

I received a brief and friendly letter today from Col. Byrd. He seems
much interested in my welfare and favor.

A wagon has arrived with chickens, and they are being brought into
camp—quite a treat, I assure you. We had very nice vegetables, however,
for dinner today, and I had a good appetite.

The present I spoke of cannot be made until you *take possession of my
house*. But it is there boxed up awaiting your arrival. It is a handsome one
is all I can tell you. I hope Mr. Hagood will regain his temper as you are
certainly deprived of much pleasure by its loss. Can't Miss Kate interpose?
Tell her that she must come back to Ala. to see you and that we will then
have peace and an opportunity of showing her some of our heroes. I
regret her impressions are not more pleasant.

---

36. Nathaniel's brother, Reginald Huger Dawson.
37. The sixty-seventh governor of South Carolina, Robert Francis Withers Allston held
office from 1856 to 1858.

I have now, my dearest, written you a long letter, which I hope you will find interesting.

With much love and many prayers for your happiness, I remain,

Your sincerely attached and affectionate friend,

N. H. R. Dawson

I always like you to write just as you feel. Such letters are pleasant even in their sadness as they convince me of your love and confidence. I love to be sad at times. It is a pleasure to think of sad things. Never let the fear of affecting me control your feelings. I always wish them to be outspoken. I am always candid with you and tell you what I feel and think. Your letters are a comfort and a solace, even one line. If you saw me nightly kissing your miniature, you would know that I was in love. I think last at night and first in the morning of my God and you, my dear Elodie.

Manassas Junction, September 8, 1861

I have just read with a great deal of pleasure your letter of Sept. 1, enclosing one to Reginald. I assure you, my dear Elodie, that the more you write me the more admiration I have for your head and heart and the more deeply do I feel how much I should thank God for having given me your love. If circumstances could only permit me to fly to you and to remain with you always afterwards, my happiness would be complete. I look forward to no happiness that is not associated with your warm heart and speaking face. No man can love more truly than I do, and no one can love more *worthily*. I think you are *peerless*. My love for you partakes of religious character. Four months of my term have expired, and only twice as long a period separates us, for I have promised you I intend to return then to keep my promise to *you and to myself*. I owe you duties paramount to any other person, and I will perform them. Why do you still write excuses for your letters? They bring me happiness and this should satisfy you. I know that my letters are far from being specimens of the style of Addison[38] or Madame de Stael.[39] Still as I am not writing for a critical age but one that is willing to overlook all deficiencies, I am not uneasy and write *currente calamo.*[40]

---

38. Joseph Addison (1672–1719) was a British poet and playwright.

39. Anne Louise Germaine de Staël-Holstein (1766–1817) was a French woman celebrated for her eloquence.

40. Latin phrase meaning "with a running hand, rapidly, offhandedly."

I am glad to hear that the ladies of Selma are still engrossed in the patriotic effort to supply our wants. They will always be thanked by grateful hearts. Let them send no articles that are not necessary as we have no way of transporting them and our soldiers are recklessly improvident, even of such articles as blankets and clothing. I will never again take command of a volunteer company, entre nous,[41] and will never take less than a Lieut. Col. commission, as I know I am more capable than many who occupy higher positions. I can afford to be vain with you, so you must excuse me. I know you think me very vain, and should not give you reason to think me more so.

Lieut. McCraw does know of our engagement confidentially, and many in camp suspect it and seem to regard it as a fact. Several persons from Selma, I understand, have mentioned it as a fact recognized there. See how much trouble you have got into by loving me? I sympathize deeply, deeply, with you, my dear Elodie, in the troubles of your family. But I do really think you should not give yourself so much anxiety as all of those who have any freedom of action are in the discharge of their duty. But I know a nature as sensitive as yours shrinks from contact with the rougher dispositions of the world, and you cannot help thinking much over the divisions that unhappily exist in your family. You speak of the arrest of your brother David. When was he arrested? I have heard nothing of it. I hope with you that he will be placed on active duty. I will forward your letter to Reginald to Richmond where he still remains. I have had the curiosity to read it, and I assure you it will be a very agreeable and welcome one to him. I approve it or I would not send it. Does this compliment satisfy you?

I am again officer of the day and am spending a part of it writing to you and hoping that you may be engaged, as it is Sunday, in writing to me. As I write I have heard three volleys of musketry over the dead of neighboring regiments. We have lost but six so far from disease. Gen. Syd Moore's brother died in our regiment a few days since. A nice young man from North Alabama. Several of the Cadets have left and are leaving on furloughs and discharges for Selma and home. Geo. F. Melton, our little drummer, will bear this letter. He had his arm dislocated and has had fever, and as he is quite young I deemed it best to send him home. Send for him and he will give you in detail all the news from camp. I think he is much attached to us and leaves reluctantly.

We have no definite information of our future movements. I think,

---

41. French, meaning "between us," "in confidence."

however, when we move from this place, it will be to some point near the Potomac. Gen's Johnston and Beauregard are very busy and vigilant. We never will attack Washington in front but may cross the river above and get into the rear, between the capital and Baltimore. Write to me at Manassas still until I write to the contrary.

The weather is that of the pleasant fall season. The woods will soon put on the drapery of Autumn, and in November we will be in winter quarters—where I cannot say. Our regiment is now about being paid off and our soldiers are in high spirits. The battle has produced a visible change in the regiment. You hear much less hilarity and joyous songs. My own company has lost some of its best men. I received a letter a few days since from Mr. Averitt, which I am tempted to enclose to you as it is very kind. I will probably send it.

I hope I will be able in the winter to get a furlough, but don't you think it better that I should wait till I go to remain, never to leave you? I should dislike to leave you again. Do you think you would be willing to return with me if we were quartered near a comfortable place where you could be and where you could see me occasionally? Mrs. Hardie will be here in the winter and the wives of many of the officers. If this question troubles you, do not answer and wait until I see you and we can talk of it then,

And now dearest I must close without having said all that I would but enough to satisfy you for the present. My kind regards to your sister and Mr. White.

Goodbye dearest. With many prayers for your happiness, I remain,

Ever yours affty,

N. H. R. Dawson

I have sent you the *Richmond Examiner* from which you will get all the last war news. It is the best paper in the city & will serve in place of *frequent letters from me*. Have you received it?

Manassas, September 10, 1861

Although I wrote you yesterday by George Melton, I cannot resist the temptation afforded by the return of Dr. Paisly[42] and Mr. Price to write

---

42. Dr. Hugh S. Paisley was a dentist before the war who enlisted as a private in Nathaniel's regiment. Mr. Price may be related to Alfred C. Price, age twenty-four, second sergeant in Nathaniel's company. Alabama Civil War Muster Rolls, 1861–1865, Alabama Department of Archives and History; 1860 Census: Selma.

you again, my very dear Elodie. I find that I love you with all my heart
and soul and next to the God who made me. To be assured of your love is
such a happiness that I can hardly believe that I am not suffering under a
delusion, but I hope one of these days to awaken to the happy reality. Do
you really think that it has been a task for me to remember you for four
months? Have I not loved and worshipped you since we returned from
the inauguration of Pres. Davis in January, and shall I ever forget that
eventful night which inaugurated a new government and a new love in my
heart which had been frozen, as I thought, never to be warmed with life
again? No, my dearest love, it would be strange that any one blessed with
the promise of your hand could love less than your humble writer, and if
I [prove] faithless to all other duties and promises I can never, while life
and sanity are mine, cease to love you with an Eastern devotion. But I can
see you laughing over this loving letter and wondering what has made me
so affectionate. I hear the sounds of violin and flute, and the soft music
carries me back to your side, recall the moonlight walk, and the hurried
parting. It is pleasant to recall these incidents. "What greater happiness
is there for two human souls than to feel that they are joined for life, to
strengthen each other in all labor, *to rest on each other in all sorrow*, to minister to each other in all pain, to be one with each other in silent, imperish-
able memories at the moment of the last parting."[43] This is the language
of one who knew the instincts of the heart, and I adopt it and ask you if
you do not feel its truth. I do and apply it to our relation to each other.

We are still here. No symptoms of our moving yet. Gen. Beauregard
has moved his headquarters to Fairfax and Gen. Johnston will change his
to Centerville, both in the direction of Alexandria. We are now erecting
batteries to command the Potomac. When this is done we will think of
advancing upon Washington. If I escape the battle it will be pleasant,
but I sometimes think it will be better for me and mine to fall upon the
battlefield, so foul have been the slanders upon my fame.

Drs. Paisly and Mr. Price will leave today and bear this letter. If you can,
please see them. They are friends of mine and will be glad to give Mrs.
White and yourself full and just accounts of the battle and of our regiment. Mr. Price behaved very gallantly, was wounded in trying to bring
Col. Jones off the field. Let this be known to the young ladies. He has
an unfortunate wound in the foot, but I tell him I wish it were mine

---

43. Nathaniel is quoting (pretty closely) a line from George Eliot's (1819–1880)
Adam Bede.

that I could have a good excuse for going home. Our regiment was paid off today, and the soldiers are all luxuriating upon chickens and other comforts in the eating line. Poor fellows, their hardships and trials are numerous but are borne with great patience.

I wrote to Richmond last week ordering the editors to send you the *Daily Examiner*. It is by far the best paper in the city and will give you all the war news. When you read it you can imagine that it is a daily letter from me.

Write me long, *original* letters and always write, my dear Elodie, as you feel. I think you should never hesitate to tell me of all your anxieties and fears. I may be able to remove some of them. What is the great luxury of love but that it permits one's heart to open itself freely to another, to tell of its joys and sorrows? When we meet to love and to be separated no more again in this world, I hope you will be able to understand fully how deeply I love you, how essential you are to my happiness. No words can express my feelings, for I love deeply, deeply. Have you never loved before?

I insist upon your telling me your *age* and birthday. You should treat my requests with more consideration than to laugh them off. I shall expect Dr. Paisly and Mr. Price to bring me the promised little present which was to assure me of your sympathy. And now dearest Tattoo has beat and taps have sounded and the camp is veiled in darkness, and I must bid you good night. I look upon your miniature as it lies before me and as I say good night I have borne it to my lips. The original I hope will not object to this sacrilege. But I must tell you farewell. May God have you in his keeping, and may pleasant dreams of future happiness visit your pillow.

Adieu my own loved Elodie.

Ever affty yours,

N. H. R. Dawson

Selma, September 15, 1861

I have just returned from church and feel my next duty is to write to you, and I wish all I had to perform were as agreeable for then I know they would be performed with the most cheerful alacrity of a ready & willing heart. All week I have been as busy as could be, sewing for soldiers, the Guards & Cadets & was glad to say there is plenty of winter clothes for them cut out & being made and they will soon receive their boxes, and hope Mrs. Hardie will no longer "be ashamed of her ragged friends, and the people of Selma." I think I would *use my fingers more* in trying to mend for them and *my tongue less* were I her tho were all to *sound their own works* she would be thrown in the shade by some of the noble and generous women of this place who are more silent. You will think I am too hard on her and perhaps I am but I have heard much of her from others and who knew her disposition better than I, and in and during my acquaintance with her I liked her well enough, but never saw much to admire, and it may be because I was prejudiced against her and I could not see her good traits that I have such an opinion of her.

We had no news from my mother since she entered Kentucky and I am very anxious to hear again. You cannot imagine how distressed I was to hear such *terrible and disgraceful* news from my birthplace. I had expected better and I almost made myself sick *crying* and bemoaning the fallen condition of my state. I am sorry to have lived to see the day when proud noble old Ky. should act in this manner. Tis true those of my family who are free to act are doing their duty, and I have yet another brother on Ky. soil, who will do his, in defending his rights or sell his life in the attempt. This is my youngest brother and my favorite. A better brother or son never lived than he has been, and I cannot give him up. Never before have we been long separated and never can our love and affection diminish for each other, even should we never meet again or should he fall I will ever fondly cherish his memory.

You see I am sad today, and you may be right in thinking I take these cares and troubles to heart too much, but I have tried in every way to drive them from me, but I cannot, tho' I employ every moment & take no time for thought, yet they find their way to me. I do not despair but hope soon the silver lining of the dark cloud now hanging o'er us will be visible, and we will be able to recognize the good intended by our trials and I know I am doing wrong to murmur so much against them.

I supposed you had seen an account of my Brother's arrest in the Richmond Papers. He was arrested for having some of the dead Yankee prisoners who had been dead a day or two in prison coffined and sent to the Qr. Master's department, as his commander told him "to be commented and gazed upon as a spectacle for the public by standing there before his (the Qr. Master's door)." I believe upon investigating the matter, it was found he had been in neglect of his duty and not my brother. At any rate I hope he will not be called on to play jailor any more.[44]

---

44. There is great disagreement as to what exactly David had done. According to his enemies, especially Northern prisoners, David had allowed an epidemic to run rampant in the jails and then become so exasperated in dealing with Yankee corpses that he "kicked

Why should you think it wrong to tell me of your cares? Do I not write you of my several ones? And it would trouble me far more to think you would hesitate to tell me anything that was annoying you, than the fact of making them all known to me. What ought I to think and feel about the subject when you express yourself as having a hesitancy in troubling me with your affairs? I did not see the letters Col. Byrd[45] had altho it was your wish that I should, because I preferred not asking Bro Clem to read them and felt perfectly satisfied with your own statement of affairs, and I think the report has died out as I do not hear it mentioned now. My blood used to boil, and I got into two difficulties about it, but they have blown over now. I *won't* knit Mr. Price any sock, he may not have intended to convey such an impression, but he should have been more particular in writing of such an important Event, and he will go without almost before I do it. I do not know any of the returned and have not seen any of them. George Mims went immediately home I think. I was very much pleased with Mr. Averitt's letter. It was kind and *pretty*. He certainly possesses some beautiful traits of character, and I think is a good man. I am glad you wrote and delivered my message. You have not a better friend, and we should overlook the faults and sometimes *very disagreeable ways* many of them have, when we see qualities to admire and that redeems them. I am telling you the best way to do, but remember *I* do not *act* always as I advise. It is easier to say than to do you know.

Evening.

I was really disappointed I did not receive a letter from you this morning. I felt just in the mood for reading one and suppose I will have to adopt your plan of reading over old ones when I fail to receive a new one. I received the paper and am very much obliged. I see every day the *Richmond*

[one] body out into the street, where it laid overnight." Having desecrated corpses, David had overstepped the bounds of moral decency so completely that Richmond's provost marshal had felt compelled to step in and relieve him of command. David's own story, as told to Elodie, suggests that he had only displayed Yankee bodies in their coffins, and then only at the behest of his superiors. Regardless, it is clear that David was part of a culture reminiscent of Abu Ghraib, where, early in a war, enemy prisoners are treated as an inhuman novelty. Berry, *House of Abraham*, 85–91.

45. Reacting to the charge of Nathaniel's cowardice, Colonel Byrd had published a card in the *Richmond Dispatch* asking the public to "suspend an unfavorable opinion until the facts were known." Nathaniel appreciated this, though he clearly wished Byrd had gone further and completely stomped out what he regarded as a malicious slander.

Dispatch, but there is so little to be known until our next battle is over that there is a general complaint of the dullness of the papers and times, but I do not intend to receive papers from you in place of letters. No indeed, I want my letters and will have them. If you do not write I shall think you are *getting tired of me* and do not wish me to write to you. I heard the other day from Mrs. Reese[46] that the 4th Alabama Regiment would be held in reserve the next battle. Is it true? I wish the anticipated battle was over and hope it may be decisive, but I fear the plan Kentucky has adopted will only add to our troubles by prolonging the war. Perhaps Southern Ky. will secede and join Tenn. My Brother-in-Law, Mr. Helm, is in the camp down about the Tenn. line with the "Southern Rights Men." Mr. Thompson is getting up another concert for the week after next. The proceeds are intended for the Ala. hospital. Ella McCraw and I are both going to assist and will doubtless sing again together. Mrs. [illegible], Mrs. [illegible], Miss Ingraham, Mr. Marshall and a Professor *Somebody* from Marion are the only ones (and Lydia Strong) to take part. The week after there will be tableaux for the M. A. Society to help in furnishing clothes for the winter. Mr. Dedman's company[47] has gone and one day last week six hundred soldiers left Selma from different parts of the community.

And now I will proceed to answer the question contained in your last, which as you are not present to witness my blushes or confusion I can make some reply to. I am willing to return with you but do not know that it would be for the best as your movements are always so uncertain and you might be compelled to leave me even there and go to Washington. I would I believe be happier there than here and think I would be equal to any hardship or privation that I might be called upon to bear. Your own example would encourage me to make an effort anyhow. Before taking any decided steps, however, I would prefer if possible to hear from my mother. If I fail in that, I'll do as I think best and not consult anybody else about the matter. I will write to a cousin in Asheville who will forward a letter for me if it can be done, but do you think of all the trouble, care, and anxiety I might occasion you? Would my *occasional society* compensate you for all this? Think well before you take more trouble. Do you

---

46. Mother of four, E. L. Reese, age forty-three, was married to J. T. Reese, a captain in Company A of Nathaniel's regiment. 1860 Census: Selma.

47. James M. Dedman organized the Phoenix Reds, a Selma company composed almost entirely of working men from the city. Dedman was severely wounded at Vicksburg. Harvey H. Jackson, *Inside Alabama: A Personal History of My State* (Tuscaloosa: University of Alabama Press, 2004), 89–90.

not feel that you are annoyed and troubled with your company and all your privations enough without having somebody to give you more than all together? I know I would feel your leaving me again more than I did at first, but still if it is better that it should be so, I am willing to bear it rather than you should not come. *I must see you*, and I'll think there is but a short time for you to remain before returning for "good and ever" and content myself in that way and as you say we can talk this matter over then. Surely I will hear from home before December if not only between us, you as Lawyer and I as *judge*, we can arrange the matter without any assistance unless you want to call in *Mr. Wetmore*, and I'll take the advice of *your friend* Tho. J. Q. S.

Kittie says she is much obliged for the ambrotype you sent her. When Mr. Wetmore sends me my photograph, I intend to be generous enough to give one that I have that she may show you in Kentucky. She still speaks of returning the first opportunity, now that we think mother will not return this winter. She seems so dissatisfied and anxious to return that it will be better. I would be in the same way if it was not for you. I could not see you or write to you there. There is some excitement in town about Mr. Charley Woods who went to Gov. Winston's[48] tent with the intention of killing him, but something fortunately prevented his doing so and no one has heard what his punishment will be. He (Gov. W) is very unpopular in the regiment and his men vowed if ever they got into an engagement they would kill him and President Davis says that regiment shall not fight. Some weeks ago one of two letters were written back here by the Blues in which all the abuse that could be heaped on anyone was given to Gov. W. They went over Selma and some one wrote to Gov. W. about them and nearly everyone suspects Dr. Mabry, and I heard two gentlemen say if it could be proved he would be mobbed, that his not given anything for the Cause had occasioned much talk and he would get into trouble. This is confidential. At least it was not intended that I should speak of it as a common thing, altho' you may have heard it as some discuss the matter freely, and no doubt the Dr. will fare better in keeping himself so quiet up the Country. Well, I cannot think of anything else to write you of (don't call me Miss *Newsy*), and I will have to stop writing until next week. Perhaps I'll get Mrs. Hardie to take you a letter. I had hoped to have sent your socks by her but have not had the yarn sent to finish them

48. John Anthony Winston (1812–1871), fifteenth governor of Alabama, held office from 1853 to 1857. As colonel of the Eighth Alabama Infantry his strict sense of discipline made him unpopular. Owen, *History of Alabama*, 4:1790.

yet and will have to wait for someone else going on. When next you write Mr. A. remember me kindly to him. Write me soon a long letter. You do not write me as often as you used to—therefore I will expect long letters now when you do. And with the earnest hope that God in his mercy may bless and keep you from harm, I am ever,

    Yours affectionately,

    Elodie

Kittie desires to be kindly presented to you.

Camp Jones, Manassas Junction, September 16, 1861

I cannot leave this place without thanking my loved Elodie for her warm and affectionate letter of the 9th September. To know from your own pen that you discredited the rumors you had heard, while entirely unnecessary to convince me that you discredited them, was a source of gratification. To be assured of the sympathy of a friend in grief is a relief.

I hope, before this time, that the testimony of those who were never in it and who kept out of the danger will have done me justice, even in the opinion of those who are not my friends. I saw Judge Graham late in the evening *after the battle* was over, when he was going to the field for a relative who had been wounded, and he has told a willful falsehood when he says that I was "walking fast." If I had been the most ardent coward in the world, I would not have been walking fast at a time when all danger was over, and especially when I was so lame that I walked with pain. The men who encouraged the circulation, clandestinely, of these reports here are now *suffering* and will do penance before the matter ends. They no doubt secretly encouraged it without my knowledge to injure me and to be benefited, but the history of the regiment will show that, like intrigues of this kind, they will be sadly disappointed. I hope the next two months will clear up the whole matter. I believe it has been a benefit to me here for it has drawn about me a circle of strong and tried friends. I only wish the facts to be known. I heard that the thoughtless boy you name had made such a statement. Lieut. Wilson informs me that the boy in question was *not in the battle.* I am surprised at Boykin Goldsby. How can I repay you for the faith you have exhibited in me? I hope that you will never have that confidence destroyed, and all I can promise you is a heart that will never cease to cherish you as long as it beats in my bosom.

I am much gratified that sister has written you. I know you will like her for she is affectionate and cheerful and very smart and quick. I am the dullest and most uninteresting of my father's children. When they know you, I have no fears that they will not love and appreciate your worth. If they do not, I will quarrel with them for my friends *must like you* or I will *dislike* them.

I will promise you, my dearest, when my term expires not to engage in the service again without *your consent.* I agree with you in thinking that there are many others who should engage in the defence of the country and give a respite to us.

I would be so much pleased to meet your brother for I wish to know him intimately for your sake and for my own. When you write to him, tell him that I am with the Fourth Ala. Rgt. in Gen. Whiting's brigade and ascertain from him to what regiment or command he is attached and let me know, if you please.

Our regiment has gone through the preparatory exercises of packing their wagons and striking tents and then of unpacking them and pitching tents this morning. It was done simply for practice and drill. We are now ordered to cook one day's rations, and if the day is good we will leave by sunrise in the morning for our new encampment about thirteen miles from Alexandria on the Occoquan river, where we will be nearer the enemy and in a better position to get into a fight. I tell you exactly what I think. We are certainly intending to advance upon Washington, and we will have to take Arlington by storm. You may look out for this, but I do not think we will take part in the affair as our duty will be in a different direction. If the Potomac is blockaded as we are now preparing to do, we may cross into Maryland and attack Washington from the rear, and, I hope, when we reach and take the capital that your kin will be far away as I wish none of them, for your sake, to fall into our hands.

I am glad that you are twenty-one as I do not think a lady should marry before that age, and I assure you the age makes no difference with me as I love you for your good *qualities*, outside of such accidental circumstances. You cannot tell me of any of your *acquirements*, which I will not *admire*. It would have been a rich feast to have been at the tableaux you mention, but the "flow of soul"[49] would have been enjoyed when *your sweet voice was heard* in the soft tones of your singing. I admire your sensitive nature

---

49. Nathaniel is referring to "the feast of reason and the flow of soul," a quote from Alexander Pope's 1733 *Satires of Horace.*

which shrinks from the observation of the idle crowd. Nothing denotes so truly the lady as her unwillingness to expose herself to the criticisms of the [illegible] vulgum, and for this reason I have always disliked public examinations and exhibitions at school. I know from my experience at school and at college how trying they are, and if a boy shrank from them I am sure a delicate girl would find them trying. I frequently think that I was intended for a woman. I hope Mr. Wetmore has returned to Selma as I have written him recently. He is a true friend. For Mrs. Parnell I shall ever have the most respectful regard. She is a lovely old lady, and I am really glad you like each other and that you will have such a kind neighbor. If she likes you, I am entirely satisfied, and you can tell her that I will accept her judgment in this case. It is pleasant to have such a friend. You tell me nothing of Mrs. Mabry and her fair daughter.[50] Have they gone to the springs?

I have asked Mr. McCraw if he commanded the company after my separation from the regt. He says that he did, as Lieut. Shortridge did not rejoin it for some time after our retreat, or rather, *rout*. This shows you how scattered we were, in a country unknown to us, grown up in pine thickets. Mr. Price never intended to reflect on me, however. I hope you will see him and knit him a pair of socks.

As I write several companies of a North Carolina regiment have marched by my tent on their way to the quartermaster's to receive their pay. Our men hail them with "Here's your money," "Here's your Confederate bonds." We are paid off in Confederate notes, which are more current than other bills as they circulate everywhere. Yesterday we had Capt. Forney[51] and Capt. Martin[52] of the 10th Ala. to dine with us. We frequently have company and are always glad to see our friends. The death of Col. Jones has made a vacancy in the office of Colonel. Col. Law will be elected without opposition. Then a Lieut. Col. will have to be chosen. I will not be a candidate. There will be a good deal of electioneering for the office, but some gentlemen who have boasted a great deal and who have been fulsomely puffed will rue the day of their vain boasting.

---

50. Gertrude Mabry.

51. William Henry Forney (1823–1893) was a captain in the Tenth Alabama Infantry, commanded by his brother Colonel John Horace Forney. Both men were seriously wounded at the Battle of Dranesville on December 20, 1861. Eicher and Eicher, *Civil War High Commands*, 239–240.

52. Alburto Martin (1830–1879) was also a captain in the Tenth Alabama Infantry. He would be wounded by a shell at the Second Battle of Manassas and remain crippled for the rest of his life. Owen, *History of Alabama*, 4:1163.

I am now quite well and in as good spirits as I ever was, away from home and you. Please when you see John tell him to take good care of my books and flowers, for I love them for you and also my choice fruit trees. I hope to pluck fruit from them for you next year.

And now, dearest Elodie, I have written you a long letter, and almost one daily for the past week. You must not expect so much in future as we will have a great deal of picket duty to perform which will take us from camp. Continue to write to me at Manassas Junction. Goodbye. May God ever guard and preserve you is the constant prayer of one who adores you. Farewell.

Ever yours sincerely,
N. H. R. Dawson

Dumfries, Virginia, September 21, 1861

I write you, my dear Elodie, from our new camp near Dumfries, one of the oldest towns in the late United States, having been settled in 1668. Its appearance is very ancient and nothing but the man of history could tell that it had once been the largest city in the colony of the virgin queen. But however little of the part is exhibited in the present, it was once the commercial metropolis of the old dominion. A very old hotel is still open, and its steps are worn by use and age. The proud forms of Washington, Lee, and other portraits have tread its halls, but like the expressive language of the Roman bard, "Ilium fuit,"[53] and the glory of Dumfries has departed. Many of its large buildings are in ruins, and its streets are grown up in weeds. It now has almost two hundred inhabitants. We left Camp Jones at 6 o'clock on the 18th and marched seventeen miles to Powder Mills by two o'clock, where we camped and remained until yesterday. Yesterday we came to our present encampment, Camp Law. We are in an open field, in view of the Potomac, which is about two miles off. Our tents are so arranged as not to be seen from the river as we are not yet ready to let the Yankees know of our presence. No drums are beat, nothing done to indicate the presence of an army. Gen. Whiting is in command of the division, consisting of about 10,000 men. I know *con-*

---

53. In the *Aeneid*, Virgil sought to capture the pastness of Troy—"Troy has been (and is no more)"—a phrase that became a common way of referring to anything that lived only in memory.

fidentially our business, as Col. Allston[54] told me this morning, and I tell you. We are now erecting nine batteries on the Potomac which command the river. When completed the intervening vessels will be cut down, and our guns will command the river, and we will have the Potomac block-aded. We are here to support those batteries in case they are attacked. This is expected as soon as the enemy discover what we are doing. I am anxious that we should have a fight as I would rather die than live with the imputation that an enemy has cast upon me. I am now more satisfied than ever with the service and for your sake, my dear Elodie, am anxious to remove this slur upon my good name. I will, however, endeavor to do no more than my duty as I have promised you to be prudent. I am quite well but suffered a little from the march. My feet blistered a little though I wore thick shoes and a pair of Mrs. Mathew's socks.

The 19th was the fifth month since our engagement, and I was mind-ful of the hour and looked out upon the light moon and thought of my absent Elodie, who, I felt, tho far away was there thinking of me. All earthly objects and places fade into insignificance when compared with the wealth of your love and the noble sentiments of your heart. How can love ever repay your generous confidence? I will love you while life lasts, my dearest, and during its duration all my energies will be bent to your happiness. Five months will soon have passed since our separation, and seven more will go by more rapidly. I still hope that I may be able to pay you a visit in December if I can bring you a *spotless name* which even the venom of an enemy cannot injure. Here I am not annoyed as all now know and feel that great injustice has been done me *for a motive*, but that motive will redound to my ultimate good and to the detriment of the men who secretly encouraged it but openly have deprecated it, and who have testified to its want of truth. How sinful is man? Dearest, your love will be the goal of all my devotion, and politics and war will henceforth have no charms for me. I promise you never to engage in the service *without your consent* as I hope never to take an important step without consulting fully with you and hope in all of them to have your concur-rence. You must not tell me that this is a promise made in the hour of love. It is made from a sense of duty, and from what I believe will be due

---

54. Benjamin Allston (1833–1900) was born in South Carolina and attended West Point. After the death of Egbert Jones and during the recuperation of Evander M. Law, All-ston acted as colonel. For more, see William Kauffman Scarborough, *The Allstons of Chicora Wood: Wealth, Honor, and Gentility in the South Carolina Lowcountry* (Baton Rouge: Louisiana State University Press, 2011).

to you as my wife. I am a good *listener* and if you will promise to talk I will promise to be your hearer. How I long for the long winter evenings that we are to pass in the luxury of our own home, *where you can occupy a chair in the corner knitting* and I can sit near you looking *into the fire.* I will be prepared for any number of certain pictures. I must now end this letter as a gentleman is waiting who will mail it at Richmond or Fredericksburg. Continue to write me *often* at Manassas Junction, which is our office. I will write you frequently and think of you always.

And now, my dearest Elodie, goodbye. May God ever bless and preserve you from all dangers.

Sincerely and affectionately,
N. H. R. Dawson

Selma, September 22, 1861

It was with much pleasure I have just read your letter of the 16th, and yet the pleasure was mixed with sadness as you mention your leaving Manassas to be nearer the enemy, and in your approximation to them you are taken so much farther from me. But I must not complain, as matters cannot be altered by doing so and perhaps the removal may be the occasion of much good in the end. I wrote you a few days ago by Dr. Harrell, but before he arrived you must have been in your new encampment. I did not see Mrs. Hardie and am now glad I could not find time to do so as my friend Miss Ella McCraw told me she left Mrs. Hardie who had spoken of much that our companies had undergone, their dangers, toils, and privations with her feelings so wrought upon and spirited that she cried all the way home. Ella is a superior girl when compared with the young ladies of this place, and besides has a warm and affectionate heart that overflows with love for her brother, of whom she often speaks to me and always ends with her brother's opinion and remarks about Capt. D. who he loves very much and I am convinced she knows all. We are excellent friends and thrown much together in our preparations for the concert on Wednesday night (25th) at which we sing a duet. I thought at the last my *public career* had ended, but I find myself deeply in for this and cannot find it in my heart to refuse when I can do anything for the benefit of the soldiers, but I hope it will be some time before another will be given as it consumes a great deal of my *precious time* to practice and is very tiresome to meet often twice a day for a week or two. Mrs. Mason and I sing a beautiful song together, very appropriate as it is of the battlefield and represents the mother and daughter praying for the safety of the son and brother. I think of you and David when I sing it and wish you could be here. Ella and I sing "Two Merry Girls,"[55] and I sing alone a song, "Thou Art so Near and Yet so Far"[56] and assist in two instrumental pieces and the choruses. You see I am telling you all I know about it, just as tho you were as much interested as I am, but I'm egotistical. However when it is over I will mention others.

I saw your *justification* in yesterday's paper. Thursday night hearing Mr. Wetmore had returned, I went over to see them. Mr. W. at once commenced to speak of you, thinking I suppose you were the subject nearest my heart and began to take out letter after letter to read to me to *prove your innocence* of the charges brought against you, but I made so much fun of his thinking I needed anything but your own statement to assure me they were false that he replaced them in his pocket after reading one, saying, "Well I shan't let you hear another word." He intends returning to Lexington in a day or two. In him you have a fair and noble friend, and I just mean to love him for acting the part of a *friend* to you, and in *trying to make me believe you were slandered* his ready willingness to read about twenty letters to remove any doubts I may have had was very kind, but struck me standing in the relation I did to you as ludicrous. I beg to be excused from delivering your message to Mrs. Parnell but have no objection to your doing so when you return as you are so fond of *telling my secret*. Now be sure and get vexed at me for saying the last few words wherein the inference is contained that *you* are a *tattler* and that will be nice and may bring on a lover's quarrel which we have not realized yet and been engaged too for five months. How unromantic! Tho to tell the truth, I am naturally so quarrelsome that you will be more than satisfied after a while without taking advantage of any opportunity I may afford you now, and you will be obliged for the sake of peace to be blind and deaf often. I am glad you write me that you had entirely recovered. I was quite sad hearing a few days ago that you were "thin and looked dread-

55. Composed by Stephen Glover, with lyrics by J. E. Carpender, "Two Merry Girls" begins: "Two merry girls from morn to night / Our might and song we mingle, / The reason why we never sigh / We both mean to keep single."

56. Composed by Alexander Riechardt and arranged by Brinley Richards, "Thou Art So Near and Yet so Far" begins: "I know an eye so softly bright, / That glistens like a star of night; / My soul it draws, with glances kind, / To heav'n's blue vault, and there I find / Another star as pure and clear / As that which mildly sparkles here. // Beloved eye, beloved star, / Thou art so near and yet so far!"

ful." Sometimes I think persons tell me such things and speak of you to
me in order to discover if possible by my countenance whether reports
they hear are true, but unless I am much mistaken they do not receive
much gratification or satisfaction.

Yes, Mrs. Mabry and her fair daughter Gertrude are at their summer
place and since she informed me she had no design on you I have felt *no
uneasiness* and consequently thought less of them. I hope on her return
to Selma she will not be taken into the confidence of Major H's family, as
I would be delighted to take them by surprise at some future day. Have
you received any more letters from your neighbor?

I am so distressed about Kentucky and alarmed for my relations and
cannot hear one word to relieve my anxiety and every day I grow more
and more restless and impatient at the silence they are forced from painful necessity to keep, and I cannot imagine now when I shall ever hear or
see any of them again, if ever. Sometimes I feel perfectly despairing, but
there is much hopefulness in my disposition, and it after a while will rise
far above in the ascendancy of my other feelings. I hope Ellick has joined
the Confederate Army and that soon an entire reaction will take place in
my loved old home, and altho late she will write her destiny with that of
the glorious Southern Confederacy.

I will deliver your message to John the first time he comes over. He has
amused me several times lately by coming over to inquire when I heard
from "Master Henry" and to give in return for my information his latest.
I hope if it is the intention of President Davis to take Washington City
that it will be done speedily and before winter. The fighting then will
be so terrible and desperate that I am heart sick when I think of it, and
that you and my brother[57] may be in it and never return, and you know
the thought will force itself on me. How can I think otherwise when all
others entertain the same fears for those they love and that a battle there
must be. Would to heaven we had never had occasion for this Unnatural
War or I had never been unfortunate enough to have such a great interest in it, but I am selfish in wanting to place my share of sorrows on the
already burdened hearts of others, and as I am writing you in a strain that
I should not indulge in will put aside my letter until my mood is better.
If Mr. Davis will only send you home this winter to guard the coast where

57. Elodie is referring to her brother David, who was by this time in Virginia with the
First Kentucky.

I can see you sometimes and feel you are not so far away, I will be better satisfied with him and everybody else. But goodbye now. I'm off for a walk with Kittie and Mr. Hagood. I went to see Parnell a few evenings ago. I believe his intellect has returned and taken possession of his head, and he sees at last that "I've no heart to give him / For another has it now."

Brother Clem has consented to wait a few moments for my letter, and I concluded to add a few more lines. Did I write you what a long letter we had received from your esteemed friend Mr. Dennis a few days ago who is still in Louisiana? I intend [to write] him today if I have time, but I think it is doubtful. I wrote to my brother and requested him to write me to which regiment he was attached and *all about himself.* He knows where you belong and his slight acquaintance proved so agreeable that I know he will if possible find you out. When you know him well you will find many noble traits to admire, but he is not *faultless* and I may overlook many being a sister that are striking to others. I had hoped to hear again from your brother and sister. Mrs. Side promised when she came to Selma this winter to come and see me, and I hope she will come soon for I am anxious to meet her.

But now I must tell you goodbye. I will write again soon and you must write when you can, and I will be more anxious now than ever about your safety. With love and a prayer for your safety and return, I am,

Ever yours affectionately,

Elodie

Dumfries, September 24, 1861

Your welcome letter of the 15th inst., was received yesterday evening. If any thing in this world could make me perfectly happy, it is the unselfish love you have for me, and I am more than grateful for the manner in which you have always acted.

I accept your comment to return with me, this winter, as an evidence of your affection that cannot be otherwise than flattering, and I will act upon it, my dear Elodie, as the circumstances that will then exist shall indicate to be best for *you.* If you can be made comfortable near our winter quarters, I will not hesitate, as I agree with you that you would be happier here than so far from me, but I will not ask you for my own sake to come unless you can have some degree of comfort and be where I will be within reach of you. You are to me now as my wife. I love you as dearly and feel as much anxiety about you now as if we were married. But I would not have you as my wife here unless you could be more comfortably situated than some of my lady acquaintances. All will depend upon my ability to obtain leave of absence from Headquarters, which I hope will be procurable. If possible this will be obtained, then the trip to you will be as rapid as the conveyances of travel will permit. You are dearer to me than life itself, and I will never be satisfied until we are joined in the holy bonds of wedlock. Dear to each other why should we be separated so long from each other? You must not speak of my *troubles* being increased by our marriage. You know, my dear Elodie, that we have many troubles on account of those whom we love, but all my troubles on your account will be undertaken as *pleasures*, to prove that my love is equal to any burthen that you may add to my anxieties. But really, I have few troubles with my Company. My officers are friends who aid me in everything, who prefer to relieve me than to see me troubled, and my men, with very few exceptions, are easily controlled, and Believe are attached to me. My relations with my company are exceedingly pleasant, and my men always oppose my leaving them upon any occasion. I have their entire confidence. During my absence two of them got into a fight and were court-martialed and punished. They are both much mortified, especially one of them who is a sensitive and high toned young man, and one of my favorites, Benj. Bell, the brother of your friend, Miss Bell. Say nothing of this as I would not have Mrs. Reece know that her son had been in trouble. I think, my dear Elodie, that you are too severe upon Mr. Price as I am confident he never meant to do me harm, tho' his remark may have been indiscreet. He is a friend of mine and very indignant at the report. He was like myself ignorant of its circulation until near a month after the battle. Did Dr. Cabell give it any credence?

As Mr. Byrd published a very unsatisfactory letter, I hope he will make use of those I sent him. They were entrusted to the discretion of Mr. Wetmore and other friends besides himself.

Last evening we got orders to march with rations for one day. We left camp at dark, but after proceeding about two miles, the order was countermanded, and we returned, much to my disappointment, as we were to make an attack upon the fleet in the river. (Confidential). I think we were not quite ready but hope we will make an assault on the Yankees this week. Our batteries are being created secretly at night in several places on the river so as to deceive the enemy and to take their attention from the principal point being fortified. On Sunday evening I rode over to the batteries with Col. Allston,[58] and met with an old So. Ca. acquaintance, Col. Pettigrew, of the 2d N.C. Regiment. Our division of the army, that of Fredericksburg, is commanded by Brig. Gen. Holmes, Mr. Wetmore's brother in law. I have not met him. Gen. G. A. Smith of Kentucky has succeeded Gen. Johnston as commander of the right wing of the Army of the Potomac, the latter being commander in chief. I have enquired for your brother David and hear that he is here, but do not know at what point.

And now, dear Elodie, let me again tell you that you are too much concerned about the troubles of your family. They are in the path of duty, like thousands besides, and you have reason to be proud of their stand and should congratulate yourself that the brothers in law of Mr. Lincoln have taken up arms against him. This fact alone should satisfy you, and I trust you will take a better and more hopeful view of things. You tell me that you have shed tears over the course of Kentucky; so have many brave men but all will yet be right, and I hope for your sake that she will be wrested from the Unionism that now overshadows her.

I see that the southerners are likely to give trouble to Gen. Anderson in that latitude, and I hope Gen. Albert Johnston[59] will bring a strong influence to bear upon the fortunes of his native state.

Near five months have now passed since we left home. Seven still intervene and I hope will pass as rapidly as the two last. The nights are now very cool, and the days warm. Yesterday it was cold enough for frost. I begin to despair of wintering in Washington city. We are near enough to hear the cannon at Arlington Heights, and we hear that they were taken yesterday. An incessant war of artillery was heard all day. We may be on the eve of great events. Please present me kindly to Miss Kittie, and tell her I hope she will return to Ala. if she should leave before I have the pleasure of seeing her. When the war is over, and we can go to Kentucky, she will certainly be willing to return with you to spend a winter, when I hope Selma will have more attractions. Like you, she may then become an Alabamian.

And now, dear Elodie, I have written you a long letter, as you desired, and I hope you will find it as pleasant to read as it has been to me to write. I will write you as often as possible, but the *Examiner* must supply you the news.

---

58. Benjamin Allston.
59. Albert Sidney Johnston would be killed at the Battle of Shiloh.

Goodbye. May God in his Providence preserve and keep you always is the prayer of one devoted to his affectionate Elodie.

Affectionately and sincerely yours,

N. H. R. Dawson

We have heard nothing about the trouble of Mr. Woods and the Blues. I regret very much this occurrence, but I have feared some trouble from what I have heard of the dissatisfaction. Do you not think it was right in Dr. Mabry as the friend of Gen. Winston, to inform him that threats had been made to kill him? Such threats I cannot regard as anything but *cowardly*, to shoot an officer in battle, *under shelter.* [illegible] Gen. W's [illegible], but I cannot approve such threats. They proceed from men who are unwilling to shoulder the responsibility of their conduct.

Confederate States of America, Selma, September 29, 1861

I was very much gratified to receive a letter from you yesterday written from your new encampment as I was anxious to hear of your safe arrival and the effects of the march on you and am glad you suffered so little. I had not heard from you before for a week, and it is not pleasant I assure you to think since your removal, I am not to hear *even as often as before*, for I do not receive letters near as often as I desire, and I cannot submit to such a small allowance of mail matter from you. I am rebelling against such a step on your part and *just won't stand it.*

The concert came off on Wednesday night and seemed to delight all who attended, but it did not please me as much as the one before, and I suppose it will be the last as there is something always said or done that renders every attempt to aid the cause in Selma unpleasant and discouraging. But so far as I am concerned I intend to be independent and *help every opportunity that offers.* When I meet with opposition so far from being discouraged and giving up, I generally find my energy and persistence aroused to the greatest extent and I *will go thro'* with what I undertake and my obstinacy helps me, for I have a generous share of the latter and sometimes to indulge in it affords me a pleasant gratification. It seems strange to me that so few are together and all helping for the one and same cause, that they cannot *work together* cheerfully and happily in place of actually working against each other and throwing as many obstacles in their way as possible, and I do not know of anything that has been tried here that has not been opposed by another party, especially if they have not entire control over matters and persons engaged. It is a pity and if a different state of feeling existed so much more would be accomplished; an intimacy of this kind has given me an insight into the true disposition of some in whom I was greatly deceived and I hope on further acquaintance I may not have proved so disagreeable to some as they have to me. But this subject will not interest you and does not me particularly, and I will discuss something more interesting to me, and try to think of something for you afterwards. See how selfish I am to be *always first?*

We received a letter from a lady yesterday who had met with my mother and sister, informing us that they were well and working hard for the *Southern cause,* and a letter from my sister informs me that my Brotherinlaw Col. B. H. Helm has command of a Kentucky Regiment under Gen. S. B. Buckner,[60] and my youngest, last and pet brother Ellick has a position in it somewhere in the Southern part of the state, and altho' I am gratified that my dear brother has gone forward without a moment's hesitation to the defense of his state and country, yet it saddens me. He is young, only in his 23rd year, and I fear the temptations and sins that surround him altho' he is a pious, conscientious member of the Church and has been exposed to them many times before. And I cannot bear the idea of giving him up. The battle monuments in different portions of our state exhibit the courage and patriotism of our family during the bloody war attending the settlement of that and other states but my respect would be diminished if he did not take part and do to the last.

My Brother David wrote me he was at "Munson's Hill"[61] enjoying a sight of Washington, and sometimes the Enemy. How I do wish the Battle at that place was over; indeed, that all were, but I fear the War will be continued much longer than we thought at the commencement, and Kentucky's troubles will add to the length of time we are to be engaged in this struggle.

I am sorry to see that you feel as you [do] about that report. I am afraid it always will trouble you and embitter your recollections of your term of service, which should be as pleasant to you who have done your duty more bravely that others as to those who have received *more credit*

---

60. Simon Bolivar Buckner (1823–1914) had graduated West Point and become an instructor there. Appointed by Kentucky's governor to enforce the state's official neutrality policy, he formally accepted a Confederate commission as brigadier general in September 1861. Eicher and Eicher, *Civil War High Commands,* 151–152.

61. The lower portion of Washington, D.C., is encircled by hills, including Munson's, which (before being partially leveled in the 1950s) commanded one of the prettiest views of the city.

than they deserve, and as you know who encouraged the circulation and the motive that prompted [it], and others are also aware of these facts, why should you longer care? You need not for my sake nor desire to get into another Engagement for I am satisfied that a greater falsehood was never uttered, and I *care not* what the world thinks, *its opinions cannot alter my feelings* or deter me from my determination to marry you, if God permits your return again, and you will always know *one* lent no believing ear to so base a slander. For your sake, I regret its creation and know your sensitive nature bears this trial as impatiently and with the same feeling of mortification and sense of great and undeserved injustice as my own would, but rest assured all will be right after a while and your trouble now will make you a *hero* in the end. I can guess in two seconds, [nay] one, who encouraged its circulation and felt a gratification, if I am not much mistaken, and he unlike other members of his family, who are exceedingly *envious*, told me the other day that a man from Marion by the name of Lockett said he met *you retreating* and that he begged you to go back and you would not. Mr. Lockett told this to a gentleman named Hunter Reeves, who told my informant, but I have not heard anything mentioned for some time and believe many here feel an interest in and a sympathy for you that were rather indifferent before this, so in the end some good may result from this evil.

I met with Dr. Paisley and had a conversation of at least two hours which was very entertaining to me. I asked him many questions and on subjects which caused him to speak of you and tell me your *parting remarks* to him, and when he spoke so kindly and in the highest terms that one could utter of another, he little dreamed that he had so interested a listener or had touched a chord in my heart and awakened anew my love and sympathy for your trials. Ella and I were very anxious to know if it was really true that the Alabamians thought more of Virginia Ladies than those of their own state, as we had heard. He replied at once, "Oh! No, you need not be afraid of losing your sweethearts if they (the Virginia ladies) are so pretty and treat them so kindly." I told him if *mine* did not love, appreciate, and feel grateful to them for their kindness I would change my opinion of him and feel my own efforts were not duly appreciated. He complimented me exceedingly for so sensible a remark and proper feeling as he termed it.

You must anticipate very *agreeable evenings*, I quietly knitting in the corner and you looking in the fire. I intend to change the evening programme. You are to do your looking and thinking in your *Law office*, and when you come home I am to be entertained by your agreeable conversation or you are to read to me from a pleasant book just as you feel

inclined and I am not going to become "old as the hills" at once and sit
in a corner knitting either. Your picture does not entirely suit me, and I
beg leave to make some changes, but not at present. When the realization of these now imaginary pictures takes place, it will be time enough,
and I must confess you look far into the future, much farther than I, for
I cannot realize or believe that I was ever destined for a life of happiness.
Sorrow and trials will no doubt continue to be my portion. I have seldom
quaffed from pleasure's cup without tasting sorrow's dregs and at present
the appearance for feeling or knowing happiness is clouded and gloomy.
All who are near and dear to me are exposed to imminent danger, even
my mother, who runs a risk of being arrested for having her sons engaged
in the Confederate service, my family all scattered and it being impossible to communicate with them. To look at these things in the best light
is sad enough, and I try to bear them and think as little as possible, but
every day I miss a mother's love, a brother's and a sister's kindness, which
time nor distance cannot make me cease to remember. You will think me
very gloomy, so I am and would be unfeeling did I not feel as I do about
these things. But I do not know that [it] is necessary to give expression
to them in writing you a letter.

For three or four days we have had very cold weather, and I thought
of our poor soldiers so exposed and dread their sufferings this winter in
the cold climate of Virginia. I have been knitting with redoubled energy,
but I am not inclined yet to furnish Mr. Price with any of my handiwork
and do not feel as sorry to see him *limping* as I would have done if he had
not written that letter to Dr. Cabell. Next time he will I hope be more
particular when he mentions you or else not trouble himself to use your
name at all.

Week after next there is to be Tableaux again. By that time most of
the absent from Selma will be at home and among them your friend and
neighbor, who if she does not soon give you information of herself, I will
have to send you news of myself. Do you not feel complimented to think
the *"Joneses"* are taking the news of your engagement to me very much
to heart? They do not like to speak to me, and it afforded me pleasure
the other day at the society to offer to assist Miss Jones[62] in sewing on
buttons and buckles and take a seat beside her and converse with her a
short time. I am glad they think so much of you and hope for their own
sake they will become reconciled and not distress themselves as I do not
attach the slightest importance to anything they say or do. *Your heart* has

---

62. Possibly M. E. Jones, age twenty, of Selma. 1860 Census: Selma.

taken a *wrong direction* for *two or three*. I am sorry to tell you old Mrs. Parnell is quite sick and looks so dreadfully I am afraid she will not live long altho' not seriously ill now. Miss Serena is as charming and delightful as ever and when you return in December you must meet with her but *not be captivated*. I am not generous enough to give you up to any one, therefore you must not fancy either Kittie or Miss P. more than myself. Kittie is very pretty, intelligent, gay, and when she desires quite entertaining. The same case with Miss Serena, and I enjoy seeing them together. Do you not dread to see a letter from me now? I write such long ones, and the size of my paper is frightful, but as I cannot talk to you, I feel as though I cannot write enough and never know when or where to stop when I begin and am fearful of saying so much when we meet that you will be tried almost to the same degree as after those long marches you have endured.

What has become of Mr. Averitt? I would be so pleased to see him but suppose when next we meet he will be a married man and I will have the pleasure of meeting his wife. I want to see him once before that time.

I cannot think of anything else to write you of, my ideas are all exhausted and I will not tax you to read any more for this time. Please just write me a long letter and tell me of *every* and *anything*, all about yourself, incidents of Camp life, & etc. You have been gone more than five months, and I am hoping to see you if but for a very little while in December. Do you really believe no one will be glad to see you on your return and think you have done your duty? Can you think of me and believe that? If so I hope to show you how mistaken you are and what injustice you do me, but now I must bid you goodbye. I will write again soon, and with the hope of seeing you soon, a constant prayer for your safety, I am as ever yours, sincerely and affectionately,

Elodie B. T.

Camp Law, Dumfries, Virginia, October 7, 1861

Your long and welcome letter of the 29th September, my dearest Elodie, was received yesterday evening and gave me both pleasure and pain. A pleasure greater than any one I now experience arrives from the receipt and perusal of your letters, which soothe and comfort me often when I am suffering from irritation and the flattering knowledge that in one heart, dearer to me than the wild dreams of youthful ambition, I am so supreme should make up for all my trials. These feelings are paramount and render your letters, as you have often been told, a rich treat to me. But I cannot refrain from sympathy when you tell me of all your anxieties about your dear brother and other relatives. I can only hope that the clouds which seemingly, now, hang so darkly over our heads, will disappear, and that happiness will yet be yours without being attended by the shades of grief and sorrow. No one, as you know, has suffered more severely than I have. Scarcely a month in the year is without its anniversary of some great sorrow, and had I yielded to the feelings of sadness which often come over me, I would be a miserable man. This is the seventh anniversary of my first great sorrow, and I have always tried to keep it sacred. I rose early this morning and wrote a long letter to dear little Lizzie, to whom I look in the future, if my life is spared, for much happiness. If I should never see her again, when she grows up, I wish you to notice her as one who was dear to me. Where have I gone for relief from all these sorrows? And where have I found it? *In your love.* All the bright hues of happiness, which dawned upon me, upon my first entrance into life, as a summer sea, have returned with the knowledge that these anticipations are not all to be realized, but with the conviction that I am to find in you the personification of all my dreams of woman, and in your love and companionship the great object of my prayers, domestic happiness.

You tell me that I live in the future. Is it wrong? Why refuse to lessen the trials of the present by looking beyond them? Does not the Christian endure more cheerfully the sorrows of life when he anticipates the pleasures of the future? Hence, my dear Elodie, you must not blame me for drawing pictures in the future of our happiness. I have no objection to the change of programme, and will especially approve your becoming the conversationalist and the *musician.* I hope you will not fall on the example of so many of our Southern women and become old as soon as you are married. I will insist upon your continuing your music and reading for they are means of happiness that should never be abandoned. For your sake and for my own, I will dismiss the report from my mind and try to forget it. My friends are all satisfied and some of my enemies, I fear, mortified to know that I behaved as well as many who have been praised most extravagantly. The regiment will mark these *gentlemen* and not permit their ambition to be gratified. I know Hunter Reeves well and have no respect for him. He has always been a man who envied all above him, a fellow of little intelligence who has been attempting for twelve years to impose himself upon some heiress. He envies me I know. I saw Mr. Lockett when I was with the wounded but did not know his name at the time. He asked me to go back to hunt for the regiment. I told him that I was unable to do so from fatigue and lameness even if *I knew* where it *was,* but that Lieut. Wilson, who was with me, and who was fresh, would go with him, but he never came to return. It is singular that others who acted as badly as they say I did blame me when in the same category. This fact I have always mentioned, as I have nothing to conceal, my brother officers, with a full knowledge of all the facts, have acquitted me of all blame. But enough, I will leave this subject, and I hope that it will be consigned to "the tomb of the Capulets." I regret that anything should have been said or done at the concert to annoy you. I have always, myself, tried to do what was expected of me on such occasions without being an entire manager. I prefer being a looker-on in service when one of her tragedies is to be enacted.

I do not see why the [illegible], or anybody else, should trouble themselves about the devotion of my heart. It has gone where I wished it, and all of their wishes will never change it. I knew, probably, that it might have been more pleasant to some in another direction, but this very knowledge generally drives me to the opposite. Do they think you have done badly in giving me your heart? Who was the fair Margaret that was to have captured me?

I hardly expect another letter from my neighbor as she has had time to write, if she intended, closing her sojourn in the mountains. This being so you must give me an account of her progress in the arts and sciences of courtship. Mrs. Hardie has returned; as I wrote you, she is staying at a farm house about a half mile from our camp, convenient to be visited by her husband. She represents Selma as a place of dullness. She comes over and dines with us occasionally and always makes herself pleasant. She brought our mess each a bottle of wine from Miss Gertrude Goodwin,[63] which we drank to her health and the health of other ladies. I feel very much gratified at this little attention and requested Mr. Shortridge to return my thanks.

I am so glad to met Dr. Paisly. He is a good man and a sincere friend of mine. I do not remember what my parting words to him were. Please tell me in your next. When he returns, I will expect a rich treat from this account of the conversation with you and Miss Kittie. I will get all out of him, what you said, how you looked, and numberless other things. His furlough expires this week. Did he tell you of the battle, how he was shot with a spent ball?

You must really be fond of deciphering my letters to ask that they should be frequent and long. I have written you recently very often. Yesterday I sent you a long letter, and now I am writing you another, for the same reason that induced you to write by Dr. Harrell. Mr. [illegible], a

---

63. Gertrude Goodwin, age twenty-one, daughter of A. M. Goodwin and R. I. Goodwin of Selma. 1860 Census: Selma.

returning recruit, leaves tomorrow and as he will bear a budget of letters I wish you to have one.

There are very few incidents of camp life that are worthy of report. I drill in the morning at nine o'clock, form companies, generally, as skirmishers; at 2 o'clock all of the officers recite Hardees tactics or go on battalion drill, when the recitation is dispensed with; dress parade at sunset. The evenings are devoted to conversation around a fire in front of our tent or in visiting some brother officer, when a cigar and the news of the day afford us the means of entertainment. We have dinner at one and generally have beef, ham, chicken, and vegetables of all kinds. We live well. Peep into my tent and you will see me sitting in a chair, writing on the tray of my trunk, used as a desk. Lieut. McCraw is reclining on our bed of straw with the oil cloth over it, reading *The Last Heiress*. The bed is enclosed by poles and looks like a little pen. Two trunks, a valise, a keg of sugar, a large bucket of molasses with sundry *empty bottles* are seen as the only furniture. Stretched on a rope across the interior of the tent are swords, boots, canteens, haversacks, and clothing. Fronting us are the company tents, in two rows, facing inwardly at each other and at the end of the row are the men cooking. This is a description of our tent and of its surroundings. Lieut. McCraw is dressed like myself, in blue pants with a blue flannel over-jacket instead of a coat, with military red top boots. Around my heck is hung a black watch guard attached to my watch pocket and impending there but hidden from all eyes is *your likeness* in a gold *locket*. My men think it is a watch and in reply to their enquiries about the time I always tell them my watch is broken. You can imagine how often this watch is consulted during the day.

On Sundays, I read several chapters of the bible to as many of my men as chance to come in and we have some good vocal music. I visit the hospital daily to see our sick and always have my heart made sad. The pallets are occupied with many who are lean looking objects suffering typhoid fever. Poor fellows, no mothers or sisters' hands are near to minister to them, and they look dejected and homesick. I always try to cheer them up, but it is a difficult duty. My little fifer boy, Jacob Mariball[?], is slowly recovering from this dreadful disease of which he has been sick over a month. I will endeavor to send him home when he is well enough. Dr. Avery,[64] of Selma, is also sick. He is a complete hypochondriac. I feel very

---

64. William M. Avery, age fifty-one, was married to Mary Avery. Their two daughters, Mary, age seventeen, and Francis, age fifteen, both make appearances in this correspondence. 1860 U.S. Federal Census, Southern Division, Macon, Ala.

much for him but can render him no aid. He is awfully *ugly* and this adds to his distressing appearance. You could never have loved me if I was half so homely.

You tell me not to fall in love with Miss Kittie or Miss Pernell. Have no fear. If you had you would not *suggest* the *idea.*

When I said none would be glad to see me at Selma, I never meant to include you in the category. I meant the people who are generally anxious to believe ill of gentlemen. I have received very kind letters from Mr. Knox,[65] Mr. E. B. Harrison, Mr. Keith, Mr. Rollins, and others, and am grateful to them. I send you Mr. Knox's to keep.

I have now written you a long letter and will expect in reply a long and affectionate one from my loved Elodie in which she must express fully all that she feels, not permitting the fear of writing *sadly* of those dear ones about whom you have so natural an anxiety to control you. *If you love me, write as you feel.* All of your anxieties should be shared with me for I assure you my heart responds to every ache in yours.

For your safety & escape from the [illegible] you anticipate, and with much love, I remain,

Very affect'y & sincerely yours,
N. H. R. Dawson

Quantico Creek, October 12, 1861[66]

My Dear Elodie,

I came down to this point on the river and am now writing you on the porch of Mrs. Otterback's residence, immediately on the banks of the Potomac. The day is one of the lovely ones which we have at this season.

---

65. William S. Knox, in Selma, who writes on September 19, 1861, "I know you have felt mortified and hurt at the report which was circulated here and at Manassas that you had abandoned your company on the day of battle, and my particular reason for writing you at this time is to say to you that in this community that report is now perfectly dead and utterly discredited."

66. This letter is preceded in the collection by a news clipping from the *Columbus Times*: "Lincoln's Sister-in-Law.—Mrs. Abraham Lincoln, wife of the President of the old Union, has two married sisters now on a visit to Montgomery, Ala. One is from Kentucky and on a visit to her sister, who resides in Selma, Ala. They are both strong secessionists and opposed to the government of their brother-in-law, Abraham Lincoln. Of course, they attract considerable attention and are the toast of Southerners. The husband of one has offered his services to Governor Moore, of Alabama, to further the cause of secession and State Rights and Republican Liberty."

Summer is putting off his ruddy cheeks, and autumn is about to put on her golden crown. The shadows of the sun and the winds whistling along the waters all wear the sad, though to me pleasant, aspect of a new season. The river is two miles wide and from this point looks like a beautiful bay. The flat shores of Maryland are dotted here and there with farm-houses and other appurtenances, while the placid stream bears upon its brow many an unfriendly sail. One is now almost within musket shot, and as I raised my eyes from the paper was coming rapidly under the wind to-wards this shore. She has tacked in now before the wind, running toward Maryland. Eleven sails are in sight. On night before last, the Yankees run up the Quantico,[67] a little estuary of the Potomac, and burned one of our largest boats under the guns of our battery. For wise purposes our bat-tery did not open upon them, but our pickets did. The vessel, however, is ruined. Our battery is in sight, but as it is masked the enemy are not aware of its dangerous proximity. When completed, which will be in a few days, it will command the river for seven miles. It is on a promontory, and the river describes a curved line around it. I wish you could sit by me and feast your vision upon the lovely picture. The quiet scene may precede the approach of the horrors of war. The negroes, cattle, and provisions have all been removed from this plantation in anticipation of an attack from the Yankees. An old servant has showed me a large shell which one of the vessels threw at a group of negroes while at work.

I am here with my company on picket duty. The company came down yesterday under the command of Lieut. Shortridge as I was attending a court of enquiry at the Hampton Legion[68] where I was detained un-til after dark. I came down this morning, and we will return tomorrow morning in time to hear Mr. Small preach, I hope. It is rather unpleasant to be on this duty two days and nights, especially when it is cold and rainy as it was last night. The men all got drenched in the rain. I dislike this service exceedingly.

At the court of enquiry, after a day spent in examining witnesses, we acquitted the accused, Captain Albert G. Clifton of the 2d Texas Regt. of the charge of intoxication while on duty.

---

67. Quantico is a thirteen-mile creek in Prince William County, Virginia.

68. Wade Hampton III (1818–1902), legislator from South Carolina, originally enlisted as a private, citing his absence of military experience, but the governor of South Carolina insisted he accept a commission as colonel. Hampton raised one of the more famous Con-federate legions (integrated units of infantry, cavalry, and artillery). Such an organization was quickly deemed impractical and Hampton's legion would be broken up in mid-1862. For more, see Robert K. Ackerman, *Wade Hampton III* (Columbia: University of South Car-olina Press, 2007).

Just as we were leaving camp this morning Mr. Brown and Rev. Tanner drove up in a wagon. They both seemed much improved. I received letters from my overseer and from Maj. Haden. I have lost one of my gray horses and regret the loss so much as I valued them very greatly. "Friend and friend departs. Who hath not lost a friend."[69]

I brought writing materials with me this morning that I might write you a letter in view of the river. I am disposed to be romantic in my disposition but have had so much to sadden me that I have outgrown a great deal of it. Scenery and circumstances by which I am surrounded always affect my disposition, and I am made sad now in reflecting upon all that surrounds me. A deserted home, a beautiful river, almost in sight of Mount Vernon, the property of a ruthless enemy, guarded at every point by gun boats. Two of these latter have been lying in the stream all day, apparently watching the shores of the river, and have turned and are coming down again. I can see the men aboard plainly and sometimes fear the sorry little wretches will throw a shell at me. Some of our sentinels may have been discovered.

I am very glad Mr. Brown brought no recruits as my company is larger now than convenient. I was very much surprised to see from the Reporter that he called for them as I have declined to receive any, and he was not authorized by me to bring them.

I fear we will suffer from the cold weather, which is fast approaching. I am now very cool tho it is not more than three in the afternoon. At home, I would have been sitting by a fire all the morning. I have walked about seven miles today from camp and around the pickets. Adieu. I will end my letter at camp.

I enclose two wild violets which I found growing alone near the Potomac.[70] They reminded me in their modest home of a flower blooming in Alabama, far away from those she loves, and I have sent them to you that you may keep them. Dearest, my heart is overflowing with love for you.

Selma, Alabama, October 13, 1861

I will not attempt to express the pleasure your letter of the 7th just read has given me. You are well aware that they are always welcome and add

69. Nathaniel is quoting British poet James Montgomery (1771–1854) and his poem "Friends": "Friend after friend departs; who hath not lost a friend? There is no union here of hearts, which finds not here an end."

70. There is a pressed flower folded into this letter.

much to my enjoyment and happiness, and I find myself after receiving one trying to count up and arrange a day in my mind as possible to again be gratified by the arrival of another; and sometimes when disappointed by the non-arrival of it you would be amused to see the extreme length of my face and its look of almost disbelief in Bro. Clem's truthfulness when he tells me, "I have none today." Especially when I have been two or three days without hearing. Do you not think I am a *vain, conceited girl* to think that my love would [illegible] you for all you have been called upon to undergo and suffer in the last few months? I did not mean to express my self as I did exactly. I meant that by many you would be appreciated and rewarded with their sympathy and highest opinion and respect and in place of losing friends whose love and respect is [illegible] you would gain more, and that I would for this reward you by giving you all I had and could, my love. But I did not think it would be sufficient to satisfy you alone, altho' it is *"fond, first love"* which the poets prize so much and which fact you desired to know a short time ago. I do not think it half enough or all that can be done for you by all your friends, *even as much as you deserve.* See how deserving I think you, but you will tire of me if I continue such a strain for you know that I do love you and intend always to try and add as far as lies in my power to your happiness and this knowledge and assurance satisfies you.

Now shall I as usual write you a gossiping letter and give you all the news afloat that I know of in Selma? Well, as you are not here to answer, I must decide for you. When I am from home I like to receive above all things a "real newsy" letter, for I want to know all that is going on during my absence, and because such is my taste abroad I think I must introduce some little items afloat. My first is sad because it records the death of Mr. H. Ware's little daughter of *poison* and his own illness now from the same. On Friday last in some manner mysterious enough poison— of what kind not confidently known tho' thought by Dr. Cabell to be cobalt—was introduced into the wine. His little daughter after sipping a little complained of being very sick and died in great agony six hours after, and Mr. W. himself was taken sick immediately. Suspicion points to a servant woman who opened the wine in place of bringing it as usual to her master to do and upon her refusing to drink it when he offered it to her and not knowing the effect it had produced as she left the room hurriedly and immediately after placing the wine on the table. Upon her own & Mr. Ware's recovery the matter will be more thoroughly investigated for there is I hear much excitement and should be for it is a dreadful thing. He forced her to drink enough to make her sick but not dangerously so. No cause can be assigned for the act as she is a favorite and indulged servant.[71] My next piece perhaps you have heard ere now, of the death of Mrs. Tom Brown (Miss Maggie Gale) of consumption. She accompanied us to Montgomery last spring, under your care, you remember.

There has been and is now in Selma a great deal of sickness and several deaths, but among children and persons unknown to me. My friend Ella has been quite sick with chills, was too unwell Friday night to act in tableaux, but I saw her looking beautifully at church this morning and better than a few days ago. Ella Watts has also been a victim, and this neighborhood seems to have been selected. So far I have escaped tho I think I may have had a slight one this morning as I now have a fever. I ought to have some excuse for looking, then, as my friends say I do, but I cannot recognize any change myself and think they imagine it. The Captain Todd you refer to must be now Col. Charles S. Todd who was minister to Russia formerly of Shelbyville Ky. but now living in Texas.[72] I have forgotten what portion but knew the family very well, particularly his son Charley.[73] If they are relations, the relationship is very distant, but my father and himself I think used to recognize each other as such and knew each other well. If Col. Allston desires to know something of his friend I could perhaps find out his present location. His daughter, Mrs. Dr. Carter,[74] is living at N. Orleans, also Charley. I met a gentleman in Ohio about eighteen months ago who married Miss Kate Robinson, a niece of Rev'd Stuart Robinson who now resides in Louisville. My two sisters Matt and Emilie were schoolmates of hers when she resided in Frankfort with her uncle. I do not remember the gentleman's name. Old Judge Robinson was the most intimate friend of my father at the time of

---

71. For more on the Ware family, see Harpers Ferry, May 10, 1861, note 44. For more on everyday slave resistance, see Stephanie M. H. Camp, *Closer to Freedom: Enslaved Women and Everyday Resistance in the Plantation South* (Chapel Hill: University of North Carolina Press, 2004).

72. Charles Stewart Todd (1791–1871) served as minister to Russia from 1841 to 1846 before becoming interested in the Texas railroad system. At the age of seventy-one he offered his services to the Union army. E. Polk Johnson, *A History of Kentucky and Kentuckians: The Leaders*, vol. 3 (Chicago: Lewis Publishing Company, 1912), 1502.

73. Charles Henry Todd (1838–1916), son of Charles Stewart Todd, took a medical degree from Tulane University in 1861 and then served as a surgeon in the Army of Northern Virginia—another example of the wider divisions in the Todd family. See Charles Henry Todd Papers, Filson Historical Society, Louisville, Ky.

74. Letitia Shelby Todd (1832–1892), daughter of Charles Stewart Todd, married Charles John H. Carter. Charles Henry Todd Papers.

his death, and I have known himself and Gen'l Leslie Combs all my life. Two days before I left Kentucky, I spent an agreeable hour with Mr. I. C. Breckenridge, Gov. Morehead, Gen'l Combs, Old Judge Robertson, and Judge Buckner, who is an uncle of Gen'l S. B. Buckner. I know Gen'l and Mrs. Buckner very well.[75]

You do not know how strangely and badly I feel when all these old familiar names are seen. A thousand memories of the past come rushing back to my mind. Some are pleasant, happy reminiscences, recalling my childhood when surrounded by all the companions of my father. Then we were altogether a happy household. Those were happy times, but now I forbear to draw the contrast, the dark view of the picture. It is more than enough to feel the difference, which I do most keenly, and am hoping each hour, each day may produce a change that will enable us once more to be a reunited family. But I fear there will be some missing from the family circle. I was very much gratified to see in the Richmond *Dispatch* containing the account of the capture and escape of J. F. Burnam of Ky. that owing to the assistance rendered him by my brother Ellick he reached his home in safety. If my family did not get their names published occasionally, I would not know they were alive. My own cousin John B. Todd of Ill.[76] I see has disgraced us. He is quartermaster of some division on the Potomac of Mr. Lincoln's forces. Is it not too bad? Here I am interrupted by some company relations of Bro. Clem's, and I must reluctantly lay aside my pen for the second time since beginning this.

On Friday night I was surprised at the tableaux by George Mims coming up to speak to me. We had a long chat. He is very much attached to you and speaks of your superiority to most of the officers in tactics and appearance, manners, and etc. He says, "ah yes, Miss Dee I have found you out." I never would have suspected anything of the kind. He then told me you had mentioned receiving a letter from a friend of his family who informed him of their being well, and she had made them a visit. He said for three weeks it was a study to imagine who the friend was, and upon his return home he asked almost the first question who made

---

75. Simon Bolivar Buckner was married to Mary Jane Kingsbury.

76. John Blair Smith Todd (1814–1872) was Mary Lincoln's first cousin. He graduated West Point in 1837 and in 1861 was appointed a brigadier general in the Union army though for most of the war he served as a representative for the Dakota Territory. Wesley C. Wilson, "General John B. S. Todd, First Delegate, Dakota Territory," *North Dakota History* 31 (July 1964): 189–194.

them a visit in June. The reply was myself. I did not deny it to him and will write to you by him as he leaves in a few days. I would send you a box but he told me he would be a week in Winchester, and the box would be too long on the route. Ella and I speak of sending one together soon. I have not, nor do I intend mentioning anything to her. There is but one lady friend I have that I would *trust with a secret*, but I think the best plan is to keep it to myself.

Monday Morning, Oct. 14

Last Evening while taking a stroll I accidentally saw Mr. Wetmore who told me he had been at home a week sick with chills. I mentioned to him your messages and that you desired to hear from him. He wrote a few days ago. I am getting *jealous of Mr. Wetmore*, you like him too much. He told me that both himself and Col. Byrd had a number of letters, but I did not feel as though I would hear them read or read them myself. I feel perfectly satisfied and do not see the necessity of putting myself to the trial of it.

Your friend George Mims came very near getting into a *left handed* fight one day last week so he told me about this same thing, but a friend interfered saying that he was wounded. George says he felt *relieved as the man was large*. From him you can learn exactly how I am looking and all you would like to know if you choose to ask. I have not seen Laura for some time. I do not suppose she will ever forgive me for not telling her, but once she was within two weeks of being married and did not make a confidante of me until the affair was all over with, so in like manner shall she be treated.

Mrs. Reese and Sallie Bell have been at Huntsville for two or three weeks and are still absent. I miss Sallie very much. I am afraid to hope you will be on the coast this winter or that I will even see you before next spring and am trying to prepare myself for a disappointment, yet I had hoped and expected you in December, and I think your Generals and Commanders just as mean as they can be. It will be a great pleasure tho' whenever I do see you again, and if it is not to be until your term expires, I will know then you are not to return. I think my patriotism has *cooled* too much to allow a thought toward your again serving.

I saw from a Virginia paper yesterday that my brotherinlaw Col. B. H. Helm was at Rochester on Greene River Ky., and that two of his brothers, sons of Ex. Gov. Helm,[77] had been arrested by the federals at Elizabeth-town. They are nothing but children, the eldest I think is not fifteen years old and the second a *cripple*. Can they be such monsters? I hope the news is incorrect.

I do not even know in what portion of Kentucky my mother is and feel very uneasy about her and desire above all things to hear from her and know where she is and what doing. Sometimes I feel very desperate and feel as tho' I can bear it no longer and that I must start and find them all.

Did you know I had a sister living in Cincinnati? Poor Mag. She cannot get away and the Vigilance Committee ran her out of the city because she would not work for the Federal soldiers and told them she was a Southern born woman and thanked God all her relations were fighting for the South, and she wouldn't work for anyone but them either. She is one of the dearest little creatures you even knew of, and I am satisfied is greatly distressed that Mr. Kellogg is compelled to remain there. You will indeed think I understand the art of writing long letters, if they do not prove agreeable. I intend writing you by George Mims who will leave in a few days. I wrote you by Mr. Price and sent you a "head protector" not for beauty, but comfort. It had no more pretensions to *beauty than I*. Do you know that if ever you write me of *my beauty* that I will set you down as a *flatterer* and *as insincere*. You are just as well aware as I am that *I am not beautiful*, and I am not gratified when any one says so. I am just as they say in Ky. the ugliest of my Mother's handsome daughters and simply plain Dee Todd. I am used to being called so, and I do not feel it at all.

I promised to write you of the Tableaux but have only time to say some [were] very beautiful. These were for the benefit of the "Guards." Each company will be remembered by Tableaux. The next for the "Cadets." Everybody will be at home then and much more will be made. I was in hopes I would hear again from your sister and brother. Where is he now? And what regiment does he belong to? I am with many others interested and anxious about the fight expected on the Potomac any day. I wish it

---

77. John LaRue Helm (1802–1867) served as both the eighteenth and the twenty-fourth governor of Kentucky, in office from 1850 to 1851 and again for a matter of days before his death in September 1867. Benjamin Hardin Helm, Emilie Todd's husband, was his oldest child. The Helms were generally harassed by Union forces during the war, and John Larue Helm was even arrested in September 1862, but the governor interceded. See *Kentucky's Governors*, ed. Lowell H. Harrison (Lexington: University Press of Kentucky, 2004), 68–70.

were over but now I must say goodbye. Write to me soon and believe me ever yours,

Elodie

Camp Law, October 17, 1861

The batteries fired a number of shots last night and about day light this morning, but we have not heard with what result.

I had a long conversation with Major McLemore, who is on duty with our regiment. He is a graduate of West Point, and has always been in the army. He proposed to me that we should return to Alabama, this winter, and raise a regiment, for the service, in Kentucky. He would be Col. and I Lieut Col. I told him I would think of it, and before doing such a thing, I deem it my duty to tell you, and to ask your permission. As I have promised not to extend my term of service without it, and have no desire to do so, unless my Country should require it. I hope before the expiration of six months, Mr. Lincoln will be convinced that we cannot be conquered, and will be willing to recognize our independence.

I see from the papers that Col. Helm has taken the field with a regiment. I hope he will have an early opportunity of distinguishing himself in the service of the states rights party. I have no doubt of the ultimate union of Kentucky with the Confederate states. We hear, as a rumor, this morning, that Gen. McClellan is advancing in large force, and that Gen. Johnston has burnt Fairfax and retired to Centreville. If this is true, we will have another great battle, at Bull Run, and I hope with better results than that of the 21st July.

Major John T. Morgan[78] was here on Sunday, and thought, if the Yankees advanced, that we would fight them at Centreville. Unless we have a battle during the month of October, or early in November, the campaign will end and we will go into winter quarters.

I promise you that I will not allow the slanders that have been silenced to make me expose myself unnecessarily. I expect to do my duty, and dare all that I should dare as a soldier and gentleman. I trust in God, and will do my duty, relying upon him for protection.

---

78. John Tyler Morgan (1824–1907) first saw action at First Manassas with the Fifth Alabama Infantry. He eventually rose to the rank of general and served as a six-term U.S. senator (and a grand dragon of the Ku Klux Klan) after the war. See John Tyler Morgan Papers, Southern Historical Collection, University of North Carolina at Chapel Hill.

The remark in my letter about Mr. Averitt being surprised that you were not an Episcopalian was a *jesting* one, and not made upon any statement of his. That you should be a Christian is more important to me than that you should be a member of the Church to which I belong, and whose services I love. And the love I bear you, my dear Elodie, will never permit me, however much it would please me that we should belong to one communion, to regret your connection with any other church. These are matters, however, upon which we are never to disagree, and I will love you as much as a Presbyterian, as I would if you were an Episcopalian.

The soldiers here were much amused at certain gentlemen *playing soldiers* on the boards of Watt's Hall, on a recent occasion.[79] I have no objections myself to their outing in this capacity.

Oct. 18.

I have nothing to add to my long letter, save the presentation of my love for you. It burns as brightly as when it was expressed in the early spring flowers and [illegible] which you received so frequently, that I was sometimes afraid of offending you with them. It is pleasant to think of our past friendship, with the hope that it is to be ripened into the closer friendship of love. I am quite well. Present me kindly to your sister. With much love, and a kiss for your hand, I remain,

 Ever affty and sincerely yours
 N. H. R. Dawson

Selma, October 20, 1861

This morning the rain is pouring down and consequently I am . . . prevented from attending Church or visiting my sick friend, Miss Serena Parnell, who is, like Kittie, a victim to chills and unable to leave her room. This morning I dosed Miss Kittie with Quinine and gave her orders not to rise until the rain ceased, and as she does not obey the orders of an elder sister too well, I am sitting beside her to witness the enforcement of them if necessary. Yesterday I received your long and interesting letter of the

---

79. In the Civil War era, W. W. Watt's Hall was a common assembly room for Selma civic events.

7th, and I felt ashamed to think of the strain in which my last letter was written, and indeed hereafter I will *try* to be more cheerful and happy, and not write you such doleful missives. I am just as selfish as I can be and take advantage of a listening ear to pour my troubles into. Between my Mother and self there has always existed great confidence and we seldom had a thought unknown to each other, never a care or sorrow, and she taught me early to come to her for comfort and sympathy, and now that she is not with me, habit and selfishness leads me to turn to some one, who will be as kind, regardless of their own deeper troubles. And yet when I know you have suffered, and are surrounded with cares and trials, I mention to you things that I should not allow to make a moment's impression on my mind. Should you never return as long as I remained here, I would carry out your request, but I would endeavor to return as quickly as possible to my native soil and spend the remainder of my days among some of my old friends and associates, and surrounded by my own family, and then, try to live as I should. I could not stay here. Memory would be sufficient, and there would be no necessity for anything else to recall the past, which would be as fresh there as here, but I do not often punish myself to think of such an event. Hope in that case has almost full sway and brightens up the picture of your return with some of its most beautiful and brilliant hues. If to live in the future causes us to live more happily, it is certainly better to do so. But do you not think that we cause ourselves often unhappiness by allowing the so bright and beautiful anticipations and imaginary pictures to take possession of us? Each moment that we give them thought but strengthens the desire to have them realized and almost unconsciously we build our air castles, and it is not until they totter and fall that we realize they were but the "baseless fabric of a vision."[80] Could we but live in the present I think we would be much happier, but to some extent I am a dreamer myself of the future.

I met Dr. Paisley at Mrs. McCraw's and he gave me an account of the entire 4th Regiment from the time of their departure from Alabama up to the day of his own from Virginia. He did not meet with my sister but perhaps saw her. I had little or no conversation indeed with Mr. Price except on the usual topics of acquaintances. Mrs. Mabry returned to Selma last evening. Miss [illegible] sent over last night with her love and some nice Apples. She has always treated me in a kind and friendly manner

---

80. Elodie is referring to a line in Shakespeare's *The Tempest*, act 4, scene 1: "And like the baseless fabric of this vision / The cloud-capped towers, the palaces, / The solemn temples, the great globe itself— / Yea, all which it inherit—shall dissolve."

and I like her exceedingly. What do you mean by keeping you informed of Mrs. M——s "progress in the Arts and Sciences of courtship"? Has she been engaged in the act lately? And whom did she seek for a Victim? You drew quite an interesting sketch of your tents and surroundings, but I would prefer your *peeping* this way in preference to taking one that way myself; it would be a pleasure to see you and my friends, but then to see such a number assembled for such a purpose would be saddening for the sight would cause sad thoughts and my look would be a short one with a hasty retreat. I do not see how Mrs. Hardie stands it, but I believe she is infatuated with Army life already.

I have no doubt the wine Miss Gertrude sent was greatly enjoyed. I hope she will send more if she intends to remember you each time. From what I have heard of her partiality for Mr. T—— I am surprised she did not send all to him like I am going to do to you by George Mims tomorrow. I sent Ella word I would send anything she desired to Lieut McCraw, and Laura Mims sent word she had something to send (I suspect for Mr. Price) and I had a *little* to send you, so I hope between the efforts of us three there will be something nice. As George Mims will remain he now thinks a week in Warrenton, I will ask him to send the things on by Mr. Crail[81] of the "Guards" who will go on directly and who leaves tomorrow with him for Virginia. You did not tell me to read Mr. Knox's letter but I did. I had too much curiosity and you did not tell me not to do so. I will take good care of all your letters, promise not to have any of them published or speak of the contents to *anyone* against your wishes. You promised to write me upon your return from Picket duty, and the result of Capt Clapton[?]'s trial, and I take a greater interest in what you write me of Camp life and duties than you imagine. I would like very much to see that handsome young cousin you speak of, that you met with lately, Mr. Hamilton,[82] I think you told me was his name.

Last Friday night the children had Tableaux which were very pretty. Miss Ickes, Elsberry and myself helped them in the way of music and playing waiting maids for 32. I was quite amused at first but grew tired when they called on me to assist them so much. They all seemed to know me and my name was convenient to call and I made myself generally useful as did the others. You see I help on all occasions. I came to the

---

81. A. W. Crail was a private in Company A of Nathaniel's regiment. Alabama Civil War Muster Rolls, 1861–1865, Alabama Department of Archives and History.

82. Elodie is undoubtedly right that the name was Hamilton as there were many Hamiltons in Nathaniel's extended family.

conclusion that I would do whenever I could be of service no matter what others said or did. I have adopted this course and mean to pursue it occasionally. I do not act in the Tableaux, but assist in the music which is very simple and unpretending. I am not a fine musician. My Instrumental performance is indifferent and but for the "cause" and to be accommodating. I would never have consented to sing in public. There are but three or four good singers in Selma. Mrs. Weaver is the best and her voice is more cultivated than any I have heard. Miss Elsberry, Miss Ickes and Miss McCraw are the other singers, and in a concert you know there must be some indifferent singers to rest others and to show them off. As I made no pretensions to music I was willing to do my best. If you favor *my style* I will promise to keep up what I know and as *I do*, to play just when I am in a mood for it and not practice regularly. I have not done so since I ceased my music lessons. There is no fear of my growing old. I am not one of that kind and will not ever be much more so than now. I love to read but have a most unfortunate memory. I am sure if I was a month reading a work irregularly I would not even remember the title. My pleasure is just at the time for I cannot recall anything I have read and never remembered a date after recitation and no doubt would like some of the girls here put Kings and Queens of one reign in with those of centuries later. At one of the Tableaux we had a good laugh at "Josephine and Hortense being at the marriage of Lady Jane Grey"[83] but it was not because they did not know better, but they were already dressed in white and served as guests for Lady Jane's wedding. Some of us noticed it and mentioned how ridiculous it was, but when some historical scenes were mentioned in getting ready for them I heard some mistakes made in regard to facts well known *that I could not have missed.*

I believe I wrote to you of Mr. Wetmore's return. I have not seen him for a week. I heard Mrs. Wetmore was indisposed but I was so engaged [during] the bright days of last week I could not steal time to visit her. Mr. Hagood told me a few nights ago he intended if they succeeded in raising a company here to enlist and go with them to guard the coast this winter and by and by. I must not forget to tell you the "Tomato Catsup" I send was made by him and he sent it to me to send knowing I was going

---

83. Lady Jane Grey (1536–1554) was married in a triple wedding in 1553 to Lord Guildford Dudley and then served as monarch of England for nine days before being convicted of high treason. Josephine de Beauharnais (1763–1814) became wife of Napoleon I, and her daughter Hortense, Napoleon's stepdaughter, became the future queen of Holland. Why exactly this historical mash-up wedding was amusing is not exactly clear.

to send it on by Mr. Mims. *I tasted it*, and told him not to put in *anything* to *season it*, when he asked if he should. He is still as kind as ever and I think I have more than once done him injustice in ascribing to him in moments of [?], and I am very sorry I did so for I am convinced I have in him a firm good friend. The rain has almost ceased enough for me to visit my friend Miss Serena. I will write to you again in the morning, but really think this letter long enough to suit and tire anyone, and I will tell you goodbye until then and hope to pick up some items of interest by that time. I have not heard from my Bro David for two or three weeks and I cannot imagine where he is, but know he will write as soon as possible.[84] Now goodbye until Morning.

yrs Dee

I have only a few moments to write in, the Boat is here and we have just finished packing a Trunk. We placed names on different articles intended for you but for fear they are rubbed off, I will try (torn) mention them. A pound cake from Matt, a can of cakes, a jar of Pickles, 2 bottles of Claret, 2 of Peach Cordial, 1 jar of jelly, 1 jar of Peaches, 1 bottle of Tomato Catsup. I do not remember anything else. I wish we had more to send, but hope these will give you a taste and reach you in good order. Ella sends her brother several articles but they hurry me and I must say Goodbye. Excuse my haste and with love believe me,

yrs Elodie

Write soon

Dumfries, October 22, 1861

I dispatched you a short note, by Mr. Downs, with a letter of Mr. Mathews's, and your last, of 6th inst. to me on yesterday morning. I will try, this evening, to redeem my promise then to write you more at length, in a few days. The first battalion moved to this place on Sunday evening, and the second came up yesterday morning. Of all places where we have yet been camped, this is the most inconvenient. We are on the side of a gravelly, sandy, hill, and as it has been raining since last night, we are now almost in a quagmire. About three o'clock yesterday afternoon, one of Gen.

---

84. After his dismissal from the Richmond prison system (and a month's rest and recreation at a Richmond hotel), David was scrambling in Colonel Tom Taylor's First Kentucky Regiment as an assistant quartermaster. Berry, *House of Abraham*, 98.

Whiting's alarming orders, to cook rations and to prepare to march, at a moment's notice, was received. The whole camp was soon engaged in its execution. Cartridges were issued and the arms inspected. At dark, a large picket guard was sent out, under command of Lieut. Shortridge, and about nine o'clock, a company was sent to support him, in case of an attack. About 10 o'clock, the Col. took all the axmen in the regiment, and went out, to clear the trees from the road, at the ford on the Accotink Creek, and orders were given that we should sleep in our clothes. At twelve o'clock, the Col. returned, and sent out another company to guard one of the approaches. All of these movements, as you can imagine, created much excitement, as they indicated the apprehension of an attack. The men, unfortunately, obtained liquor, in the neighborhood, and many of them were drinking, and made a great deal of noise. At one o'clock the rain began to pour, in torrents, and our tents, including mine, were flooded. Imagine the tents of a regiment, without straw, on the ground, and filled with water. Blankets and those who slept on them, wet with streams of rain water, and you have a picture of our condition. The night wore our wearily, and all were up, early in the morning, to pass almost as unpleasant a day. My feet have been wet until recently, but I am now in my tent, for the evening, sitting upon an oil cloth, with my writing materials on my knees, writing to you.

No Yankees attacked us, and the over-cautiousness of our officers, or their disposition to give false alarms, caused us to pass a most unpleasant night. It was said the enemy were about twelve miles off, approaching us, to flank the batteries, at Evansport. But we hear no more of the rumor today, and I hope the news was untrue, at all events, that they will not attack us in this weather.

The season is rapidly closing, and the beautiful hues of autumn are fast [illegible] the forests. As we marched over, on Sunday, while I was admiring the woods, I thought of your last letter, in which you speak so *prettily* of your preference for this season of the year. I love it more than I do the other seasons, which brings with it the beautiful flowers. I love to see summer, laying down his golden crown, and losing the purple from his ruddy cheeks, and winter gathering to her bosom the rich fruits of her royal spouse. Like you, when other stars overshadowed me and while the flush of youth was up on my brow, I used to spend hours alone in the woods, at this season. The deep love I have always had, in my nature, for domestic scenes, made me almost a recluse, and I never felt less *alone* than when I was permitted solitarily to roam the beautiful live oak grove of Gardenia. My father's mansion was surrounded by beautiful gardens,

which in time were bordered by a large park of these magnificent trees
in which many of the happiest hours of my childhood were passed. With
my loved mother, how often have I trod the walks under those venerable
trees and looked up into her face as she recounted the deeds of Robin
Hood and his men. Alas that we ever live to wake up to the stern realities
of life. And what would life be without the influence of our *Elodie?* God,
who made man, saw that woman alone could fill the gaping void of companionship in his bosom, and also created her that her love might teach
him the love he should bear to his creator. I do not think men could
have received the revelations of the gospel, without the inspiring faith
of the gentler sex to lead him to an appreciation of the truth. All of the
virtuous impulses I ever feel are attributed to the teachings of my sainted
mother and the influence of your sex. Without them I would have been a
barbarian, and I have only to look around at the depravity of our soldiers
to be convinced of this truth. I do not think any other feeling than one
of duty could induce me, with my present feelings, to adopt war as my
occupation.

But, alas, how forgetful? I have filled three pages of a letter to my
loved Elodie without one word of affection. Are you not surprised when
you remember how my letters have been usually filled to the brim with
words and protestations of love? But I have tried to write you more inter-
estingly, and let you take for granted how much you are loved. Can you
tell me that you have always liked the *tone* of my letters? Have I not been
too loving to please you? You must excuse me, however, for loving you so
fondly. It is my nature to be ardent in all my feelings, except that of hate.
I hate no one, but when I have a dislike, I always try to avoid the person,
when I love, I always like to be near. I begin to fear that it will be out of
my power to get a furlough, and that six months must pass before we see
each other. I assure you the prospect of a dreary winter, in our tents, is
not at all encouraging. I expect to sleep most of the time away. Reading
will be out of the question, as the great effort will be to keep warm, and I
can see no better mode than to lay in our beds day and night.

We are now reduced to the strictest point with our baggage. The men
are allowed to carry nothing but their cooking utensils and tents on the
wagons. The company officers are allowed a mass chest, and a small
trunk or valise. I came near losing mine at Camp Law, but hope to hold
on to it until we get into winter quarters. The ladies send a good many
articles that are useless, and which are thrown away upon occasions of
moving. I think really they are imposed upon. We have now everything
that we require, except *hats*, a winter uniform and overcoats. I have ordered the hats and overcoats from the Quartermaster department, and

they will be paid for out of the clothing money allowed to the men. Really we have more money than our friends at home. I tell you these things to show you that we are not suffering. The things sent by Mrs. Hardie have not reached us, and will not be brought to us until we get permanently quartered for the winter. I saw Mrs. H. on Sunday morning. She has been quite sick recently.

Several of my company will be leaving for home in a few days, having been honorably discharged for inability to perform their duties. Among them are Boykin Goldsby, Dr. Avery, Billy Harrison, and others not known to you. I will write you by some of them. Mr. Kennedy[85] left this evening, but I did not care to entrust a letter to him, as he is not a man I like or admire, and I will ask you not to allow him to pay you any but unavoidable attention. He leaves very few friends behind him, and tho' under obligations to me, is not by any means a man upon whose friendship I would rely, or one from whom I could receive a favor. We are friendly, but I keep him at a distance. He is not a man to whom our hospitalities should be extended.

How pleasantly and happily I could spend this dark rainy evening with you. How I would look up into your beaming eyes, and see the beams that have been so softly shed upon others turned upon me, but another year must pass before I can spend a winter evening with you, unless my furlough is obtained. What a luxury it will be to sit, and talk, and read together, before a blazing hearth. You are the sweet angel that is to bless me, and reward me with your love. Such love as mine for you can *only end in Heaven, it is a foreshadowing of the love we will enjoy there.* I reciprocate your desire to talk with me, and I promise to be a good *listener.* My love and admiration for you increase every day. Have you seen Rev. Mr. Small? He is a friend of mine, and from Mr. Byrd, and himself you will no doubt receive more interesting details of our mode of life, appearance, and military bearing. I will leave off for tonight. Adieu. May God bless and keep you my darling and loved Elodie.

Sincerely and affectionately yours,

N. H. R. Dawson

Oct. 23. I have just returned from selecting a better encampment near by in the woods. We will prepare it this evening, and move there tomorrow.

---

85. Both Arch E. Kennedy and George D. Kennedy were enlisted in Nathaniel's regiment. The context does not make it clear whether Nathaniel is referring to one of these soldiers or to a visiting member of their family. Alabama Civil War Muster Rolls, 1861–1865, Alabama Department of Archives and History.

We are now on the plantation of Lord Fairfax, "Free Stone Point," within cannon shot of the Potomac. Near by lie the remains of a British officer, who was buried in *1698*. The epitaph speaks of him as a good Britain and a gallant officer. There is no tradition in regard to his death. I will visit the grave, and in my next letter will send you the epitaph. I am fond of these old monuments. They serve to remind me of our own mortality and of the records we are to leave behind us, when we shall shuffle off this mortal coil.

I was quite unwell last night, but the bright sunshine has dissipated my bad feelings. I try to be content with our situation, and endeavor to repress all disposition to murmur at our privations. We must be patient, and relief will come. Our Independence is a fait accompli. I have read parts of Mr. Breckenridge's address with great admiration. He's a true man, and will have all Kentuckians, who love their state, to his standard. Do you know anything of our mutual friend, whom I met at Baltimore, in the Kentucky delegation? His name has escaped me, but you will remember him, as he spoke of you frequently.

I must now close dear Elodie. I will write you again in a few days. If a battle takes place, I will telegraph Maj. Haden, so that you will hear the result. There is an office at Dumfries. Present my respectful compliments to your sister. My heart still keeps your image sacred, and my love is as faithful as the shadows to the object they reflect.

With much love, and a kiss for your hand, I remain,

Very affectionately and sincerely your attached,

N. H. R. Dawson

Selma, November 2, 1861

Altho' I wrote you a few days since, I cannot allow the opportunity of Mr. Averitt's returning to pass without sending you a letter especially as he has been kind enough to ask me to send one by him. He has just left us, paid his parting visit and I feel as I could [illegible] it a scene so sorry do I feel, if I could only give my own [illegible] to giving away to my feelings, but I know it is wrong and I will try to bear everything as bravely as possible a little while longer. I received a letter from you and a package of my own by Mr. Byrd on Wednesday, also a letter last night dated the 22nd and I am *much obliged* to you for complying so hastily and truthfully to my request of long letters and such interesting ones as you have recently penned. I am like yourself always gratified to receive one, as they afford me more pleasure than anything else. Indeed I may say with truth, they are my only happiness for you know I am a suffering exile too from my loved home and too dear friends. Not even a line is received to assure me of their safety and well being of those dear ones. I often wonder if I have not seen and kissed my dear old Mother and my loved brother[86] for the last time, and if it can be that I am indeed never again to behold them. I try to prepare myself in vain to even receive such a thought [but] I cannot, and pine to be in Kentucky "up and doing" with them and the noble women there who are exerting themselves to do all in their power to aid our and their own cause. I cannot let my old State throw off her tyrannical yoke and be a silent inactive looker on during its glorious struggle. I cannot interest myself I want and must do something myself that will aid if it be but the smallest amount in the whole effort and I hope for a chance very soon, which will afford me so great a happiness. But I must write of something else beside old Kentucky but it seems to me if I have my wits turned, that will be the subject for the love and interest I have for it increase every day, but I will not say another word about Ky in my letter *if I can avoid it.*

Mr. Small has returned I hear. I have not seen him or heard repeated any of his conversations on the subject of his sojourn among the soldiers. You should not have written to me that the soldiers were so much more comfortable than I imagined them for I am affected forthwith with a feeling of downright indolence in consequence and I hope no one else will hear it, for fear they will be affected in the same manner. I knit Mr. Averitt a "Head Protector" and Kittie knit one for his friend Col. Ashby[87] at his request. Sister Matt has added a Comfort to our little package of mementoes. He told me of his *secret* and asked me to promise that he should marry me but I would not do so then, but promised afterwards as I had promised you the same thing a short time since. The more I see of Mr. Averitt the more I admire and like him, he is so good that I wish I could always be surrounded with his influence. You need not fear Mr. Kennedy's paying any attention, he never has, and you know from the beginning and extent of my acquaintance with him as it began at the same time yours did, but if he should have any desire to do so at this late day, I will certainly do as you request me and avoid them and him. He has

---

86. She probably means Alexander Todd, who had remained in Kentucky near his mother.

87. Probably Turner Ashby Jr. (1828–1862), the Confederate cavalry commander who would be killed at the Battle of Good's Farm.

lady friends who are greater admired than I, altho' I really think him an agreeable and pleasant man. Our friend Mr. Wetmore has been elected Captain of a new company formed there for the Coast defense, and took to the honor with such ill grace that he was seized with chills and has not recovered yet from the effects. The favorite you mention must be Mr. Leach. I am unable to give you the slightest information of him since last spring the tidings then were favorable and to his credit, but I see the horror[?] of several friends who have gone on the *other side* among them Col. John Harlan[88] a very talented brave man, with an *Indiana wife*, that is.

I wrote you I have called to see Mrs. Mabry and Miss Tatt but strange to say they have not returned my visit with their characteristic promptness. They do not keep up their former interest in me. The ladies Military aid society has been reorganized. Miss Ferguson and Miss Perkinan are Secretaries, so prepare yourself for interesting documents there is so much indignation expressed by many ladies and gentlemen about the partiality shown the "Blues" that I would not be surprised if there was not a society organized for them especially. I want to be *Secretary*, but will have to begin and practice penmanship and business letters.

You tell me that you are fearful you cannot obtain a furlough, now do you not feel ashamed to have raised my hopes and expectations of an early meeting to become so soon dashed? You ought. I am indeed very anxious to see you and do not relish the idea of so many months passing before I can do so and hope you will succeed in your efforts to obtain one. Your friend Col. Law will *receive a piece of my mind* if he does not aid you as far as lies in his power. I could put up a very pitiful face if he was near and touch his good heart, but I will be just as "brave as a soldier" and bear the disappointment in such a manner that you would compliment me if you were present to witness it unknown to me. Yes I was astonished at your *cooling off so much*, but I took for granted you meant and felt what you did not say. I am so vain, unless you had just met with some beautiful and accomplished Lady whose *charms* had caused your heart to turn astray, but then I thought it would turn back again after a while and did not distress myself in the least, for if you forget I will treat you in the same manner and smile on some of my old admirers. But I am too vain

---

88. John Marshall Harlan (1833–1911) was a lawyer and politician from Kentucky who had mustered into the Tenth Kentucky Infantry and after the war served on the U.S. Supreme Court, offering famous lone dissents in the *Civil Rights Cases* (1883) and *Plessy v. Ferguson* (1896). For more, see Linda Przybyszewski, *The Republic according to John Marshall Harlan* (Chapel Hill: University of North Carolina Press, 1999).

and conceited to think of such a thing and think that if you do not see me until your time has expired you will be like myself, *still in love*. Mother used to tell me that I would never marry because I could not make up my mind and select from my beaux, and that if she were a suitor, she would bring a clergyman with her whenever she asked the important question, and have it over at once, if the answer was favorable. I told her "just wait until I see the right one." How much injustice she did me, for I declare my heart has been perfectly stationary for six months with a constancy that would do credit to any one.

Camp Law, November 7, 1861

I have received your two letters, by Geo. Mims, of the 13th, and of the 27th, both on yesterday, and am, as ever, much gratified to know that your thoughts are so frequently turned towards me. When the trunk arrives, as it will today, ample justice will be done to your nice things, and I will have the satisfaction of knowing that you provided them.

Your last letter is to me most welcome, as it brings me, next to your avowal of affection for me, the assurance of your willingness to become a member of my church. It was what I have no reason to expect, as I knew your early teachings have been in a church to which your mother was attached, and in which all of your religious impressions were received. I accept this as the best evidence you could give of your love and affection.

You need not apologize for the tone of your letters, in mentioning your troubles and trials. I am never so well pleased as when you write freely upon these subjects, for they show where you turn, in the absence of a dear mother, for sympathy, and I think I deserve the confidence, as I have placed it in you. And I will even do it now. The election for Lieut-Col. took place yesterday and the day previous. There were six candidates, Captains Bowles & Dawson, Maj. McLemore and Lieuts Geo. D. Johnston of Marion, Jas. Hardie of Selma, and Thos. Coleman of Union Town. On the first ballot, we stood in the following order Dryer, Johnston, Coleman, Dawson, Hardie, and McLemore. On second ballot Hardie & McLemore were dropped. My vote increased on third [and] ran up to 146 votes, four candidates in field. I then withdrew, but my company again cast its vote for me. On next ballot Johnston withdrew, and we put Capt Goldsby in the field and elected him after three ballots. I received the unanimous vote of my own company, save one, every time, with that of the Guards after Mr. Hardie withdrew. But he, after having promised to support me, did all he could to influence his company to vote against me, but I am glad to say I beat him in his company, and his candidate afterwards, and we elected Capt Goldsby against all combinations. Mr. Hardie has *played out* to use an old phrase, and in his own company is ruined. This morning an election for the Captain of the Guards was held. It is just over, and Mr. Kidd, the orderly sergeant, beat him, receiving 52 votes to 6 for Mr. Hardie. This ruins him. I am much gratified at the vote I received. The largest vote by any candidate, except Col. Goldsby on last ballot, was 213, my largest 146. The regiment was so equally divided between the six candidates that we could never have made one election.

I will now mention a disgraceful thing that occurred last evening. Lieut Shortridge, in a fit of intoxication, and much offensive language to me, drew his knife, and insulted me most wantonly. I did not strike him, and he was taken off. This morning, I addressed a note to him, by [illegible] Goldsby, demanding a retraction. He has just written me retracting his language. I can never have for him the same feelings I have entertained. He read law in my office, and I had reason to regard him as a friend. His conduct seems to have arisen from a suspicion in his mind that I like Lieut McCraw better than himself. Did you ever hear of such infatuation? It may become a jealous lover but not a man. Has anyone a right to hate me because I love you above all others? I tell you this *confidentially*, but to show you how much confidence I have in you, and how much I love you. I fear it is troubling you too much.

Until Major Scott returns, I will act as Major, as I am now the senior Captain. We hear that Gen Moore has requested Pres. Davis to send this reg't to Mobile, but I fear the Pres. will not do so from motives of policy. It is now becoming cold. Last night was almost as cold as we ever have it in Ala. This is a bright beautiful day. The forests are changing their Autumn color for the deeper mourning of winter. I was apprized of Mr. Averitt's visit to Ala. by a letter from him on his way.

Geo. Mims is here. He tells me a great deal of you, and seems to know that we are engaged. I received from Mrs. Fannier yesterday a beautiful "comforter" and have written my thanks this morning. I will thank Mrs. Parnell for the cake, and try to write a handsome note, as she will show it to you. I hope you will forgive Mr. Byrd for his indiscretion. He certainly acted from good motives, and is truly my friend. I am glad you have changed your opinion of Mr. H.

I do not think I will remain in the army after this year. I must certainly return home to you, to remain at least one year before doing so, unless there is an imperative duty. As your husband, I will never leave without your consent, or without a sense of duty.

I am quite well, and hope soon to be gratified by receiving another of your letters. There is a post office at Dumfries, where I will mail letters, but you better continue to write me at Manassas, as we have frequent opportunities from there, and our remaining here is uncertain. I have written you frequently by mail and by persons. Please always indicate the date and channel thro' which you send my letters.

I cannot consent to the burning of your letters. I expect much pleasure from them in the future.

With my kind regards to your sister, and much love for yourself, and many prayers for your happiness, I am

    Yours devotedly and affectionately
      N. H. R. Dawson

Selma, November 9, 1861

Altho' this is not my usual day for writing, yet my inclination to do so is so great, that I have put aside my knitting to indulge. I am too home-sick and sad tonight to utter one word and too much of a *woman* to cry, and concluded to dispel my moodiness by talking to you on Paper. I have been anxious and uneasy ever since hearing of the Battle at Columbus Kentucky fearing my brother and brother-in-law may have been engaged,[89] and I am ignorant of their whereabouts, and you know I am perfectly dependent on the Telegraphic column for my information, but I will try to be cheerful and hope for the best until I hear to the contrary as I will hear of many Battles before the War is over and must accustom myself to the suspense. I received your letter of the 2nd of November last night, and am glad to hear you have again returned to "Camp Law" and your few comforts indeed. I sympathize very much with you, that so many seemingly unnecessary marches are forced upon you, and more hardships and privations, and I fear the Winter will prove too much for some and perhaps thin your ranks as they are so severe in comparison to those of the sunny South. I never enjoyed the extensive cold weather

---

89. Elodie is referring to Benjamin Hardin Helm and his aide-de-camp, her brother Alexander Todd.

and always preferred admiring the snow as beautiful, throwing over the Earth and trees its white robe, thro' the windows, to taking sleigh rides and snow balling matches even when I had a nice entertaining beau. I thought it more sensible and pleasant to sit by a cheerful fire. I love the Fall Months. They are sufficiently cool to please me, and the pleasure of seeing summer also is great, especially the leaves. A few evenings since, I walked in the woods and amused myself for some time collecting a beautiful bouquet of richly tinted leaves but gathered so many that I am obliged to throw away some. I believe I could have spent the day gazing on the trees of so many different colors. This time a year ago I used to go hunting with my Brother[90] and enjoyed myself to my heart's content rambling in the woods of dear old Ky. I wish I was there now, but how foolish to make so vain a wish, one so impossible just at present.

I did not call on Miss Avery. I believed she made no stay here. My cousin Mrs. Craighead was making us a visit and I could not have accomplished the call had Miss A. remained, but will certainly do so if she returns to the Convention. I have often heard Matt speak of her in the highest terms of admiration as a noble and good woman and together with your admiration for her am prepared before knowing her to appreciate her many excellent qualities. I believe Dr. Avery is as yet the only one who has returned, the others must have been detained on the wayside to bid farewell to their *Virginia Sweethearts* who have usurped our places and thrown us so completely in the shade as I have not seen or heard of their arrival. Indeed, I am not like yourself, in the habit of limiting the love of any one for one. You may love me just as much as you desire and *perhaps more*, and if you can accomplish the wonderful stretch of imagination required to think me beautiful I will not even object to that. It seems strange to me that any one having such an affectionate disposition as your relations all give you credit for possessing can to all appearances be so *haughty* and *cold*. I used to think you terribly so and must confess to great astonishment when I discovered you had like others feeling and more love and kindness then the generality of human beings. Your Aunt makes me believe I have secured the jewel in the Land or I should say *tries*, as I do not think all her recommendations have remained hidden from my eyes or that she *likes you any better than I do*. I am sure I shall love her for I can from her letter fancy her a charming woman and imagine that your sister in many respects resembles her. I hope you have assured

90. Probably Alexander Todd.

her of my being heart and soul with the Confederate states, and those
of my family who are able to accomplish anything to aid in the cause
are also, and that I have in *Mother's kin* and please to remember that I
am a Southerner myself, for when I am at home we Kentuckians think
ourselves as much Southerners as anybody. The inhabitants of this little
town think because Kentucky is not on a Cotton Plantation that there is
no difference between me and a Northerner, and I sometimes let them
know of their mistake. So I shall be apt to remind her if ever I meet her,
and she does not acknowledge me as such. We were so distressed to hear
the Federals had seized Fort Royal and Ft. Walker, and I hope their victory is not so great as now represented.

Can I not knit you a pair of socks like Mrs. Shaw's?[91] Which kind were
they? Tell me all about them and in the meantime I will try to find out myself, and I will knit you a pair, if you will come home for them, and then
I can have an opportunity of seeing all those changes you speak of. You
know I am a great admirer of gray hair, but not so partial to wrinkles. If
you had not mentioned a short time ago the fact of some of your friends
thinking you looked better than they ever saw you, I would believe you
were "grey headed" and looked "five years older." I heard a Lady (a young
Lady at that) expressing her admiration of your handsome looks and
military bearing, and her opinion that the Photograph at [illegible]'s did
not do you justice, this morning while there so if you are so changed you
must keep out of her sight or lose her admiration. I met your neighbors
yesterday. The young lady is as charming as ever and her mother as polite
and kind and I shall be sorry to lose her friendship, but will not allow it
to distress me as I am not to blame.

May I just here ask you a question, but I do not wish you to answer it
if you feel a hesitancy and I have no right to another's secret, are Miss T.
and Mr. Haden engaged? I have heard so and then I have heard that
altho' they were pleased with each other, that Mrs. M. did not exactly
agree to it, and many think she is engaged to you, but I do not think it
is to either, or anyone. The Dr is in Montgomery and all I have heard of
or from him is "that the coffee at the Hotel is terrible." While I write the
rain is falling in torrents, the weather for a week has been beautiful and
so mild but now I fear it will be cold and damp and I will be compelled
to forego the pleasure of my walk every Evening. Yes you heard me say I

91. Probably Mrs. S. Shaw, age fifty-one, mother of four married to R. Shaw, of Selma.
1860 Census: Selma.

loved to ride horseback, that was my favorite, indeed my only exercise at home and I am almost masculine in my fondness for a beautiful horse, and would much prefer such a pet to any other. I would prize your war steed very much, but to be a Hero you must have it killed under you in some way, have its head shot off. I think that would appear the funniest. I would be afraid as I am out of the habit of riding to mount a blind steed or headless one either, but I must bid you goodnight and finish my letter as usual tomorrow Evening,

Yrs affectionately, Elodie.

Sunday Evening, November 10, 1861

This evening I went to Mr. Small who preached the best Sermon I have ever heard him deliver, and the first time since his return from Virginia. This Evening Mr. Hagood spent with me and I showed him your Ambrotype which I promised to do at the end of three months when I received it and I wanted him to know it. He evidently suspected and was somewhat prepared. I have heard today that the Bridges between Chattanooga and Atlanta and thro East Tenn were burned and I feel further off from home than ever. It is a great pity and I suppose they will be rebuilt immediately as they are so necessary. I am sorry I mentioned not being well as it made you uneasy. I am now very well and think the cold weather and plenty of exercise will keep me so. Kittie has been quite unwell for two or three Weeks and I think would have accomplished [illegible] home if she had been sufficiently well. A change would do her good and I would like one myself and I think I will pay a visit to Marengo[92] also for I am heartily disgusted with Selma. The longer I stay the more disagreeable it is and if it were not for a *few families that I like and visit* I could not stay, but I ought not to write you of your home in this way, but nevertheless it is true that I feel so and am one of the kind that gives utterance to her likes and dislikes plainly and for this reason have not many friends, but I have no desire to be *popular.* Give me one, two or three *sincere* and *pleasant friends* and I can be independent of the whole community. Yet I would prefer having no Enemies and would not seek them. And would of course wish to be kindly thought of, but friends are "few and far between" yet I have more and better ones than I deserve and I appreciate them and never

92. Marengo County, Alabama, was due west of Dallas County.

can forget them altho miles now separate us and we may never meet again on Earth but I hope we will be reunited in Heaven.

I have seen Mr. Wetmore several times this week but had little conversation with him. Mrs. W. is still having chills but looks remarkably well. I believe I wrote you of your other neighbors. They are well but I am inclined to think something has gone wrong as they have not returned my call yet and usually they are so prompt. We received a letter from my Brother[93] a few days ago. He is at Centreville and writes very cheerfully. By this time you must have seen or heard from Mr. Averitt. He told me he had written to you to meet him in Richmond and he anticipated the pleasure of meeting you there, but here I have filled six pages of what? To you nothing worth reading, so I will cease hoping soon to have the pleasure of talking in place of writing, and then I will try to do my best in entertaining you, but goodbye. Write me soon a long letter and with love believe me I am ever yours

Affectionately and sincerely, Elodie

To Capt. N. H. R. Dawson
Manassas Junction
Virginia

Please tell me if I direct your letters correctly. I do not think so but know of no other way.

Camp Law, November 12, 1861

I was the recipient yesterday of a large package of letters by Mr. Averitt, and the most welcome one was yours of the 2nd inst. I assure you its length was not objectionable and never will be with me. You must remember that reading long letters is a part of a lawyer's duties and that I am not to be wearied by those from you. Mr. Averitt wrote me that he had a most pleasant visit, and I envy him the pleasure of having seen you, but I look forward to our meeting with hope, and know that it is a pleasure worth many trials. I believe that it would be best for both of us to defer the meeting until I can remain, to claim you as mine. I feel deeply your situation, as "an exile," from your native soil, but do not think you should return before we are married. You could be of little service, except as a

93. This letter from Alexander Todd does not survive in the collection.

source of comfort for your friends, and you would be widely separated from me. I hope you entertain no ideas of going back. If I could control you, I would exercise the *power* to restrain your intention. If I am not mistaken your home, Frankfort, is now in the hands of the Federalists. Am I correct? Your heart has been stationary for six months, but I can say that mine has been since Mr. Davis's reception, 22d Feb'y. There are no charms that can make it deviate from its anchorage. I am drawn a captive at the wheel of your chariot. And you must not now discard me. But I have no fears upon the point.

I have seen in the Montgomery Mail of 29th at the Flag speech of Col. Battle, at Norfolk. He makes a beautiful allusion to our flag, but is wrong in saying that we lost it through the battle of Manassas. I will try to get the extract for you.

The Confederate Army has a new flag. The Southern Cross, upon a field of Pink, yellow borders—blue cross from the corners—with white stars. The General sent us one, and it was presented to the reg't by Col. Law in a beautiful little speech. You know it is my favorite, and we all like it better than the *stars and bars*.

Sunday the whole regiment went down to Evansport, and bivouacked there that night. I visited the batteries, and found one of them under command of an old friend from Ala. now an officer in the Arkansas regiment, Lieut Bussy. Evansport is the farm of a gentleman, bearing that name. The house is within one hundred yards of the river, and is a comfortable farm home. One of the Yankee streamers shelled it, while the family were at breakfast, and shot a ball through the room where they were. The home is now deserted, and the place about in a state of ruin. I send you a rose leaf from the garden, and a piece of a boll of cotton which grew near by. The Yankees are opposite Evansport, in Maryland. I saw their battery distinctly. They may intend to make an attack. When I looked at Maryland, and thought of her condition, I reverted to Kentucky, and was glad that her sons were struggling for liberty. I heard the evening we went down of the battle at Belmont, where we defeated the Federals. We, also, hear that their fleet has taken the forts near Beaufort, So. Ca. My mother was born there, and I have many relatives in the town. Lieut. Hamilton of the Hampton Legion lives there. He is very anxious to hear from his father. I heard from Mr. Wetmore yesterday. He tells me that he has not heard from me for some time, but that he has several times seen a friend who seems interested in my welfare. I leave you to judge who he means. He tells me of the honor done him in electing him captain of the new company. I do not know whether it is a subject for congratulations or not.

Did I fail to tell you how deeply I would be disappointed if the furlough could not be obtained, and that it was a great disappointment? The plans of our Generals depend entirely upon those of Gen. McClellan. We will not go into winter quarters until the Yankees do, and while this state of things continues, no furloughs will be granted. We are in a state of uncertainty and perplexity too in regard to our movements. We will suffer a great deal if we winter here.

Geo. Mims has gone to Warrenton, on sick leave for ten days. I wish he had not returned at all. He has lost the trunk, and I fear the nice things will be thrown away. Mrs. Parnell will receive a note of thanks from me, for the cake, and you must not tell her that it was not recd.

I have a trunk with Mr. Averitt, but it has not made its appearance yet. None of the articles brought on by Mrs. Hardie have reached us. We lose almost anything that our friends send us.

I hope you will not become secretary for any aid society. The ladies have been very useful and kind, but I would prefer that you remain an independent contributor. I am opposed to all female societies, as I have never seen one, not even a Bible or church society, where unpleasant controversies did not arise. A lady should let her influence always be felt, in all good works, but she should never expose herself to the calumnies of the evil minded. For this reason, I have admired your prudence in withholding from an entire participation in these things, but nevertheless, always showing a willingness to render your aid. You can do this most effectually by not being an entire partisan. I have been amused at the remark of a little friend of mine, who wrote me recently. She said, "I go to the Aid Society every week. The people do nothing but talk. I have knit a pair of gloves for the Gen. and will send you a pair." Should I be honored with a communication from the fair secretary, at Selma, I will respond in beaming style.

I hope you will like Selma better when you live there longer. I have many true friends among the citizens, and I know you have only to be known to be appreciated. We will have Mrs. Wetmore and Mrs. Parnell for neighbors. While at Cahaba you will have in Mr. Mathews' family those who will love you dearly. I see nothing in the Selma papers. We now hear a very heavy cannonade in the direction of Centreville. It may mean something, but we are so accustomed to hearing cannon that it never disturbs us. I have a chimney in my tent, which gives smoke and heat enough to keep us quite warm. I wish you could see us at night sitting around and playing whist. We pass our evenings frequently at cards. I must now tell you goodbye. I will write you again Sunday, sending you two letters a week.

With many messages of love, I remain,

ever Sincerely and affty yours

N. H. R. Dawson

Selma, November 17, 1861

I have not received a line from you since the 3rd of the month, and can only account for your long silence by thinking you are indisposed or have forgotten me however I concluded this morning to try and find out what the matter was by writing myself. I have a wretched cold and yesterday suffered from a sore throat, something new for me. And altho I feel better today I did not go Church, thinking I might be improved by afternoon service and be more inclined to hear a sermon then. We have had company all week with us among our guests is Laura Mims but she is today with Mrs. McCraw.

Kittie is going over to Dayton to visit Mrs. Craighead and will be absent two or three weeks and I expect to be very lonely while she is away, but I think a change is absolutely necessary for her health, and hope she will be rid of chills. I received a letter from my Brother Ellick a few days ago, written from Bowling Green, the 13th day of October. He has been acting as aide to Genl Sloan[?] but has been transferred to my Brother-in-law's staff (Genl. Helm) and is acting as assistant Q Master, and yesterday I heard from David, so you see what good fortune has befallen me in one week but I assure you I missed *my other letters* very much. These do not satisfy me alone. You have spoiled me, and I think you terribly neglectful when I do not receive a letter every few days, and I can scarcely excuse this long silence. But for fear this may find you sick I will not scold any more, but hold in reserve the rest for similar conduct if you cannot give an excellent excuse. I have not an item today calculated to add the least interest to a letter and am as dull as can be myself and feel as tho I shall be inflicting punishment enough on you by sending you such a letter as this will be.

Next week the Convention meets and the half grown girls give a Tableaux for the benefit of the Maryland soldiers, and on Wednesday Miss

Maggie Fitts is to be married to Mr. Harris[94] of Tuscaloosa, but now a member of Capt. Smith's company at Mobile, and I think she is to accompany him. Week after next the young ladies I believe give Tableaux for the "Cadets" and just here my knowledge of the winter programme ends, unless the week after that forms some of the indignant ladies into a society for the Guards and Cadets in opposition to the worshippers of the chivalrous "Blues" of which company you have perhaps heard Mr. Robert McCreary is Capt., Dr. Kent having resigned two or three weeks ago.[95]

Monday Evening Nov 18th 1861

I was interrupted yesterday and compelled to put aside my letter until today. Laura and Kittie have both gone, Matt is paying attention to housekeeping and sick servants, so I will be lonesome, unless I am careful to employ my time in divers ways. I was gratified exceedingly today by your letter of the 7th of Nov. Why could it have been delayed so long on the route? I imagined you sick or marching. Indeed my imagination was roaming at large in order to conjecture some good reason for your silence, but now I must allow my ill will to vent itself on the mail. I had heard of the Election in the Regt for Lt. Col. and if *I was not afraid would tell you* I preferred you not being elected because I think you are becoming too much attached to the Army and will never be satisfied anywhere else, and my partiality for it is limited by a small amount of preferment. I regret the occurrence of the difficulty between yourself and Mr. Shortridge, as it will necessarily change your former opinion of him. I know of nothing more unpleasant than to be deceived in those who once were regarded in high esteem by us and compelled to be thrown with them after our feelings are changed. I have no acquaintance with Mr. S. but have met with him frequently at different houses in Selma. Indeed he was at Bro. Clem's several times during my previous visit here attending little sociables but never considered it was the duty of a gentleman to be intro-

---

94. The couple did marry and a few months later, Elodie wrote Nathaniel, "We have heard that Dr. Harris, the husband of Miss Maggie Fitts, was dead. Is it so?" Nathaniel's response does not survive in the collection. Marriage certificate, Margaret L. Fitts and John J. Harris, Dallas County, Ala., *Alabama, Select Marriages, 1816–1942.*

95. Robert A. McCreary was a member of the Twenty-Sixth Alabama Infantry. Alabama Civil War Muster Rolls, 1861–1865, Alabama Department of Archives and History.

duced to the young lady to whom they were given, and I never regretted it as I seldom heard anything of him to his credit. He and Mr. I. Q. Smith rank about equal in my estimation, perhaps I think less of Mr. I. Q. who you know has joined a company, Capt. Wetmore's, but there is felt by many a doubt as to his bravery carrying him as far even as Mobile, and I am sure I do not wish him left to guard Selma in the absence of others.

How I do wish Mr. Davis would give his consent to the 4th Regt coming to guard the Coast, or the Officers would allow furloughs, or a surprise of the same nature as that of Mr. Averitt's would I assure you be far more enjoyed. But I am trying to reconcile myself to the disappointment of not seeing you until next Spring and think I will be able to bear it quite bravely if you adhere to your resolution of not returning again, unless [illegible] compels, but I have no idea you will. I think your patriotism will be entirely too great to allow you to remain at home idle if a dozen go to fill your vacancy. I think it is to be regretted that so few at home who are of service to themselves or anybody else would not become imbued with the spirit or enough of it to leave and fill the places of those who should be at home.

Mrs. Framier is a pleasant lady and I will like her better than ever since her no doubt acceptable gift to you. I think I will have a small "souvenir" myself ere long to send you. Do you know anyone who will return next month that I can send by? I prefer sending by someone going on immediately to sending by Express as you may not receive the package. I am afraid the delay George Mims made at Wannactoa ruined all that was nice in your Trunk. If so I think you must punish him slightly as I charged him particularly to send it on if he contemplated making a trip on the roadside. If I meet with an opportunity I will try to do better as I may not have perhaps the same disadvantages in getting things ready to send next time. We collected and packed things in about twenty minutes.

We are enjoying such delightful weather and today is so bright and pleasant that I believe I am perfectly restored to health and have spent the morning knitting very industriously. I have not accomplished my visit to Mrs. Shaw yet and for fear I may not will rely on you for a good description of her present to Genl. Johnston so that I may be able to send you one also like it. I saw from the evening paper there had been a Battle at Pikeville Ky. We have had no news of my Mother since the 18th of September. It is just a year today since I came to Selma, little dreaming then that today I would be here, or that so many and varying changes would occur in that space of time. Much has transpired. A new Government has been formed and our fair and loved country plunged by a revolution

into a bleeding, weeping land with monuments of fallen Hero's, which will serve as landmarks to strangers who may perhaps visit our Southern Confederacy made more dear to us by the shedding of their blood, but alas! that the year ever arrived to cause this terrible change which will require years to recover from. But really I have written you a long dull letter and should apologize as certainly something is out of order that causes me to send such a written letter to you, but just blame my "pen, ink and Paper" and not the writer for misspelling and omitting so many words and a general carelessness pervading the whole letter. But I will not give you as usual another sheet to decipher this Evening. Write to me soon and tell me you are coming home next month and I will write you a *handsome letter if I can.* But goodbye believe me as ever yrs affectionately
   Elodie

Camp Law. Nov. 21. 1861.

I received, two days ago, my dear Elodie, your welcome letter of 10 and 11th insts, and have to thank you again for your affectionate interest in my welfare. I assure you nothing gives me so much happiness as the knowledge that in one heart, worth to me a thousand hearts, I am supreme, and that I there reign, as you do, in mine, without a rival to claim the smallest part of its domain. I cheerfully acknowledge your right to ask me any question, and therefore willingly answer yours in regard to Mr. H. and Miss G. He addressed her, but received no encouragement at the time. I think she alleged her extreme youth as a sufficient reason to excuse her, and I do not think there is an understanding between them. He is however much attached, and may renew his suit, when he returns home. *I* am not engaged to her, *as you know,* and never felt inspired by any of her charms. I have always liked her, and as a girl, she was and is still a favorite. I hope you are mistaken in regard to any change of feeling, but you know my friends *must* be yours, or cease to be mine.

   At last, the trunk, brought by Mr. Averitt, has arrived. It was full of packages for different persons, with a comforter and pair of gloves for me, but without any indication from whom I received them. Did Mrs. White send them? If so, please thank her, and tell her that they are most acceptable mementoes of her remembrance. Geo. Mims's trunk is still on the way. The Leggings sent Gen. Johnston by Mrs. Shaw were knit, and cover the boots. You must make me a pair and I will claim them *in person,* if possible, but you must make haste, as the winter is fast approaching.

Yesterday Maj. McLemore,[96] Lieut Johnston and myself went to Evans-port. We were fortunate enough to overtake Gen. Johnston, who was on a tour of inspection to this division of the army. He was accompanied by Maj. Genl. Holmes, Mr. Wetmore's brother-in-law, Brig. Generals French, Wigfall, and Whiting, besides a large retinue of aids, cavalry, etc. It was a splendid cavalcade of gallant gentlemen, all in uniform, and mounted upon noble steeds. As the train rode, at a gallop, over hill and dale, thro' the woods, beautiful in their autumnal robes of crimson, my mind reverted to the days of Ivanhoe, and I thought the comparison would have been complete, if my Elodie had been in the lead, upon a black charger. We were in the rear, and bid adieu to the company at Evansport. We visited all of the batteries, and saw those of Gen. Sickles's brigade on the other side of the river. We heard their drums beating. Just as we were approaching the batteries, they exchanged several broadsides with each other, and one of the shells burst near the chaplain of Col. Judge's Ala. regt. and roused him from a pleasant service. No damage was done us, but our shells exploded in their fort and sent them scampering in any direction. The morning was cold. We rode through *frozen puddles of water*. What think you of this for the 20th November? We dined with Cols. Judge and Baine, old friends. They had just selected their camp, and were in a state of disorder, but such things are every day occurrences with us, and did not interfere with the pleasure of the visit. After a hearty repast, and a glass of Virginia *brandy*, we mounted our horses and returned to Camp Law. You should have seen three officers buying candy at the ancient town of Dumfries. One of them got a pound of *rosin* by mistake. I will not tell you which of us was so unfortunate.

Gen. Holmes is a large portly gentleman, and was handsomely dressed. One of the aids told us that the old gentleman was deeply in love with Miss Baxter,[97] of Fredericksburg, and would soon marry her. His head-quarters are near that town. How will Mr. Wetmore like this news? On our return to Camp, we found that Gen. Johnston and staff had visited the regt. and had reviewed it, on his return to Gen. Whiting's headquarters. We also heard of the battle, at Springfield, in Mo. and the victory of Gen.

---

96. Owen Kenan McLemore had been transferred from the Fourteenth Alabama to the Fourth, where he served as lieutenant colonel, helping to help fill the officer void after the losses at Bull Run. For more, see Ben H. Severance, *Portraits of Conflict: A Photographic History of Alabama in the Civil War* (Fayetteville: University of Arkansas Press, 2012), 92.

97. Theophilus Hunter Holmes had lost his wife in 1859. If he was pursuing Miss Baxter, he was apparently not successful.

Price over the Federal army. I hope this news is correct.[98] I have just been handed a package from Cahaba. It enclosed a beautiful comforter from Rebecca Mathews. This is the fourth I have received. I will put the prettiest aside for you. I feel that I have more friends than I deserve.

I hope you will like Selma better in the future. I have many friends in Dallas, and Selma is the best place for me to reside, as it is central, and will one day have the Court House, and as I must pursue my profession diligently for *your sake* and *mine*, I prefer it to any place in the county. I am now permanently located there, and am, in a measure, identified with its improvement and interest. Under these circumstances, I know you will endeavor to like the place. Like you, I have no great love for its multitude. I have never darkened the doors of a dozen houses in the town. You may judge of the extent of my intercourse from this fact. It has no doubt been my own fault, as I was so happily situated, so much immersed in business, that I never felt like leaving home, when I returned to it. This will be the case in future, and you will hardly be annoyed by the large circle of my acquaintance. Selma is in no sense of the term a sociable place. It is almost too new. I know you will like Selma better. You will have many things to occupy your mind, as a matron, that you have not at this time. The duties of a mistress and housewife are numerous, and will take up much time. Then you will have *me* to *take care of* and *to pet*, which will hardly give you a moment to devote to *less important* matters. I am in earnest. I am as fond of being petted as a girl.

You judge me rightly, when you give me credit for some affection and feeling. I love the few whom I do love warmly, and admit no doubts or objections to oppose me. I will put up with the infirmities of a friend, but cannot with his vices. I know that I am misunderstood, and I have never been anxious enough to correct the impression, except in those cases where I desired to obtain the good opinion of persons. I rejoice that you feel that you are *warmly* and *affectionately loved*. The hour when you will be mine will make me the happiest of men, as it will place, under my care and protection, one dearer to me than life, and will give me the right to confess that love before the world. Why will you insist that it is a stretch of the imagination, in me, to think you beautiful? When others have always proclaimed it. While I know that you are beautiful, I assure you that I love qualities of *mind* and *disposition* in you which are far more essential to happiness than mere comeliness of person. It is the right of woman to

---

98. The First Battle of Springfield, October 25, 1861, was a Union victory.

be beautiful, her *mission* to be *good*. Eve was beautiful, and good, and I can only think of her as described by Milton.[99] As she was the type, so I regard you as the *prototype* of woman.

I have just seen a copy of the *Louisville Courier*, published now at Nashville, and I will have it sent to you. It will keep you informed of all that passes in Kentucky, and I hope will frequently bear you good news from those you love.

I see that Gen. Breckenridge has taken command of a brigade at Bowling Green. I hope he will soon have an opportunity to distinguish himself and that he will live to see your native state redeemed from the rule of Republicanism. Just here, I want to tell you that I regard you as a southerner, but as one entitled to more credit than if you had been a Carolinian. Your family has had everything to tempt its loyalty, and has not been found wanting. I assure you that my Aunt, Mrs. Strothart, knows this, and has too much delicacy of feeling, if she did not, to say one word that could wound your feelings. Care not for the opinions of those you mention nearer home, who have not the sense to appreciate merit, and whose jealousies would always make them unkind to those they feel to be their superiors.

I hope soon to be your guardian, ready at all times to sympathize with you, in all of your sorrows, and thus, to *divide* them, to share your joys, and thus to *double* them. We must be prepared to have sorrows in this life of ours, but we must be equally prepared to meet them cheerfully. With you to aid me in struggling with them, I know they will be greatly diminished. I am almost selfish in my love for you. I would be the sole person to contribute to your happiness, but I know how wrong would be the indulgence of such a feeling.

Ever and affectionately yours,

N.H.R. Dawson

Selma, Nov 23rd 1861.

Many thanks for your entertaining letter of the 12th received a few days ago, and which you know was greeted with a warm welcome, as is usually

---

99. It is hard to be sure precisely what Nathaniel is implying or how well he knows his Milton. In John Milton's *Paradise Lost*, Eve is thoroughly beautiful and deeply curious; she loves Adam but also finds him suffocating and is bored by their routine. This is probably not what Nathaniel meant.

the case with all of yours. I had become uneasy from not hearing for *ten days* and wondered at your silence, but since the arrival of your last two letters acquit you of all blame, and charge the mail with being anything but punctual or managed with the care and attention it should be. . . .

My friend Miss Serena leaves on Monday to visit her sister in Columbus Miss. and expects to be absent a month or six weeks. I shall miss her exceedingly and hope to see her earlier than she bids us hope. I have promised to stay with Mrs. Parnell when she has no one else with her during her absence. She is a dear old lady and I love her so much. I do not think if I should meet with an opportunity and could go to my mother that I would refrain from doing so. My mother is old and at this time ought to have the care and attention of one of her daughters, and not be dependent on anyone else for them. It is true they will be bestowed by relatives, but I would like to be with her and am afraid your bird would fly if it could, but when I see any chance for going *I will let you know before I start and* I hope since things have become so much brighter and more decided that it will not be long before Genl. Johnston will clear a pathway thro our state, and I do not think I could keep from going if he did so before five or six months, but as there is no hope of doing so at present and all looks so clouded and gloomy I need not say anything more on the subject. Indeed I assure you I was but jesting and thought I mentioned it in that way, when I spoke of becoming secretary for the new Society. I know too much of them to *ever become a member* and agree with you perfectly in your views on this subject, and beg you to have no fears as I have no serious intentions of doing any such thing. I am always willing to assist in sewing and knitting for them but do not desire to belong in any way to the sisterhood of uncharitable Gossipers, because I already possess enough of that *trait*, and do not want it increased. I think your Flag must be without a doubt perfectly horrid, the *stars* and *bars* were ugly enough, but to whose brain do we owe gratitude for such a device and selection or combination of colors? I wish they would adopt the Southern cross, a crimson field blue cross and white stars, or a *white field, crimson cross* and blue stars, with a red, white and blue border as it to my taste is far more beautiful than the stars and bars which resemble too much our old flag.

Sunday Evening   November 24th, 1861.

I wrote you the above hastily yesterday, not knowing that I would have it in my power to write you as usual this afternoon and was compelled very reluctantly to lay aside my pen to fulfill an Engagement and I spent nearly the entire day calling. I have just had the pleasure of reading your letter of the 17th and you would have been amused to have seen me on my return from church seat myself quietly before removing my bonnet or cloak to wait for my letter, knowing I would receive one today, and having seen Bro. Clem returning home, you can scarcely imagine the gratification your letters give or you would write as often as you once did, but doubtless when your duties are performed you feel little like corresponding, and as I have such a great dislike myself for writing letters I ought not to say one word on the subject. I find Lizzie's letter quite entertaining, and if she continues to improve, as she has since her first letter to you, she will certainly give you cause for being very proud of her and will add much to your comfort and happiness. I have heard that she is a very interesting child, and from the tone of her letter I judge that the heart and head are both being cultivated at the same time. I did not know before that you had but one brother. I do not remember to have heard you speak of him, tell me something of him when you write again.

I have a cousin Robt. B. Todd[100] of Louisiana who lives very near the line, whom I met with in N. O. two years ago. He has been a member of the Legislature two or three times and is a polished elegant gentleman. His wife was a Miss Bingham[101] of La. and last summer her Father stopped here to see us on his way to Montgomery to enter his son in the army. Cousin Robert is my Father's nephew, but I do not know whether he has a brother or not. Uncle David[102] lived in Mo. but I have never seen any but this cousin of his family. I love my Father's relations more than my mother's but have been thrown but little with those who live in Kentucky. Someday it will give me pleasure to tell you of some of them. When you write to your Brother will you please make some inquiries concerning the relatives he makes mention of for my special gratification. I am so glad Kentucky even at this late day is redeeming herself so nobly. If

---

100. Born in Lexington, Kentucky, Robert Barr Todd (1826–1901) was one of the earliest graduates of the University of Missouri; he went off to be a justice of the Supreme Court of Louisiana from 1880 to 1888. He died at the residence of his daughter, Sallie C. Todd, in Brooklyn, New York. His wife was Ann Ruth Bingham, the daughter of James Harvey Bingham and Sarah Davidson Bingham. Mary Barile, *Forgotten Tales of Missouri* (Charleston, S.C.: The History Press, 2012), 135–136.

101. Ann Ruth Bingham (1827–1900) was the daughter of James Harvey Bingham and Sarah Davidson Bingham. She married Robert Barr Todd.

102. David Todd (1786–1859) was an older brother of Elodie's father, Robert Smith Todd.

I was but there to see the struggle I cannot bear the idea of the whole of Kentucky's daughters being at home aiding at this time and I here doing not the slightest act, but perfectly idle. Do you feel sorry that you cannot go to South Carolina to fight now? I feel sorry for you as I imagine so many have the same feeling of patriotism, for their native state. My Bro. David was anxious to fight in Ky but has contented himself by joining Col. Tom Taylor's Regt.[103] We heard this morning the fighting was renewed at Pensacola, but no particulars. I do not fancy their fighting us so far south a particle and am fearful if they get a foot hold all my courage and threats to stand and encourage those who were to fight for me to the last will vanish unless I can get a brave *S. Carolinian* to shoulder his musket in my defense. It will be dreadful for the citizens of Mobile it is said.

Mr. Dennis left this morning. He desired me to send his kind regards when I wrote you with sundry messages; those I will reserve until we meet. I do not wish you to take me by surprise. I wish the pleasure of anticipating your return and being prepared to realize the happiness it will give me the moment you arrive so as I will not lose a moment of your short stay in trying to believe my eyes which I would do if you were to return without giving me notice. Mrs. Philpott told Mrs. Parnell the trunk had been lost and she had her confirmation from Etta. Mrs. P. will suppose some told you of her sending it and your anticipation will be nothing. I never mention you first to anyone but when asked or teased about you then speak of you. I saw your neighbors yesterday, they both astonished me with a kiss!! Wonderful to relate. Matt stopped to meet the Misses Avery this morning and they told her they intended calling tomorrow before leaving for home, so I will have an opportunity of meeting Miss Mary. We have had two or three days of cold weather and I am debating in my own mind whether I will go to church or not this evening but little Willie is so urgent that I think I shall have to go with him. He insists that Mr. Averitt is my sweetheart and cooly informed some one the other day "That Miss Dee was knitting him a beautiful pair of socks" and before I could say a word brought one to satisfy their gaze, but they happened to be yours and I will send them the first opportunity. Old Mrs. Parnell

---

103. A veteran of Mexican-American War, Thomas Hart Taylor (1825–1901) was a lawyer and cattleman before the war. He served as commander of the First Kentucky Infantry before being transferred to brigade command and then to serve as a provost marshal of the Department of Alabama and East Mississippi. For more, see *Kentuckians in Gray: Confederate Generals and Field Officers of the Bluegrass State,* ed. Bruce S. Allardice and Lawrence Lee Hewitt (Lexington: University Press of Kentucky, 2008), 258–263.

insisted on my going to church every day last week and once she insisted on my telling her my reason for not going and I replied I did not wish to do so. She threw up her hands with holy horror exclaiming "oh Miss Dee Mr. Dawson would be so shocked to hear you say so" and I am prepared now that her company has gone to receive a good lecture during my next visit. But I must say goodbye with a prayer for your safety. Believe me to be ever yrs affectionately

    Elodie

Camp Law. Dumfries Va., Nov. 25. 1861.

I wrote you on the 21st, but must not lose the opportunity of doing so again by Captain Reese.

Since writing, I have improved and am well enough today to anticipate, with pleasure, a dinner upon roast turkey and oysters, dainties which a soldier seldom sees in camp, but which a cheating huckster sometimes brings to tempt the hungry and to deplete their purses. Men here seem to place no value upon money. If to be had the price of a thing is not regarded if within the means of the purchaser.

The weather is very cold, and I am in my tent, writing over a fire, which the ingenuity of the Yankees has enabled me to have. You may have seen a description of the fireplace, in the newspapers. It is very simple, a hole two feet deep and square, with a place underground to carry the smoke to the exterior, a barrel being placed over the outside opening to draw the smoke. I adopted the idea and now they have become common. We are to change our location this week, for a new camp, more conveniently situated, and less exposed to the winds. It is about a mile from Camp Law.

We will commence building huts for winter, as the weather is too cold for tents, and even if we have to leave them, we will be more comfortable while we remain in this vicinity.

I hear that Dr. Kent has resigned and returned home, and that he abuses Col. Winston, assigning his dislike to him as a way to excuse his resignation. It is singular that a Captain would extricate himself from an unpleasant position, and still leave his men there. Have you seen Mrs. Goldsby? I have seen gentlemen from Yorktown who speak in high terms of Col. W. as an officer. You must not believe all that you hear of Cols. or Captains. They are apt to be unpopular and to have enemies, as they are compelled to do unpleasant duties at times. Col. Allston was very unpopular in this regt. but he was the best officer we have or ever will have. He

was strict, and always conscientious in the discharge of his duties, and required others to discharge theirs. But, I will not quarrel with the friends
or enemies of Col. W. but leave them to quarrel among themselves, having matters of more importance to occupy my mind. I will always avoid
being the partisan of a man who is not my friend, and whose friendship
I can rely upon in an exigency.

Geo. Mims has just returned, but without *the trunk*. He says it is now
at the station, and I will still endeavor to get it, tho' I fear many of the
articles are injured.

I long for the time when we will be able to hold communion with
each other, in our own home, where we will have all the happiness you
so richly deserve, and I so much desire. If I were to return home, on
furlough, which I now despair of, how would you wish me to treat you?
Would you wish my attentions to be guarded, or would you let me visit
you frequently? Do you think the good people of Selma would trouble
themselves about us? Seven months of the term have gone into the repertory of the Past, and five more will find me at your side, if life and liberty
are given me by a gracious Providence. I find that the nearer the end
approaches, the more anxious I become to grasp your hand, and to kneel
at your feet to claim you as my blushing bride. You know how a girl feels
in the first dreams of womanhood, when life is buoyant, and when hope
gilds the horizon with bright harbingers of happiness, when the poetry
and feeling of the soul are stirred, and no cloud darkens the picture. Just
so I now feel, tho' experience teaches me that such a picture has been
frequently blasted, and that the fairest hopes have been destroyed by an
"untimely frost."[104] Have you ever read *Romeo and Juliet*, or the *Lady of
Lyons*?[105] They contain the most beautiful touches of feeling and of love I
have ever met in language. How full of love must have been the hearts of
their author's, tho' the unhappy difficulties of Edward and his wife would
lead to a different conclusion. I anticipate great pleasure from reading
with you many of the beauties of the English classics, and rejoice that you
have a taste for them. Nothing will give you so much real satisfaction as
reading. It will be an attempt that can never be taken from you, and you
will find it in moments of unhappiness a solace or relief. I remember a
period of my life when I could not sleep, and I took to reading, at night,

---

104. Nathaniel is quoting Shakespeare's *Romeo and Juliet*, act 4, scene 5: "Death lies on
her like an untimely frost."

105. *The Lady of Lyons; or, Love and Pride* was a romantic drama, written by Edward
Bulwer-Lytton, and first produced for the stage in New York in 1838.

of which I have always been fond, with the avidity of an opium eater. From this habit I derived more relief than from the society of friends, or from constant travel. I mention it to show how valuable the habit of reading is, in addition to the pleasure it gives, and its improving effects on the mind and feelings, when properly directed and [illegible]. But I fancy you are smiling at my [illegible]. Your love and companionship will make me entirely happy, and I will not be surprised to devote the time to you that necessity forced me to give to books. The luxury of having a library, with you in addition, will be great, and I hope I will thank a kind Providence for the double blessing. I love you, my dearest Elodie, with all my heart and soul, and your image is ever near me, in all my trials, and present too, when anything occurs to give me pleasure. If I have any [illegible]tions they are now founded upon a desire to enhance your happiness. I could pass the remainder of my life away from the world, if you and a few others, whom I love, were near. I look forward with faith and hope to the happiness of our married life, when love will wed us as it did Adam and Eve.

I see from the papers that the "salt question"[106] is causing much excitement in our little city. I wish these spectators could be forced into the service of the country and made to show their patriotism in a better mode. I have no opinions of such shylocks, and I hope Public opinion will bring them back to their propriety. The state would permit no speculation by monopolists in articles of prime necessity. In some parts of this state these "salt mice" have been threatened by Judge Lynch. Salt has been scarce here in the army on account of this disgraceful monopoly. Such heartless men are not friendly to the Confederate states. I think I can guess who some of them are about Selma.

An effort will be made to keep this regiment in the service after its term of enlistment expires, but it will meet with little favor from officers or men. The government would do better to disband us in December, and call for us in the spring. A large majority would then return. I promise you however to decide upon no plans until I can see you in person, and then we can decide together upon our plans. How do you like this?

I have now written you a long letter. I got letters of 15th today from home, but none from you. Write to Dumfries, while we remain here. If at a loss, at any time, how to direct, address to Manassas.

---

106. See Ella Lonn, *Salt as a Factor in the Confederacy* (New York: Walter Neale, 1933).

And now dearest, Goodbye. May God ever bless and protect you.
   Your attached and devoted
   N. H. R. Dawson

I send a package of letters under cover to Mr. White.

Camp Law. Dec. 1. 1861.

I have been more unwell since writing you, on Wednesday, than I have been, with one exception, since leaving home. I was in bed all of Friday, and for four or five hours was what might really be termed quite sick. Yesterday I passed unpleasantly as the day was damp, and I suffered much from the effects of morphine and opium.

Today, however, I am up, and will endeavor to write you my usual letter. It is not a labor to write you as you have been often told, but one of the few pleasures afforded in camp life. If you receive a short letter you must assign it to the want of materials and to my bad feelings, and content yourself with the letter enclosed, from the Dispatch, giving an account of the history of Dumfries. It is well written, and will give a good idea of the dilapidated place.

If you do not wish your secrets known you must not confide them to Geo. Mims. He told Col. Law how much interested a young lady was in me, and no doubt in the fullness of his heart has told others. He went to Warrenton on Thursday, and is an applicant for a discharge. The trunk has not yet come. I know of no Mr. Carrigan to whom you can entrust a "Souvenir," but you could leave it with Mr. White, who no doubt will see some person coming on directly. A great many visitors come from Marion and Union Town. I will not put you to the trouble of making the leggings, but will take a pair of gloves in their place.

We will commence building huts for winter this week. I will have one 15 by 15, and will then feel like an African prince in his wigwam. How comparative is happiness!

I had quite an animated discussion with several gentlemen yesterday upon the propriety of using the term intimate friend in connection with a lady. I took the ground that a gentleman could only speak of being intimate with his mother, sister or affiance, but that he would not be so with a lady friend. I have no right to claim to be intimate with a lady. It presumes a friendship which I do not feel for any one that I do not love. I might say that you were an intimate friend, but with what propriety could I say so of Mrs. Pegues? What think you of my opinion? Have you ever met Mrs. Pegues since our engagement? She suspected my attachment to you, previous to the 19th April. You know she saw me with you in Montgomery, where I paid you no more than the general attention than a gentleman would show to *an interesting* young lady from his town. She is very smart, however, and may have seen deeper into my heart than you did. You have never told me where you first thought me interested? Will you not tell me in your next letter? How sweet it will be to commune with you when we meet, to talk over the hopes and fears that have filled our hearts in the last nine months.

You mention the 18th of Nov. as the anniversary of your arrival at Selma. I remember the day. Mrs. Troy came down on the boat with you, and mentioned your arrival to me, telling me that Mrs. Lincoln's sister had come on with Mrs. Watts.[107] I had a distinct remembrance of having seen you, a year or so before, on the street, near Mr. Clark's book store. I never have forgotten the impression made upon me by your expression when I turned[?] as the lady you were with was an acquaintance. I thought I never had seen such lovely eyes, and when I returned home, enquired who you were. I little dreamed that those eyes would one day grow brighter when I came, and that their owner was an angel on earth to tow me back to happiness and to life.

I have no recollection of having seen you previous to our meeting in Montgomery. I had frequently heard you spoken of as being very much admired by Dr. Gil and Mr. Hagood, and thought you would marry one of them. But Heaven was kinder than I deserved, and "the beautiful belle of Kentucky" has given her heart to a stranger to her at that time. I will always like Mr. Dennis. He is a great friend of yours, and said you were too nice a lady to marry either of the two, that they would not and could not make you happy, as you deserved. I hope it will be my happiness to make you happy. Have you no doubts? No fears that you will be disappointed in me? Has your young heart, now overflowing with its dreams of "first-love", and believing that the chosen object is all that your fond imagination pictures, never thrilled with the thought of the risk you run of having all those hopes shipwrecked? How frail and easily broken is your heart? How sensitive the nature that would shudder at a word of unkindness? Have you thought of all these, my dearest? And have I all

107. Louisa M. Watts, age thirty-six, was the mother of Ella Watts. 1860 Census: Selma.

your confidence, after being weighed in the balanced? The answer to that question will tell you how much I must do to make you happy, and how great is your faith. I promise all, however, and will do all to deserve so much love. I love you beyond all earthly honors, and will be content to wear none that your love will not bestow. I yearn for home and its happiness, a home now associated with you. If it were not that I was to claim you as the partner of my life, I would not care to return home, for it would have few attractions to satisfy me, none that might not as well be obtained elsewhere. How much do you think that I love you?

Do you like me to write such letters as this, or do you prefer simple details of the camp? This is the first day of our eighth month, and I think the remainder of our term will pass quickly, much more so than the first five months. We will necessarily be stationary, during the time, and the days are now becoming short. Reading will usurp the place of the drill, and cards will occupy the evenings. I confine my playing to whist and euchre. I can fancy you reading and playing on the Piano to while away the long evenings. Do you remember how I frequently intruded a note upon you, last winter, under the pretence of sending you books and flowers? Did you not then see that I was making love, and using the means to please you? I wish I were near enough to see you *occasionally*, as I did then, when I was afraid to be in your sight, but anxious to know that you were near. I wish I could be near you this spring, to send you the first early flowers, and jasmines, as I did last year. I must write John a note to remind him of his duty. Is he still attentive in carrying you flowers and fruit? You have not mentioned him in your letters for a long time.

My overseer wrote me that he had a number of turkeys, and wished to know what to do with them. I have directed him how to do, and instructed him to send Mrs. White a pair of large ones, for Christmas. Please tell Mrs. White that the present is to her. I hope my letter to him will not miscarry. I told him to send to several other of my friends who have been kind to me, during my absence, and whose kindness I wished them to know was appreciated. Among them Mrs. Fourier. I am glad you like her. She is a very deserving lady and I have always respected her.

I assure you my return to the army will be the result of necessity, and will be regarded as an evil. I hope the necessity will not arise, but I will certainly remain at home until next winter. I hope the next campaign will decide the way, and acquire our independence. Six months will certainly bring about important changes in the condition of our affairs. France and England will certainly take some stand. Can you tell me how Kentucky is divided, and what your relations there think of our prospects in the state? I can form no idea from the papers. The war will now be conducted in Ky. and Mo. and probably in Maryland, if we ever cross the Potomac. We hear nothing more of a battle. The enemy seems to bear patiently the blockade of the river. He may have sent large forces to Ky. and Mo. and have retained only enough to defend his lines, in front of Washington. The weather and roads will now prevent a movement in much force. The idea of being idle all winter is exceedingly annoying. Don't you think we could be better employed at home? I feel so, and the feeling, pervading all, is making a decided impression upon the discipline of the regiment . . .

Confederate States of America, Selma, December 1st

You may imagine me seated this Evening by an open window, unanswered letters and loose papers scattered around me attempting to write you my usual letter but my face is covered with ugly frowns. My mood is one of general dissatisfaction, sadly out of harmony with the warm and genial afternoon, and all owing to the non arrival of my usual Tuesday letter from you and I feel very decidedly like indulging in a good quarrel with you for your silence, no news for a week and this the second or third time you have been guilty of this offense. Must I think that absence has begun to dim your remembrance of me or that I write you such dull long letters that you are tired of hearing from me? I thought I was having commiseration enough for you when I only indulged myself in the pleasure of writing once a week, but as you cannot see that a wee smile is playing on my face and do not perhaps know that I am too vain to believe exactly all I have written on the subject of your silence I will tell you I am not in earnest in what I write, but am not pleased but really ill tempered because I was so greatly disappointed on my return from church.

I have been unable the past week to collect anything calculated to make a letter interesting altho' there was some excitement created by the citizens of Selma to aid them in equipping their Company which has been accepted. I did not attend owing to the inclemency of the weather, which did not however prevent others more patriotic from doing so, and I have heard their success was beyond their expectations. Your fair neighbor was there, and is engaged with some others in soliciting subscriptions. All the ministers besides Col. Byrd, Dr. Henry, and the Capt. indulged in speeches. Did I write you Bro. Clem had joined as a private and Mr. J. Lapsley[108] as a Lieutenant? Mr. W. is now absent recruiting. The Federal Pioneers also caused a great deal of talk and many felt disappointed that the Boat passed down during the night and they were denied the gratification of a gaze at them. I did not feel inclined to see them after hearing my Father's nephew had been captured (Capt. Robert Todd of Mo.) somewhere on the Potomac, because I would have felt dreadfully to have recognized him among them. I am in hopes the news may prove untrue. I wish the only three relations I have in Mr. L's service uncaught, unharmed by the Confederates.

Another piece of news is the marriage of Miss Ella Weedon and Mr. Ditmass on Thursday morning and their immediate departure to Pensacola on a Bridal Tour. My friend Miss Serena left on Monday for Columbus, Miss. and thinks of remaining a month or six weeks. I miss her exceedingly and Kittie is still absent, and writes me that she is enjoying herself so much that she does not think of returning for some time, so I am alone. My friend Mr. H. has not even been to see me for a week, but I have not felt lonesome, every spare moment I have devoted to reading when I finished my task of knitting. Ella paid me a little visit yesterday, and told me she had been quite sick for a few days but she looked so beautiful I could scarcely bring myself to believing her.

We both gave George M. "a piece of our minds" for his negligence of the Trunk. I have not heard from any of my family for two or three weeks, and for two or three days have bestowed so much thought on them all, especially my mother and sister in Ohio,[109] that I feel as tho' I am going to hear from them in some manner, but last night I dreamed I was nursing my youngest brother[110] who was dreadfully wounded, and the whole scene was so vivid and life like in all its minutiae, and I was so distressed that I awoke myself sobbing, and I must say the dream has made quite an impression, but there has been no fighting in Ky, and I am expecting a letter from him every day also from David. Mrs. Jeffries[111] is staying with Mrs. Parnell and seems so sad, thinking there will be a Battle in Virginia, near Centreville, near which place he now is, it seems to be the general impression, but I cannot think so, as such has been the thought and hope of the community for quite two months, without the slightest realization. The Ladies are very anxious that some more Tableaux be given

108. Possibly J. W. Lapsley of Selma. 1850 Census: Selma.

109. Margaret Todd Kellogg.

110. Alexander Todd, who will be killed by friendly fire in 1862.

111. Possibly Ann E. Jeffries, age twenty-one, of Pences, Dallas County, Alabama. 1860 U.S. Federal Census, Pences, Dallas County, Ala.

for their benefit as they are so much in debt and Matt and I are thinking of getting one up for them after which the "Cadets" and "Blues" are to be remembered also. I understand Mrs. Fournier is getting up a Concert for the express purpose of showing off Mrs. Weaver's vocal powers. Miss Truitt has been asked to assist and I heard of it as coming from her, but I have been left out, with Misses Ellsberry and Ickes. I did not suppose Madam F. would ask me, and my only regret is that I could not have *the extreme gratification of refusing to take part. It would have pleased me so much.* Did you imagine I was so spiteful and eager to be disobliging? Yes Capt. Kent has resigned and is at home with his family. Some seem to think he expects to be Lt. Col. of Col. Conoley's Regiment but if he resigned on account of his health, I should think he would be unable also to accept that position.

The ladies are busy sewing for Capt. Gardner's Company which belongs to that regiment and are very destitute altho' Mrs. Gardner and Maggie have begged over the almost entire county yet could not raise anything. The family have given $800 toward the equipment of the Company. As you tell me not to look for you this month I will not expect to see you until your time has expired, and perhaps it is for the best as I would not part with you again so cheerfully or apparently, tho' I have no idea you intend remaining out of Service and have made up my mind to hear of your re-enlistment for the War with your entire Company. You cannot give up the glory of the "4th Ala." so soon.

The sun is sinking to west and the air is cool and the daylight becoming so faint that I will be obliged in self defense to bring my letter to a close. Have you heard from your Aunt since the Landing of the Troops in South Carolina, was that not too bad? An attack is anticipated at Mobile and some fears are entertained for the safety of Forts Morgan and Garner. I hope they will be able to stand the fleet unharmed for the sakes of our Confederacy and the special sake of the few friends I have stationed there. But now I must goodbye. I hope to hear from you soon and with a prayer for your success and safety, I am ever yours truly

Elodie.

Selma, Dec 8th 1861

I received your letters of the 21st and 25th a few days since, also a package of my own by Capt. Reese, and this morning your neighbor informed me that she had just seen J. T. Morgan who reported you as looking "splendidly." I am glad to hear so and envy those who have the gratification of seeing and judging for themselves of your appearance. I was agreeably surprised on Thursday by a visit from your sister, with whom I was perfectly delighted. Her kind and affectionate manner won me at once, and I would be exceedingly pleased if I could think I had made half so favorable an impression. She does not resemble you in personal appearance, indeed I should not have supposed for one instant there existed the slightest relationship, so totally unlike do you seem. I regret her stay was so brief, that I was unable to meet with her but once. She returned the morning after I saw her.

Matt and I have been very busily engaged for the last few days getting up Tableaux for Gen. C. Conoley's Regiment which is reported as being very destitute and numbers 260 sick. I hope we will succeed in raising money enough to render them comfortable for a short time by providing for their absolute necessities. They will come off Thursday night, and if the weather only continues to be as beautiful as at present, the citizens will have no excuse for staying at home. My sympathy is always enlisted for the poor Soldier and altho' I am by no means partial to cold weather, yet I think I would cheerfully exchange the warm beautiful weather we are enjoying for the cold freezing winter our soldiers are suffering from in Kentucky and Virginia and indeed many little comforts I have if they would relieve them from the many privations and hardships they are called on to undergo, and I think the women of the whole South feel the same way and are more anxious and willing to do than ever for them each day that the War continues will but strengthen our patriotism and cause us to do our part with redoubled ardor and devotion to the Cause we all love so much and are interested in. I have been for two months expecting a Battle of the Potomac, but will no doubt be taken by surprise when it does occur as I was when the Battle of Manassas was fought. I dread one there and at Bowling Green so much, indeed really fear for one in Kentucky as our Army at Bowling Green is so much smaller than I thought. Mr. Baker who is just from Ky and Tenn was giving me all the latest information of affairs there last night, and I do not feel so confident of success as I did before hearing the simple truth from an Eye witness of the amount and position of the Confederate forces there. I must thank you for the *Courier* which made its appearance last week. How can I ever repay you for all your kind consideration? Each act of kindness and attention that I receive from those who love me renders but more apparent the fact that I am so utterly unworthy and undeserving of their love and kindness.

As I finished the last word I heard the Bells for afternoon service and laid aside my letter to attend and now I am hurried as I must go over and spend the night with Mrs. Parnell who is alone and I promised Miss Serena to stay with her when she had no one else. I have been unfortunate enough to displease your neighbor. This morning when leaving church she took the pains to stop me and tell me she had just seen Mr. Morgan who reported you as "looking splendidly." I immediately asked her, "Are you glad to hear it?" She laughed and said she thought I would be. I said yes I had no objection to hearing so at all and this Evening coming from Church she said "Good Evening Miss Todd do you wish another opportunity for sarcasm?" I asked what she meant and the reply was, "I can assure you it does not hurt me. I do not feel it." I hope she will give no more opportunities for sarcasm as she terms it for as *she has never spared me* I will surely not allow an opportunity to go *unimproved*. My friend Mr. H., I told of my Engagement to you about two weeks ago, and he has not been up since until this Evening, and I did not see him. He looks very *doleful* and *sorry* but I think some of it *is put on*. Am I not particularly unfortunate?

What did you do me so for? Sending those Photographs to excite my curiosity? I do not know who they are and cannot conjecture. They are very handsome and might *do some harm* if I allowed myself to look at them often. Do tell me who the original is, as I do not expect to see you until spring. I will not then restrict you in your attentions to me but will allow you to pay me as much as you wish. I shall not care then. Does this satisfy you? I never expect to like Selma any better unless it improves, but I did not wish you to think I could not stay here as I suppose I shall be able to do without the society of some without any trouble if your friends will not trouble me, my few will not worry you. I do not desire nor ask you to leave Selma on my account. I know I am not more partial to agreeable society than you are and I can certainly do without it, also, if you promise to make yourself very entertaining for after the few commonplace subjects of the day are discussed I expect to be your *interested listener*. Yesterday Evening I saw a Soldier dressed in Military and before catching a glimpse of his face thought it yourself. I felt disappointed, but really do not expect you after what you wrote but would be glad to see you exceedingly so, but almost eight months have passed and then but few remain until you return, *perhaps to remain*!! And I mean to employ my time so well that it will pass rapidly but I feel impatient to think of it.

You ask about my brother. Really every time I hear from him he is something else. When he wrote last he was acting as Assistant Quartermaster in the 1st Ky Regt., Col. Tom Taylor's, and eager to go home to fight but I feel he is safer in Va and I wish my dear Ellick was there too or they had a larger Army. I see the Confederates are going into Lexington, my birthplace and home until a few years ago, but the home of my own and Mother's and Father's friends. My Mother is 15 miles from there now. I am so anxious to hear from her. But really I must say goodnight and goodbye, hoping to hear soon and that you may be secure from harm and danger and I remain as ever yrs, Elodie B. T.

The Ladies intend sending the "Guards and Cadets" boxes. Perhaps I may send your "socks" in that way unless I hear of another.

Camp Law. Dec. 11. 1861.

I received last night your letter of the first instant, and it is needless to assure you, my loved Elodie, that it gave me much pleasure. I regret, however, that the failure of the mails should cause you so frequently to wear a *desponding face*, and, I regret, again, that I cannot be present to drive away the *frowns* that usurp the play of your *smiles* and to witness the brightening eyes that would mark my advent. I believe that on such an occasion, I would not be overcome by your tears.

> "So bright the tear in beauty's eye
> Love half regrets to kiss it dry."[112]

It makes me frown sadly, when I am disappointed, day after day, and week after week, in not receiving the *weekly* letter you send, but I never blame my love for the failure, always attributing it to some other person, and *fearing* to think that her duty has not been done. I see you every Sunday evening, with pen in hand, inditing your letter, and I then love to go away out of sight, to look at your *beautiful likeness.* Love makes me seek solitude, because I can then commune in spirit, and in mind with you. I have not failed for two months to write you regularly twice a week, Sundays and Wednesdays, and sometimes oftener, but I am afraid to tax you more frequently, lest my letters will become stale. The picture you draw of yourself, in the opening of your letter, is certainly an unjust one, for I cannot imagine that you look like "Patience, on a monument, smiling at grief",[113] and yet your description would warrant the inference. I imagine a different picture.

---

112. Nathaniel is quoting Lord Byron's *The Bride of Abydos,* canto 1, stanza 8.
113. Nathaniel is quoting Shakespeare's *Twelfth Night,* act 2, scene 4.

I see my Elodie, bearing cheerfully all her trails, like a *brave Southern woman*, who would have the man she loved, at his post of duty, daring all and enduring all for his country, and to share in the glory of clearing with my sword her path to liberty and independence. I am determined to see you and to unite my destiny with yours, *unless you decline*, before I take any additional step, or make any new pledges to Mr. Davis. All is *secondary* to my anxiety to see you, and to become the sole and proper guardian, and custodian of your love. I have regretted always that I did not ask you to marry me on the morning of my departure from Selma, and when my term of service is over, my first duty will be to you, and to lay all that I am at the feet of my loved and priceless Elodie.

Are you indeed *too vain*, as you tell me, to think that my heart has broken its chains and been captured by some fair Flora, or that forgetfulness has been enthroned in your place? No fairer form can it imagine, and forgetfulness will never usurp your love, until the dark waters of Lethé shall close over me.

I am interested in all you write. Do you know *being behind the scenes*, I see much to amuse me in the proceedings of the people at home, in regard to the absent soldiers? Do you know that the Government gives them money to purchase their clothing, and that large sums are squandered in gambling, which should be expended for better purposes? If they have wants they are themselves to blame. The best uniformed body I have seen in the service is a Battalion of Maryland artillery. Why don't the ladies do something for the Kentucky volunteers? They are greatly deserving. Our regiment will be paid off for Sep. and Oct. in a few days, when each man will receive $29 for clothing, which is paid to the Captains. My company will not spend it in clothing, as the men are generally bountifully supplied. I will persuade some of them to send this money home to their mother's who no doubt need it more than they do. It will ruin the country if everything at home and in the treasury is given to the soldiers. The ladies better devote their energies to the support of *Hospitals*, for the sick and wounded. These are *charities* that would be most beneficial. If our regiment had been stationary, so that we could have kept all the clothing that we have received, we could have given away, at the end of our term, enough to equip two new regiments, but as we have been kept moving, we have lost nearly all. A soldier should not have more than can be carried in his knapsack. I mention these particulars that you may not have your sensibilities unnecessarily taxed. Let others however proceed in their good work.

I have learned a great deal of human nature in eight months, and in that respect have been freely remunerated for any inconveniences that have been suffered. I am sometimes vexed to hear men talk of their sufferings. Well men do not suffer, but the sick do, and they have my sympathies always. Nothing disturbs me more than to walk through the gloomy wards of a regimental hospital.

I hope Captain Wetmore all success and prosperity in his new vocation, but he will find "Jordan a hard road to travel".[114] A captain and Col. have hard duties to discharge, and generally receive a full share of thanks from the inconsiderate and thankless.

I regret to hear that Mr. White is a volunteer, as he is too delicate to stand the fatigue of camp life. Tell him for me, by all means, to have a servant, and no superfluous or unnecessary clothing. I think Mr. H. should have gone in his place. Who are the Lieutenants? I have heard that Mr. Siddons, Geo. Lapsley, and my *law student*, P. G. Moore, were the officers. Are they destined for the "Mercy ground," as your state will certainly be the theatre of war?

I am glad Mrs. Fourrier did not invite you to join her concert. I deem it a compliment, and would always prefer to see you a "looker on in service". I hope you will take it as a complimentary tribute to your sense and taste. Now I must tell you something of what has been transpiring in this quarter of our large world.

The batteries at Evansport have been firing as usual at all vessels attempting to break the blockade. On Monday night one of their guns exploded, injuring seriously some of the gunners, but not mortally.

On Monday morning the *Harriett Lane*[115] shelled our pickets on the Potomac, near the mouth of the [illegible] and sent a small party ashore, who set fire to the mansion of Col. Fairfax, and burnt up his barn with a large quantity of wheat and hay. We saw the smoke distinctly from here.

On Sunday and Monday, we saw the balloon of the Yankees,[116] on the opposite side of the river. It was elevated to see our positions. The Aeronaut was seen, by a glass, by Dr. Paisley, who was at the battery. Our bat-

114. "Jordan Is a Hard Road to Travel" was an 1853 minstrel song, composed by American songwriter Dan Emmett.

115. *Harriet Lane* was a U.S. naval vessel named for the niece of former president James Buchanan.

116. The U.S. Balloon Corps had begun operations in October 1861. For more, see F. Stansbury Haydon, *Military Ballooning during the Early Civil War* (Baltimore: Johns Hopkins University Press, 1941).

teries sometimes open on it, but so far without effort, as it is several miles distant. On Tuesday our pickets inveigled five Yankees over in boats and took them prisoners.

Our guards are all expecting a battle at this point, but I do not, as the enemy has certainly been singularly remiss in waiting so long. There is a Telegraph from here, and in the event of a fight, and I am not injured, you will hear of the result, as I will dispatch Maj. Haden. I have heard no more of the report of our being sent home.

The weather for a week has been singularly mild and beautiful, as temperate as our early fall days. Now, however, a change is taking place, and the clouds have blown off since morning, and it is becoming cold. We are preparing for winter quarters, and will have our huts ready in January. Yesterday Capt. King and myself visited the old church yard near the [illegible] city of Dumfries. It is around the site of the old Episcopal Church erected in Colonial times and at an era when Dumfries rejoiced in her large trade with England. The ground is covered with crumbling memorials of the dead, and but few monuments are in a state of preservation. These owe their safety to the care of the living, who are the descendants of the sleeping inhabitants of this Necropolis. I spent two hours in exploring its devious paths all overgrown with vines and chaparral. Great trees have grown from graves, and have no doubt flourished upon the elements of man. This is one of the laws of matter, that nothing perishes, and here it is beautifully exemplified. Umbrageous oaks, and crouching vines, have been formed from the ashes of the dead, and are again luxuriating in the pleasures of [illegible] of life. You know, I am fond of such places. They teach us of the uncertainty of life, and always carry to me a touching lesson of our mortality. In all my travels, I have uniformly sought an acquaintance with the living through the silent instructions of the cemetery. Show me a beautiful monument, with a chaste inscription, and I will always know that a warm heart, and a virtuous mind erected it. Nothing is so touching as these tributes of the departed, and they generally indicate the *status* of the living and of the dead. By this standard, Dumfries once had cultivated and refined inhabitants, as you will see from the tone of some of the inscriptions, which are enclosed. Ask Mrs. White if she does not agree with me.

After deriving so much pleasure from the visit, I thought you would like to see the notes taken, and I have transcribed some of them for you.

I am quite well, rejoicing that each day brings me nearer to you and to happiness. I will not tell you how much you are loved, lest you think me too lavish in my protestations. Write soon and with a heart full of love, and many prayers for your happiness, believe me, my dearest, ever affectionately and sincerely yours

N. H. R. Dawson

Camp Law. Dec. 18. 1861.

I have not heard from my loved Elodie since the receipt of her letter of the first of December, and I know that she would scold me if she had been half so long without a letter. I will not do as she might do me, but will write as usual, knowing that her letter is somewhere on the way, and hoping soon to have my wishes gratified by its receipt.

I wrote you last Saturday, hurriedly, from the 5th Ala. where I was on a visit to Mr. Pegues. Col. Goldsby and myself returned on Sunday, having had quite a pleasant time with our friends in that quarter of the army. The service has treated some of them roughly, and I noticed grey heads and wrinkles, in many instances, where I did not expect to find them. Field service is laborious and you must be prepared to see changes in your acquaintances and friends, which an earlier knowledge of would cause you many regrets.

Upon my return, I found that Capt. King had gone to Richmond, to meet Mrs. King, who had arrived there. He will be gone ten days, and I hope will bring us good news in regard to our furloughs. I enclosed you Mr. Robt Smith's[117] letter in regard to obtaining one for us. As you see, I have done all in my power to obtain one. As the expected time draws near, I almost feel unwilling to return, as I know the separation from you again in so short a time will give us both much pain, but I will risk it, as the principle of love rules all, and enters into all of our feelings. My love for you increases every day, and I will rejoice, when I shall become free again, and at liberty to pursue my own wishes, and not be trammeled by the law of war. I received last night a long letter from Mr. Mathews. He desires me not to return to the service, unless I am given a much higher position than I now have, as he thinks my experience and position entitle me to preferment. He will only consent to my return upon these terms, and I am determined to adhere to his suggestions. I know you will approve them. I have never felt so anxious, upon any subject, as to close

---

117. Robert Hardy Smith (1814–1878) was a lawyer and Confederate congressman from Mobile, Alabama. Owen, *History of Alabama*, 4:1592.

the term of my service, in order that I might be with my loved Elodie. *She is my country*, and without her, I would have no country, to live for, and to die for. I would make a better soldier, if you were now my wife, as you could take publicly an interest in my welfare, and not be subjected to many annoyances that must now disturb you.

I love you, my dearest, with an Eastern devotion, and when I picture the happiness that you will bring me, I cannot express the feeling of my heart. You are the ideal of all my dreams, the sweet image that woos me to sleep, an apparition that never disturbs my composure. We are having as balmy and delightful weather as you describe in your letter of Dec. 1st. I have never seen such mildness in winter before. For ten days we have had cold enough to freeze the water, but it is not half as unpleasant as the same character of weather in Alabama. I am now sitting in my tent, without fire, Geo. Mims has just arrived to get his discharge. He will leave in the morning, and as he promises to take care of a letter, and to deliver it, I will entrust this to him, especially as you complain of the slowness of the mail. I hope he will keep his word, if he does not you must scold him well. Our regiment is now busily employed in building log cabins for winter. Mine has not been commenced, as axes are scarce, and I wish the privates to have the use of them first. I will have a cabin 20 by 20 feet square, large enough to accommodate all of my furniture. In the other regiments, the men have already put up their tents, with fire places, and are very comfortable. I hope soon to be well fixed, and trust that the Yankees will not run us out of them some cold night this winter.

Gen. Rodes[118] told me on Saturday that he expected a battle before the campaign closed. He thinks Gen. McClellan will gradually close in upon our lines, so that he can throw a large force upon any one point, in one night. This may be so, but I am almost incredulous. We are so accustomed to the danger that we do not mind it. There is a cannonading on the river every day, and the muttering of the heavy guns is even now heard on the river. Hampton's Legion ran off two of their vessels last week, near the mouth of the Occoquan. "Nobody hurt" on our side. I fear this war is to become a grand quarrel that will last a long while. Mr. Lincoln makes no suggestions looking to peace, but his treasury has been nearly depleted, and the national debt on the first of next July will exceed the enormous

118. Robert Emmett Rodes (1829–1864) was born in Virginia but moved to Tuscaloosa and served as a colonel of the Fifth Alabama Infantry. He was later killed at the Third Battle of Winchester. Eicher and Eicher, *Civil War High Commands*, 459.

sum of Eight hundred millions of dollars. Such a debt, yearly doubling, will soon exhaust any nation, and he will have to continue the war on a smaller scale, or abandon all hope of subjecting the South.

Capt. Todd, of the Federal army, was really captured. Is he not the officer whom Maj. Allerton[?] met traveling in Europe?

Our regiment will be paid off this week, when each private proposes to pay one dollar towards relieving the sufferings by the fire in Charleston. The Miss. Regiments have already done so. We will raise about one thousand dollars.

How harrowing must this blow be to those who are separated from their families at such a time. The Institute Hall was the handsomest room of the kind I ever saw, superior to the halls in Baltimore, or in New York, that I have seen. What a spectacle. A beautiful city in ruins! And more than the loss of handsome structures, the desolation of so many families. In many cases, preparations were doubtless being made to celebrate the coming Christmas, but hearths which have witnessed the burning of the yule log for many generations will no longer gather around them the cheerful, happy reunion of the family circle. Long years must elapse before this wound can be cured.

But my loved Elodie will no doubt grow tired of a letter of such little interest, unless I add something more agreeable. Tell me when Capt. Wetmore will leave for Kentucky, and who his officers are. I would like to see him before he leaves, as I could give him many hints that experience alone will suggest. Can't you tell him for me to have as *light* and *small* a trunk as possible, and a camp chest that will carry the largest quantity in the smallest space? The campaign in Kentucky will doubtless be an energetic one, and the means of transportation will be limited.

Not many of our men will accept the provisions of the act of congress allowing them furloughs where they reenlist. Those who look to the war as a means of subsistence will all take it, but those who do not will return at the end of their term and enlist at their pleasure.

I hope to hear from you by the next mail. You should see my face when I fail to get a letter. It has been long ever since your last letter was read, and I hope for the sake of *my face* that you will write me regularly. I saw a gentleman with a long letter from his "ladie love" this morning, and it caused me very sad feelings.

Write me soon, and in the meantime, accept the assurances of my love, and of my prayers for your continued health and happiness.

Ever sincerely and truly yours

N. H. R. Dawson

Camp Law. Dec. 22d. 1861.

Your sweet letter of 8th inst was received on Thursday evening, after my letter of the 18th was dispatched by William. I was glad, it is needless to tell you, to hear of your health, but regretted that anything unpleasant had occurred to jar your feelings. I am sure you can never suffer, in an encounter of wit or sarcasm, with your neighbor, but do you not think it will be generous in you not to cross swords with her? I think she had no cause of outrage in your remark, and that her subsequent reference to it indicated plainly that, tho' unintentional on your part, she was evidently "hurt." I hope, my dear Elodie, you will not permit yourself to be troubled by the *ill bred inquisitiveness* of others, and that your *dignified reticence* will heap coals of fire on their heads. Such a course will hurt and make them respect and admire you. A lady is never so amiable as when she preserves her composure and indignantly repels, *with a silent look,* the efforts of the ill bred to annoy her feelings. I would not have you, remember, submit to insolence without a proper punishment, but I would dislike to know that you are engaged in a *duel* of *sarcasm* with any one. You have too much character and cannot afford to be drawn into it by any one. Mrs. M. is well known as a person of great pretension, and no one appreciates her character more than the writer. Hence I take the liberty of speaking freely to one who is so dear to me as you are. She is insane upon the subject of what has come to her late in life, *position in society,* and like persons educated late in life, is always uneasy, lest she is guilty of mistakes. I never saw her easy or natural in all of my intercourse with the family. Number her among your acquaintances, not in the list of your friends.

Let me turn to a pleasanter topic. I am rejoiced that you met Sister. She has a warm heart, and I knew you would like her. She is very quick, and has that naiveté of manner that is so well calculated to prepossess. She resembles my father, while I am like my mother, quiet, sensitive, but under a reserved exterior warm and affectionate to those I love. You must not tell me that my kindness makes you feel unworthy of my love. I flatter myself I could not be prepossessed with a lady unworthy of my love, and every day convinces me that I have been extremely fortunate in securing yours. The little attentions shown you have only been the evidences of my desire to shower your path with happiness, were it in my power. You would grace any position, and I am fortunate in having induced you to share my humble fortunes. I tremble lest you shall be disappointed when you come to know my many frailties. "In your prayers let all my sins be remembered."

I did not intend to excite your curiosity, with the Photographs, but presumed that they would have been labeled. They are likenesses of Gen. Barnard E. Bee, of So. Ca.

Our lamented Commander, who fell at the battle of Manassas, I thought you would like to have his likeness among your things of interest and ordered them from the photographer at Augusta, where I saw they were to be had. The third brigade, composed of the 6th N.C. 1st Tennessee, 2d and 11th Miss. and 4th Ala. regiments will always lament their heroic leader. He was very handsome, and prepossessing in his manners. He was loved by his soldiers. I hope you will see Mr. Morgan himself before he returns, and hear from him how well I look. He will not know that you are an interested listener.

Our regiment has contributed near $1300 to the sufferers by the recent fire in Charleston. This sum was sent on yesterday by a special messenger, and I hope the example will be followed, as I think, by the entire army of the Potomac. This will surprise those who imagined that they are in a starving condition. No private contributed less than one dollar. Our company gave $340, one 350, and third came the Cadets and Marion Co. each $100. I have only 65 men in my company present.

We are very much amused at the favors shown the Blues, and I have heard it said that a plan was afoot to take up a subscription here for their benefit. They have not endured half the privations that we have, but I am glad they have made such loud laments. Their praises should certainly be sung by some chroniclers.

Reginald is better. He has had a severe attack of typhoid fever, was in bed for six weeks, and was very ill. He writes that he is convalescing, and will return to Ala. on sick leave, as soon as he is able to travel. We heard of the rupture between England and the United States yesterday by telegraph from Richmond, and from its directness hope there is truth in the report. If it be true that the demand has been made, and rejected, for the delivery of Messrs Mason and Slidell,[119] war will be inevitable, and we may expect an early peace. I am credulous enough to believe the rumor. Mr. Lincoln and his Cabinet are certainly infatuated. They are instrumentalists in the hands of God to punish a vainglorious and sinful

---

119. Two Confederate diplomats, James Mason and John Slidell, were on their way to Great Britain to request international support for the Confederacy when a Union captain intercepted and detained them, creating the first major diplomatic imbroglio of the war. For more, see Charles M. Hubbard, *The Burden of Confederate Diplomacy* (Knoxville: University of Tennessee Press, 1998).

people. The end draweth near, and soon the spectacle of a humiliated nation will be presented to the world. I have heard that some persons, members of Mr. Wetmore's company, were now refusing to go on the ground that they did not wish to fight for Kentucky. If there are such cowards in his ranks, he should be anxious to leave them behind. When we reached Harper's Ferry, on 14th May, we found there a regiment of Kentuckians, who had abandoned their homes, before their state was revolutionized, to vindicate the liberties of the Confederate states, then trembling in the balances. These brave men are still in the army of the Potomac, and are commanded by Col. Taylor. I hope your effort to raise funds for Gen. Aubry's regiment was crowned with success. The more I know of your nature, the more I love and admire you, my dear Elodie. I have been uneasy about Turner Vaughan until today. He has been quite sick, but is now much better and out of danger. I wrote his father yesterday. He is one of the most exemplary young men I know, and I would say any lady would do well to catch him in her silken meshes. He has no superior, hardly and equal in the company. The weather has become colder, but is clear and beautiful. Gen. McClellan must certainly be afraid to commence his harvest of glory.

My letters, since the 18th October, have been mailed at Dumfries, but I fear you have not received them all. I was obliged at first to pay the postage, in money, as stamps were not to be had, and I suspect the P.M. generally kept that change and suppressed the letters. He is suspected of having done so in other cases. I have written you regularly since middle of November, on Wednesdays and Sundays, and occasionally have sent you long letters. You can calculate now the days upon which you should get my letters.

Intelligence reached me last night of an engagement, at Granville, on our line, between four of our regiments, and twelve of the Yankees, in which we were forced to retire, with small loss. Among the killed is said to be Col. Forney of the 11th Ala. I hope is it not so, as he was a fine officer, and a gentleman whom I liked very much. I hope your friend Mr. H. will cease to annoy you with his attentions. If he does not, after your disclosure of our engagement, he will deserve a rebuke at other hands. He has evidently been interested in you a long time, and has no very kind feelings for me. I am sorry for him, but hope he will now shoulder his musket and go to the seat of danger. I notice what you say about Selma. The place must and will improve, and I know you will like it better. We will make *home* the *centre* of our happiness, and it will, I hope, be so pleasant there, that neither of us will want to go elsewhere. I could live in a wilderness, with you, and never wish to leave its forests or its sands. You will have books and flowers to amuse all of your leisure hours, and all of mine will be given to you. I have drawn in my own mind a beautiful picture of the future and every one of its features is colored with the tints of that happiness, which you are to bestow, and which I am to share. Heaven grant that it may be realized! Eight months have elapsed since you confessed that my love was returned, and in four, I will be near to claim you as my blushing bride, if my life is spared. Will you appoint an early day after my return?

I can never hope to repay you, my loved angel, for all you have given. I only hope to be worthy of so much confidence. I wish I would be with you at Christmas, the festal season, where age is rejuvenated and lives again in the merry carols of youth. I will devote a part of the day to you, and will try to write you an interesting letter.

Our brigade is about to be reformed, and we will be transferred to an Ala. brigade. The change may lead to our removal from this place. If so it will be hard on us, as we have nearly half of our cabins done. Mine is not commenced. Col. Law went to Centreville yesterday to endeavor to have the order for our removal rescinded, but I fear will be unsuccessful. I will write you upon the charge, and direct you how to write. Manassas will be one office, I think, as we will probably be thrown in Gen. Rodes brigade.

And now dearest Goodbye. May God bless and keep you always, and may it be mine to deserve the love you have given.

Ever affectionately and sincerely
N. H. R. Dawson

I will number my letters, so that you will know when you receive them regularly.

Selma, Dec 22nd 1861.

I have been exceedingly fortunate in receiving news from you this week. On Wednesday I received your letters of the 7th and 11th, and today was again pleased to have one handed me of the 14th, written from the 5th Ala. Regt. I feel assured that your visit to Mrs. Pegues will prove beneficial. I commenced a letter to you this morning but was interrupted by Kittie's returning from Dayton with two of my young cousins who will spend their Christmas with us, and Mr. Hagood in spite of *wind, rain and weather* came up and only left a little while ago, and tonight I hesitated about writing you my usual letter as I feel so very sad.

We received a dispatch today announcing the Fight at Dranesville in which my Bro. David was engaged and poor Col. Tom Taylor killed. No other names were mentioned or any particulars given. I am uneasy and anxious to hear of his safety and hope since no mention is made of him that he is unharmed. I sometimes think I cannot bear the suspense a moment longer and this together with not hearing from Ky seems indeed hard to bear and I feel almost like giving up entirely and there is no telling when there will be an end to it. What must I say to you about re-enlisting? I had hoped such a step would not be necessary for you to take again, and now you speak of reenlisting for two years or the War. I think one year is quite enough for one man to serve, but I have nothing else to say as doubtless you consider it your duty to do so and would not be satisfied to remain at home, but I do feel sorry that there is a prospect of War for such a length of time, and that I must be *secondary to my country* for two more years with just a good look at you in the meantime. I did wish you to go and serve a short time for I would not for any consideration marry a man who would not go and fight for his country and endeavor by his courage and sword to maintain his rights and liberties, but I would be satisfied with one year, however I will not say anything against your doing so, if you desire to do so, and you need not wait to see me before taking such a step, if such is your inclination, as I would not for the world (if I could) deter you from doing what you think *is right and your duty.* I know we must persevere in our undertaking and that we must have soldiers to carry it out and that all must sacrifice their feelings in giving up those they love to obtain for us the sacred object of a cause so dear, and I hope we will all prove ourselves equal to the trail and not hesitate. I for one will try to do as I should. I will not promise very cheerfully or contentedly at first but will try and grow reconciled as the time approaches, but I will drop this subject and try and give you some of the news afloat. The first piece I heard is that I am to be married to you *this week* or in Jany, where or from whom this information came I cannot hear and doubtless eyes are looking for your daily arrival being silly enough to give credence to such an idle rumor.

On Wednesday night the opposition Tableaux, Charades, and etc. gotten up by the friend of the "Blues" and for their benefit comes off. I had intended going but after seeing the programme in which I see my Brotherinlaw Mr. Lincoln is to be introduced twice I have declined, as all my feeling and self respect have not taken wings and flown. I must confess that I have never been more hurt or indignant in my life than since this last step has been taken. What have we ever done to deserve this attempt to personally insult and wound our feelings in so public a manner? We have suffered what they never have and perhaps never will in severing ties of blood. We have done all we could to aid the cause in which our Country is enlisted both in doing what was necessary to add to the comfort of the soldiers, and giving our three brothers to aid in the struggle, and this is the reward from those who have not one that is dear to them absent for such a purpose. Dr. Hendree and Mrs. Hendree last summer proposed that on one of our Tableaux we should introduce the two scenes which they propose entertaining their audience with Tuesday night, and I then in their *own home* showed the indignation that I felt at a proposition made to wound me. I thought when my visitors used to wish Mr. Lincoln would be caught and *hung* to me that that was enough but I feel I can never feel kindly again toward those who take part in this. You do not know all we have taken from some of the people of this place, no not one half, and *pride* has kept us from showing how we felt. I am afraid I shall never love Selma and I feel thankful that I am not dependent on its inhabitants for my happiness. Hereafter I will stay to myself and keep out of the light and way of those to whom my presence seems to be obnoxious. I cannot refrain from expressing myself tonight and hope those who have aroused my temper will not come near me until it is exhausted as I am afraid I would say something I would afterwards regret.

I believe I wrote you of the benefit for the "Cadets". Those two nights are the whole and sole amount of our Christmas entertainment. I am going to spend mine in reading, which will be a treat, as I do not often indulge. Yes I knew the soldiers were paid and could afford to buy their clothes, but thought it was impossible to obtain them where they were, and that they were unable to spend their money in this manner when they felt inclined, but since you tell me there is no necessity of working so hard I will rest a while with thanks for your hint. The Miss Edmonia Todd of whom you speak is no relation of mine. I know who she is, and used to hear of her frequently when she visited her relations in Frankfort, among them Col. Tom's father. I met with a Major Roberts of Mo., a very fine looking gentleman and wounded hero of Springfield Battle who informed me that my relations there were on the Confederate side. I had not heard from them. My Father's brother, a very old man now, is an aid of Gov. Jackson. He has served before and cannot be far from 70. He is not quite or more than that age. But what a long dull complaining letter. I have written last week I will do better or not write at all. I must not forget to thank you for your Inscriptions and your agreeable account of your visit to the Cemetery at Dumfries. I quite agree with you in thinking a well kept Cemetery with neat and handsome memorials of affection indicate the refinement and culture of the inhabitants, what says the one here? I am keeping my cousin up and as she is tired will take compassion on you both. I hope to get a letter soon and now I will say goodnight and goodbye, hoping God may bless and keep you and I am as ever yours

Elodie

Letter No 2., Camp Law. Dec 25. 1861

The revolving year has again buried the seasons in its repertory, and the recurrence of this Holy day brings up many memories of the past. The many hours of childhood, when church and home were dressed in evergreen, when the Christmas tree was hung with gifts, and Santa Claus made his annual round, and "all went merry as a marriage bell"[120] will never be forgotten. Families gathered around the festive board, and the links of friendship were strengthened in this annual reunion. The images of two indulgent parents, who always tried to increase the pleasure of those hours, mingle with their recollection. Then comes the remembrance of darker days, when the family altar was hung in mourning for the departure of father and mother to that "bourne from which no traveller returns", and darker, sadder still than those comes the remembrance of two "bright liveried saints" who have put on the robes of immortality. The scene changes, the dark cloud that a twelvemonth since lowered upon me, rendering life almost a burthen, has passed, and the new light of a fair maiden's love gladdens and warms my heart. My Elodie, beautiful in person, and graceful in mind and mien as a Grecian goddess, requites my love, and ere another year shall end its course, promises to be mine. If I have ever failed to thank you for your love, I do so now, on this day, when all the memories of the past are clustering around me. Near a year has elapsed since I met and loved you. Long did I linger, between hope and fear, before the confession was ventured. Had this unfortunate war not arisen, we would have been keeping this day together, and have entered upon our journey of wedded life. Tho far away, I am hovering near you in spirit, and imagine that I hear your merry laugh winging on the ear, and have wished you

---

120. Nathaniel is quoting Lord Bryon's *The Eve of Waterloo*.

many happy returns of the season. You must think of me among your absent friends and give me the largest place in your heart of hearts.

Winter is now fairly upon us. Since writing you it has rained, and now the day is beautiful, but cold. I am in my tent this morning writing while all are out enjoying the Christmas. Bad whiskey is abundant and pleasure is sought and sorrow drowned in large potations. Last night we had an egg nog, and late in the night I heard the revels of a party of Irishmen who were celebrating the approach of Christmas. They sang and drank until daylight. I fear we will have too much drinking. A friend writing to me says, "I saw your friend Miss T. at church the other night, during the Episcopal convention, she was looking in full bloom and beauty." Sister mentions her visit to you, and was delighted with your "beauty" and "graceful manners" so you see others beside myself appreciate you. She saw Miss G. T. at Maj. Haden's and says it is not known in Selma whether I am pleased with you or her, and adds "I admire your selection." You have certainly made a very favorable impression as you always do. I wrote her yesterday that she could not have gratified me more than by calling to see you. Reginald has gone home on sick leave. I hope he will call to see you should he be in Selma. I love you so well and dearly, that I wish all of my friends to love you. Is it not a proper feeling? Reginald has been recommended for major of his regiment, by Col. Fry[121] and Gen. McGender, and I suppose will receive the appointment.

You have heard of the unfortunate affair at Drainsville.[122] It exemplifies the importance of attacking a well posted enemy without a knowledge of his position. Judge Martin[123] fell upon a vanquished field, and the end of his brilliant career is sad indeed. How much more glorious to have had his last moments cheered by a retreating foe. I hope never to die in such a field. I would prefer to fall in a great battle where our flag waved over me in victory. Colonel Forney had his arm broken in two places. Mr. Spence of Selma is severely wounded.[124] I have felt anxious about your

121. Birkett D. Fry was colonel of the Thirteenth Alabama Infantry, of which Nathaniel's brother Reginald was also an officer.

122. The Battle of Dranesville, December 20, 1861, occurred when two winter foraging forces collided at a crossroads village in Fairfax County, Virginia. The result was a Union victory.

123. James Benson Martin (1825–1861) of Talladega, Alabama, was lieutenant colonel of the Tenth Alabama Infantry. He also served as a district judge and had obtained leave to hold his courts but postponed his trip to participate in the battle. Owen, *History of Alabama*, 4:1164.

124. There are two Spences listed on the roster of the Tenth Alabama Infantry: B. J. Spence and James Spence, both privates in company E. Alabama Civil War Muster Rolls, 1861–1865, Alabama Department of Archives and History.

brother, as Col. Taylor's regiment was one engaged, and have sent up to Centreville by a friend to inquire about him. If he is injured, I will go to see him. I have seen no account of the battle, but have heard many rumors. Col. Law returned from Centreville last night. We will go in winter quarters here, which is quite satisfactory to our men, as they have made considerable progress with their cabins.

The news from England is very hopeful. It can result in no injury to our cause, and will certainly damage the Yankees. If the blockade of our ports is raised, the war is virtually decided in our favor. I wish this could be affected, as it would relieve the pecuniary distress of the country, and enable us to sell cotton. I have made the largest cotton crop I have ever raised, and it avails nothing. I do not know what our planters, who are dependent on their crops, will do. We must learn to live independently, and to make everything at home. I would like so much to live on my plantation, and to see the raising of fine horses and cattle. It is the natural occupation of man. The curse upon Cain was a blessing in disguise intended to make life sufferable by making labor one of its conditions. Sister writes me that the shrubbery about my place is very much in need of trimming. I am afraid to tell John to undertake it. Is there a white gardener in Selma now? I am very fond of flowers, and expect you to take an interest in them. I will plant the cabbages and potatoes and leave them to you.

I hear Mr. Wetmore will be unable to raise his company. I regret it as I am anxious that Kentucky shall be redeemed. Are you not surprised at the course of Gov. Magoffin? Wonders will never cease. And now, my dearest Elodie, I must bid you adieu. May God bless you, and may your future life be crowded with all the happiness you so richly deserve.

Present me respectfully, with the compliments of the day, to Mrs. White and Miss Katie. Ever affectionately and sincerely

yours, N. H. R. Dawson

Friday night Dec 27th 1861.

I have wished for several days to write you a letter but it seems from the unusual amount of visiting this week that I am only to sit with folded hands and entertain, however tonight I am almost alone having with me little Willie and Jennie Craighead.[125] Matt and Kittie have gone to spend

125. Jennie Craighead was Elodie's cousin and a child of Jane P. Craighead.

the Evening at Mrs. Goodwin's to make arrangements for Tableaux and supper on New Year's Eve, but I am quite indisposed from a wretched cold and do not think any inducement could have prevailed on my leaving my comfortable Arm chair and the nice cheerful fire, particularly after the mood of writing to you seized me.

I received your letter sent by George Mims on Christmas Evening with those of my own delivered I think by a Servant. George did not come near me. I felt quite disappointed that I did not have them Christmas morning and thought I would not hear until the last of the week and my face brightened considerably when they were handed me. Kittie and I attended Church in the morning and after Tea we spent a pleasant Evening at Miss Gertrude Goodwin's where we met nearly all the young people in Selma collected to drink an Egg Nogg together. Two of the 4th Ala were present, Mr. *Waddell* and Mr. *Huggins,* whom I for the first time met. I believe Mr. W. is a "Cadet". Mrs. Weaver and Mrs. Calvin Norris had "Sociables" also the same night Miss Flannigan of Charlottesville was at Mrs. G's. I intend to call on her if she stays until I am well enough to do so.

Last night we had a few young persons to spend the Evening with us, and I think it passed off pleasantly to all, as they did not leave until after one o'clock. We played cards, Backgammon or danced nearly the whole time, and introduced the Lancers[126] which was quite amusing as several had never danced them before and many mistakes were made. I stood and prompted during the dancing, the rest [having] declined, [including] gentlemen too that they could not, and I enjoyed it more than I would have to have indulged myself. I did not forget that it was just eight months since you left, and I wished for you and think your presence among us would have added much to our pleasure. I know that my own would have been greatly increased and I think I will reserve my dancing until your return, provided it is to remain. Perhaps between Mr. Mathews and myself we may be able finally to drive all ideas of reenlisting out of your brain, even if you can secure a higher position, tho' to speak in earnest and plain terms, I do not think either one of us ought to try and influence you but allow you to act as your inclination and conscience dictate and I will not *quarrel* with you for doing *this once* just exactly as you choose altho' from the manner in which I have written you lately,

126. The Lancers was a series of dance steps similar to the French quadrille and noted for being slower and having more graceful gestures than the American quadrille.

one would think I was terribly opposed to your doing anything that I did
not wish. Mr. Willie Knox, Mr. W. Fitts, Mr. Francis of the Guards are all
here and Mr. Becker is daily expected and Mr. W. Byrd also, so it seems
something like old times to hear the frequent mention of their names. I
have not seen them all. Mr. Kennedy is remarkably quiet. I have not seen
him and never hear his name mentioned. How delightful it would be to
welcome all our old friends home.

Saturday Night. Dec 28th 1861.

Last night I felt too unwell to finish my letter and as Matt and Kittie
are absent again and I feel so much better, I concluded I could spend
my Evening more pleasantly in writing and remained at home for the
purpose of doing so in preference to going to the Hall to discuss the
Entertainment of New Year's Eve. Thank fortune some other in Town
have at last taken the trouble ("for the Blues") to get up such things
("Tableaux") and as there has been already opposition and rivalry stirred
up, Matt has concluded not to have any more after the Benefit for the
"Cadets." I wish she never had been connected with them. If the Soldiers
knew what it cost to raise for them money I know they would send a
Petition to cease our efforts at once. I for one am satisfied to hereafter exert myself only in sewing and knitting as all I have endeavored to
do has proved unfortunate to myself. Indeed I am puzzled what to do:
if I refuse to assist I am accused of *sympathizing with the North* and if I
cheerfully aid them "I am officious" and "usurp the place of some girl
in Town" and "I do not live here and have no *right* to do anything, so
say some," and from this time I think I will do to please myself and not
entertain for a moment the idea of pleasing the Town or any body *now
in it.* You will wonder what is the matter with me. Well I just wish you
were here and I could relieve myself by telling you, for I am all out of
sorts, *indignant* and *angry,* and am foolish enough to take notice of what
the people will say about me, and unfortunately those who profess to be
friends take pleasure in communicating all they hear. What a pity I did
not return to Kentucky with my mother and then some one else would
have taken my place and satisfied those who take such a great interest in
me or I should say *pretend to.* This Evening I walked down the street and
it really looked something like old times to see Mr. Fitts, Francis Byrd,
Knox, Waddell, Huggins and several others who have been absent so

long walking about as usual, but I miss so many others that I do not like to meet them.

We are beginning already to make our arrangements for the return of the Guards and Cadets. [illegible] in talking some propose our going to Montgomery to meet them. Others that we stay at home and ornament the whole town with Evergreens made into Arches, and etc in honor of their arrival among us, but I am afraid more will be *said* than *done*, however not all agree in avowing that our happiness will be almost complete when our gallant bands are once again with us, and I do hope there will be no necessity for them again departing for the Battlefield. As yet there are no signs of peace and I believe England will do no harm. I think they have just as much *courage* and *spirit* as the *Yankees* yet if they do resent the condition of the North, we might then be let alone as they will find it impossible to fight both. Since the fighting at Dranesville we have not heard a word from my Brother. We Telegraphed on Monday to Col. Taylor but have had no answer and I feel my brother is safe or think we would have heard before now, but I shall be in trouble until the Battle at or near Bowling Green is over. Until July I never dreamed how horrible war was, and now every day it grows more dreadful to me, how much worse must it be to those who are in the midst of trouble and danger and feel the effects so much more in every way than we who can hardly realize from what *we see* how changed affairs are. Mrs. M. and Miss G. have recovered from my *sarcasm* and are very pleasant indeed. Miss G. spent Thursday Evening with us and looked so sweet and pretty, I would not blame any one for loving her. I believe I could not help liking her exceedingly myself were I to try. On Thursday Evening at four o'clock Willie had a little party. At least *forty* were present, and I have not enjoyed anything so much for some time. I played with them for some time, all their *kissing games* with so much interest that they thought Miss Dee *played so pretty* that to rid myself of them I proposed their dancing and played on the Piano for them. Some came beautifully dressed and very fancifully, and the happy little creatures formed a beautiful sight.

Mr. Hagood told me on Christmas that your brother had returned and was looking very badly. Miss Lide told me he had been extremely ill. For the last few days the weather has been intensely cold and is still so, but I hope we will soon have pleasant weather. I do not like winter and will hail with joy the return of spring. Until *you do return* I will not even try to indite a handsome letter and perhaps then I will beg you to excuse

me from attempting such a *Task* for I would labor unsuccessfully I fear.
I have written you a long letter. My head and eyes are both beginning to
ache me and I will finish hoping to receive your usual letter tomorrow.
So goodbye and believe me to be every yours affectionately
 Elodie

You have no excuse for wearing a frown. I have written *you regularly* and
suppose you must blame the mail, but sometime I am longer in hearing
from you than you are from me and frequently receive two or three letters at once.

No 4. Camp Law. Dec 31. 1861

I dedicate the last hour of this day to you, wishing you a happy new
year, and the realization of all your prayers. The year opens with much
brighter prospects for our new born confederacy and I hope at its close
we shall have vindicated and maintained our liberties. National prosperity must precede individual happiness, and I join in your prayers for a
speedy and honourable conclusion of your troubles.

   The bright sun and the mild temperature render the day a fit one to
inaugurate the new year. But I am sad, nevertheless, as a member of my
company, James Doneghay,[127] is lying at the point of death. He has been
sick for two weeks, but not until last Friday was he considered in danger.
I go to see him twice a day, and try to make him as comfortable as circumstances will allow. Yesterday I carried him an orange, which a friend
had given me, and you should have seen how grateful the poor boy was.
I have chicken soup made for him every morning by Andrew. He lies on
a *pallet of straw*, the best bed in our camp, and far away from home, and
attentions which woman, in the character of mother, sister or wife, can
alone give. I had rather see my men killed on the battle field than to
waste away by disease. These are the trials that most trouble an officer.
Poor fellow, the regiment was mustered yesterday and he answered to his
name on our roll for the last time, I am afraid. It was an affecting scene.
I notice that Captain Gardner has written quite a big letter, in regard to
the aid given his company by the ladies. Is he just when he speaks of their

---

127. James G. Donegay was a twenty-year-old private in Nathaniel's company. Alabama
Civil War Muster Rolls, 1861–1865, Alabama Department of Archives and History.

"preferred professed disposition" to aid his country? You know my opinion is that much of the time and money spent upon the soldiers would be better given to the "poor at home". We have trials that are *unavailable*, that no human aid can lessen. If we had good homes and comfortable hospitals for our sick, we would not require anything. When articles are sent we have no way of disposing of them properly. We are not settled at home and with store rooms and locks and keys. We are much gratified that we have friends at home alive to our interests and our welfare and thank them from the bottom of our hearts. If we were in garrison for any definite time, we could enjoy the presents from home. If we were to leave here now suddenly, not one *fourth* of our baggage could be carried with us. I have kept mine down to the standard, but I will venture to say there are few in my condition. I have less than I started with, having learned by experience that more than absolutely necessary is an encumbrance and vexation.

I received a very kind, I might say affectionate letter from Mr. Mathews yesterday. He is unwilling that I shall remain in the army, unless I have a higher position given me. I am certainly unwilling to remain upon any terms, if it can be avoided, but I fear our condition next year will require all of our men, and more patriotism than we have. No steps are being taken to raise our army. The govt seems to depend on our remaining in the service, but I am confident a large majority of this regiment will return home. I am not satisfied to remain in it as now organized. If the field officers were all my equals, *as officers*, I would then be willing, but I am not content as things now stand, and this is a common feeling here. I must see you before I can make any definite plans.

I hope the Mason and Slidell imbroglio will lead to a favorable result and involve England and the U.S. in war. Mr. Seward, however, seems willing to make amends, and to humble himself before the throne of England. "What a fall" from his high, hectoring, mien of only a month ago.

I hope Mrs. Pegues has recovered her equanimity by this time. I did not tell you she is the *only* lady that ever treated me rudely. I have long since forgiven her, as it occurred when I was just grown.

How will you like it if I wrote you *once a week* instead of twice? Not half of my letters can reach you. An order has been received here from Headquarters forbidding any leaves of absence to officers or men. The advance of the enemy is assigned as the reason. Gen. Whiting told me he would give me a furlough, as soon as he was authorized.

Col. Allston has been transferred to the army of the Peninsula, and if you were to send him the comforter, he would hardly even receive it, so I do not regret the scarcity of the material. I heard from Mr. Wetmore on Sunday. He is afraid that he will not succeed in raising his company to the required number, and *entre nous*, wishes to come on to join my company. I have advised him to not to do so, but if he still decides to do so, I will receive him with pleasure. I will expect to hear from you by him. I do not think that he should leave home, or that he should be expected to leave at this time, when he has done all in his power to organize his command.

I did not hear from you yesterday as I expected. Your letter of 22d is due and should have reached me. Mr. Mathews's of 22d came from Cahaba.

I thought of you last evening as a ministering angel, engaged in the benefit of the Cadets. An improvised bank of musicians serenaded. As the sound of the voluptuous music rose upon the evening air and harmonized with the soft moonlight, I involuntarily turned to you, my dear Elodie, and my heart was filled with sweet remembrances of you. How strong is the sentiment of love? I know young ladies laugh at the idea, as an abstraction that is never in part realized, but I am willing to plead guilty to the soft impeachment, so far as you are concerned.

Jany 1. 1862.

I here put pen to paper, first, to wish you my dear Elodie a happy, happy new year. The sun has just risen, and the morning is balmy and beautiful. I hope it is an augury of happiness for you, and promises an early and honourable peace.

Poor James Doneghay died yesterday as the sun was setting. He fell asleep calmly and quietly. I had not left him more than an hour, to attend the dress parade. He will be buried this evening.

I must now close this letter as Dr. Paisly goes to Dumfries immediately after breakfast. I would even try to make it the usual length of my letters, but can find nothing to make a letter interesting. You remember my friend, Col. E. C. Bullock, who was at the theatre with us in Montgomery last winter? He too has been numbered with the illustrious dead of 1861.

I will expect a letter from you by tomorrow's mail. With much love, I remain,

    yours very affectionately

    N. H. R. Dawson

Camp Law. Jany. 1. 1862.

I wrote you my regular letter, but cannot lose the opportunity of writing you a short letter by Mr. Garrett.[128] He goes home to escort the remains of Mr. Jas. Doneghay, who died yesterday evening.

Gen. Whiting has been very kind in allowing me to send an escort with his body. I made a great effort, as I knew it would gratify Mr. Doneghay. I have been busied all day in attending to this matter, and am now wearied, but not too tired to devote an hour to communion with one so dear to me as my loved Elodie.

I wish I were a gentle wind that I might breathe softly upon your damask cheek, or that I could transfer to this paper the emotions that now kindle at the mention of your name. The first hour of the morning of this day was devoted to you, and night finds me still endeavoring to compass your pleasure. How heartily do I pray for Peace, that we may know how pleasant are its ways, and how happiness is to be enjoyed. I will appreciate the comforts of home, as never they were before. When I say this, I do not mean the creative comforts, for I care little for them, but I mean the nameless little kindnesses, which, in the end, make up the whole of happiness, and win our love. The love which would induce me to anticipate every wish of your life also makes me anxious to be near you, that I might minister to your happiness. I promise to do all in my power to secure the love you have given. I hope you will see Mr. Garrett. He is a good little man, and makes a fine corporal. He has been almost crazy to see his wife, and it has given me much pleasure to detail him. Dr. Paisley and himself are the only married men in the Cadets. When he returns, I will expect both a letter and souvenir from you. You do not value *souvenirs* I believe, tell me, are you a matter of fact person? Do you believe all I tell you? These two plain questions can be answered in *one letter*.

The 14th Ala. regiment, which has been encamped near us has been sent to Richmond. The mortality has been dreadful. Over one hundred men have died in less than two months, as many as five have died in one day. I do not know what this winter will do, but so far we have been very fortunate.

---

128. Robert E. Garrett of Selma, age twenty-nine, a corporal in Nathaniel's company. 1860 U.S. Federal Census, Union, Dallas County, Ala.; Alabama Civil War Muster Rolls, 1861–1865, Alabama Department of Archives and History.

The wind is very high, and it is too *warm* for *fires* in our tents. Is it not singular weather for the season?

Col. Law had his tent burned today, with most of his clothing.

I must now bid you goodnight and goodbye, as I have other letters to write.

With much love and my respectful regards to your sisters, I remain,

My Dear Elodie,

Sincerely and affectionately

N. H. R. Dawson

Selma, January 1st 1862.

As Sister Matt is writing you tonight a note I concluded to enclose a few lines also, although it is late and I am exceedingly tired having worked hard both last night and today for the Cadets and I am happy to tell you we met with usual success. A large crowd was in attendance at the Hall last night when we had Tableaux, a beautiful table of Presents, and a bountiful supply of delicacies, which drew forth praise and money (the latter was most acceptable), and this morning we had a nice Lunch from 12 until 2 o'clock. As this is to be the last Benefit in which we are to take any part I am exceedingly gratified that the affair terminated in every respect so well for there is an "opposition Blue party" who desire to take things into their own hands and we prefer giving way rather than creating any more rivalry than now exists between the Companies, but I must not fill my *short* letter with the "Benefit" as I assure you when I received your two letters this Evening (No "1 & 2") that I forgot everything but the great pleasure they afforded me, and really enjoyed them very much, and altogether my New Year's day has been quite agreeable and I hope this year will prove a happier one than the past has been, yet perhaps I should not regret everything that is now past, for doubtless it will all end at last for my good and happiness.

How shall I thank you for your kindness concerning my Brother? This is but another proof of your goodness and kindheartedness. We telegraphed to Col. Taylor but have not yet received an answer or even a line from my Brother. I think perhaps if he is unimproved that he may be on his way to New Orleans, as he wrote me word that it would be necessary for him to return on business as his partner was dead, and promised to stop and see us so I hope he will answer the Telegram in person. I do not know how Mr. Wetmore's Company is progressing, when I last heard

it numbered 36, and I did not hear that anyone had been so ungener-
ous as to express themselves, as unwilling to assist the oppressed, but I
am not astonished in the least, for such is the way of the world, and I
am *old enough* to have experienced its selfishness and ingratitude, but
thank Heaven the Kentuckians are *able now and willing* to help themselves and I know they *can* and *will*, for they will never give up now and
History will testify to their *bravery* yet. I am pained to see that many of
my friends and the first and most talented of our state have gone on the
other side to fight. How can they be so blinded to their own interest and
happiness? I am not surprised at Gov. Magoffin's course and predicted
it from the commencement of our troubles. He is a *weak conceited* dissipated man and totally unfitted for the position *he occupied.* He could
never have been brought on our side with *good liquor* and *Compliments.*
His new Son-in-law and *Secretary of State* is a cousin of Tom Munroe,[129]
a nephew of Judge Monroe's wife, Mr. Gaither, and an old friend of
mine, and from his conduct shows himself to be a very different man
from Mr. Munroe.

Your neighbors have entirely to all appearances recovered their usual
kind and attentive manner to me, and I hope do not treasure an unkind
thought against my *unintentional Sarcasm* and I hope I have convinced
them by my manner that I did not mean it. I will not have a *Duel of any
kind* I hope but from appearances may have to indulge sometimes in
speaking my mind freely. You need not be troubled about your shrubbery as the yard has jut been very prettily trimmed, by John, and looks
very well. I saw him engaged at it two or three weeks ago. Mrs. M. says "it
will afford her pleasure to have it done whenever it is necessary altho'
you have plenty of servants" but John has saved her the trouble and the
idea that it should be done entered his brain about the same time it did
hers. Last Monday morning Lt. Whiting called to see me. He is stationed
at Fort Gaines and is both handsome and agreeable, an acquaintance
I made three years ago in Montgomery, and speaking of Montgomery
acquaintances reminds me of Col. Ballock and his death. I regretted it
so much. But Matt and David Craighead[130] are begging me to stop as it
is so late and indeed since I think of it I must. I will write again soon and

---

129. Nathaniel Gaither (1835–1894) served as Kentucky's secretary of state from October 1861 to August 1862. He married Susan Shelby Magoffin, the daughter of Kentucky's
governor, Beriah Magoffin.

130. David Craighead was another of Elodie's cousins and one of the children of Jane P.
Craighead.

in the meanwhile hope to hear from you. With love and kind wishes for a happy New Year, I am as ever, yrs truly, Elodie

Do overlook the errors my haste has occasioned.
    To Capt. N. H. R. Dawson

Selma January 5th 1862.

I was quite disappointed at the non arrival of your usual letter today, but have observed when it does not arrive on the Sabbath that on Wednesday I am the recipient of two. I wrote you a hasty letter on New Year's night, acknowledging I believe the pleasure of your last letters of the 22nd and 25th, if not you may now accept my thanks. Our Christmas is almost over and has proved far more agreeable than I for a moment imagined, quite a number of small parties were given which were pleasant to us all. Matt gave one to Miss Ferguson on Thursday night. Mrs. Ellsberry intends giving one this week and I think this will be our last.

You must know that in the last three weeks society has undergone a change and is now divided into two distinct classes, in the 1st belong the Weavers, Weedows, Fourniers, Morrises, Mrs. Steele, Perkinsons, Watts, Miss Echols, Misses Sikes and Carroley. In the *second* by order of the *first* belong ourselves, Mrs. Mabry, Misses Goodwin and Elsberry, Misses Ferguson and Bell. The rest of the inhabitants have been allowed the privilege of placing their own position. The consequence is that many persons do not speak, and the first class give their surprise Parties and omit the second class entirely. We are congratulating ourselves that they classed us *No 2*. There has been a *war here in words* and the *Victory* is not yet awarded to the "Whites" and "anti-Whites" as the two parties call themselves. This all arose from the opposition Tableaux given for the Benefit of the "Blues" and I think they will be sorry enough before the matter is settled. *Mrs. M., your neighbor*, is very sociable since this happened and says she prefers belonging to class No 2. Can you stand having a sweetheart who does not belong to the first circle of Selma society? I am sorry to see such a state of affairs, but this trouble has been ready to burst on the community for several months, but I am actually "gossiping," you will think I am afraid from my letter that I am endowed with no propensity in that way, but I think you want to know all that is transpiring during your absence even if it is a fuss among the females, but I consider the classing of society quite an important item. Where will you be placed I wonder? But I will change the subject for I have heard enough of it.

I received a letter from David on Thursday giving me the pleasing intelligence of his perfect safety and the particulars of the Engagement, and he adds that he has applied for leave of absence for thirty days, and if it is granted will return to N.C. and see us on his way. I hope he will soon arrive. He writes that he does not believe he will ever quit the service as it suits his taste better than any other profession. How many will feel just as he does and adopt an Army life? I would prefer his electing a more quiet settled life, but of course would not endeavor to dissuade him from it at this time when all men should feel as he does, ready and willing to fight to the last. The surrender of Mason and Slidell was true to the *bravery* of the Northerners and they had actually Yankee sense enough to know that they had more in hand now than they would ever accomplish. To subjugate the South had proved a dangerous play to them and England would make them feel unpleasantly too. I only wish Foreign aid in breaking the blockade. We could then do very well, but I am sure have little cause as yet for complaint. I am in hopes *some day* to hear of *Peace*, but so little fighting has been done, that the day I fear is far in the future every day I hear of new Companies and Regiments being formed so there will be no scarcity of soldiers no matter how long the war lasts. Poor Kentucky is to be made the Battle ground and I think them *so slow* up there, and grow more and more impatient every day to hear from my mother and friends. Do you not know I will enjoy the first letter I receive from my Mother and the first time I meet with her and the dear ones at Home? I will think it the happiest hour of my life. I wish I was a bird indeed. I would be willing to be an *Owl* long enough to fly and see them all.

Do you remember Mr. Butler? He came to see me a day or two ago and always calls when he is in Selma. I never fancied him particularly, but he can make himself quite pleasant and is very polite. I did not write you we had made $205 for the "Cadets" and $30 for the "Guards," but I believe some expenses are to be deducted. *I wish you would accept for the "Cadets"* no matter what use you put the proceeds to. Will you? I know you do not need the money, but put it aside and it can be given [to] those of the Company who reenlist or very early appeared to some purpose. I am seriously opposed to the "Aid Society" getting it. Some people think the Cadets *need no help, no money, no anything* and do not want them to have any given them but as I helped to make this, I wish them to enjoy the little sum, I care not how. I have not had any conversation for a long time with Mr. Wetmore but he is now at home. I hear of but few additions to his Company. Messrs Lapsley Wood and Favel are his Lieutenants. I do not think Mr. H. remained at home on my account, but from a disinclination to participate in the struggle now going on. He has quietly resigned all hope and evidently sees he can occupy but a friend's place and as such behaves himself. I find it difficult to realize but four months are to elapse before your return, but I am delighted that so few remain, even if you intend returning I will get a glimpse of you and that will be some consolation and gratification. Well as usual I am writing a long letter and considering you received an *extra one* last week I had better show some consideration and make a finish of this. I hope to hear from you very soon, but Mrs. Knox says you are to return this week. If such is the truth I need not expect to. *Did you write her word before me?* But good-bye and goodnight. Write me soon a long letter and believe me to be as ever yours

    Elodie.

Kittie desires to be remembered to you, also Willie but he is ignorant of whom I am writing to however he often speaks of you and has not forgotten either yourself or Mr. A.

No 6. Camp Law, Jany 5, 1861. [1862]

I wrote you twice on Wednesday, and two days ago received yours of the 22 December.

    I am glad that the sadness under which you labored, at the time, on account of the Drainsville affair has been removed by later intelligence.

    I presume that your Christmas festivities have all passed. I will hope that you had some share of enjoyment in them. The inconsiderate introduction of Mr. Lincoln is well calculated to annoy you, but when you remember that ignorance of the amenities due to our neighbors was perhaps the cause, you will pardon the authors. I have no idea that it was done to offend you. I hope not, for I can see or imagine no reason for such a presumption. The community would not tolerate such insolence or I am mistaken in its tone. That you have persons who are curious of you is probably true, but they will conceal their feelings under their bonnets. Mr. Lincoln has become almost the personification of our enemies, and the partisan feeling of the south holds him responsible, but it is only so in a *political sense*, but good breeding would require persons to speak of him respectfully, or not at all, in your presence.

Here I will mention a little thing, of Lizzie, that Mr. Mathews tells me, in one of his letters, which speaks well of the sense of propriety of the dear little child. He heard Josh, his little son, about her age, speaking to her of Mr. Lincoln. He spoke of him as "Uncle Abe" and "Old Abe." She told him that he was wrong, that Mr. Lincoln was a grown gentleman, and that he should call him Mr. Mr. Mathews was very much pleased, and mentioned it to me.

These things happen frequently to others, by the conduct of the inconsiderate and malicious. I have reason to know that my friend, Mrs. Goldsby, has had her feelings frequently wounded on account of her father. Dr. H. is a very foolish old man, and is frequently guilty of being ridiculous. His brother in law I hear is a "salt [illegible]" and it would be well to have him held up to the public. Dr. Shortridge is also one, but my kind feelings for Mr. McCraw prevent me from ever alluding to the question, as much as I detest and dislike his serpentine relative.

I enter into your feelings fully in regard to my reenlistment. I intend to return in May, and when I reenter the service, it will be as your *husband*, unless you refuse to become my wife, in which event I will risk the service as a refuge and asylum. This was the first regiment that flew to the standard of the south, and many of us left home hurriedly, and are therefore illy prepared to remain for our business. We have been in the front during the entire campaign, and the voice of our country and of our generals has given us some credit for good conduct at the battle of Manassas, when our independence was practically won. We have made forced marches with our men, sometimes barefooted. We claim in all this to have done nothing but our duty. We are now facing the cold wind and shows of a northern climate, in tents, and our sentinels, as they make their rounds, at night, have their beard upon their faces frozen. We are now informed that we should reenlist for the war, and that public opinion at home requires it. Public opinion, we know, is made up of men who have seen service, and who are anxious to share its exposures. Some we hear are impelled by *climatic*, others by *patriotic* motives. Some object to the cold, others that they have no desire to fight for Kentucky, as she was too laggard in joining the Confederacy. It may be that these gentlemen, who enjoy the comforts of home, who are in the habit of indulging in the luxury of their Havanas and who occasionally steal reluctantly an hour of sleep from their precious time, are better patriots and more impartial judges of duty than the worn and beaten soldiers. It may be proper that some, who are fattening upon the necessities of the poor, where time is spent in the acquisition of money, and who are even willing to supply the article of salt at ten dollars per sack, should sit in judgment upon our conduct.

We have an opinion of our own upon the subject. If our presence were necessary here, every man would be willing to remain. But when there are plenty to take our places, we cannot appreciate the reason for remaining. We will return to allow others, equally interested, an opportunity of exhibiting their love of liberty and their willingness to give their lives and fortunes in its defense. We care not to monopolize all the glory of winning our independence. We know that public opinion will give us the honors, but we see that the patriots who remain at home will claim all the [illegible] of freedom. It is strange that patriotic men who have large estates, who have wives and children, and who are becoming corpulent from the ennui of tranquility and ease should be willing to let us have all the glory of this war. I am astounded when I hear such a generous and [illegible] determination on their part. Injustice is certainly above them, as they are honorable men! When they shall have served one year, and know the pleasures of the service, they will be unwilling to return to their homes and families, preferring the dangers of the battle field and the routine of camp life. They will lose all relish for mince pies, and the little niceties of the table. It is hoped that this small class of gentlemen will consent to accept field or staff commissions from Mr. Davis, that their children may point with pride to the portraits of their much patriotic ancestors. I have given you my views upon this subject, almost in identical language as I have written to a friend. I wish more gentlemen could see themselves as others see them, and appreciate others as they appreciate themselves. I got a letter from John last night dated 28 Dec. and one from Miss Emily Ferguson, informing me of the shipment of a box of clothing and jellies for the Cadets. I have acknowledged it, and in order that you may see that I do not infringe upon the rules of propriety in writing to a young lady, enclose you copies.

The weather is bitterly cold. The ground is covered with sleet and frozen hard, too cold for snow.

Our cabin will be done next week. Mine is now commenced, and will be ready by the end of the week.

Lieut. McCraw is a little unwell. We heard yesterday of the surrender of Mason and Slidell, and of the renewal of the fight at Pensacola. I hope it will now be decided. I anticipate a war between the U. States and England, before our difficulties are settled.

And now, my dearest, goodbye. May God protect and keep you always. With my earnest prayers and much love, I remain yours,

    affectionately and sincerely

      N. H. R. Dawson

It is now snowing.

Selma, January 12th 1862.

Since writing last I have been the gratified recipient of three letters from you and which afforded me much pleasure by the perusal of them, that I feel myself very much more than usual your debtor. For three weeks there has been an unusual amount of gaiety, and on Friday night Miss Ellsberry gave a very pleasant party and I hope it will be the last. I am so entirely out of the habit of going to Parties or into scenes of pleasure that it has actually become an unpleasant task and all else that changes the "even tenor of our way." A life for eight or nine, yes I may say more, months of almost perfect monotony, cannot in three weeks regain its old ways without an effort, besides the circumstances which now surround me were never felt before, and seemed to sadden me and add to my disinclination to participate in the pleasure of a season so enjoyed at home generally by a united and happy family.

My Brother Ellick writes that he has captured two Yankees and four guns already and seems very well satisfied with the life of a Soldier and mentions quite a number of our young friends who are in the Confederate Army, but we hear not a word from my mother and have not since last summer. How happy I would be to hear from her *just once* but I stand the separation now much better than at first, and hope soon that we may be able at least to hear from her. Sister Emma has written to Kittie begging her to come to Nashville and stay with her as she is so lonely and I would not be surprised if she did soon as Selma affords her no pleasure and she thinks that now she may have an opportunity of slipping thro' sooner than remaining here.

I wrote you of the division made in *Society* and the *quarreling* and *fussing*. On Wednesday the young ladies of the 1st class went around and begged all the young ladies in town except Kittie and myself and Miss

Ellsberry to take part in a Tableaux which would be one of reconciliation remarking that the division had been made to "cut the Todds" and to make as *they thought the cut deeper* we were omitted and Miss E. for being our friend and Mr. Hagood for the same reason was the only gentleman left out. Mrs. Fournier and Mrs. Weaver are to manage the Tableaux, and if the girls had not so suddenly disliked us, Mr. And Mrs. F. are the *bitterest Enemies* I have or ever had and would have influenced them to behave as they have and may have done so, but I never have visited but two or three places in Town except in a formal manner and can stand being put aside and spend my time more profitably and pleasantly in divers ways than in visiting them. I hope they will enjoy it, but fear I do not attach importance or feel it enough for that. Mrs. F. did not have her Concert, but I think will probably have it combined with the Tableaux.

I saw Mrs. Wetmore a few days ago and she told me Mr. W. thought of going on to your company next week. I do not think Mr. W. should stay at home. There are hundreds in the field who sacrifice even far more than he. There is no business here for him to be engaged in, consequently he makes nothing and for every day he remains in the Army he is remunerated and only risks with others his life and his life is not more valuable than that of anybody else. I do not think it right that some men should be allowed to stay at home, kept by nothing but by disinclination to go, and others make all the sacrifices which they will not, to fight for their rights and risk in Battle after Battle their lives those stay at homes think so precious, and if the patriots fall, they reap the benefits they died fighting for. If you should fall, which of the stay at home men just here do you suppose will ever give you any thanks or credit for shedding your blood, sacrificing your life for the maintenance of their rights just as much as your own? If I were President Davis I would force every man to serve one year or at least six months and not permit the fighting to be done entirely by brave and patriotic men whose lives, just one, is equal to that of *five who have not the courage to go to the field of Battle.*

I have not the slightest item of news to give you and you must excuse a dull letter. I wrote you *begging* you would accept the money for the Cadets. There are no persons really suffering here. Those who ask charity will not eat *Corn Bread*, throw away *Peas*, and are tired of *Sweet Potatoes* and when some had means given them one bought a *Bracelet*, one gave a party, one took at a *trip*. The coming Tableaux are for the Poor. If you do not accept the little sum the "SAS" expect to get it. They bought some clothing for the Blues a short time since and expected the money received from the Blues Tableaux to pay for them, but the young ladies would not give it to them and placed it in the Bank, now they want *your money* to pay for them but Matt told me to tell you if you had written declining she would keep the letter until you wrote another accepting. I do not wish the Blues to have one cent of it, because we are friends of the Cadets and Guards. We are placed in the 2nd class and altho' have something for the Blues there are some trying to make the Blues believe us unfriendly to them and did tell Mr. Knox and Byrd so.

I have become very much interested in the "Rise of the Dutch Republic"[131] which I have at last found time to commence reading and as my visitors will be fewer I can find more time to spend in reading, but I must close my letter as Kittie wishes me to walk with her. She says she would not receive such a long letter from me for any consideration and wonders how you can stand it. You ask how I will like your writing once a week. I do not think I will enjoy it very much, but if your inclination does not prompt you to do so oftener or it is inconvenient why do not do so. I can do nothing but receive as few or as many as you write. I am not particularly matter of fact nor romantic. Sometimes I fancy I am a little romantic and sentimental. I must confess I have some *doubts sometimes* as to *believing everything you say*. Now you have answers to all your questions and candid ones. I believe you like candor do you not? I do above all things. I will certainly write and send you something of Mr. Garritt who leaves I find in two weeks, and by every opportunity. Now goodbye

No 9, Camp Alabama, Jany 14. 1862.

As Capt. Porter King leaves in the morning, I avail myself of his offer to take letters, to write you. He heard yesterday of his father's death, and has obtained leave of absence, on account of ill health. I mention this to account for my failure to accompany him. He is a man of warm and tender heart, and I sympathize with him, in his affliction.

Your letter of 5th inst. was recd last evening, and I was glad to hear that you had passed so pleasant a Christmas and hope it is a harbinger of happier days for my much loved Elodie.

I received yours of first January, with Mrs. White's note. I replied to both, immediately, thanking Mrs. W. and accepting the proceeds of the Tableaux for the Cadets. I mention this as you express an anxiety that I

---

131. Written by American historian and diplomat John Lothrop Motley in 1856.

should accept. Please tell Mrs. White. I feel an anxiety myself to accept the fund, since seeing a notice in the Reporter of the 3d. The Aid society has done *little* but to profess for our company, and I am under no great obligations. They shall never be informed of our wants, nor *begged* to aid us in any way, and I am willing to pay them for all they have ever done. Because we have been prudent, and have husbanded our means, it is no reason that everything should be given to the Blues. But I am impatient when I think of the subject, and I must not let you see that I have a *temper*. Tell Mrs. White that I tried to write her a *handsome* note, because I felt that she deserved it, at my hands, and I only said what I felt.

I regret that society has been so clarified. All of my sympathies are with you, and if allowed to select my own position, I will not become a member of the "first circle." I have never been honored with an invitation to one of the homes you name, and trust they will always remain in blissful ignorance of my shadow. I hope "surprise parties" are only fashionable with them as I eschew them as intrusions upon a lady's hospitality. They were introduced from New England, and I hope the tone of Southern society will taboo them entirely. I have many peculiar ideas, and fear you will find me unmanageable, on many points, but if I have weaknesses I will never attempt to conceal them from you. I rejoice that you agree with me about societies of all kinds. I never wish to see you a member of one, but will always desire that you should do your full share in works of charity and benevolence. The poor will always, if my wishes influence, call you friend. I love you so much that I would never have you placed where even the hypocritical could imagine that you did wrong. I hope, before this time, that you have met your brother, and I know you will be happy when you hear from your mother. I think I could communicate with her by writing through Col. Helm or Gen. Breckenridge, at Bowling Green. They have opportunities of communicating with friends in Kentucky. Have you ever tried this expedient? Mr. Pegues left me this morning, having been with me since Sunday. He came down with Col. Allan Jones and Capt. Blackford of the 5th Ala. I went with them yesterday to Evansport to see the batteries, with which they were much pleased. The *Pensacola* went down on Sunday night without being discovered until she had passed nearly out of the range of two of the batteries, quite a disappointment. The sentinels at the upper battery will be court-martialed for their negligence, and I hope will be punished. The Yankees are erecting winter quarters in Maryland. I can say to you that our works are strong. I saw one of the guns brought over by the Bermuda from England. It weighs 9,000 lbs. and carried a shell weighing 126 lbs., and throws it four miles.

Mr. Pegues has enlisted for the war, with thirty men in his company. All of them will go home on furlough. He desires me to go home to see to the affairs of P. P. and D. Is he not very kind to wish me to leave the army? My company will not reenlist, and I do not think its captain will, as he has strong inducements to return. The time is speeding rapidly, and it will soon be ninety days to the 26th of April. I always remember the 19th of the month as the day of our engagement and the 26th as that upon which I bid you a long farewell. I wish you could select the 19th of April as your bridal day, if I could be at home then.

You must prepare for an early request to celebrate our marriage after my return, and I hope you will consent. We certainly know each other well enough, and I am exceedingly anxious to take you under my protection. I dreamed a few nights ago of being at a party with you, but it was all a dream, however pleasant the delusion. I have not seen a lady to converse with since bidding Miss Mary Preston Cochran adieu at Charlottesville in August. She is a sweet girl, and if I had not met you, I think she would have had an opportunity of emigrating to Ala. I wrote you of her, I think, when at Charlottesville.

The night is bitter cold, and it is now sleeting. It snowed heavily last night and this morning. The whole face of the country is white, and the snow freezes as it falls. I have been in doors all day trying to keep warm, but it has been difficult. The guard is now going round, and I pity the poor fellows. How can some people, at home, envy the little comforts our friends would send us? Why do some desire the Cadets to have nothing? Poor souls, their sweethearts, among the Blues, are no doubt so dainty that they are unable to eat the army rations. Hence the many boxes sent them. It is a fancy command and altho' I have friends among them, I cannot appreciate their sufferings.

I do not think we will have a battle here this winter, as the roads will prevent an advance even if the Yankees desired to make one. We will hardly be able to get provisions. I called to see Col. Petigrew of the So. Ca. line yesterday. He was at dinner, and had nothing but old ham and a few biscuits. For six months his regiment has been guarding our batteries. The men go on duty every *fourth* night, *bivouacking*. What think you of such service in this weather, when the same vigilance is required as in the pleasant months of summer? We will never get our reward from the people who remain at home, hence I am willing to remain myself.

Capt. Blackford has Capt. Todd's sword, and Gen. Rodes his horse and accoutrements. Capt. B. insists that Capt. Todd of the Lincoln cavalry, who was taken prisoner, is a Yankee, and not the cousin of Mrs. Lincoln.

What say you? It is late, and my paper bids me end. Goodnight my loved
angel. May angels guard and protect your sweet slumbers.

   Write me a long letter, and with much love, I remain,

      Ever affectionately yours
      N. H. R. Dawson

I send you all of your letters.

Selma, January 17th 1862.

As Mr. Francis leaves tomorrow to rejoin the Guards I concluded to send
you a letter by him and your socks also, which have been waiting so long.
Accept my thanks for your letter of the 8th received today. Altho' short
it gave the gratifying and pleasing assurance of your health and safety. I
am glad you have not put your plan of *writing once a week* into execution,
as it will deprive me of much pleasure, and when you begin to do so I
will drop you off of my list of correspondents unless you are *terribly tired
of writing to me.*

   But let me tell you of another pleasure, that of a visit from your agreeable Brother. I *liked him even better* than I imagined I would, and soon
found myself chatting away to [him] as if with an old friend, with an ease
and freedom, which since I think of it doubtless amused and surprised.
You should have heard me talk of you to him and opposing him in regards to his views of your reenlisting. He told me he knew you would do
so because he has put his own foot into it for the War. Now Mr. Dawson
you say Public opinion in Ala. expects you to reenter the Army. What
right has public opinion to do so and pray who constitutes public opinion in Ala.? But too many men who have not courage to go and fight
or even give their money to maintain their *rights* and *liberties,* which you
are risking your life and fortune for, but they have the courage and gen-
erosity to try and take from you that of all things the most *valuable* and
desirable, your fair name, and were you to *die ten deaths* you would receive
about the same credit you have and justice would not be done you even
in your own home, for many here who *profess* to be your *friends* are Enemies cloaked under the disguise of Friendship. Do not think my Patriotism has departed for I assure you if there is a change it has increased,
but until I see the necessity of your returning my opinion is the same in
regards to your doing so. Your Brother wishes you to, but he also desires

your securing a higher office and I believe if *you must* I would too. But I do not fancy your leaving to go back much in any capacity. *Do you not feel ashamed* at pretending to me you were anxious to return on a short furlough even and then to tell others you "just did not desire to return and stay only a few days?" I am *finding you out already*, but as much as I wished to see you and do now I think it was for the best you did not return tho I suppose by May I *will have almost forgotten you*. Of course I am in earnest.

I cannot refrain from expressing my admiration of Lizzie's propriety and respect for her elders and think if some of the grown people were imbued with the same, it would be better for them. I assure you I have every reason to *know* and believe the act I mentioned was *intended personally*, and when you return I *can tell you enough to convince you* so too. What we have been subjugated to many would not believe and now since I have "declared my Independence" Selmians will see that I can maintain it. I ask you now as Col. Byrd did the public to suspend judgment until you hear both sides of the story. You will hear from none until you return perhaps the side very much against us *especially*.

I do not dislike Col. B. I do not know anything about and do not take interest enough in him to care for him in any way. Mrs. Parnell (the old lady) is the warmest friend I have and I believe loves me very much. She is always speaking of you to me but refuses to tell me whom she derived her information from. I imagine Mrs. W. Her and your neighbors and [illegible] informed. I have never acknowledged it to her. She says she intends to knit for you.

There has been some excitement in Town about Mr. Baker inviting two Yankee Officers to dine with him and several other Yankees in town to meet there all of which turns out to be a *story* and invented by some *busy bodies* who know everything and nothing actually. Things have come to such a pass people can do and say nothing without a fuss. I never believed the report as I thought Mr. B. would have more sense and discretion, even if he sympathized with the North, than to so publicly make it known by such an act. You will see his and Mr. Bill's card in the "Reporter" of today.

I have begun already to count the months and weeks until I see you, soon will count the days. Do you think I will be glad to welcome you back? I do not know when Mr. Wetmore speaks of going to Virginia but hope he will let me know as I will write by him. I have not seen him for a long time. Your other neighbors I have seen frequently of late. Miss G. has improved so much in talking and is really lively at times and makes herself very pleasant, as does her Mother. I have been in hopes there would be a Battle fought in Kentucky before this time and matters more decided, but I fear nothing will be done until Spring either there or in Va. If we are tired waiting here for a fight what must you Soldiers be?

Mr. Herman gives a concert for the Soldiers tonight. All the churches took up a Collection for the poor on Sunday last and the Reconciliation Tableau is for the Charleston sufferers but I do not know when it is to take place. Miss Bell and Miss Ellsberry declined acting with them.

I am writing you a long letter today but do not expect me to write on Sunday as my ideas will all be exhausted in this, do you not feel sorry for them? Do tell me were you transferred from Genl. Whiting's Brigade? Some say you were, other not. I do not know. You only wrote me that Col. Law was doing what he could to prevent it. In your next tell me and where you are now stationed and if in your winter Quarters. I heard the 1st Ky Regt had been ordered to Ky. My Brother is I think in New Orleans. I do not think he will see us it is so much out of his way and he doubtless will be hurried. I believe you think I am *jealous* in disposition from sending me those notes. Indeed I am not and would not be if you visited ladies which I suspect you have and never said a word about it to me. As to answering in your *last* and *candidly* I won't do it. That is for me to know and you to find out if you can. *Mr. questioning Lawyer* I have answered quite enough to satisfy any one and to *convince you of what you want to know.* I think I will begin and ask you some and see if you will be as candid as I have been. The weather is cold and rainy and my hands are almost stiff this morning. I have not stopped to warm them since I commenced. I hope very soon to receive a long letter and now will end mine. Hoping you will soon return in safety, I remain as ever *yours truly*

Elodie.

Selma, Feby 1st. 1862.

I have been fortunate this week in receiving letters which contained pleasant intelligence. Two have arrived from you, and it is needless to tell you how welcome they were, and the happiness and gratification they gave. Another came from my Brother at Bowling Green, who informed us that he had received a *letter* from my dear mother a few days before writing, and that she was well, and at that time safe. This is the first intelligence we have had since *July*, and you can imagine the great happiness it caused us, as we did not know whether she was alive, where she was, or anything about her, and only conjectured her whereabouts because she intended returning home, but now we have the satisfaction of *knowing something*, and that she can correspond irregularly with my Brother, even an occasional letter will give us so much joy, and relieve some of our continual and deep anxiety.

But I must not fill up *your letter* with my feelings occasioned by another, when I have something else to write of, and so much to *retract*, that was contained in one of my late letters, and yet I am almost determined not to do so, for you ought to know that I was not in earnest when I inflicted the "unkindest cut of all", and at which you seem to take umbrage. Have I not always expressed the confidence I placed in you? And surely if I doubted that you loved me I could not have felt any to express. I simply thought your question an unnecessary one, did not care particularly to answer it, and did not aim to give satisfaction, yet did not think you would notice it as you did. Now say that I am a good girl and that "nobody is hurt" or angry, since I have made such a retraction and my *first*. I think someone else must be more "guarded in future" as to what she writes.

We have had for several days very disagreeable rainy weather, which has kept us closely confined to the house but together with the cards, sewing, reading and Music, and the presence of my friend Miss Sallie Bell we kept the "blues" off completely and successfully, but the Sun lent us a few beams this Evening but met with a cold reception, and soon withdrew, yet I hope to feel its warmth tomorrow.

We have heard of the failure of the Burnside Expedition, and that Genl. Price has captured St. Louis, that I doubt, as well as this rumor of a Battle at Bowling Green, in which the Northerners acknowledge they were whipped, but if it were true, I would have heard from my Brother or Brotherinlaw to that effect and think it a Yankee invention. I am much obliged to you for your advice concerning Tableaux and etc., and if *ever I am disposed to assist* in anything of the kind again, I will promise to take it. I was never among the *acting* young ladies but once, and that was owing to the withdrawal of one, at the last moment, and it was left to me to be obliging and take her part in one scene or allow it to be omitted. To be accommodating I consented, the more willingly because two thick net screens concealed me from the audience, *but sixteen could not now induce me to do so*. Besides no one wants me to. I have been omitted in the invitations, and so has Ella McCraw unless she has been asked since I saw her last, and a week or two after all the others were. I assure you I am giving myself no concern about the *fusses*, and *speak only when I am spoken to*. As you expect to continue in the Service and desire a higher position, I hope you will succeed in obtaining the appointment for which you have been recommended. I have made up my mind to your returning to the Army sooner than I expected and with more contentment than I thought I would.

Sunday Morning, Feby 2nd

The lateness of the hour compelled me to lay aside my pen last night before I finished my letter, and this morning I again resume it, as excessive rain prevents my attending church and I fear I do not regret it as much as I should, but I sometimes think I commit as much sin going to Church once or twice a day, even when I am compelled to listen to an indifferent sermon, because I was raised to do so and taught to consider it my duty to do so by a pious and good mother. I believe I prefer your not going to Kentucky. I think our most terrible Battles will be fought there, and I would rather have you in a safer place, tho' really there is not much safety anywhere in War, and the places we now consider the safest may in the end prove to be the most dangerous. How I do wish we would have peace, or that France and England would recognize us, if they intended to. I confess I have little patience left, and wish we could take our time in allowing them to have Cotton when their necessity forces them to recognize the Confederate States. I hope they will pay for their tardiness in giving an enormous price, but I should not be so *spiteful*, but I never could tolerate the English and will not acknowledge like some members of the family that we are of English descent. I prefer being *Irish* and certainly possess some Irish traits. I leave you to find them out, if they have remained concealed. I remember Lt. Johnston of Marion. I met him I think in Montgomery and was struck with his resemblance to Mr. J. C. Breckenridge, is it not the same one? Mr. Ramsey married an old acquaintance of mine I believe, Miss Meta Redwood of Mobile. I knew her when I was a little girl, but have never seen her since. We received your letter of acceptance and had it published and you must have seen it before now in the Reporter and I received your last on Thursday enclosing the one from your Aunt. I did not know you had so many Relatives, but thought you stood almost alone in the World. I always thought it a misfortune to have many relatives, and am now convinced of it since the War began, as mine cause me so much anxiety and thought. I have one cousin who I dearly love whose home is in Mo. and I am perfectly ignorant of him not having heard from or of him since the War began. I am also his favorite, and we have spent many many happy hours together and

I would be delighted to hear from him. When I think of my friends and relatives at home, and think perhaps I shall never meet with them again, I am almost perfectly miserable, and my heart yearns for the love which they lavished upon me and which then I did not properly appreciate, and which I do not receive here. The friendships I have formed and may form here will never be like those at home, altho' I have some friends whom I love very much here and who I think like me, but sighs for the past, and murmurs against the present, will not unite separated friends and will not ameliorate matters, so I will only hope for a happier future, and hoping end this subject.

The Rain has kept me at home and friends from calling so I have no news or gossip for you this week. Mr. C. Woods called to see us a few days ago, looking remarkably well. He leaves tomorrow to visit his Parents, and will return from his home to Va. *Three* young ladies *claim him* and I suppose the sight of him made glad their hearts. I judge them by myself under the same circumstances, without the *two rivals*. I am glad I did not fall in love with a *Blue* as they are in such demand that when they return there will be great disagreements and squabbling, besides I think I would have showed a great want of taste to have overlooked the "Cadets". I am quite interested in the *Rise of the Netherlands*, have nearly finished the second volume, and *Killed off* poor Egmont and Horn and have William of Orange in Germany trying to raise an Army against Philip. I have read Prescott's Philip but have such a treacherous memory, that I read portions of this work which is very similar I am told with the same avidity with which I would seize something I had never seen before, as I too do not read *for show*, but for a love of reading. I do not feel the disappointment at not retaining what I read, as others who read from a different motive do. Ella McCraw is a great reader and I expect one of the best informed girls in Selma. She visits very seldom and is now engaged in teaching a little School, and says she likes it and as she is amiable and patient I suppose it does afford her interest, but it would not me. But I am writing quite a long letter considering I had nothing to write of.

I saw Mrs. Mabry and Miss G. a few moments last Evening. They are exceedingly friendly and begged Kittie and I to go in and take Tea with them sociably, but we declined. I think the difficulty has had the effect of creating much more sociability among the different parties, and among some the unkind feeling that at first existed is dying away. I am hoping for my usual letter from you today, and as I have written you such a long letter today I shall expect you to return the Compliment soon. I will be so glad when I can talk to you in place of writing and the time is speeding away which separates us, but now I must say goodbye. Write soon. Over-look all the errors contained in this and believe me to be with love, ever yours devotedly, Elodie.

I will direct my letters to Manassas as you receive them sooner than from Dumfries until you write to do otherwise.

March 8, 1862.[132]

I send my loved Elodie two *Dispatches*, one of them will inform her of the death of Willie Lincoln, and give her the melancholy particulars.
 I hope to see you this evening, as I may have to leave on Monday.
  Sincerely and affty
   N. H. R. Dawson
   March 8/62

Opeliker Ala. March 14. 1862.

The railroad track was injured, yesterday, by a train running off, about twenty miles from Montgomery, and we were detained until evening. Not having made the connection, Col. Goldsby and myself remained here, in preference to spending the night at West Point. We take the train at 12 today and will go by Columbus and Macon, as the route by Atlanta will probably be much crowded. I do not regret the detention as every day from our camp now is so much gained. I look forward to the time to be spent with the regiment with no sort of pleasure, and wish for many rea-sons that my term had expired. I look forward to our marriage, my dear Elodie, with much pleasure and anxiety. It is the goal of my hopes, and the love you have given me is a guerdon greater than I desire. I know that you will make me happy. As I have frequently told you, the Christian has no firmer faith in the promises of his Savior than I have in your being all that a woman can be. I hope and trust that I may be allowed to devote a long life to your happiness.
 I got up early this morning to admire and kiss your likeness, which still accompanies me. When I reached the boat, at Selma, I found that

---

132. Nathaniel has returned to Alabama.

in changing my vest I had omitted to take the locket. You may imagine my feelings, as I went back home to get this valuable "little gem." Mr. Wetmore failed to get breakfast yesterday at Montgomery and you should have seen him, when we were detained, walking to a house near the cars to get this essential meal. The owner declined to furnish the meal and you cannot imagine his despair. He made a note of the man's name in his diary, and no doubt the unfortunate fellow will descend to posterity unhonoured and unsung by our hungry friend. At last [illegible] a soldier on the cars invited Mr. W. to partake of his Haversack, and he was regaled upon ham and bread. He went on to West Point, and we will not see each other, as we travel in different directions.

The news of the battle in Arkansas was rather discouraging in Montgomery. We hope to hear more favorable accounts this morning. Our reverses are unaccountable. We must change the tide.

We remained in Montgomery only long enough to take breakfast. I hope you have received my two notes. You must write me regularly. I will send you frequent letters.

And now with much love, I remain, my dear Elodie,

    Yours affectionately and sincerely,

      N. H. R. Dawson.

The spirit of volunteering in this part of the state is very fine. Two new regiments are now in camp, at [illegible] on the rail road, about 10 miles from this place. They will be organized in a few days. The whole country seems alive to our dangers, and it is to be hoped that we will shake off the lethargy of the past eight months.

Columbia, So. Ca., March 16/62

Leaving Augusta this morning at 8 o'clock, we reached Kingsville at 2, and making a detour from the Wilmington route, came on to this beautiful city, and will continue our journey, via Charlotte and Raleigh, in the morning. A disposition to please ourselves, and a desire to see this place, were the reasons, and I might add, with some show of truth, that we were both disinclined to travel on so cold a night, especially as I had a touch of rheumatism, in one of my knees. At all events we put up at the "Congaree House" and have been amply paid for our trouble.

We arrived at 4 o'clock, and as soon after as possible, we strolled out, and walked over the city. The main street is wide and shaded with three rows of water oaks. This is the promenade of the town, and is built up with fine residences, most of them having beautiful gardens and shrubberies. Col. John S. Preston's residence is very handsome, indeed it may be termed palatial in its style and surroundings. It is of marble, and has around it a shrubbery that Shenstone might have envied. I enclose a piece of Jasmine and of woodvine from the garden. We visited the college buildings, which are prettily situated, and look like University buildings generally do. We were attracted to one of the student's rooms by the name of Legare being carved on the wall, and went into it. It was occupied by him, and is now remembered as the habitation, during his college life, of this great Carolinian. We also walked around the new capitol. The walls are complete, but the building is not covered. The style is very handsome, Grecian. The columns and capitals are Corinthian. The medallions of Robt. Y. Hayne[133] and Geo. McDuffie[134] are carved on each side of the door of the upper entrance, while niches are prepared for the statues of Calhoun and other departed worthies. I have never seen a building so eminently chaste and well adapted to the deliberations of the representatives of a chivalrous people. At sunset, we returned to the Congaree, and were soon sitting at the supper table, enjoying the luxury of a cup of pure coffee, which I have not had since leaving Selma. It was indeed refreshing, and I do not wonder at the fondness of the Turks for this delightful beverage.

We have news of a battle at New Bern N.C. on Friday, in which we lost 700 men and the Yankees 2500, the town being burned by the citizens. If this be true the enemy may have possession of the road at Goldsboro, and we may have acted wisely in taking this route. I saw in the *Charleston Courier,* of yesterday, a letter from the *Savannah Republican,* in which the writer introduces Mr. Kellogg as a warm advocate of our cause. I took the liberty of enclosing it in an envelope to Mrs. Helm, that she might call his attention to it, as it may get him into some trouble with his Yankee cousins. I send you the extract, referring to him.

I have thought of you all day, my loved Elodie, and when admiring the beautiful gardens and residences of this city, I wished so much that we could be allowed in peace and quiet to enjoy even a modicum of domestic comfort and happiness. I love to think of you among the flowers, and long for the hour when we shall be made one at the altar. We are now one

---

133. Robert Y. Hayne (1791–1839) was governor of South Carolina from 1832 to 1834.
134. George McDuffie (1790–1851) was governor of South Carolina from 1834 to 1836.

in all save the ceremonials of the law. I think of you, and pray for you, as the loved partner of my happiness. If we were married, I believe I could bear our separation better. I would then feel that, in case of my death, you could be the inheritor of many things, which I have a dread of passing into the hands of persons who do not love me, as you only, my own dearest angel, can love me. My servants would have a mistress to care for and protect them and my little daughters would have a friend to guard them, in after years, from the alluring temptations of society. My love for you is deep and strong. I see nothing beautiful that does not remind me of you. I imagine that you are now, or have been this evening, occupied in writing to me, in lieu of an opportunity of conversing with me, as you have done since my return to Selma. Last Sunday evening, I gave you the first flowers of spring, and this evening, in a distant city, I have plucked for you the same wild flowers. Ah dearest, I trust that ere another spring shall bloom, that we may be enjoying the happiness of wedded love, and that Peace may have poised her wings over our now convulsed and bleeding country. I look to our marriage for a great deal of happiness. I see you possessed of all of the qualities so essential to make home a paradise on earth, entertaining none of the foolish notions that some ambitious women do, of leading the town, and of taking the lead in society. I will be glad to see our home the welcome resort of cultivated and refined gentlemen & ladies, but not the place for [illegible] and assemblies, and I wish to see you the accomplished and elegant hostess, at home always to your friends. I have no desire to see you rivaling Mrs. Weaver or Mrs. Pegues for the mastery of the circles of Selma [illegible]. But why should I repeat when you have so often told me, of your views of life and duty?

The moon is shining brightly, and its rays beam softly into the window reminding me, as the clock is striking nine, that another eye than mine is fixed upon it, that another heart is beating with the love for one that he lavished upon you. I will write again from the first stopping place.

Goodnight and goodbye, my dearest. May angels watch and guard your slumbers. Adieu.

Affectionately and devotedly yours

N. H. R. Dawson

Selma, March 16th 1862.

According to promise I have taken my writing materials to send you my usual Sunday letter, and the one promised on your departure, but you remember I did not speak of how interesting it would be, and it is well that I did not, for I have not an item worthy of record or of sufficient interest to transfer to paper, therefore I will be compelled to write of myself, which you have sometimes informed me proved entertaining.

After you left me on Wednesday I felt very low spirited and I know ten other ways at least and I thought nothing but a good cry, woman's resort under all trouble, would do me the least possible good, but upon sober second thought, I concluded that altho' I did feel badly, and a cry would relieve me, yet you would not like to see me give way to tears, when it was my duty to bear bravely all trials which my poor country at this time caused others to feel as well as myself, so I stifled back my sighs and tears and behaved myself in a manner that day and since which I think Mr. Dawson would have approved of and Complimented.

My Brother has not returned yet, but has been since Friday at Perryville and Radfordville buying Arms which he heard were to be purchased there, and to my surprise has not returned, but I think his prolonged absence is owing to the recent rain, which has swollen the creeks. He looks badly, being just recovered from Typhoid Fever and Pneumonia, and certainly requires rest. He had a great deal to tell us of our acquaintances, and many amusing incidents of his Camp life in the last six months, but notwithstanding the great happiness it afforded me to meet him again, yet it did not compensate for the pain of parting with you. Every moment I miss you and think of you and really believe I shall think the next two months longer in revolving than have been the ten which are past, and I can imagine how much worse reenlisting for the War will be, unless the Ky and Tenn Generals whip not the Federals as have Genl. Van Dorn. This last Victory caused merry smiling faces and exclamations of delight today, and I would have been more gratified if we had not lost so many ourselves.

Mr. Pegues came up today bringing with him the children who spent the day with Willie. I did not see Mr. Pegues. The children seem very affectionate but in other respects to have been exceedingly neglected. I mean the boys. George and I became in a short time quite friendly. His manner of conversation amused me. Fannie told me her Mother was ten weeks in Mobile, but that she became very tired as she preferred home to any other place. I have not seen Mrs. M. since you left or indeed any one scarcely. The Weather has been so unpleasant, raining and blowing, until today which has proved more welcome as it brought the sunshine with it, and innumerable birds whose happiness, judging from their sweet notes, is to be envied. I fully expected a letter from you ere this, but suppose you made no stay in Montgomery and could not write elsewhere, and to think "no news is good news," but hope very soon to receive a long letter telling me of your trip and all that has transpired since you left Selma. I think I will be more interested and better satisfied when I begin again to receive my accustomed letters but which will cause me to regret more than ever the Evenings so enjoyed and past, but I hope there are others in store for us, and that we will meet again in a few weeks. This I try to believe and think, and to only look forward to a bright and happy future, but so many hopes as bright as mine have been blasted and hearts as loving as mine been broken that I cannot but think sometimes that I may not escape the common lot of suffering, allotted to us all, but when I begin to write you in this strain I know I should cease at once, feeling that I am wrong to do so, since these are not such letters as a patriotic soldier should receive, but I am afraid some of his patriotism is taking flight when he tells me he is "willing to make his country secondary to his love." This must not be at such a moment when Country should be first with *all* and until every Yankee is whipped entirely off our soil and we [are] proclaimed a free and independent people once more. This will I believe soon be the case, and from the number I hear that are enlisting is by all determined on. It does me good to hear of new companies and regiments being formed, for I think then by the time the 12th month Volunteers expire, that there will be men enough in field to let them rest a short time, if not entirely. My *patriotism* is *only resting*! But I must end my letter this Evening. When I hear from you I will write a longer one and I hope a more agreeable one also. Write to me often and soon, and believe me with prayers for your safe return, your own loving,

Elodie.

Richmond, March 21. 1862.

I wrote you yesterday, my loved Elodie, and then thought I would go to Fredericksburg this morning, but a mistake in the hour at which the train leaves has kept me here another day, and we will have the pleasure of reaching *home* tomorrow.

I received a duplicate of my authority to raise a regiment yesterday. The original was granted and forwarded on the 5th March. I will make an effort to get leave of absence, but have no idea that it will be granted.

I have made up my mind to remain in the army quietly until my term expires, when I will be free to act as I please, and will be at liberty, untrammeled, to enter your service, I hope, for a long term of *years* and *happiness.*

I met with quite a piece of good fortune yesterday. Mr. Jackson of Cahaba, and a number of Mr. Pegues Co. brought me my pistol & all of my missing articles. It seems that my trunk flew open and was closed by the conductor before he discovered that any of the contents had fallen out. Mr. G., seeing my name on the trunk, kindly took charge of the articles, and brought them on for me.

Richmond is very quiet. Parties who profess to know, say that we are on the eve of great events. It seems to be conceded that a great battle is to be fought, and must be won, near Corinth in Miss. McClellan is advancing on Richmond, and we may have a battle on our line before summer.

I will try to get "My Maryland," and if successful, will send it to you by mail today. I find it will be prudent to leave my trunk in this city, and confine all of my wants to a carpet bag, such is life. I have seen all of our congressmen. I have heard with much pleasure that Mr. Leach, of Ky., is in the army of Gen. Johnston, and is fighting gallantly for our rights and liberties. Mr. Burnett of the Blues gave me this information.

Pres. Davis left on the central cars, this morning, for Gardensville, where Gen. Johnston has his headquarters. This is reliable, as his private secretary told Judge Dargon of Iredell, who told me. We can only speculate upon the motives, but hope all is for a good purpose. Mr. Clay is in better health than his friends could ever have hoped to see him. I was greatly surprised. I think of calling on Mr. Clay today.

I found in my trunk one of your letters, which is enclosed. I dislike to burn anything that you write, especially when my dear Elodie is keeping all of her letters for me.

How happy will my safe return to Ala, in May, render us? I hope our marriage will unite us for many year and that you will never have reason to regret the step. I look forward to it with a certainty of happiness.

I would write you more but have now to give up my seat to a congressman, as the body is about to convene. I have been disappointed in not hearing from you this morning, but am certain the letter is on the way.

With much love, and the hope that God will keep you safely, I remain,
    Yours most affty
    N. H. R. Dawson

Selma, April 1st 1862.

I have been exceedingly gratified this Evening by the reception of two letters from Richmond bearing the dates of the 23rd and 24th of last month. I was surprised at your long detention there, but do not regret it knowing among so many agreeable acquaintances that your time spent among them passed both rapidly and pleasantly, and much more so than in Camp, but I missed those Evenings you were spending so far away and wished for your presence often to cheer me up when feeling sad and lonely, as I so frequently do, when you are away and exposed to danger, but I hope soon to see you again and dwell with pleasure upon the thought that so few weeks intervene between our meeting, but the days do not pass as briefly as I desire and time seems really very long and I fear my usually small amount of patience will become exhausted before the 1st of May. I believe I have received all of your letters and beg permission to differ with you in regards to their being interesting or not, for I think some of them exceedingly so, without meaning to flatter or Compliment, which you know is not a fault of mine.

Tonight is my birthnight and I feel older than ever, but not enough so to behave myself as prettily as I ought. I concluded to take advantage of today and play some April pranks, and fooled Miss Serena elegantly. She fooled me however in the end by sending me over a nice supper which I feared to remove the napkin from, for fear of seeing an empty waiter, and I think I would have troubled you too, if you had been at home. The Ladies held a meeting this Evening for the purpose of turning the Institute into a Hospital for the benefit of Col. Kent's regt which is to go into Camp here, or any sick soldiers that may be sent here to be nursed. Mrs. Hooker[135] was elected Matron, and several assistant nurses. I was not present but hope to do my share when the time comes. For us to have sick soldiers in our midst, I will cheerfully do all in my power to relieve their suffering. I have not heard directly from my Brother since he left, but hear that he is at Corinth, and indeed the entire Army of Gen'l Johnston. My sister Mrs. Helms is here and will remain a month or two I hope. Both of her children are sick with measles and for two nights I have been nursing them and begin to feel fatigued but suppose the rest of the children, Willie and two little darkies, will be the next, and we will have a time of

---

135. The Selma census lists an S. J. Hooker as a female head of household running a boardinghouse. It also lists a Sallie L. Hooker, age forty-eight, as living in the same household. The Mrs. Hooker referred to here is probably one of the two. 1860 Census: Selma.

it, but I will be an experienced nurse for the Hospital. Everything is very quiet, more so than usual. I hear tho' among the different rumors afloat that Miss Echol is to be married very soon to a Mr. Williams of Mobile. I sincerely hope it may be true, and believe Selma will be improved by her absence. Neither Mrs. M. or Miss G. have called since you left and I have not met with them but once.

Bro. Clem has volunteered and leaves on Friday for Mobile. The entire militia excepting five, volunteered, fearing they would be drafted. I fear Bro. Clem will do no good and require constant nursing tho' Dr. Cabell says the change may improve him, and indeed I hope so. He will be absent three months. You desired me to tell you my favorite combination of colors. I think all you mentioned are pretty but could not decide which, unless I know for what, as I might admire green and gold for one thing and crimson and gold for another. I do not fancy blue particularly I believe, so I fear my *advice* and *preference* will not benefit you much. You must tell me why you wished to know. I am so glad to know that Mr. Leech is fighting. Emilie tells me Mrs. Buckner has gone to New Orleans on a *pleasure trip*, and speaking of that city reminds me of our friend Mr. Dennis, who is at Fort Pillow, and my oldest Brother also. I regret to hear of Mr. Williams being a Prisoner and hope he may soon be released. I must not forget to thank you for "My Maryland" which I think very pretty and will sing it with pleasure for you on your return. Already I have had the pleasure of singing for one soldier, but it was not such as I would have experienced singing for you. Will you excuse my short letter? My eyes ache me badly tonight, besides the hour is late and all have sought sweet slumber but myself long since so I will bid you goodnight, hoping God will bless you and keep you and restore you again in safety to your affectionate Elodie.

　　To Capt. Dawson
　　　Magnolia Cadets
　　　4th Ala Regt Vol.

Camp Bartow, Fredericksburg Va. April 2d. 1862

I am writing alone in my tent in a dark, cold and gloomy night—cheerless because my loved Elodie is far distant, because dark shadows hang upon our future. When will the bright sunlight break thro' the clouds, when will all we have hoped be realized? These are questions which the future alone can solve; they lie buried in its unfathomed bosom.

I am perhaps too sad, because I may be too apprehensive of the effect of the new military bill proposed by Pres. Davis. If it includes the 12 mos. volunteers, as I believe it is intended, I see no way of escaping, but will have to bear gracefully a hardship that cannot be. My only opposition to the measure is that it separates us again, places an ominous hedge between us, and will defer a happy union, to which I had looked with so much anticipation, in a few weeks. I am so anxious, for many reasons, that you should be under my protection, that the disappointment will be a great one. If allowed to do so, honorably, I will resign my commission rather than remain and postpone our marriage. Now a furlough of ten days would be eagerly embraced, as I could in that period go to Ala. and ask you to give me your hand.

But I will not determine that Congress will do us so great an injustice as to keep us in the service, but will hope for better treatment, for all we have done. A few days will determine. The volunteers are very indignant at the attempt to coerce them, but will have to acquiesce. The Yankees are fighting us on every side, and all things indicate a speedy attempt on their part to march to Richmond. Our generals in their orders are evidently preparing us for a great emergency of some kind. Oh for a great leader to [illegible] our arms to victory, and to carry us safely through the [illegible]. Our armies have done little but throw up lines of fortification, to be abandoned when approached by the enemy. Our great men wrangle in Congress over their pay, while the great arteries of the country are bleeding profusely. But we will not despair.

I wish I had foreseen the state of things. We might have been prepared to bear it better, and I never would have left home without celebrating, with your consent, our marriage. Can I not be married by proxy? I will get a friend to sign the contract for me. Then you can come on to me and a minister could unite us formally. I must devise some plan of seeing you in order to be married. I cannot consent to postpone it until the war is over, for it may never end. Is it not a grievous wrong that we should be deprived of our liberty & locomotion for three years?

I wrote you yesterday, on your 21st birthday, hope you have received the letter, not because there is much in it, beside the assurance of my love for you. Tomorrow I am field officer of the Brigade and will have my hands full.

McCraw has gone to spend the night at Fredericksburg with the [illegible]. It is late, after tattoo; I must close.

I have heard from you but once, but hope soon to receive a long, *loving* letter.

May God in his greatness and mercy, my Dear Elodie, protect us, and in his good time, unite us in all of our hopes.

Goodnight, with much love.

    affectionately and humbly

       N. H. R. Dawson

Fredericksburg. April 6. 1862.

Your welcome note of 20th ulto. long in anticipation, like a truant friend, at last made its appearance yesterday, and I was glad once more to hear of your continued health and happiness. As you have my address I hope now to hear regularly once a week. It is one year today, my dear Elodie, since my first visit was paid you, and how long has dragged the time. Flowers have blossomed and faded, and again are blooming, and still our hopes are unfulfilled. But I hope the end of our probation draws near, and that ere another moon shall fill its hours, we will be happily wedded, and will begin a long life of love and contentment, that we will go up its weary hill, bearing lightly its burdens, and that after the heat of the day is over, we will descend in the evening, quietly and calmly, to the repose of Eternity. Whatever fate shall be mine, I hope for you happiness and the prosperity, which gilds the hours of the good and beautiful.

I rejoice that you have so good a friend in Miss Serena, and hope you will always find her faithful. Mrs. Parnell I love, and I love you the more, since she loves you so much. Please remember me most kindly to the old lady, and tell her that I prize her friendship very highly.

I am glad that you are willing to marry me, immediately, upon my return to Selma. There will be no necessity for delay. I fear your bridal trip will be to accompany me to the army, as there seems no option left even now. We must all make up our minds to fight, and to go into the service. I will endeavor to leave this regt. and to obtain a better position. I have heard nothing from Dr. Tallind about his progress in making up his regiment. The conscript law has not yet passed, but I presume it will. I will endeavor to avoid its operation here. I suppose some provision will allow me to vacate my commission. If not, I will have to depend upon the success of my being in a regiment with Dr. Tallind, or upon the chances of a short furlough to return and bring you back, at any rate to marry you. I think of you now as mine, and I am determined, with your consent, to be married as soon as possible. When there is a will, there is a way. The weather today is beautiful and it must be quite warm in Ala. as the sun is unpleasant here. A large number of my company have gone to Church at Fredericksburg. Lieuts. McCraw and Wilson with them. I remained to write to you and others. You no doubt are now at church, and I can shut my eyes and see you plainly. Oh for Peace, and a pretty little cottage, in the shadow of a mountain, where we could live so happily.

I hope this campaign will end the war. The Yankees are now bending under a terrible pressure, and I hope will have to yield. We too are hard pressed, but are fighting for all, and can therefore bear burdens more easily. I think we will fall back from here towards Richmond, when the Yankees advance. This seems to be our policy, to concentrate our lines at some point, from which our forces can be thrown to any point of attack. You must be satisfied with short letters, as I write so frequently. Hereafter I will write semi weekly and do better. Did you receive none of my letters on the way to Richmond? And now, my dear Elodie, goodbye. May God preserve and keep you from all harm. With a kiss and much love, I remain

yours devotedly

N. H. R. Dawson

Selma, April 15th 1862.

For a long week I have been anxiously expecting a letter, and today thanks to you came two dated the 4th and 6th, and to my surprise from Fredericksburg. Owing to a rumor in Town to the effect that the 4th Ala was at Goldsboro or Yorktown, I did not write as usual on Sabbath hoping a letter would arrive informing me of your whereabouts. I am now provoked to think that I lent a listening ear to such a report. We have had quite a Hospital for two weeks. [illegible] disease, Measles, now we have four sick, three with Measles, and I will be delighted when all are entirely restored to health. I have been suffering from a cold which settled in my throat and Ear, but after ten days complaining I find myself today almost well again. Speaking of Invalids reminds me of a visit I paid to the *Selma Hospital* on Monday for Col. Kent's Regt especially. I was surprised to see everything so nicely arranged in so short a time, but highly amused at all I saw. We found eighteen men, recovering from Measles but lounging idly around. Two were confined to their room and I suppose ere this have been killed from excessive kindness. The mantelpiece was perfectly crowded with choice Bouquets, willed by the fair hands of *class no. 1* who go daily, I should say *twice* a day to visit the sick, and seem to be untiring in their devotions and efforts to relieve their suffering, but of all crowds, the roughest *I ever saw* are established in the Selma Hospital, petted and caressed, until, I predict when three weeks roll around they will be so *spoilt* and *lazy* that there will be no tolerating them. No one seems to understand what their duty is, and I had one good laugh at their ignorance and the pains they are taking, for I do not know what, but enough of fun making. [Ere?] this you have seen all the particulars of the Battle at Corinth, and the death of Genl. Johnson. I feel so sorry about it and regret he did not live long enough to prove himself free from the blame attached to him in his retreat from Tenn. I felt very uneasy for three days about my Brother Ellick and Mr. Helm who I found were there, but Mr. H. telegraphed from Tuscumbia saying he was still there, but as we have not heard since I think it probable they have been ordered to Corinth. Really these Battles and rumored battles keep me miserable all the time and the changes so constantly being made render it utterly impossible to keep posted as to the whereabouts of my Brothers, or any one else with any degree of certainty. I believe I wrote you Bro. Clem had gone down below Mobile. We have had no recent news from him and know nothing more of him than the rest. I am astonished at your being in such a bad humor with Congress, altho' I agree with you in thinking the bill you fear will be passed very unjust. At the same time it is *better to bear now for a little while* than by releasing the 12 month's men, when they are so much needed at this time, to suffer forever from the Tyranny of the North, and if the Government think it for the good of our country to take such a step me must not turn against our President, but try and help him as much as we can, and if in no other way, bear cheerfully this new trial. You know it is no pleasure to me, to be separated from you, or that your being absent so long and at a time when danger seems to surround you on every side, does but add to the other anxieties and troubles which it seems my lot to bear, and I hope I will be as able to bear my part of sorrow and trouble, caused by so glorious a struggle for liberty, with as much firmness as any of my countrywomen. After my spirits flag and when I think of home and friends whom I perhaps may never see again, and of myself a stranger in a strange land, *unloved*, I feel as tho' I could bear no more but I know I am not doing my duty or right in giving way and force back many a sign and tear, which it seems but natural I should give vent to. Since our battle at Corinth I feel more hopeful as to our War being one of short duration. I think from all I can see and hear that we will certainly and soon whip them off our soil and pray that Victory may be ours from this time forward. I think too, that notwithstanding Mr. Dawson's fears, that he will soon be at home and *I will be very much delighted to meet with him.* As you do not seem to know why the Comforter was not sent by you I can very easily account for it. There is not one [illegible] of course they wished nothing done that would *discourage you,* and at the same time wished to keep Mr. H. hanging on as a beau. Why should not Daughter *be a belle* when such is Mother's highest ambition. I know I have no objection, so long as they do not catch for her *my beau.* I received a few evenings ago a letter from Mrs. Lide, in which she made quite a number of inquiries about you, and which I endeavored to answer satisfactorily.

But now I must ask you to please excuse this miserable scrawl and try and read it, and to say goodnight. All have been buried in slumber for sometime, and I alone am sitting up at wee small hours. Write soon a long letter and believe me with prayers for your safety every yours affectionately

Elodie

To Capt. N. H. R. Dawson
Wednesday Morning 16th

This morning I was awakened by a note from my Brother-in-law Mr. Kellogg informing me that he was a *prisoner* on board the Southern Republic and on his way to Montgomery, and also informing us of the death of my Brother Sam, killed in the Battle of Corinth.[136] We have Telegraphed to New Orleans hoping to hear this sad news untrue. I little thought another day would bring with it two such trials and sorrows. Mr. K. has been with our Army for 6 weeks and said while Gen'l Johnston lived he had no trouble and was with *our side* during the Battle but I suppose did not participate. I went to see him but the Boat had gone, but Mr. Hagood saw him and gave me all the particulars of his conversation with him. I fear we can do but little for him, and will be obliged to wait for time to prove him a friend to our cause. I am greatly distressed on my poor Sister's account and deeply regret he ever came to hear of, or see us, but I trust in

136. Samuel Todd, Elodie's older brother, had joined Company H of the Louisiana Crescent Regiment as a private. On April 7, the second day of the Battle of Shiloh, he was shot through the back while retreating. His intestines protruding from the exit wound above his groin, he said to an officer, "Ah, Lieut., I believe they have got me this time." He was right; he died on the way to the hospital and was buried by the side of the road. Berry, *House of Abraham,* 115.

One who can and will aid us in all our troubles. I see the bill has passed as you thought. I cannot write more this morning, but will soon, with
love yours
Elodie

Williamsburg Va., April 18, 1862.

After a march of Eighty miles from Ashland we are resting the morning in sight of Williamsburg, on our way to Yorktown, where we arrive this afternoon.

I have stood the march well, suffering only a little with my feet. Gen. Whiting has just told us we were ordered to the front, Yorktown, the most dangerous point, and that a terrible battle was impending, soon to take place.

The result will tell immensely, and I would not, if I could, avoid being in it. I wish it for many reasons.

I have been engaged to you one year today, tomorrow being the anniversary, and my love is fresh, ardent, as ever. I love you as my own soul, my dear Elodie, and God grant that life may be spared me to be blessed with your affections. The conscript keeps us all in service, but I do not think it applies to officers. At present, I do not think of being a candidate for Captain of my Company, tho' the men are anxious that I should. If I do not, I will return in 40 days from the 26th inst. and will be enrolled in the reserve. My love for you is supreme, and I wish to be married at once, even if I remain in the service. You must write me to Yorktown. I have not heard from you since your letter of 20th March. Was greatly disappointed in not getting a letter by Mr. Price, tho Mr. L. and Kidd may have one. I write on the leaves of my note book, excuse it, as I have no paper.

And now adieu. Think of me always as devoted to you, loving you. [Nathaniel]

Select Bibliography

Alabama Civil War Muster Rolls, 1861–1865, Alabama Department of Archives and History, Montgomery, Ala.

Allardice, Bruce S., and Lawrence Lee Hewitt, eds. *Kentuckians in Gray: Confederate Generals and Field Officers of the Bluegrass State.* Lexington: University Press of Kentucky, 2008.

Baker, Jean. *Mary Todd Lincoln: A Biography.* New York: W. W. Norton, 1987.

Berry, Stephen. *House of Abraham: Lincoln and the Todds, a Family Divided by War.* New York: Houghton Mifflin, 2007.

Clinton, Catherine. *Mrs. Lincoln: A Life.* New York: Harper, 2009.

Davis, William C. *Battle at Bull Run: A History of the First Major Campaign of the Civil War.* Garden City, N.Y.: Doubleday, 1977.

———. *The Orphan Brigade: The Kentucky Confederates Who Couldn't Go Home.* New York: Doubleday, 1980.

Dubay, Robert W. *John Jones Pettus, Mississippi Fire-Eater: His Life and Times, 1813–1867.* Jackson: University Press of Mississippi, 1975.

DuBose, Joel Campbell. *Notable Men of Alabama.* Atlanta: Southern Historical Association, 1904.

Elder, Angela Esco. "'We Weep over Our Dead Together': Emilie Todd Helm and Confederate Widowhood." In *Kentucky Women: Their Lives and Times.* Edited by Tom Appleton and Melissa McEuen. Athens: University of Georgia Press, 2015.

Evans, W. A. *Mrs. Abraham Lincoln: A Study of Her Personality and Her Influence on Lincoln.* New York: Knopf, 1932.

Grimsley, Elizabeth Todd. "Six Months in the White House." *Journal of the Illinois State Historical Society* 19 (1926–1927): 43–73.

Helm, Katherine. *The True Story of Mary, Wife of Lincoln: Containing the Recollections of Mary Lincoln's Sister Emilie (Mrs. Ben Hardin Helm), Extracts from Her War-Time Diary, Numerous Letters and Other Documents Now First Published.* New York: Harper, 1928.

Hubbs, G. Ward, ed. *Voices from Company D.: Diaries by the Greensboro Guards, Fifth Alabama Infantry Regiment, Army of Northern Virginia.* Athens: University of Georgia Press, 2003.

Jackson, Harvey H. *Inside Alabama: A Personal History of My State.* Tuscaloosa: University of Alabama Press, 2004.

Johnson, E. Polk. *A History of Kentucky and Kentuckians: The Leaders.* Chicago: Lewis Publishing Company, 1912.

Jones, Kenneth W. "The Fourth Alabama Infantry: First Blood." *Alabama Historical Quarterly* 36 (1974): 35–53.

Kirwan, Albert D. *John J. Crittenden: The Struggle for the Union.* Lexington: University of Kentucky Press, 1962.

Klotter, James C. *The Breckinridges of Kentucky, 1790–1981.* Lexington: University Press of Kentucky, 1986.

Lane, J. Gary, and Morris M. Penny. *Law's Alabama Brigade in the War between the Union and the Confederacy.* Shippensburg, Pa.: White Mane Publishing, 1996.

Marshall, Anne E. *Creating a Confederate Kentucky: The Lost Cause and Civil War Memory in a Border State.* Chapel Hill: University of North Carolina Press, 2010.

Neely, Mark E., and Harold Holzer. *The Lincoln Family Album.* New York: Doubleday, 1990.

Owen, Thomas McAdory. *History of Alabama and Dictionary of Alabama Biography.* Chicago: S. J. Clarke Publishing Company, 1921.

Scott, D. M. "Selma and Dallas County, Ala." *Confederate Veteran* 24 (1916): 214–222.

Stocker, Jeffrey D., ed. *From Huntsville to Appomattox: R. T. Coles's History of 4th Regiment, Alabama Volunteer Infantry, C.S.A., Army of Northern Virginia.* Knoxville: University of Tennessee Press, 1996.

Taylor, Amy Murrell. *The Divided Family in Civil War America.* Chapel Hill: University of North Carolina Press, 2005.

Townsend, William H. *Lincoln and the Bluegrass: Slavery and Civil War in Kentucky.* Lexington: University of Press of Kentucky, 1955.

Turner, Justin G., and Linda Levitt Turner. *Mary Todd Lincoln: Her Life and Letters.* New York: Knopf, 1972.

Wilson, Douglas L., and Rodney O. Davis. *Herndon's Informants: Letters, Interviews, and Statements about Abraham Lincoln.* Urbana: University of Illinois Press, 1998.

Index

Abelard, Peter, 96
Adams, Robert, 57
Adams, William S., 131
Adkins, Agrippa, 131
Allston, Ben, 186, 200, 206, 254, 285–286
Allston, Robert Francis Withers, 186
Anderson, G. T., 170
Anderson, Pauline, 170
Anderson, Robert, 84
Andrew (slave of Nathaniel), 179
Ashby, Turner, 233
Averitt, James Battle, 25, 53, 114, 150, 185, 211, 224, 232, 241; as correspondent of company, 26; engagement of, 93, 98–99, 119–120, 166; friendship with Nathaniel of, 110–111; Nathaniel's opinion of, 51, 59, 153; ordination of, 74
Avery, Francis, 214
Avery, Mary, 214
Avery, William C., 131
Avery, William M., 214–215

Baker, Eli W., 131
Barker, James, 162
Beattie, Thomas K., 131
Beauregard, P. G. T., 36, 96
Beckham, Fontaine, 53
Bee, Barnard, 95, 108, 115, 142, 273
Bell, Benjamin, 205
Bell, Bush W., 131
Bell, Sallie, 221
Bingham, Ann Ruth, 252
Bingham, James Harvey, 252
Bohannon, Robert B., 131, 137
Bradley, Hugh C., 131
Breckenridge, John C., 90, 95, 151, 156, 232, 250, 298, 304

Briggs, Charles H., 131
Brown, Benjamin Gratz, 114
Brown, James G., 131
Brown, John, 53, 58
Brown, Maggie, 219
Buckner, Mary Jane, 220
Buckner, Simon Bolivar, 209, 220
Bullock, E. C., 286
Bulwer-Lytton, Edward, 58, 81
Burnam, J. F., 220
Burt, Erasmus, 158
Byrd, Francis, 282
Byrd, William G., 131

Caball, Patter H., 111, 183
Campbell, John Archibald, 46
Caughtry, Joseph R., 131
Chadwick, S. W., 164
Chapman, Reuben, 166
Charleston Mercury (newspaper), 145
Claiborne, J. F. H., 147
Cleveland, George W., 132, 137
Cleveland, Grover, 14
Cleveland, Pulaski, 132
Clifton, Albert G., 216
Cochran, Mary Preston, 170, 186, 299
Cohen, Lewis, 131
Cole, George W., 132
Coleman, Caroline A., 112, 140
Coles, R. T., 32
Collins, Wilkie, 165
Cook, Benson, 131
Cook, James W., 131
Cook, Thomas M., 131
Coursey, William W., 132
Craighead, David, 289
Craighead, James B., 154
Craighead, Jane P., 111, 154, 176, 238

Crail, A. W., 226
Crittenden, George, 1
Crittenden, John Jordan, 1
Crittenden, Thomas, 1
Cunningham, Frank M., 132
Curry, Ann, 129

Dallas Rangers, 56
Daniel, John R., 132
Daniel, Lucian A., 131
Daniels, T. C., 63, 157
Davis, Jefferson, 4, 190, 203–204, 312
Dawson, Elizabeth M. (daughter of
    Nathaniel), 75, 172–173, 185, 212,
    252, 301
Dawson, Henry Rhodes (son of Nathaniel
    and Elodie), 12
Dawson, Nathaniel: Averitt, Nathaniel's
    opinion of, 87–88, 153; on Battle of
    Manassas, 137–138, 141–142, 149,
    180–181; childhood and parents of,
    229–230, 242; children of, 11, 12,
    172–173; on Confederate flag, 242;
    courtship history of, 3–7; cowardice
    charge of, 181–182, 184–185, 193,
    196, 200–201, 208–209, 212–213; on
    disease in army, 167, 284–285; financial
    status of, 13; graveyards and, 13, 164,
    268; health of, 174, 200; on his own
    nature, 272; home of, 12; hope of, for
    furlough, 189; hope of, that Kittie will
    live in Alabama, 206; image of, 122; on
    Jones, Egbert J., 7; on Kentucky and its
    neutrality, 81, 108, 259–260; on letters
    and importance of, 73; on Lincolns, 5,
    32, 41, 45, 53, 73, 107, 108, 120, 149,
    157, 174, 292–293; love of reading and,
    255–256; marching, soreness from,
    43–44, 200; marital history of, 3, 30,
    212; overseer of, 259; plans after term of
    enlistment of, 293–294; postwar career
    of, 14; predictions for war and, 81; on
    prospect of European intervention,
    259; religious attitudes of, 88–89, 94,
    148, 165, 168–169, 177; reported
    killing of, 142; on romance as religion,
    73; on rumors of battle, 76, 82, 106,
    118, 178, 223, 229; on salt shortage in
    Confederacy, 256; on Selma, Ala., 249;
    on slavery, 6; slaves of, 309; on smoking,
    74; on supplies for company, 230, 298;
    on Union finances, 271; on Virginia
    landscape, 118–119; wounding of, 141,
    167–168
Dawson, Percy (son of Nathaniel and
    Elodie), 12
Dawson, Reginald Huger (brother of
    Nathaniel), 113, 158, 186, 279, 300
Dedman, James M., 150, 194
Densler, John E., 132
Donegay, James G., 132, 284, 286–287
Dranesville, Battle of, 276, 279–280, 283
Duncan, Blanton, 44, 61
Duncan, Garret, 44

Edwards, Ninian Wirt, 128
Ellsworth, Elmer, 33, 49, 63, 84–85
Evans, George R., 4

Ferguson, Emily, 294
Fiquet, William, 75, 93
Fitts, Margaret L., 245
Ford, Joseph H., 132
Forney, John Horace, 116, 166, 198
Fort Hatteras, Battle of, 184
Fort Morgan (Ala.), 151
Friday, Hilliard J., 132
Friday, James L., 132
Friday, John C., 132
Fry, Birkett D., 279

Gaither, Nathaniel, 289
Garrett, Robert E., 131, 287
Goldsby, Boykin, 107, 131, 145, 173, 196,
    231
Goldsby, Mary A., 112
Goldsby, Thomas Jefferson, 112
Goodwin, Gertrude, 213, 226, 281
Grice, Henry F., 132

Haden, James Grey, 96, 132, 232, 239
Hagood, Robert, 28, 35, 55, 115, 140, 147,
    157, 160, 186, 240, 283, 292
Hampton, Wade, 216

Hannon, William H., Jr., 132
Hannon, William H., Sr., 132
Hardie, James, 235
Hardie, Joseph, 32, 44, 53, 87, 186
Hardie, Margaret Isbell, 32, 44, 66, 67, 87,
    173, 186, 189, 191–192, 195, 201, 213
Harlan, John Marshall, 234
Harper's Ferry, Va., 43, 52
Harper's Weekly (newspaper), 155
Harriet Lane (ship), 267
Harrill, Thornton R., 132
Harris, John J., 245
Harrison, Billy, 169, 231
Harrison, William H., 137
Hayden, James G., 61
Hayne, Robert Y., 308
Heard, Nannie, 162
Helm, Benjamin Hardin, 50, 221–222,
    223, 237, 298, 303, 318; biography of,
    47; enlists in Confederate army, 57;
    military positions of, 11, 194, 208, 244
Helm, John LaRue, 222
Henry, Judith, 142
Hobbs, S. J., 100, 107, 140
Hodge, William L., 132
Holmes, Theophilus Hunter, 97–98, 248
Home Again (song), 62
Hooks, William A., 132
Hopkins, Juliet, 178

Jackson, Felix W., 132
Jackson, Thomas J., 105
Jeffries, Ann E., 261
John (slave of Nathaniel), 30, 72, 89, 153
Johnston, Albert Sidney, 68, 80, 206
Johnston, George D., 235
Johnston, Joseph Eggleston, 68, 149
Jones, Allan, 298
Jones, Egbert J., 29, 91, 142, 167–168,
    180, 190, 198
Jones, William, 132
Jordan, James M., 132

Keitt, Laurence M., 23
Kellogg, Charles, 47, 129, 222, 308, 319
Kellogg, Margaret, 47, 129, 222, 261
Kennedy, Arch E., 132, 231

Kennedy, George D., 132, 231
Kent, James, 34
King, Porter, 116, 125, 297
King, William R., 132
Knox, William, 215, 282
Ku Klux Klan, 13

Lady of Lyons (Bulwer-Lytton), 255
Lamar, John H., 132
Lamson, Frank R., 132
Lane, William B., 132
Lapsley, George, 267
Lapsley, J. W., 261
Last Heiress, The, 214
Law, Evander M., 29, 138, 180, 198, 233,
    257, 275, 280, 288
Lide, Cornelius Mandeville, 30
Lincoln, Abraham: effect of Todd family
    on, 1–2; as subject of Selma tableaux, 8,
    276–277
Lincoln, Mary Todd, 299; childhood of,
    2; criticism of brother David by, 157;
    effect of divided family on, 1; letter from
    Kittie to, 72; letter to Elodie from, 69;
    relationship with Elodie of, 2
Lincoln, Willie, 306
Littleton, Thomas B., 132
Louisville Courier (newspaper), 250
Lowry, Uriah, 132
Lowry, William A., 132, 137
Luske, John M., 132

Mabry, Albert Gallatin, 34, 108, 195
Magnolia Cadets (Fourth Alabama,
    Company C), 4, 7; camps and
    movements of, 24, 40, 148, 254, 270,
    275; disease in, 284; drinking on
    Christmas of, 279; flag of, 123; illness
    in, 167; leadership of, 91; singing, 62;
    tensions with Selma Blues, 8, 27–28, 49,
    61, 93; typical camp routine of, 38
Magoffin, Beriah, 33, 280, 289
Magoffin, Susan Shelby, 289
Manassas, Battle of, 9–10; map of,
    125–127
Marshall, Jacob, 131
Martin, Alburto, 198

Martin, James Benson, 132, 279
Mason, James Murray, 46, 273
Mather, Thomas S., 132
Mathews, Elizabeth, 30, 66–67, 117, 185, 200
Mathews, Rebecca, 249
Maury, Harry, 151
May, Syd M., 132
May, William V., 132
McCraw, Ella L., 47, 184, 194, 201, 219, 221, 225, 226–227, 303, 305
McCraw, S. Newton, 47, 131, 178, 184, 188, 198, 214, 226, 315
McCreary, Robert, 245
McDonald, Angus William, 93
McDuffie, George, 308
McKerning, John W., 133
McLemore, Owen Kenan, 248
McNeal, George S., 133
Meade, William, 74
Melton, George F., 131, 188, 189
Melton, Thomas J., 132
Miller, Stephen J., 132
Mims, George, 132, 220, 221, 226, 236, 257, 270, 281; biography of, 65–66; loses trunk, 243, 246, 255; wounding and recovery of, 169, 180–181
Mims, Laura, 27, 97, 244
Moody, William R., 132
Moore, P. G., 267
Moore, Syd, 188
Morgan, John Tyler, 223, 262–263
Mosely, Andrew B., 133
Motley, John Lothrop, 89
Munroe, Tom, 289
My Maryland (song), 312

Napoleon, Prince, 168
Norfolk, Va., 60

O'Neal, William, 133
Overton, John B., 88, 133
Overton, Thomas W., 133

Paisley, Hugh S., 133, 189, 209
Parkman, Alla, 91, 92
Parkman, James M., 91

Parkman, John M., 92
Parkman, M. R., 91
Parnell, Serena, 72, 211, 224, 228, 251, 264, 316
Patterson, Robert, 105, 117
Peeples, Frank W., 133
Pegues, Christopher Claudius, 34, 107, 112
Pensacola (ship), 298
Pettus, Edmund Winston, 13, 30, 75
Phoenix Reds, 7
Preston, Henrietta, 80
Preston, John Montgomery, 170
Preston, John S., 308
Price, Alfred C., 131
Pryor, John W., 133
Pryor, Robert O., 133

quinine, 40, 224
Quitman, John A., 147

Raiford, William C., 133
Randolph, Thomas Jefferson, 174
Redwood, Meta, 304
Reese, E. L., 194, 205
Reese, J. T., 194
Reeves, Hunter, 209, 212
Reinhardt, George L., 133
Richmond Dispatch (newspaper), 193–194
Richmond Examiner (newspaper), 189, 191
Riggs, Martha, 108
Rise of the Dutch Republic (Motley), 297, 305
Robbins, John L., 133
Robinson, Kate, 219
Robinson, Stuart, 219
Rodes, Robert Emmett, 270
Rollins, John, 169
Romeo and Juliet (Shakespeare), 255
Rucker, Henry, 133
Rucker, Lindsay, 133

"salt mice," 256
Scott, Charles L., 29, 138, 142, 180
Scott, Winfield, 151
Searles, Louisa Ann, 128
Selma, Ala.: Civil War and, 12; Ladies Memorial Association and, 13; map of,

124; Nathaniel's opinion of, 243, 249;
social divisions within, 8, 276–277,
282–283, 288, 290–291, 295–296
Selma Blues, 7, 27–28; captain of, 63;
tensions with Magnolia Cadet partisans
and, 8, 61, 71, 93, 234, 276–277,
290–291, 296–297, 298
Selma Grays, 56
Selma Reporter (newspaper), 142
Sewell's Point, 60
Shakespeare, William, 255
Shiner, David H., 133
Shortridge, George David, 47, 90, 131,
213, 216
Simpson, John, Jr., 45, 141, 144
slaves, 6; held by Nathaniel, 30, 72, 89,
153, 179; poisoning and, 218–219;
working for Confederate army, 216
Slidell, John, 273
Smith, Clark Mouton, 128
Smith, Edmund Kirby, 158
Smith, I. Q., 246
Smith, Robert Hardy, 269
Southern Cross, The (song), 25
Springfield, Battle of, 249
Stewett, Mayor D., 133
Stokes, William C., 133
Stone, John W., 133, 137
Strong, Lydia, 194

Tartt, Gertrude, 108, 116
Tarver, Ben J., 133
Tarver, Mary E., 30
Taylor, Thomas Hart, 253, 274, 276, 283,
288
Taylor, William E., 133, 137
Terry, Thomas B., 133
Thomas, Lewis, 133
Thompson, John S., 133
Thompson, William E., 133
Thou Art So Near and Yet So Far (song), 202
Todd, Alexander, 11, 101, 103, 203, 208,
233, 237, 244, 261, 264–265, 318;
biography of, 129–130; capture of, 295;
death of, 10, 11, 129–130, 161
Todd, Catherine (Kitty), 12, 50, 61,
130, 195, 206, 244, 275, 295, 305;

appearance of, 79; Ellsworth and, 63,
68–69, 79; Hagood and, 157; letter
to Mary Lincoln of, 72; return of, to
Kentucky, 176; on Selma's dullness,
77–78, 172, 176; sickness of, 224
Todd, Charles H., 219
Todd, Charles S., 219
Todd, David, 26, 66, 148, 208, 261,
264–265, 283, 288, 291, 302; as
assistant quartermaster for First
Kentucky Regiment, 228, 244; in
Battle at Dranesville, 276; biography
of, 129; as commandant at Richmond's
Libby Prison, 172, 183, 188, 192, 228;
estrangement from George Todd, 161;
Lincoln's reaction to Confederate
service of, 139
Todd, Edmonia, 277
Todd, Elizabeth "Betsey" Humphries,
33, 61, 100, 192, 246, 261; attitude of,
toward Elodie's marriage, 64, 69, 154;
Elodie's opinion of, 79; politics of, 71,
146; return of, to Kentucky, 140
Todd, Elizabeth Porter, 128
Todd, Elodie: attitudes of, toward
Kentucky, 146, 159, 252–253; on
Averitt, 79, 193; birthday of, 158;
childhood of, 2; children of, 11, 12;
on Confederate flag, 251; courtship
history of, 3–7; dancing and, 281, 283;
death of, 12–13; on Ellsworth, 79;
family tree of, 128; on Hagood, 160,
292; on her family, 1, 5–6, 35, 65, 161,
182–183, 192, 233, 261, 277–278,
302–303; on her growing distaste for
war, 283; on her looks, 3, 222; home of,
12; image of, 121; on Lincoln, Abraham,
102, 159, 276–277; on making light of
Nathaniel's injury, 175; on mother, 79;
on Nathaniel's career options, 83; on
Nathaniel's potential death, 78–79, 102;
nightmare of, 261; relationship with
sister Martha, 3, 141; relationship with
sister Mary, 2, 102, 139; religion of, 161,
168–169, 224; as seamstress, 85, 156;
secessionist politics of, 101–102, 139,
150, 159, 239, 311; on Selma, Ala., and

Todd, Elodie (*continued*)
  its divisions, 8–9, 71, 93, 102, 109–110,
    207, 234, 276–277, 282–283, 290–291,
    295–296; on Selma, Ala., generally, 77;
    on sickness in household, 313–314,
    317; singing of, 85, 109, 201, 226–227;
    on slavery, 6; temper of, 140
Todd, Emilie, 12, 64, 129, 219, 295, 308,
  313
Todd, Frances Jane, 128
Todd, George Rogers Clark, 129, 148, 161
Todd, John Blair Smith, 220
Todd, Letitia Shelby, 219
Todd, Levi Owen, 128
Todd, Mary Ann, 128
Todd, Robert Barr, 252
Todd, Robert Smith, 128, 161, 252
Todd, Samuel, 10, 11, 129
Trent Affair, 273–274, 285, 294–295
Turner, Daniel M., 133
Two Merry Girls (song), 202

Ursory, Edward G., 133, 137

Vallandigham, Clement Laird, 140, 156
Vaughn, P. Turner, 96, 133, 274

Waddell, Edward R., 131
Wallace, William Smith, 128

Ware, H. H., 41, 218–219
Ware, Ida, 41
Watts, Ella F., 64–65, 84, 219
Watts, Louisa M., 258
Weaver, Legrand, 109
Weaver, Leroy, 109
Whallon, Daniel, 133
White, Clement Billingslea, 23, 28, 36, 48,
  79, 147, 160; Confederate service of,
    260–261, 314; marriage of, 2–3; weak
    health of, 90, 101, 111, 151–152
White, Martha Todd, 129; education of,
  219; home of, 51; marriage of, 2–3;
    relationship with sister Elodie, 3, 48, 141
White, Willie, 68, 253, 313
Whiting, William Henry Chase, 167, 197,
  199, 229, 285
Williams, Mary Louise Dunbar, 93,
  119–120
Williams, Philip, 45
Wilson, James H., 12
Wilson, John R., 131, 180
Winston, John Anthony, 195, 207
Woman in White, The (Collins), 165
Wood, Lapsley, 292
Woods, Charley, 195
Woodson, F. A., 84
Woodson, Maria T., 84
Wrenn, Theodore J., 133

Printed in the United States
By Bookmasters